AL-QAEDA

AL-QAEDA

CASTING A SHADOW OF TERROR

JASON BURKE

I.B. TAURIS
LONDON · NEW YORK

Published in 2003 by I.B.Tauris & Co Ltd
6 Salem Road, London W2 4BU
175 Fifth Avenue, New York NY 10010
www.ibtauris.com

In the United States of America and in Canada distributed by
Palgrave Macmillan, a division of St Martin's Press
175 Fifth Avenue, New York NY 10010

ISBN 1 85043 396 8

A full CIP record for this book is available from the British Library
A full CIP record for this book is available from the Library of Congress

Library of Congress catalog card: available

Typeset in Palatino Linotype by Steve Tribe, Andover
Printed and bound in Great Britain by MPG Books Ltd, Bodmin

CONTENTS

ACKNOWLEDGEMENTS

I have many people to thank. I am particularly indebted to my colleagues at *The Observer*. Roger Alton, Paul Webster, Andy Malone, John Mulholland, Allan Jenkins and many others have taught me a huge amount and have provided unfailing support. Other reporters on the newspaper, especially Martin Bright, have been generous with their time and contacts. I owe Peter Beaumont, a great reporter and friend, a lot. For their faith in my days as a penurious freelancer, thanks are due to Leonard Doyle and Ian Birrell at the *Independent*. Without Ciaran Byrne's advice at Lambeth town hall in 1993, things would have been very different.

I also have to thank the many colleagues outside the newspaper who have been so generous with their own work, advice and resources both during the writing of this book and on innumerable days in the field. They must include Abdul Bari Atwan, Scott Peterson, Adrian Levy, Alex Milner, Paul Danahar, Munir Ahmed, Zaffar Abbas, Ahmed Zaidan, Janaullah Hashimzada, Rory McCarthy, Ibrahim, Said Aburish, John Aglionby, Stephen Farrell, Luke Hunt, Syed Salahuddin, Fareed, Mirwais, Abdullah, Ahmed Shah and Azzam in Kabul, Peter Popham, Tim Judah, Ben Brown, Scott Peterson and Dilip Hiro. There are many, many others who have been excellent company on long journeys in strange places, far too many to list here.

I was enormously lucky to be able to tap the profound scholarship of Malise Ruthven, who very kindly read much of my manuscript at very short notice and made many invaluable suggestions. Peter Bergen gave me the benefit of his own deep knowledge with a similarly detailed reading of the book. Brian Whitaker was generous and patient as were Gilles Kepel, Owen Bennett Jones, Camille Tawil, Peter Marsden and Alice Perman. I am very grateful to them all. My thanks to Simon Reeve too.

Ilyas Masih is the best driver in Pakistan. His brother, Taj is the second best. Ershad Mahmud of Islamabad's IPS and Alexander Evans have been particularly helpful. Ala Talabani of the Patriotic Union of Kurdistan was a huge help in northern Iraq. In five years living or working in Pakistan and Afghanistan, there are many, many people who have assisted me in one way or another. Hundreds of people from prime ministers and presidents to shepherds and kebab-sellers enabled me to travel and work in safety in such interesting times. My thanks to Karen Davies as well. There are many others, diplomats, policemen and security officials in the UK, the Middle East and the Far East, whom I cannot thank by name. They know who they are and I am grateful to them. I owe Ashleigh Lezard thanks too.

Above all I have to thank Mohammed Ekram Shinwari. Ekram is a fantastic reporter, and a good friend. His understanding of Afghanistan, contacts, news judgment, unflagging enthusiasm, energy, sense of humour and hospitality are without equal. His mental computer, an archive of contemporary Afghan history, is a national asset as valuable as the Bagram ivories. Without him this book simply could not have been written. With him, it has been a lot easier, and a lot more fun.

Nor, of course, could this book have been written without Turi Munthe, my editor at I.B.Tauris, and Toby Eady, my agent, both consummate professionals with enthusiasm, understanding, erudition and experience.

Raf Nieto, Denise Bailey, Roger, Brian and everyone else, student or sensei, involved with Zen-do have done a magnificent job of keeping me sane and vaguely fit over the last five years.

For all the support and the forbearance of all my friends I am profoundly grateful.

I would like to thank my brothers and sisters, Adam, Sonya, Patrick and Anna, and my parents, my grandmother and Mike and Sally, all of whom are always there. I can remember days spent reading on Nina's dining-room table.

This book is dedicated to my grandfathers, Sidney Marks and Samuel Burke. Both were truly good men, full of dry humour, respect for others, honesty, tolerance and integrity. I miss them both.

In the memory of
Samuel Burke and Sidney Marks.

In the memory of victims of terrorism
and victims of the war on terrorism.

Regardless if Osama is killed or survives, the awakening has started, praise be to God.

Osama bin Laden, videoed speech, broadcast 27 December 2001

He was no man of action; he was not even an orator of torrential eloquence, sweeping the masses along in the rushing noise and foam of a great enthusiasm. With a more subtle intention, he took the part of an insolent and venomous evoker of sinister impulses which lurk in the blind envy and misery of poverty, in all the hopeful and noble illusions of righteous anger, pity, and revolt... The way of even the most justifiable revolutions is prepared by personal impulses disguised into creeds.

Joseph Conrad, The Secret Agent

Brute force without wisdom falls by its own weight.

Horace, Odes, *iv, 65*

BELORUSSIA
RUSSIA
Kiev
UKRAINE
Volgograd
MOL.
ROM.
Astrakhan
Akyubinsk
KAZAKHSTAN
Semeypalatinsk
Balkash
Aral Sea
Black Sea
BULG.
Istanbul
Chechnya
GEORGIA
Tiblisi
Dagestan
Caspian Sea
Shevchenko
UZBEKISTAN
Alma Ata
Bishkek
ARMENIA
AZERBAIJAN
Baku
Tashkent
Ferghana
Ankara
TURKEY
Yerevan
TURKMENISTAN
Bukhara
CHINA
Izmir
Konya
Tabriz
Askhabad
Dushanbe
Kashi
Yarkhand
Kurdistan
Mary
Mosul
Tehran
Mashad
CYPRUS
SYRIA
Hamadan
Qom
AFGHANISTAN
LEBANON
IRAQ
IRAN
Herat
Kabul
Jalalabad
Peshawar
Islamabad
Mediterranean Sea
Beirut
Damascus
Bagdad
Isfahan
Tel Aviv
Karbala
Amman
Najaf
Persepolis
Kerman
Kandahar
Lahore
ISRAEL-PALESTINE
JORDAN
Basra
Quetta
Cairo
Kuwait
PAKISTAN
Deoband
SAUDI ARABIA
KUWAIT
New Delhi
BAHRAIN
Buraydah
Khubar

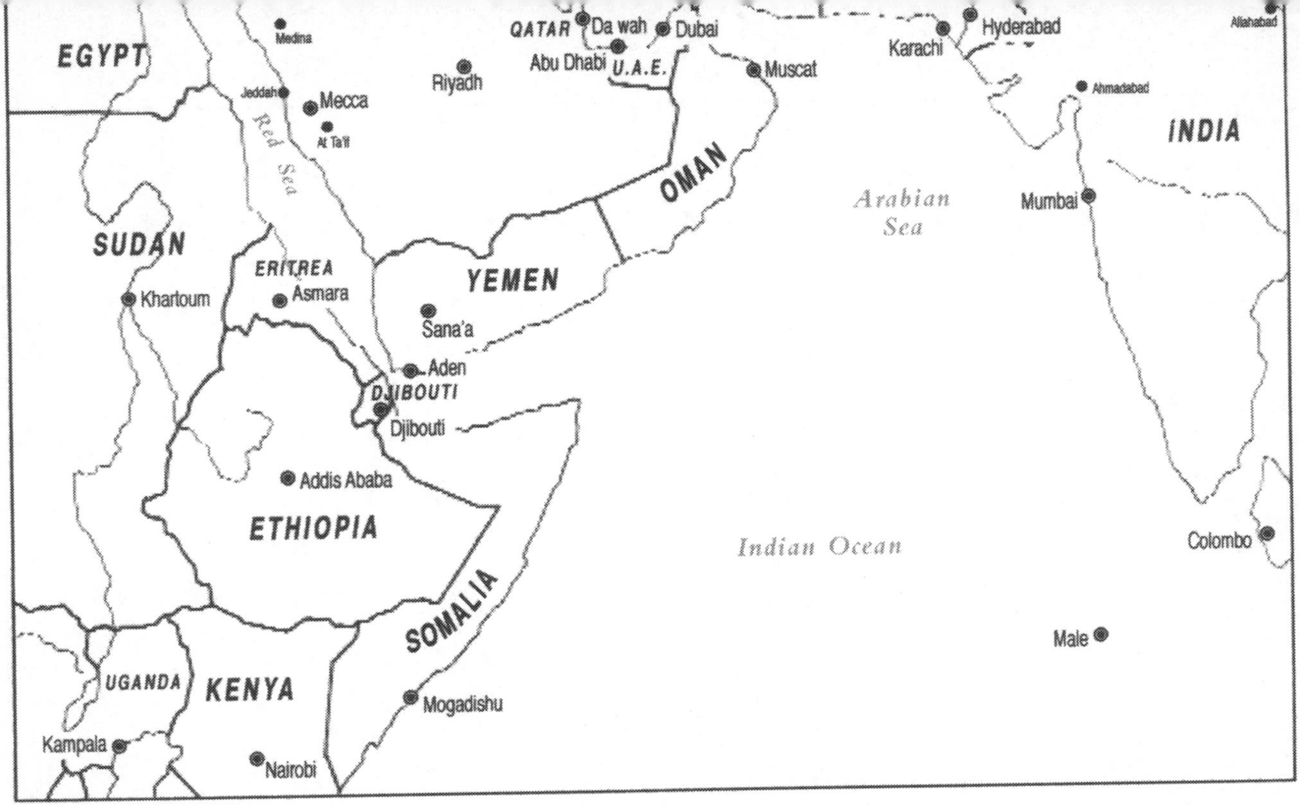
EGYPT
Medina
QATAR
Da wah
Dubai
Hyderabad
Allahabad
Karachi
Abu Dhabi
U.A.E.
Muscat
Riyadh
Jeddah
Mecca
Ahmadabad
At Ta'if
Red Sea
INDIA
OMAN
Arabian Sea
Mumbai
SUDAN
ERITREA
YEMEN
Asmara
Khartoum
Sana'a
Aden
DJIBOUTI
Djibouti
Addis Ababa
ETHIOPIA
Indian Ocean
Colombo
SOMALIA
Male
UGANDA
KENYA
Mogadishu
Kampala
Nairobi

TURKMENISTAN
UZBEKISTAN
TAJIKISTAN
TAJIKISTAN
IRAN
AFGHANISTAN
PAKISTAN
INDIA
Amu Darya R.
Amu Darya R.
WAKHAN CORRIDOR
Termez
Imam Saheb
Faizabad
Jowzjan
Taloqan
Shiberghan
Balkh
Mazar-e Sharif
Kunduz
Kunduz
Badakhshan
Faryab
Takhar
Torgundi
Maimana
Samangan
Kushk
Murghab
SALANG TUNNEL
Baghlan
R. Indus
Bamiyan
Jabel us Seraj
Charicar
Laghman
Asadabad
Badghis
Ghor
Kapisa
Bagram
Herat
Yakawlang
Bamiyan
Kabul
Sorobi
Jalabad
KHYBER PASS
Maidan Shahr
Tora Bora
Peshawar
Torkham
Islamabad
Shindand
Oruzgan
Kabul
Gardez
Kohat
Rawalpindi
Birjand
Khost
Ghazni
R. Indus
Jhelum
Jhelum R.
Chenab R.
Kalat
Paktia
Farah
Gareshk
Lashgkar Gab
Kandahar
Lahore
Zabul
Faisalabad
Helmand
Nimroz
Kandahar
KHOJAK PASS
Sutlej R.
Dara Ghazi Khan
Multan
Helmand R.
Quetta

INTRODUCTION

THE SHADOW OF TERROR

The fighters came back in the middle of the night. Their weapons and the ammunition slung around their shoulders reflected the dull red glow given out by the embers of the fire. The men sleeping in the room sat up and moved to make space by the fire for the new arrivals. Outside it was cold enough for frost to form wherever there was standing water.

During the day, two men had been taken prisoner and several others killed or wounded and the fighters did not talk much. One of them cleaned and checked a captured light machine gun while the others ate the remnants of a thin chicken stew cooked several hours earlier. It was 3am and everyone knew, at least if the routine established over the previous two days continued, that the bombing would not start again for two or three hours and now was the time to sleep.

Throughout the day and for much of the night the B-52s had been overhead. We had watched their distinctive quadruple contrails tracking in straight lines from the north towards their targets. Then they would make a sharp turn to the west and we would see great gouts of smoke, dirt, rock and flame on the steep slopes above us. A second or so later the noise and the blast would reach us, tugging at our clothes.

But now there was no noise. The fighters were sleeping or eating or talking softly to each other. In the next room, where the commanders were sitting on the floor drinking tea and dozing, a radio set on the dirt floor crackled out bursts of conversations and static.

When I woke three hours later all the men in the room were awake and most were standing. They had already eaten and stowed some dry bread for later in the day and had hung chains of bullets for the captured light machine gun around their necks. Then they wrapped their blankets over their thin *shalwar kameez*, hitched the straps of their Kalashnikovs over their shoulders, put magazines in their pockets or in the home-stitched webbing and, talking in low, muffled, uninflected voices, moved outside into the cold. Many of their blankets, bought in the bazaars of the city of Jalalabad some 30 miles away, had been imported from Iran and were bright green and pink and covered in gold prints of large flowers. There was the occasional abrupt laugh and then, with the blankets still wrapped over their thin clothes, the men moved off in small groups towards the pick-up trucks that would take them up to their assault positions.

The sky had begun to lighten and long files of men were now marching along the ridge towards the steep, dark, forested slopes that rose towards the snowy mountains. To the north, behind us, lay the city of Jalalabad and the dirt-coloured desert around it. Strands of mist hung over the irrigated lands around the Kabul River. Beyond it the ground banked up in a series of crumpled dry valleys, cliffs and plateaux to another long, low ridge of snow-covered summits. I heard the dull double or treble crack of the big 20-year-old Soviet antiaircraft guns that the mujahideen were using as ground support weapons.

Then high overhead, above the mountains to the north, scoring confident white lines across the pale sky like a steel cutter across glass, I could see the first set of the quadruple vapour trails of the B-52s of the day. When they appeared, the trails were white against the dawn sky. But the rays of the early morning sun, though yet to hit the mountain tops, were angled up into the sky like searchlights and when they struck the vapour trails, at an altitude of 10,000 feet, they turned them a pink as lurid and as bright and as out of place as the printed flowers on the blankets wrapped around the soldiers' thin shoulders. The trails powered forwards towards the mountains and then dipped elegantly away to the west. And then came the boiling, orange flames and the oily, dark smoke, indistinct in the half-light as if through a smeared windowpane. The noise came rolling over the hills.

The Americans had started bombing the caves, on a spur of the Spin Ghar mountains and less than ten miles from the Pakistani border, on 30 November 2001. They were known locally as Tora Bora. Seventeen days earlier, the Taliban and their Arab and Pakistani auxiliaries had pulled out of Kabul and the troops of the Northern Alliance had advanced across the Shomali plains to enter the city they had abandoned just over five years before. With a group of mujahideen, I had smuggled myself across the border and arrived in Jalalabad a few hours after it had been liberated. Two days later I drove the road to Kabul, hours before four reporters were killed on it, swung through Gardez and finally, after nearly a week, reached the eastern Afghan city of Khost, the heart of Islamic militancy in Afghanistan. My hosts, fighters loyal to the local warlord, told me I was the first Westerner in the city for five years. The Arabs, they said, had all gone.

Over the next weeks American warplanes scoured Afghanistan mopping up retreating Taliban and al-Qaeda fighters. Resistance was minimal. The Taliban virtually evaporated. Those commanders who had hitched themselves to the movement as it had swept through the country from 1994 to 1998 defected as quickly as they had joined up. By early December the southern desert city of Kandahar, the spiritual home and administrative headquarters of the Taliban, was in the hands of warlords and Mullah Mohammed Omar, the reclusive cleric who had led the hardline Islamic militia, was a fugitive.

Osama bin Laden was in Kandahar when the air strikes started.[1] By early November he had moved up to Jalalabad. Shortly before the fall of the city bin Laden, his close aides and several hundred of his Arab followers moved up into the hills to its south. The area, known locally as the Milawa Valley, included the former mujahideen base centred on the caves of Tora Bora.[2]

The battle of Tora Bora lasted for 18 days. On the ground, Afghan fighters and small groups of British and American special forces pressed on up the rough, boulder-strewn slopes. On 16 December, the Afghan warlords in charge of the assault on the cave complex declared 'victory'. A few ragged prisoners, mainly Afghans too poor or stupid to attempt escape, were paraded before the international media. Bin Laden and his senior aides, the Taliban high command, and hundreds of other al-Qaeda fighters had slipped the net.

I left Tora Bora, spent a few days in Jalalabad and then drove out to Pakistan. I arrived in London in time for the office Christmas party.

For me, the sight of cluster bombs exploding over the dry Afghan hills had been profoundly shocking. Though I had been reporting on Afghanistan, Pakistan and bin Laden almost full time for nearly four years, and had been covering conflicts, coups and natural disasters for a decade, nothing had prepared me for what I had seen. In fact, living and working in the region for so long had made the shock altogether more powerful. As I drove the short familiar road from Jalalabad to the border point at Torkham, I was profoundly troubled by what I had seen. In the years I had been travelling in and out of Afghanistan and Pakistan

I had watched executions and bombardments, been shot at, sniped at, mortared and shelled, held up at gunpoint and nearly died on several helicopters. I had listened to fathers describing the deaths of their children in missile attacks or at the hands of bandits, watched infants in the final stages of hunger-induced illnesses in filthy hospital wards, walked away from countless scenes of grief and deprivation but, though horrific and tragic, everything I had witnessed seemed to make sense. It was partly what had drawn me to Afghanistan initially. It seemed somehow to be part of the essence of the place. What I had seen at Tora Bora did not make any sense at all and I desperately wanted to understand how it had come to be.

It was clear that it was impossible to explain what had happened merely by looking at developments in Afghanistan and Pakistan. As I began to look beyond the region it swiftly became very clear that what had occurred at Tora Bora was the culmination of a huge and complex historical process. The men who had been under those bombs on those slopes above us were from the Yemen, Egypt, the Sudan and Algeria as well as from southwest Asia. The reason for what had happened at Tora Bora involved their histories as much as those of the Afghans.

I also wanted to answer other questions. Like many others I was scared. What was the nature of the threat that now confronted my way of life, my culture, my values, my own personal security and that of those I love? Should I genuinely be frightened of bombs on the London Underground, hijackings at Paris Orly, gas attacks in Los Angeles or dirty bombs in Chicago?

As the months passed, I found that none of these questions were being answered by the myriad articles and books published on 'the war on terror' and its supposed targets. I became increasingly concerned about the misconceptions that were gaining currency. Foremost among them was the idea that bin Laden led a cohesive and structured terrorist organisation called 'al-Qaeda'. Every piece of evidence I came across in my own work contradicted this notion of al-Qaeda as an 'Evil Empire' with an evil mastermind at its head. Such an idea was undoubtedly comforting – destroy the man and his henchmen and the problem goes away – but it was clearly misguided. As a result the debate over the prosecution of the ongoing 'war on terror' had been skewed. Instead of there being a reasoned and honest look at the root causes of resurgent Islamic radicalism, the discussion of strategies in the war against terror had been almost entirely dominated by the 'counter-terrorist experts' with their language of high-tech weaponry, militarism and eradication.

The latter may be useful to treat the symptom but does not, and will never, treat the disease.

The nearest thing to 'al-Qaeda', as popularly understood, existed for a short period, between 1996 and 2001. Its base had been Afghanistan and what I had seen at Tora Bora were the final scenes of its destruction. What we have currently is a broad and diverse movement of radical Islamic militancy. Its roots go back decades at the very least. Elements can be traced back to the earliest days of Islam. It involves tens of thousands of people, some merely individuals, some who have formed groups. These groups shift and change and grow and disappear. Similarly individuals become active and then cease their involvement. Others take their place. This movement is growing. Osama bin Laden did not create it nor will his death or incarceration end it. For all but five (or arguably three) years of his life, bin Laden was a peripheral player in modern Islamic militancy. He may have been the most charismatic and the best known but there were, and are, and will be, many others who have the will and the capacity to foment violence, murder innocents and sow chaos around the world.

Bin Laden and al-Qaeda are the radical, extremist fringe of the broad movement that is modern Islamic militancy. Their grievances are political but articulated in religious terms and with reference to a religious worldview. The movement is rooted in social, economic and political contingencies. Over the past 15 years, tens of thousands of young Muslim men made their way to training camps in Afghanistan. Many, as late as 1998, had never even heard of Osama bin Laden. Their motivations were varied but profound and genuinely felt. They were neither kidnapped nor compelled to travel in search of Jihad. Similarly, the men who sought out bin Laden's assistance, hoping to find the help that they needed to realise their dreams of violent actions against the West, travelled for what they felt were good reasons. The smoke and the vapour trails over Tora Bora may have signalled the end of Afghanistan as a favoured destination for aspirant terrorists but it did nothing to eradicate the reasons for the volunteers wanting to go there.

The threat is grave. Thirty years ago a new Islamic political ideology began to resonate amongst millions of young men and women across the Muslim world. This ideology was a sophisticated and genuine intellectual effort to find an Islamic answer to the challenges posed by the West's cultural, economic and political superiority. Over the decades that ideology has changed and mutated into something different. Once Islamic activists thought primarily in terms of achieving power or reforming their own nation. There was room in their programme for gradualism and compromise. There was room in their movement for a huge multiplicity of different strands of political thought. There was room for the parochial, radical and conservative movements of rural areas and for the clever, educated and aware ideologues of the cities. There was even room for those extremists who were committed to violence and who saw the world as a battlefield between the forces of good and evil, of belief and unbelief.

But increasingly, and this is a trend that is accelerating, the extremists are no longer perceived as the 'lunatic fringe'. Instead they are seen as the standard-bearers. And their language is now the dominant discourse in modern Islamic political activism. Their debased, violent, nihilistic, anti-rational millenarianism has become the standard ideology aspired to by angry young Muslim men. This is a tragedy.

In this book, I attempt to provide a detailed deconstruction of 'al-Qaeda', place Osama bin Laden in the context of radical modern Islam and, to an extent, trace out the movement's roots. The first two chapters introduce some of the concepts and ideas that I believe are important to understanding the phenomenon of al-Qaeda. Chapters Three to Eight outline bin Laden's early life and examine, in some depth, the historical events that formed him and formed the movement of which he became a part. There follows a close analysis of al-Qaeda and its operations between 1996 and 2001. This allows us to draw conclusions, in the final chapters, about the nature of the threat we face today.

In the weeks immediately following the tragedy of September 11th there was a genuine interest in understanding 'why'. *Why* 'they' hate us, *why* 'they' were prepared to kill themselves, *why* such a thing could happen. That curiosity has dwindled and is being replaced by other questions: *how* did it happen, *how* many of 'them' are there, *how* many are there left to capture and kill. Anyone who tries to 'explain' the roots of the threat now facing all of us, to answer the 'why', to elaborate who 'they are', risks being dismissed as ineffectual or cowardly. To ask 'why' is to lay oneself open to accusations of lacking the moral courage to face up to the 'genuine' threat and the need to meet it with force and aggression. Many characterise this threat, dangerously and wrongly, as rooted in a 'clash of civilisations.' This attitude not only plays into the hands of the extremists but, by denigrating the importance of genuine causes, risks encouraging tactics that are counterproductive. I hope, with this book, to redress the balance. As I watched the bombs falling at Tora Bora I had asked the question *why*. This is my attempt to find some answers.

CHAPTER ONE

WHAT IS AL-QAEDA?

So, what is 'al-Qaeda'? Ask even well-informed Westerners what they believe al-Qaeda to be and they will tell you that it describes a terrorist organisation founded more than a decade ago by a hugely wealthy Saudi Arabian religious fanatic that has grown into a fantastically powerful network, comprising thousands of trained and motivated men, watching and waiting in every city, in every country, on every continent, ready to carry out the orders of their leader, Osama bin Laden, ready to kill and maim for their cause.

The good news is that this al-Qaeda does not exist. The bad news is that the threat now facing the world is far more dangerous than any single terrorist leader with an army, however large, of loyal cadres. Instead, the threat that faces us is new and different, complex and diverse, dynamic and protean and profoundly difficult to characterise. Currently there is no vocabulary available to describe it. This leads to problems. 'Al-Qaeda' is a messy and rough designation, often applied carelessly in the absence of a more useful term. Before attempting any analysis we need to look at the name, where it came from and why.

The word itself is critical. 'Al-Qaeda' comes from the Arabic root *qaf-ayn-dal*. It can mean a base, as in a camp or a home, or a foundation, such as what is under a house. It can mean a pedestal that supports a column. It can also mean a precept, rule, principle, maxim, formula, method, model or pattern.

The word or phrase 'al-Qaeda' was certainly in use by the mid 1980s among the Islamic radicals drawn from all over the Muslim world to fight the Soviets in Afghanistan alongside the local resistance groups. Given that it is a common Arabic word this should not surprise us. For most of them it was used in a relatively mundane sense: to describe the base from which they operated.[1]

However, the word 'al-Qaeda' was also used by the most extreme elements among the radicals fighting in Afghanistan, particularly those who decided that their struggle did not end with the withdrawal of the Soviets from the country in 1989. Abdullah Azzam, the chief ideologue of the non-Afghan militants drawn to fight alongside the mujahideen and an early spiritual mentor of bin Laden, used the word to describe the role he envisaged the most committed of the volunteers playing once the war against the Soviets was over. In 1987, he wrote:

> Every principle needs a vanguard to carry it forward and [to] put up with heavy tasks and enormous sacrifices. There is no ideology, neither earthly nor heavenly, that does not require... a vanguard that gives everything it possesses in order to achieve victory... It carries the flag all along the sheer, endless and difficult path until it reaches its destination in the reality of life, since Allah has destined that it should make it and manifest itself. This vanguard constitutes the strong foundation (*al qaeda al-sulbah*) for the expected society.[2]

It seems clear, not least from the constant references to vanguards elsewhere in radical Islamic thought at the time and previously, that Azzam was talking about a mode of activism and a tactic, not talking about an organisation. The word is used to denote a purpose and a function, not an extant organisation.[3]

Bin Laden and a number of close associates acted on Azzam's suggestion and, sometime between 1988 and 1989, set up a militant group in Peshawar. The war in Afghanistan was over and the unity that a common purpose had forced on the disparate groups of Islamic extremists who had fought the Soviets was disintegrating. To bin Laden's great distress, national and ethnic divisions reasserted themselves strongly among the volunteers. 'Al-Qaeda' was formed with the express aim of overcoming those divisions and creating an 'international army' which would defend Muslims from oppression. The group was small, comprising not more than a dozen men, and there was little to distinguish it from the scores of other groups operating, forming and dissolving in Pakistan, Afghanistan and elsewhere in the Islamic world. Nor did it have the monopoly on the idea of internationalising the struggle. Though most of the larger groups were focused on campaigning against their own governments there were plenty of individuals or smaller groups, beside bin Laden and his small band, who, radicalised and enthused by their experiences in Afghanistan, were committed to a wider battle.

It is unclear if those involved with bin Laden called themselves 'al-Qaeda' at all at this stage. Some activists who were in Peshawar at the time say that it was known that a group attached to bin Laden was referred to as 'al-Qaeda' as early as 1990. Others say they never heard the term, though they knew of bin Laden. Certainly an 'Encyclopedia of the Jihad', an 11-volume compilation of the tactics and techniques of modern irregular warfare and terrorism compiled in Pakistan sometime between 1991 and 1993 by veterans of the war against the Soviets for use in other theatres of conflict, does not mention 'al-Qaeda'. Instead, it thanks Azzam, bin Laden and, the only group or organisation mentioned, Azzam's Maktab al-Khidamat (offices of services).[4] In 1993, a bomb exploded under the World Trade Center in New York. A few months earlier, Ahmed Ajaj, who was to be convicted for his role in attack, was detained on arrival at JFK airport with a bag full of terrorist training manuals. One was entitled *Al-Qaeda*. It was translated by American investigators, correctly in my view, as 'the basic rules'. Again, this is not the name of a group but is being used in its sense of 'a maxim' or 'the fundamentals'.[5]

Bin Laden left Pakistan in 1989 and returned to his homeland of Saudi Arabia. In 1990, when Saddam Hussein invaded Kuwait, bin Laden, several other Arab veterans of the war in Afghanistan and a number of Afghan commanders, offered to form an army of Islamic militants to protect Saudi Arabia. Rebuffed, bin Laden devoted most of his energies to reform of his own country. The al-Qaeda project languished. In 1991, bin Laden left his native land and fled, via Pakistan, to Sudan, where he remained until 1996.

American intelligence officials have been criticised for 'missing' al-Qaeda during this period. This is unfair. In his first few years in Sudan, bin Laden was at least as interested in experimental arboriculture and road construction as he was in creating an international legion of Islamic militants. His own group had barely expanded beyond the dozen or so individuals who had pledged allegiance to him back in 1989 and he was heavily reliant on the know-how and resources of larger and more established militant outfits. Nor was he connected to the raft of attacks there were in this period.

American intelligence reports in the early 1990s talk about 'Middle Eastern extremists... working together to further the cause of radical Islam' but do not use the term 'al-Qaeda'. After the attempted bombing of the World Trade Center in 1993, FBI investigators were aware of bin Laden but only 'as one name among thousands.'[6] In the summer of 1995, during the trials of a group of Islamic terrorists who had tried to blow up a series of targets in New York two years earlier, 'Osam ben Laden' (sic) was mentioned by prosecutors once; 'al-Qaeda' was not.[7]

The 1995 US State Department report *Patterns of Global Terrorism* explains that 'individuals and group-sponsored terrorist acts [now] overshadow state-sponsored terrorism'. It says:

> Many of these terrorists – some loosely organized and some representing groups – claimed to act for Islam and operated, increasingly, on a global scale. These trans-national terrorists benefit from modern communications and transportation, have global sources of funding, are knowledgeable about modern explosives and weapons, and are much more difficult to track and apprehend than members of the old established groups or those sponsored by states.[8]

This is an accurate assessment of the situation. Bin Laden is mentioned in passing as a 'major financier'. Some analysts see this as evidence that al-Qaeda existed as a huge and powerful terrorist organisation at the time but was simply so secret that no one, militant or counter-terrorist agent, mentioned it. This is facile doublethink.

A CIA report compiled in 1996 actually uses the term 'al-Qaeda' but does so ambiguously. It says that 'by 1985 bin Laden had... organized an Islamic Salvation Front, or al-Qaeda' to support mujahideen in Afghanistan. It is unclear if the author is referring to a group acting as an 'al-Qaeda' or called 'al-Qaeda'. Though the memo, entitled 'Usama bin Laden: Islamic extremist financier', goes into exhaustive detail about bin Laden's activities up to 1995, it does not mention 'al-Qaeda' again.[9] In 1996, he is described similarly and only in 1997, in the report compiled in the early months of 1998, does the State Department use the term 'al-Qaeda' for the first time. It is described not as an organised group but, again accurately, as 'an operational hub, predominantly for like-minded Sunni extremists'.[10]

In 1996, bin Laden moved from Sudan to Afghanistan. This provided the first real opportunity for him to build something that could genuinely be described as an organised terrorist group. It still centred around a small number – somewhere between 50 and 100 – of experienced and committed militants but, with a series of coincidental factors working in his favour, bin Laden was able to turn his earlier vision into something approximating reality. Again though, it is important to avoid seeing 'al-

Qaeda' as a coherent and structured terrorist organisation with cells everywhere. This would be to profoundly misconceive its nature.

In the immediate aftermath of the double bombings of American embassies in east Africa in 1998, President Clinton merely described the target of the retaliatory missile attack he ordered as 'the network of radical groups affiliated with and funded by Usama (sic) bin Laden, perhaps the pre-eminent organizer and financer of international terrorism in the world today.' Sensibly, Clinton talks of 'the bin Laden network', not of 'al-Qaeda'.[11] In fact, it is only during the FBI-led investigation into those bombings that the term first starts to be used to describe a traditionally structured terrorist organisation. A related concept that starts appearing in legal documents prepared by the FBI is the idea that there are 'al-Qaeda members' who swear allegiance to the organisation, not to bin Laden, through a *bayat* or an oath. In fact, a bayat can only be a pledge of loyalty to an individual. The change is a significant one and the reasons behind the shift are obvious. The culture of the FBI is focused on achieving convictions and the teams working on the prosecution of those responsible for the East African Embassy bombings of August 1998 had to work within the extant laws, particularly those of conspiracy. Such laws were designed to deal with coherent and structured criminal enterprises not with amorphous and dispersed politico-religious movements where responsibility for any one single act is very difficult to pin down. Evidence that someone is a member of an organisation is thus extremely useful. Unfortunately, in the case of 'al-Qaeda', it completely misrepresents the nature of the entity under investigation.

The FBI's main source was Jamal al-Fadl, a Sudanese militant who fled bin Laden's circle after stealing a large sum of money from him in 1995. He subsequently hawked himself around a series of Middle Eastern security agencies before being picked up by the Americans in 1996. As a prosecution witness in USA vs Usama bin Laden (sic), he had a strong interest in exaggerating the role of the main defendant. Most analysts rely heavily on his account of the formation of 'al-Qaeda' in 1989.

But al-Fadl's insistence that a coherent group by the name of al-Qaeda was up and running by the late 1980s is challenged by an exchange on day 19 of the trial, when an FBI agent gave the court details of his interrogation of Khalfan Khamis Muhamed, one of the suspected bombers:

> Prosecution: Did you ever ask KK Muhamed whether or not he ever heard of the term *bayat*?
>
> FBI: Yes, we did.

P: What did he say?

FBI: He said he had not.

P: And did you ask him about the term al-Qaeda?

FBI: Yes we did.

P: And what did he say?

FBI: He said that *al-Qaeda was a formula system* for what they carried out, talking about the bombing.

P: And did you ask him whether or not he'd heard of a group called al-Qaeda?

FBI: We did.

P: And what did he say in response?

FBI: He *claimed* he'd never heard of a group called al-Qaeda.[12]

This exchange clearly shows KK Muhamed's understanding that the phrase 'al-Qaeda' described a function, not an entity. KK Muhamed is a minor figure whose involvement with serious players close to bin Laden was minimal and who fulfilled a menial role in the actual bombing. But his understanding of 'al-Qaeda' is significant. The exchange also makes very clear that the US investigators were very keen to find a group, led by an identifiable figure, and to give it a name.

This is not to say that al-Qaeda does not exist but merely that the labelling implies that bin Laden's group is something it is not. To see it as a coherent and tight-knit organisation, with 'tentacles everywhere', with a defined ideology and personnel, *that had emerged as early as the late 1980s,* is to misunderstand not only its true nature but also the nature of Islamic radicalism then and now. The contingent, dynamic and local elements of what is a broad and ill-defined movement rooted in historical trends of great complexity are lost.

What bin Laden was able to do, between late 1996 and late 2001, was to provide a central focus for many of these disparate elements. This led not to the formation of a huge and disciplined group, but to a temporary focus of many different strands within modern Islamic militancy on Afghanistan and what, in terms of resources and facilities, bin Laden and his three dozen close associates were able to provide there. These resources – training, expertise, money, munitions and a safe haven – were what many militants, either as individuals or working as groups, had spent the years since the end of the war in Afghanistan trying, with varying degrees of success, to find.

This period is when 'al-Qaeda' matured. Yet it was still far from the structured terrorist group envisaged by many commentators. 'Al-Qaeda' at the time consisted of three elements. This tripartite division is essential to understanding the nature of both the 'al-Qaeda' phenomenon and of modern Islamic militancy.

The first element is the 'al-Qaeda hardcore'. In addition to the dozen or so associates who had stayed with him since the late 1980s, bin Laden was able to attract many of the pre-eminent militants active at the time. Most came for purely pragmatic reasons. Afghanistan between 1996 and 2001 was an excellent place to be. For militants who had spent years trying to mobilise and act, struggling all the while with domestic security services, Afghanistan was like a department store designed for Islamic terrorists. Recruits, knowledge, ideas and even cash could be had off the shelf. Bin Laden and his associates were running a whole floor, the biggest, the best stocked and the most glitzy.

By the time of the September 11th attacks, bin Laden and his dozen or so close associates had been able to attract and retain the loyalty of around a hundred highly motivated individuals from throughout the Islamic world who all had key skills and expertise and were committed to a similar agenda. A substantial proportion of these men were also veterans of the Afghan war. Many had also taken part in fighting in Bosnia or Chechnya. They acted as trainers and administrators in Afghanistan and, on occasion, were sent overseas to recruit for the group, to act as emissaries or ambassadors to other militant organisations or, more rarely, to run specific terrorist operations. It is a mistake to see even this hardcore as monolithic in any way. Even among the few dozen individuals who have remained physically and ideologically close to bin Laden from the end of the Afghan war to the present day, there have been, and currently are, significant divergences of opinion over methods, tactics, political and religious beliefs. Nonetheless, these hundred or so men, with the dozen or so long-term associates at their centre, can be considered the 'al-Qaeda hardcore'. Many had indeed taken an oath of allegiance to bin Laden at some stage. It seems fair to designate this group as the 'al-Qaeda hardcore', given its own perception of its role as a vanguard. It is a clumsy term but a useful one.

There was nothing inevitable about the emergence of this group, or any of the individuals within it, as pre-eminent. Modern Islamic militancy predated the war against the Soviets in Afghanistan by several decades and drew on a tradition going back to the very earliest days of the Muslim faith. There were many hundreds of groups and many potential leaders among the thousands of militants radicalised, hardened and inspired by their military victory in Afghanistan. In 1989, scores of men had, like bin Laden, expertise, charisma, access to funds and motivation. This situation has not changed and bin Laden must still be considered merely *primus inter pares*. Even five years ago his current pre-eminence was far from foreseeable. It is likely to prove merely a temporary phase in the history of modern Islamic militant activism.

A second element of 'al-Qaeda' as popularly conceived involves the scores of other militant Islamic groups around the world. Again, a careful examination of the situation shows that the idea that there is an international network of active groups answering to bin Laden is wrong.

To label local groups such as the Lebanese Asbat ul Ansar or the Islamic movement of Uzbekistan as 'al-Qaeda' is to denigrate the particular local factors that led to their emergence. It is true that elements within these groups may have some associations, though often very tenuous ones, with the 'al-Qaeda hardcore'. Some links date back to the late 1980s, some members may have been trained in 'al-Qaeda' camps post-1996, some leaders may have had contact with senior figures within the 'al-Qaeda hardcore' or received funds or training or other help from bin Laden himself or from his associates at various times. But similar links tie almost all Islamic radical groups and individuals active in the world today. There are many other sources of funding and of expertise and training beyond bin Laden. Groups and individuals have multiple associations and multiple lines of support. Groups, or elements within them, may cooperate with each other or with bin Laden on occasion if they feel it suits their purpose. But, though they may see bin Laden as a heroic figure, symbolic of their collective struggle, individuals and groups have their own leaders and their own agenda, often ones that are deeply parochial and which they will not subordinate to those of bin Laden or his close associates. Until very recently many were deeply antipathetic to bin Laden. As many remain rivals of bin Laden as have become allies.

Even within individual movements different factions can have different relations with 'al-Qaeda'. The Ansar ul Islam group that emerged in Kurdish-controlled northern Iraq in the autumn of 2001 comprised three different factions. Two set off to Afghanistan to meet senior al-Qaeda leaders in the spring of 2001. A third had been unwilling to deal with bin Laden or those around him. By the end of 2001, Ansar ul Islam was joined by Arab fighters who had fled the US-led onslaught in Afghanistan, some of whom had been close to bin Laden. One movement, three different relationships to 'al-Qaeda'.

And there was a fourth relationship to al-Qaeda too. Ansar ul Islam also comprised individuals who were not interested in any broader agenda beyond Kurdistan. One (failed) Iraqi Kurdish suicide bomber told me in the summer of 2002 that he did not want to go to Afghanistan for training because 'he did not want to travel' and was interested only in the affairs of his own country.[13] These men did not care for in bin Laden or his vision of an international struggle. It did not interest them at all. Others have rebuffed bin Laden's advances. In the early 1990s, the Algerian GIA rejected the aid of bin Laden on the basis that his agenda was vastly different from their own. Leaders of the GSPC, the GIA splinter group, refused to meet emissaries sent by bin Laden in the summer of 2002. The leader of the Indonesian Lashkar Jihad group refused to ally with bin Laden because to do so would have involved a significant sacrifice of autonomy.[14] At least one radical Palestinian Islamic group has rebuffed his advances too, concerned that links with the Saudi would have a negative impact on their image at home and overseas.

So how does one make sense of the enormously diffuse phenomenon of modern radical Islamic militancy? Some ways of conceptualising it work better than others. None are perfect. One model might be the anti-globalisation movement. There is as little in common between Italian anarchists with criminal records for drug use and violent assault and middle-class housewives campaigning against vivisection as there is between an Algerian peasant from a small town near Tizi Ouzu, recruited into the Armée de Salvation Islamique in 1994, and Yazid Sufaat, a university-educated, Malaysian clinical pharmaceutical salesman who ended up hosting a meeting of the September 11th hijackers at his apartment in Kuala Lumpur in January 2000.[15] As with the anti-globalisation movement, sometimes component groups' aims and methods coincide, often they do not. There is a constant tension between thinking global and acting local. The factionalism, competition and infighting of NGOs and lobby groups mirror the radical Islamic groups. In late 2002, I watched dozens of different groups on an anti-war protest in Florence marching under pictures of Che Guevara. The parallel is obvious.

Of course there are some links between bin Laden and other groups. As pointed out previously, bin Laden's 'department store' in Afghanistan was extremely popular. Leaders of many militant groups from all over the world sought him out. One way of characterising the relationship between bin Laden and many of these groups would be by analogy with that of the USSR or America and their various proxies during the Cold War. The US State Department's 1998 report on terrorism outlined the advantages of state support for a militant group. 'With state sponsorship a... group often receives a safe haven, money, weapons, training, logistic support or use of diplomatic facilities. Some of the most violent terrorist attacks on record would not have been possible without such sponsorship'.[16] Here the 'hardcore of al-Qaeda' outlined above plays the role of the state. By late 2001, bin Laden and the men around him had access to huge resources, both symbolic and material, which they could use to project their power and influence internationally. They even had a country they could virtually call their own. They were thus able to offer everything a state could offer to a militant group by way of support. As it had been during the Cold War, this was a two-way process. The local groups had their roots in a whole variety of local factors, often stretching back decades or even longer but, for a variety of short-term reasons, were keen to ally with the major power. Indeed many had been proxies before. One tactic used both by Washington and Moscow during the Cold War and now adopted by bin Laden and his associates is that of attempting to broker deals between warring factions of local groups. If successful, al-Qaeda establishes a degree of influence over both.

There are other models too that can be of use. Al-Qaeda can be seen as a venture capitalist firm, sponsoring projects submitted by a variety of groups or individuals in the hope that they will be profitable. Or viewed as a commissioning editor, providing funds and expertise to enable the production of the ideas of someone else.

Together these links, some tenuous, some more direct, allow us to speak of a loose 'network of networks'. This is not an 'al-Qaeda network'. It is a way of describing those elements within the broad movement of Islamic militancy who have some connections to the 'al-Qaeda hardcore' however varied and indistinct. Along with the 'al-Qaeda hardcore' and the 'network of networks' is a third element: the idea, worldview, ideology of 'al-Qaeda' and those who subscribe to it.

Bin Laden does not have the power to issue orders that are instantly obeyed. He is not the commander-in-chief of an army. In fact, any military analogies, despite the martial-sounding names assumed by many Islamic groups, are unhelpful in understanding their nature. Bin Laden does not kidnap young men and brainwash them. Both the young men who flocked to Afghanistan to seek military and terrorist training and the leaders of the more established groups who were happy to link themselves with bin Laden's group did so of their own volition. As is clear from the testimony of recruits in the training camps run by the 'al-Qaeda hardcore' in Afghanistan between 1996 and 2001, nobody was kept there against their will. Most overcame considerable obstacles to reach the camps. In the last years of the twentieth century, bin Laden's associates spent much of their time selecting which of the myriad requests for assistance they would grant. They came from everywhere from Morocco to Malaysia. These were not requests for money for refugee camps or new mosques. They were requests for help with bomb attacks, assassinations and murder on a horrific scale.

These requests, like the recruits who carried them, originated in the huge swathe of largely young men who are sufficiently motivated to want to devote substantial proportions of their lives and energies to the most extreme end of Islamic militancy. In very broad terms they share the key ideas, and the key objectives, of bin Laden and the 'al-Qaeda hardcore'. They subscribe, whether involved in a radical group or not, to the 'al-Qaeda' worldview. They speak the 'al-Qaeda' language. This is a difficult concept and is examined in greater detail in the following chapter but it is perhaps the most helpful of the various ways of conceiving of al-Qaeda. It is not about being part of a group. It is a way of thinking about the world, a way of understanding events, of interpreting and behaving. It is the composite of the common elements of all the various strands of modern Islamic radical thought and currently it is the most widespread, and the fastest growing, of the various elements that make up, to my mind, the phenomenon currently, and largely erroneously, labelled 'al-Qaeda'.

Yet the misconceptions about 'al-Qaeda' are proving as persistent as medieval depictions of Mohammed as a philanderer or of Muslims as saturnine sensualists. Why is this?

The first reason is that it is convenient and reassuring. It is enormously difficult to conceive of the nature of modern radical Islamic militancy without simple ideas that make sense of a hugely varied and shifting phenomenon. Blaming bin Laden implies that his removal will end any problem. Conceiving of 'al-Qaeda' as a traditional terrorist group constructs something that can be conventionally defeated.

Labelling opponents 'al-Qaeda' also allows repressive governments to do what they want with limited international criticism. After September 11th, governments can expect American support, both material and moral, to help counter any perceived Islamic extremist threat. During the autumn of 2001, al-Qaeda cells, previously

Self-fulfilling prophecy?

undetected, were 'discovered' in scores of countries. Tashkent suddenly branded the Islamic Movement of Uzbekistan, a group whose links to bin Laden are tenuous, as 'al-Qaeda'. For Beijing, it was the Uighur Muslims who were designated as the local branch of bin Laden's network, despite the fact that, though some individuals in some of the various Muslim groups resisting Chinese rule in the southeast of China may, at one time or another, have spent time in Afghan training camps, unrest in the region dates back to the first moments of Chinese domination. In Thailand, local police chiefs tried to blame a series of bomb explosions in the south of the country on 'al-Qaeda'. In fact, they were part of a long-running turf battle between the police and the military over protection and the smuggling rackets in which local Islamic groups were sometimes involved. The prime minister of Thailand immediately slapped down the claim. In Macedonia in March 2002, eight young Pakistani men were shot dead by police. The minister of the interior was swift to proclaim a victory for his, fairly unsavoury, government in the war against bin Laden. The men were merely illegal economic migrants.[17] When I visited the Tunisian embassy in London in January 2002, I was shown a list of 'Muslim extremists living in the UK linked to bin Laden'. This list comprised well-known, largely leftwing dissidents that the Tunisians had been trying to quieten for a decade or more.

The Abu Sayyaf group in the southern Philippines was formed by radicals returning from the war in Afghanistan as an offshoot of a far older Islamic movement that has roots in the struggle of local Muslims against the Christian dominance that resulted from colonial rule. Its links to bin Laden are tangential, and completely unsubstantiated. Its founder, Abdurajak Janjalani, died in 1998 and since then the group has largely abandoned militant Islam in favour of crime, particularly the kidnapping of wealthy Westerners. This does not stop the Philippine government labelling the group 'al-Qaeda' and Washington deploying hundreds of troops to the country to help to eradicate it.

The fact that bin Laden has never shown any real interest in Kashmir, let alone tried to go there, has not stopped repeated attempts by Indian intelligence to claim his presence in the contested mountain state. Usually India's regional rival, Pakistan, is blamed. Predictably, as tensions rose between Islamabad and New Delhi at the beginning of 2002, the claim that bin Laden was in Kashmir surfaced again. The London *Daily Telegraph* reported that, according to Indian intelligence, bin Laden was being hunted by a British special forces team there.[18] Quite why the 6ft 4" fugitive, one of the most instantly recognisable men in the world, would choose a war-torn province in a hostile nation garrisoned by more than 700,000 troops and paramilitary policemen as a refuge was not made clear. The claim re-emerged during another period of tension six months later. The US Defense Secretary, Donald Rumsfeld, following a briefing by the Indian prime minister in New Delhi announced that al-Qaeda were operating in Kashmir. Islamabad protested strongly; Rumsfeld checked with his own specialists and then retracted his statement.

Intelligence services lie, cheat and deceive. Propaganda is one of their primary functions. On 4 October 2001, a dossier was presented to the press on the 'responsibility for the terrorist atrocities in the US, 11 September 2001' by the British government. It included the line that '[al-Qaeda] activity includes substantial exploitation of the illegal drugs trade from Afghanistan' and claimed that bin Laden's 'drugs stockpiles' were protected by the Taliban. There has never been any evidence that bin Laden has ever been involved in narcotics production, and everyone involved in the trade in Pakistan, Afghanistan and elsewhere, from farmers through to the United Nations experts monitoring drugs production, denies the allegation. The dossier also claimed that 'from 1989 until 1991 [bin Laden] was based in Afghanistan and Peshawar, Pakistan. In 1991 he moved to Sudan, where he stayed until 1996.' Bin Laden's tumultuous two-year stay (from early 1990 to late 1992) in Saudi Arabia was omitted. The dossier also said that 'in the spring of 1993 operatives of al-Qaeda participated in the attack on US military personnel serving in Somalia.' This refers to the battle in Mogadishu in which 18 American servicemen were killed. This claim is almost certainly untrue as well.

The British intelligence specialists must have known that the dossier they gave to the prime minister to reveal to parliament and the British public to justify involvement in a major conflict included demonstrably false material but felt the war in Afghanistan needed to be fought and the public needed to be convinced of it. Painting bin Laden as profiting from the heroin trade served the same purpose as atrocity stories about Germans in the First World War,[19] and Saudi Arabia is a key ally that needs protecting. Yet there was no need to exaggerate the threat from bin Laden or al-Qaeda, in all its shapes and forms, in the weeks after September 11th. That it was necessary to dismantle bin Laden's terrorist complex in Afghanistan was widely accepted.

Similar tactics were used to prepare a reluctant public for a war with Iraq. In late 2001, senior former CIA officers and American politicians briefed journalists that Mohammed Atta had met an Iraqi agent in Prague prior to the September 11th attacks. Investigations by the FBI, the CIA and British and other European intelligence services showed the claim, itself retracted by the local intelligence service, to be untrue. Credit card documents proved Atta to have been in America at the time of the alleged meeting. In the summer of 2002, President George W Bush, White House hawks, and Tony Blair, the British prime minister, started talking about 'broad linkages' between Saddam's regime and al-Qaeda. I travelled to Iraqi Kurdistan to investigate the allegations and found them to be utterly unfounded.[20] When Tony Blair issued his long-awaited dossier of evidence aimed at convincing the British public of the need for war in Iraq, it did not mention al-Qaeda at all.

Oddly, a convention seems to have developed whereby something from a 'security source' acquires a degree of veracity. Such material thus appears to be exempted from normal journalistic practices. The fact that it cannot be confirmed independently is seen as a confirmation of the utility of the information rather than the opposite. There are, of course, no al-Qaeda press officers to approach for official confirmation. One frequently repeated claim is that bin Laden himself lived a life of debauchery in Beirut in his mid teens. Bin Laden was in fact a pious, studious, polite and somewhat shy teenager who was married at 17. Neither is there any evidence that bin Laden is an Arsenal fan who personally ordered the assassination of England and Manchester United football star David Beckham.[21] For the record, nor does bin Laden have a small or deformed penis nor is he homosexual.

I know from experience that selling a story to a news editor is a lot easier if you can involve bin Laden. When, as a penurious freelancer in the autumn of 1998, I reported an attempt by Russian smugglers to sell supposed 'enriched uranium' in Peshawar, the foreign editor of the tabloid I was working for said he was interested only if bin Laden was the putative buyer. When, on 28 August, Kerim Chatty was arrested in Stockholm's Vasteras airport with a gun in his toilet bag, the mere fact that he had been travelling on a plane with a group of Muslims who were on their way to a conference on the Salafi strand of Islam in Birmingham was enough for several British newspapers to splash a 'bin Laden link' on their front pages. Prosecutors have found no such connection or indeed any terrorist intent at all.[22]

Bin Laden is of course complicit in the confusion over the true nature and capability of his group. He has never directly claimed credit or admitted responsibility, at least not wittingly, for an attack. This clearly does not make the task of working out exactly for what he is responsible any easier. It does not mean however that we should leap to conclusions. Bin Laden did not claim credit for the embassy bombings in 1998, though he has claimed a role in instigating them, even though we know they were one of the operations run closely and directly by his close associates. With other attacks, such as those in Saudi Arabia in 1995 or in New York in 1993, he has praised the perpetrators. He has sometimes claimed a major role in Somalia, though in fact he did little. On other occasions he has denied involvement altogether. There have been various reasons for these inconsistencies. One is his own changing security environment. While a guest of the Taliban, bin Laden was careful not to irritate his hosts.[23] It is also true that strict Muslims believe it is wrong to claim credit for an act that has been successful solely due to the will of God. It is particularly wrong to claim credit for something with a view to improving one's position in some material way. There are tactical considerations too: bin Laden, though explicit about his status as a 'vanguard', is aware that this minority status should be played down as much as possible. Support in the broader community should be emphasised instead. From this point of view, it is better to imply that unknown 'brothers' rose up of their own will.

On the whole, however, bin Laden and the various elements outlined above share an interest in emphasising his role in modern Islamic militancy. A dialectic is thus set up. Myth breeds more myth. History gets re-written.

One history that is currently being revised is that of the training camps that were maintained in Pakistan and Afghanistan following the end of the war against the Soviets. Currently the dozens of facilities where militants trained in the 1990 to 1996 period are referred to as 'bin Laden camps'. The implication is that all those who trained there during this period, and the terrorist acts that many committed at the time or went on to commit later, were instigated, inspired, facilitated, indeed even directly commissioned, by bin Laden. Yet there is no evidence for any significant involvement of bin Laden in the dozens of establishments set up by Afghan and Pakistani religious hardliners at the time. The 1995 US State Department report on terrorism says that 'all the factions', including 'the regime in Kabul', are 'involved in harbouring or facilitating camps that have trained terrorists from many nations who have been active in worldwide terrorist activity'. It does not mention bin Laden; instead the report fingers one particular warlord, Abd al-Rab al-Rasul Sayyaf, for 'continuing to harbor and train potential terrorists in his camps in Afghanistan and Pakistan'.[24] The simple truth is that bin Laden was a marginal player at the time. Men like Sayyaf, one of the most hardline religious and political players in Afghanistan and a man who has excellent contacts with wealthy and devout Saudis who contribute huge sums to his coffers, were far more important. Grasping this is critical for understanding later developments.

Contemporary Islamic militancy is a diverse and complex historical phenomenon. To blame it all, or even a substantial portion of it, on one man is a gross over-simplification. Building bin Laden up to be a global mastermind directing a well-organised and effective network of terror is counter-productive. Now, with the 'al-Qaeda hardcore' scattered by the US-led action in Afghanistan and under enormous pressure from security services in the wake of September 11th, understanding the true nature of 'al-Qaeda', and thus of the threat we face, is more important than ever.

But, much as we must guard against exaggerating bin Laden's personal role, so we must be careful not to turn to other over-simplifications. One of the most pernicious is the idea that the September 11th attacks were a product of some kind of inevitable 'clash of civilisations' between the Islamic and Judaeo-Christian worlds. If there is no evil mastermind, the argument seems to run, then it is Islam that is at fault. But is it?

CHAPTER TWO

SEPTEMBER 11TH, TERROR AND ISLAM

On 11 September 2001, 19 men flew four planes into three buildings killing 3,315 people. The question of whether Islam itself could be blamed for the attack was swiftly asked. In later chapters, I explore the broader elements which may have motivated the hijackers, look at the slow unfurling of the major historical processes and minor events that together resulted in the September 11th attacks and define the situation we now find ourselves in. However, the hijackers found some resources within Islam itself. Though it is impossible to offer any comprehensive survey of Islam and the roots of modern Islamic militancy in only a few thousand words, certain elements are of critical importance.

As in the last chapter, definitions are important. There are multiple ways of defining terrorism and all are subjective. Most define terrorism as 'the use or threat of serious violence' to advance some kind of 'cause'. Some state clearly which types of group ('sub-national', 'non-state') or cause (political, ideological, religious) to which they refer. Others merely rely on the instinct of most people when confronted with an act that involves innocent civilians being killed or maimed by men armed with explosives, firearms or other weapons. None is satisfactory and grave problems with the use of the term persist. Terrorism is after all a tactic. The term 'war on terrorism' is thus effectively nonsensical. As there is no space here to explore this involved and difficult debate, my preference is, on the whole, for the less loaded term 'militancy'. This is not an attempt to condone such actions, merely to analyse them in a clearer way.

As with the term 'al-Qaeda', 'Islamic terrorism' is a catch-all of dubious use in helping us comprehend the phenomenon, and address the threat, confronting us. Like 'al-Qaeda' it is a useful shorthand, and is thus likely to be employed frequently and for the foreseeable future by journalists, policymakers and security agencies alike. One very simple reason for this is that repeatedly writing 'terrorist violence legitimised by a particular reading of Islam but rooted in a largely political project defined by local contingencies' is simply impractical.

Some would argue that the thought and aims of bin Laden and his associates are exclusively religious and that 'politics' as commonly conceived is of little interest to them. However a cursory glance at bin Laden's statements in recent years shows this not to be the case. Bin Laden is an activist with a very clear sense of what he wants and how he hopes to achieve it. Those means may be far outside the norms of political activity as we usually understand it but his agenda is a basically political one, though it is couched, of course, in religious language and imagery.

Bin Laden's views grew out of a strong, and continuing, tradition of dissent in Saudi Arabia, his native land, and the Islamic world more generally. Since 1996, bin Laden has demanded, among other things, the withdrawal of American troops from Saudi Arabia, tax, currency and sanitation reform in the kingdom, the lifting of sanctions on Iraq and an end to what he calls the oppression of the Palestinian, the Chechen and the Kashmiri peoples. He has condemned America for its use of atomic bombs in the Second World War, for its continuing development of weapons of mass destruction, for alleged 'human rights' abuses and for its support of Israel. In early autumn 2002, associates of bin Laden posted a 'letter to America', apparently authored by him, on the internet. Among the reasons for branding America 'the worst civilization ever' was the charge that the US is 'the biggest nation that destroys our natural surroundings and pollutes it with industrial waste'. 'You then refuse to sign the KYOTO agreement, so that you can continue to profit from these industries, whilst leaving a world barely inhabitable for our children,' it said.[1] In late 2001, Ayman al-Zawahiri , the Egyptian activist who was a major influence on bin Laden's political thinking, listed the 'tools' adopted by 'the Western forces' to fight Islam. They included:

> (1) The United Nations. (2) The friendly rulers of the Muslim peoples. (3) The multinational corporations. (4) The international communications and data exchange systems. (5) The international news agencies and satellite media channels. (6) The international relief agencies.[2]

The parallels with the favourite targets of secular activists on the far right or far left is obvious.

Some 'Islamic terrorists' share most of bin Laden's aims, some share a few, some share none. The hundreds of groups, cells, movements, even individuals, lumped together under the rubric 'Islamic terrorism' is enormously diverse. Individuals, and groups, turn to terrorism for a variety of reasons, some of which, though not all, may be shared with others. The motivation of Mohammed Atta, who led the September 11th hijackers, and Ramzi Yousef, who tried to blow up the World Trade Center in 1993, may superficially seem similar. They both appear to be driven by a fanatical anti-Americanism based in a radical interpretation of Islam. Yet Yousef saw himself as a playboy terrorist, leered at women in the courtroom and was far from observant in his own religious practice. Yousef saw his acts as a personal achievement. In contrast, Atta felt compelled to attack Western targets, much as he felt compelled to pray five times a day or avoid eating pork. He saw his actions as an unavoidable religious duty. Similarly, the motivations, tactics, and worldviews of the Indonesian Lashkar Jihad, the Egyptian al-Gamaa al-Islamiyya, the Bangladeshi Jihad Movement and the Pakistani/Kashmiri Jaish-e-Mohammed, though they share certain elements, are, as we shall see, very different. All these are Sunni Muslim groups. There are also hundreds of Shia groups. Branding them all 'Islamic terrorists' conceals the importance of local contingencies in the evolution of any group and hides the essentially political nature of their aim of creating a perfect, or at least a better, society. The anger of the Algerian GSPC, Egyptian Islamic Jihad, the Islamic Movement of Uzbekistan or the Libyan Fighting Group may be misguided, unjustified and have horrific and morally abhorrent consequences but the grievances that they are seeking to resolve are not in any way metaphysical. Their sense of grievance might be extreme but it is rooted in reality. In their manifestos they refer to real events and real people and what are perceived to be real problems. While bin Laden's discourse is based on an interpretation of Islamic history, his power is derived from playing on the current social, economic and political problems of the Muslim world.[3] Just because a lack of graduate employment, decent housing, social mobility, food etc is explained by an individual by reference to a religion does not make it a religious grievance. It remains a political grievance articulated with reference to a particular religious worldview. Other discourses, such as Marxist-Leninist dialectical materialism, can fulfil a similar function and indeed did throughout much of the Islamic world until relatively recently. At least one distinguished modern historian has referred to al-Qaeda as the extremist wing of a political religion, a term occasionally used to capture the nature of Nazism.[4] The influence of modern leftwing, and occasionally rightwing language and thought on bin Laden, his associates and many other modern Islamic radicals is clear from their public statements.

Almost all terrorists consider themselves to be soldiers who are 'at war'. American right-wingers use the greeting 'RAHOWA' which stands for 'racial holy war'. Their tracts announce that they 'believe there is a battle being fought this day between the children of darkness (today known as the Jews) and the children of light (God), the Aryan race'. Like most religious terrorists, they are convinced that a 'cosmic war' is underway around them. Hamas, the Palestinian Islamic extremist terror group, say they too are 'at war'. Meir Kahane's Jewish extremists talk of war between Jews and Arabs.[5] In his 1998 fatwa, bin Laden announced that the American actions in the Middle East were 'a clear declaration of war on God, His messenger and Muslims'.

If the world is understood as dominated by a cosmic struggle between good and evil all problems are explained. An individual can explain personal and communal suffering and humiliation. Even better, they can blame someone for both. A battle involves a clear and present danger from an obvious enemy. Seeing the world as a battlefield enables an individual to deploy a whole series of myths, cultural and religious references. This is hugely empowering. Those who take part in the cosmic struggle are holy warriors, proud, strong, deserving of respect and prestige.

Moreover, being at war implies both the possibility of victory and offers a vision of the means to achieve it. When the war is seen as cosmic, this triumph can be understood as the moment of social and personal transformation when an individual casts off all limitations. As the scholar and sociologist Mark Juergensmeyer comments: 'To be without such images of war is almost to be without hope itself.'[6] The idea of a cosmic struggle is thus enormously attractive. Yet though it is clear that resources that enable such worldviews of cosmic struggle exist in all religions (and in revolutionary leftwing thought too) there are elements within Islam that are peculiarly powerful in this regard.

Islam is a more explicitly political religion than many others and this makes its use to explain political grievances and, most importantly, to suggest a course of action to remedy any given situation far easier and far more potent. There are also other elements within Islam which, as we shall see, have been lent enormous power and significance by developments in entirely non-religious areas, such as technology.

Muslims believe that the Prophet Mohammed was picked by God or Allah to be His messenger to bring to the human race His final instructions on how to live in the material world. Mohammed, who lived in the Hijaz, now part of Saudi Arabia, between about 570 and 632CE, aurally received a text, known as the Qur'an, that was delivered as the word of God. The Qur'an is a 'revealed text' 'sent down' by God or Allah and is thus perfect, unchanging and unchangeable. Mohammed is the latest, and the last, in a series of prophets, who include Jesus and Moses, sent to bring the word of God to man. Alongside the Qur'an is the collection of narrative traditions that relate the behaviour and sayings, the example of the Prophet, called the *sunna*. These texts are known as the *hadith*. The hadith were collected by Mohammed's followers and compiled into collections after a long period of oral transmission by later Muslims, and are thus of varying authority and so are traditionally quoted with a description of their provenance. The hadith, on the whole, are not 'revealed' but originate in the acts and sayings of Mohammed in his capacity as a human being, whereas the Qur'an is understood to be the direct words of God without any human input. Mohammed, though chosen by God to be His messenger, was very much a man. Muslims do not worship Mohammed or the Qur'an but Allah and Allah alone. Any suggestion that Mohammed, as distinct from God, can be worshipped will be seen by pious Muslims as detracting from the absolute primacy and unity of God. This theological principle of oneness or unity, known as *tauhid*, is a fundamental, and deeply political, concept. Many Muslims, including bin Laden, believe it should be given political expression through the eradication of divisions, national or other, among Muslims and the unification of the *umma*, or Muslim community.

Mohammed was a warrior, a merchant, a philosopher, a judge and a radical social reformer. The Meccan community in which he grew up was riddled with hierarchy, inequality, greed, violence, tribalism and factionalism. To him, this was symbolised by the polytheism practised locally. War and feuding were a constant among the Arabian tribes and left them vulnerable to the threat of the superpowers of the day, the Persians and the Byzantine Romans. Mohammed's demand that the only recognisable authority was God was genuinely revolutionary, directly challenging the powerful tribal oligarchy that ruled Mecca. The fundamental message of the Qur'an was that the community on earth had strayed from God's instructions over the years, and was now riven with social injustice and wrongdoing as a result. Unsurprisingly, the young Islamic community faced many powerful and well-armed enemies. These were eventually overcome and the internal peace established. This, conservative Muslims believe, was as a result of

Mohammed's success in implementing Allah's instructions. The nature of the society of these first Muslims, the forefathers or *salaf*, and the incredible expansion of the Islamic community throughout the Arabian peninsular and beyond towards the Maghreb and south and central Asia during the time of the Prophet and his immediate successors has been proof to devout Muslims ever since that following the instructions of Allah and the examples of the Prophet will ensure a just and peaceable society and the concomitant cultural, military and political superiority of the Islamic world. The texts and the example of the first generations of believers thus provide an ideal, a reference point, that can be compared, inevitably unfavourably, with any given extant government, situation or ruler. They offer a vision of an 'authentic' and 'true' Islamic society, against which reality rarely stands much comparison. This is a political resource of enormous power. The core texts of the Qur'an and the hadith are thus 'closed', in that they are unchangeable, but also 'open', in that they are infinitely flexible, providing answers in principle to all questions of behaviour at all times. The former quality means they have an autonomy that prevents manipulation by anyone hoping for short-term gain in a specific local or political context, the latter means they can be made appropriate for all people in all situations.[7] This again means that Islam is always politically engaged as it allows dissident movements in the Islamic world to appeal to the 'purity' of an, often imagined, earlier society or religio-political order, predicated on a 'true', authentic reading of the Holy texts. There is thus an obvious religious answer, and proscribed programme for action, for any political grievance. If the corrupting elements are purged, the logic runs, a fair and just and happy society will be established.

To ensure their continued relevance in the real world, the Qur'an and the hadith need to be interpreted. Though some of their message is clear, much needs to be drawn out through a process of exegesis, particularly when looking for answers to elements that simply did not exist in seventh-century Arabia. This was recognised by Mohammed himself, who explicitly condoned reasoned argument, leading to a consensus ruling, over such issues. The process of interpreting the texts to provide guidance on an issue that is not ruled on directly by the Qur'an is known as *ijtihad* and, though Islam recognises no clergy with intercessionary powers, a corps of specialised experts in such reasoning and the sciences associated with it emerged. They were known as *ulema* (singular *alim*), 'the learned'.

Reformist movements, based on a 'return' to the Qur'an and the

Prophet's sunna, have been a recurring pattern in Islamic history. There have been successive waves of dissent and schism, all of which have been rooted in a specific social and political context. An early example was Islam's split into Sunni and Shia branches, within a century of Mohammed's death, over whether a direct descendant of the Prophet should be appointed over the broader community's favoured candidate when appointing the *caliph*, the leader of the umma, a position in which were vested significant military and political powers, but no inherent religious authority. The origins of the split were political and personal, though the division later became enshrined in doctrine (and, many scholars say, by ethnic divisions between Persians and Arabs).[8] The Shias felt that to appoint anyone but a descendant of the Prophet was a departure from, and thus a corruption of, the ideals of the Prophet. Another early example is that of the *Kharijites*, 'those who go out' (from the Arabic *kharaja*), who preached a radical, puritanical egalitarianism accusing the successors of Mohammed of foregoing his true message. The Assassins, a radical Shia group, are another example. Over the centuries, many Muslim dissident movements have accused the ulema of being complicit with the corruption of the Islamic message. The clergy, whose influence is often underestimated by Western commentators, are often seen as self-serving, co-opted partners of an evil wordly elite.[9]

A key dissident for contemporary radical thinkers, often quoted by bin Laden and modern Islamic militants, is the fourteenth-century conservative Islamic scholar, Taqi al-Din ibn Taimiya. Ibn Taimiya is seen as the spiritual father of modern radical revolutionary Sunni Islamic activism. The fall of Baghdad to the Mongols in 1258 had been an appalling shock for devout Muslims at the time. After centuries of military expansion, political and cultural superiority, most Muslims had considered the conquest of the caliphate and of Islam by infidels to be impossible. A similar shock was to be felt more than five centuries later on Napoleon's invasion of Egypt. Ibn Taimiya reasoned that the weakness that had allowed the defeat was a result of the failure of the Muslim community, or umma, to properly follow the injunctions of the early Holy texts. He was hounded into exile in Damascus where he continued his campaigning, spending much of his life in prison as a result.

Several key concepts within Islam have a powerful resonance in current times. The division of the world into categories, including the *dar ul harb* (the realm or house of war) and the *dar ul Islam* (the realm of Islam), is one and has been repeatedly quoted by bin Laden. Another key resource is what Malise Ruthven calls the 'Mohammedan

Paradigm'.[10] Mohammed was forced to flee Mecca by the wealthy rulers who liked neither his rejection of their authority in favour of God's nor his attacks on the worship of the idols in the main shrine in the city, the Ka'aba, on which a lucrative pilgrim industry was based. Mohammed, unable to practise his religion, secretly left for the city of Medina, then called Yathrib, with a small group of followers. His flight in 622AD is known as the *hijra* and its significance is such that the Islamic calendar is dated from that event, not Mohammed's birthday or his first revelation. Such a flight in the face of oppression is explicitly recommended by the Qur'an.[11] The next years were hard, with Mohammed caught between the suspicion of many of the people of Medina and the military might of Mecca. But he prevailed, defeating the Meccans at the battle of al-Badr in 624AD and eventually winning over the people of Medina. He was able to return to his home city in triumph in 630AD, dying two years later. Muslim reformists, from the Kharijites through the Assassins to bin Laden, have consciously mimicked the hijra and withdrawn from a society that opposes them to live as 'true' Muslims and to launch a campaign that they believe will, like Mohammed's, eventually be successful. Following the Mohammedan Paradigm they understand that they will be tried by periods of oppression and difficulty but, as they follow Allah's will and Mohammed's injunctions, they, or the generations that follow them, will eventually triumph. For bin Laden and his associates, this model of flight (hijra) and struggle (*jihad*) is hugely powerful and frequently features in their statements. But it brings practical problems. The withdrawal isolates the enlightened from the masses that they need to mobilise to achieve their aims.

On his return to Mecca, Mohammed established a society known ever since among Muslims for its justice. Justice, and its opposite, injustice, is again a very powerful motivating resource within Islam and has obvious social and political elements. As with the anticlericalism directed at the 'establishment' ulema, this stress will be familiar to anyone who has studied Western European, and indeed American, revolutionary or dissident movements. It is disappointed aspirations, a sense of unfairness, that are critical in motivating much 'revolutionary' political action, not absolute deprivation, and this helps explain bin Laden's constant reference to the 'humiliation' of the umma. The aspiration is not world conquest but world leadership by the umma, conceived of as a replication of the political, cultural, military and social superiority enjoyed by Muslims between the seventh century and the time of the European Renaissance. The opposite of justice, tyranny, or *zulm*, can and must be resisted, as it was by the Prophet and his earliest followers, by ibn Taimiya and by so many other movements over the centuries.

The struggle against zulm is jihad. Indeed an effort against, or for, many things, is jihad. The root of the word is the Arabic *Jhd*, meaning strain, effort, struggle, endeavour or striving. The word ijtihad, the effort to interpret, comes from the same root. According to one well-known hadith, Mohammed distinguished two jihads: the greater, against oneself, and the lesser, against another. It does not necessarily mean 'holy war' as is so often said. Indeed one can have the jihad of the heart, of the pen, of the tongue, of the sword and so on. Islamic scholars and jurists have argued over the exact definition of jihad throughout Islamic history.

The problems of defining jihad condense many of the key issues highlighted above. Mohammed's pronouncements on jihad vary and, taken together, show clearly how political and engaged Islam has always been. Early Islamic scholars dealt with the ambiguities by showing how Mohammed's injunctions were appropriate to the various stages of his struggle. Early Qur'anic verses, delivered to Mohammed between 610 and 623AD while his community was small, unpopular and barely tolerated by vastly superior forces, urge patience and the spreading of the word of Islam through non-violent means alone. 'There is no compulsion in religion, for the right way is clear from the wrong way,' the Qur'an says (2:256). After the time of the hijra, Allah appears to have given permission for Muslims to engage in defensive warfare.[12] Later verses, received by Mohammed when at the height of his power, enjoined an offensive against unbelievers: 'fight and slay the pagans wherever ye find them and seize them, beleaguer them and lie in wait for them' (9:5). These verses, known as the 'Sword verses', were held by the ulema of the powerful and expansionist Ummayad and Abbasid dynasties to abrogate the previous more pacifistic Qur'anic injunctions. This interpretation provided a religious justification for armed expansion by the newly confident dominant ruling group. Though modern moderates prefer to quote the early verses, contemporary radicals, such as bin Laden, following the ideologues of the Ummayads and the Abbasids, maintain that they are abrogated by the later more aggressive verses. Abdallah Azzam makes this point explicitly. Writing in 1986 he said: 'The Sword verses abrogate around 140 verses on jihad… revealed previously… They give a definite answer to anyone who questions [the Qur'an's] clear definition [of jihad].'[13] In November 2002, Mohammed al-Massari, the British-based Saudi Arabian dissident, circulated a lengthy rebuttal of moderate Muslims' claims, post-September 11th, that the jihad of bin Laden and the hijackers was wrongly conceived. These moderates, his circular said, were trying to 'water down Islam to make it more palatable for their Christian and Zionist masters'. The only true definition of jihad 'is fighting for the sake of Allah... True believers will never be deflected from this task... The highest jihad is having your blood spilled'.[14]

So, like almost all Islamic practice and belief, the doctrine of jihad is the product of various readings and applications of the principles of the sacred texts, each in specific historical and political contexts.[15] Despite this, there are a number of elements in the doctrine of jihad that are widely accepted and are important to any attempt to comprehend September 11th or any other modern act of 'Islamic terrorism'. There are, for example, both defensive and offensive elements in the contemporary Islamic militant's understanding of jihad. In the 'cosmic struggle' between the forces of good and evil, jihad is seen as largely defensive. A sense of last-ditch defence is a common theme in the writings of bin Laden and other Islamic militants. It is not sophistry but a manifestation of a genuine sense that they are warriors engaged in a desperate struggle for survival against an aggressive and powerful enemy intent on humiliating, weakening and eventually destroying them.

However, their views are also informed by a more offensive reading of jihad, as outlined by Syed Qutb, the Egyptian radical thinker seen as the principal ideologue of modern Sunni Islamic radicalism.[16] Because Islam aims 'to abolish those oppressive political systems under which people are prevented from expressing their freedom to choose whatever beliefs they want' the aim of jihad is thus to tackle 'the material obstacles' such as 'political power resting on a complex of interrelated ideological, racial, class, social and economic structures' that are responsible for the perpetuation of oppression.[17] 'After annihilating the tyrannical force, whether political or a racial tyranny, or domination of one class over the other within the same race, Islam establishes a new social and economic political system, in which all men enjoy real freedom.'[18] Jihad is thus an obligation on all Muslims. The political elements of Qutb's thinking and the influence of contemporary leftwing thought (Qutb was writing in the early 1960s) is clear.

However, it is a mistake to see jihad as merely a tactic aimed at achieving a specific worldly goal. This point is critical in understanding why acts of spectacular terror, especially those involving the suicides of the attackers, occur. Fundamentally, acts of jihad are conceived of as demonstrations of faith performed for God by an individual. The immediate local aims or enemies are largely irrelevant. Jihad is part of the cosmic struggle and thus to expect an immediate result from it would be presumptuous and wrong. 'The scope of this struggle is not limited to this earth or to this life. The observers of this struggle are not merely a generation of men,' says Qutb.[19] In early 2002, Suleiman abu Gaith, a spokesman for bin Laden, said it again:

> We believe we are still at the beginning of this war... So if we are killed or captured or the enemies of Allah manage to achieve one victory... we should not forget that this path is long and it is a path that the Muslims have to walk upon until judgement day.[20]

Though jihad will eventually result in victory, should Allah will it, that victory may be generations, centuries, even millennia away. It is the act that is important, not its results. Jihad is conceived of as an eternal process of affirming faith that should be performed by all Muslims at all times. As pointed out above, the struggle of living as a good Muslim in a world of trial and temptation is jihad. Like so many other key Islamic concepts, jihad is thus uniquely transferable to any geographic or political context.[21]

This demonstrative, sacrificial quality in jihad combines with another essential element of Islam, the *Shahadah,* the 'testament' or the bearing witness, with a potency that is of critical importance for understanding what happened on 11 September.

The Shahadah is the first of the five 'pillars' of Islam, that make a Muslim a Muslim.[22] The call to prayer, the *adhan*, includes the lines '*ash-hadu an la illaha illallah, ash-hadu Mohammed ur rasulullah*', which are usually translated as 'I bear witness that there is no god but Allah, I bear witness that Mohammed is His prophet'. This submission to the sovereignty of God, and one God alone, is a political act. All other authority, whether that of the tribal leaders who ruled the Arabian peninsular before Mohammed received and propagated his message or the current Egyptian, Algerian or Saudi government, is superseded by God's. The Shahadah is both a statement of profound personal faith and a declaration to others, a 'bearing witness'. Being a witness needs someone other than God, who is after all omniscient, as an audience. The testament was aimed, understandably given Mohammed's desire to make converts, at a believer's fellow men. Jihad shares this demonstrative quality, particularly when combined with that ultimate affirmation of faith – martyrdom.

Indeed, the Arabic Qur'anic word for a martyr or the martyred, *shahid*, also means witness. It comes from the same root as 'shahadah'. This is critical for understanding the worldview and the motivations of contemporary Islamic militants. In the last paragraph of the final instructions that Mohammed Atta gave the hijackers on the eve of the September 11th attack is the injunction to 'let [their] last words be 'There is no god but God and Mohammed is his prophet'.[23] They knew that the witnesses to the testament they verbalised with the Shahadah and demonstrated at that moment with their martyrdom would, thanks to satellite television, be counted in billions.

Such a spectacular martyrdom is thus the ultimate demonstration of jihad as a testament. The primary audience is of course God but, in addition, martyrdom involves a demonstration of faith to various audiences for various purposes. Primarily it affirms the strength of the martyr's own faith, courage and bravery and right to belong, to their own close community. (To those outside that community, understandably, it demonstrates cowardice and fanaticism.) It also demonstrates to the enemies of the faith that, though there may be an obvious disparity in their material strength, the combatants engaged in the 'cosmic struggle' are in fact fighting an equal fight. There has been no conflict yet where both sides have used suicide bombers. A suicide attack is designed to demonstrate that faith is lacking on one side and exists on the other and so to force all aware of the martyr's action (all 'witnesses') to conclude that, despite the apparent imbalance of forces, when the most important quality is considered – the faith that is necessary for victory in the long run – it is the suicide bomber who has it in greatest depth. In an interview in September 2002, al-Zawahiri stated this explicitly, saying: 'It is the love of death in the path of Allah, that is the weapon that will annihilate this evil empire of America, by the permission of Allah.'[24]

Finally the suicide attack demonstrates faith and strength to those the bomber, and his commanders, hope to motivate. It makes it impossible to ignore what the martyr believes and suggests strongly that only something with inherent value, authenticity and power could provoke such an act. Similarly it suggests that the 'cosmic struggle' is also a reality. On top of all this, there is also a shaming element. A suicide attack, an incredible sacrifice carried out 'on their behalf', presents a challenge to a spectator's own lack of faith or inaction.

The problem for bin Laden and others is that the vast majority of Muslims, though they may feel profound sympathy with the Palestinians, oppose actions in Iraq, feel humiliated by the presence of American troops in Saudi Arabia and elsewhere in the Middle East and are concerned by burgeoning Western cultural and political hegemony, do not sympathise with his methods and reject his extremism. Bin Laden and other extremists are aware that, of the many Muslims sympathetic to them, very, very few are going to act on those sentiments. Though they may be pleased, sometimes secretly, that bin Laden is taking a stand and feel a profound, though complex, identification with his cause, the vast majority of Muslims do not condone his methods and are not disposed to take up arms. The extremists thus see their task, like that of all political activists, as being to mobilise and radicalise. Bin Laden outlined his aim explicitly in an interview with al-Jazeera, the Qatari TV channel in 1999: 'We seek to instigate the [Islamic] nation to get up and liberate its land, to fight for the sake of God and to make the Islamic law the highest law and the word of God the highest word of all.'[25]

However, there are considerable practical problems facing modern extremists. They reject the gradualism of many Islamic thinkers, on the basis that there can be no compromise with the forces of unbelief and no divergence from the true path. Yet a gradual approach, as the Egyptian Muslim Brotherhood has shown, is possibly the only strategy that will be successful. The alternative is hijra, the Qur'anically prescribed flight to an environment where true Islam can be practiced. Two of the extremists' problems remain unresolved by flight however. The first is understanding why 99 percent of Muslims still reject their radical teachings. The second is changing this situation, but from a position of exile, with all the practical problems this entails.

Here, the thought of bin Laden and his associates owes as much to contemporary leftwing thought as to the holy texts, their exegetes and the examples of dozens of radical reformist movements before them. The lack of sympathy their radical views elicit among most Muslims is attributed to 'false consciousness'. So al-Zawahiri describes the hordes that turned out at the funeral held for the very secular Gamal Abdel Nasser on his death in 1970 as:

> only the residue of *the state of unconsciousness* that prevailed among the Egyptian masses thanks to his strong media and a kind of farewell by the Egyptians to their ruler. Soon they replaced him with another ruler, who took another turn and started to sell them *a new illusion*.

Currently, al-Zawahiri says, there is a huge 'gap in understanding between the jihad movement and the common people'. He attributes this to 'the media siege imposed on the message of the jihad movement as well as the campaign of deception mounted by the government media'.[26]

To wake the masses, a 'vanguard' is needed to lead by example. Here again, the thought of the modern Islamic radical fuses elements of religious tradition with modern secular revolutionary theory to create uniquely powerful, attractive and convincing ideas. Sura 2:249 of the Qur'an says: 'God replied: "Many a small band has, by God's grace, vanquished a mighty army. God is with those who endure with fortitude."' Bin Laden repeatedly uses this reference. The tradition of revolutionary vanguards in leftwing thought is well established. In the Middle East, the model of a small group of militants using violence to seize control of a state and then being greeted with grateful acclamation is a familiar one to nationalists, Arabists and Islamists alike.[27] Abdallah Azzam's 1987 reference to 'al-Qaeda' as a vanguard was mentioned in Chapter One. Azzam returned to the theme again and again:

> When the *umma* goes astray… God sends an individual or small group of people who will rescue it from perdition and restore it to the path of truth. This small elite are the ones who carry conviction and ambitions. And an even smaller group from this band are those who flee from the worldly life in order to spread and act upon these ambitions. And an even smaller group from this elite… are those who sacrifice their souls and their blood in order to bring victory to these ambitions and principles.[28]

It is here that the concepts of jihad and martyrdom, and of the spectacular, are so key. In his book, al-Zawahiri warns: 'we must mobilize the nation in the battle of Islam against infidelity. We caution against the risk of… Muslim vanguards getting killed *in silence*.' For by using modern communications the vanguard in self-imposed (and more secure) exile can reach out to the population at large without the possibly compromising, and lengthy, process of mobilisation through grassroots organisation and activism. In his statement on 7 October 2001, bin Laden specifically referred to the September 11th attackers as a 'vanguard of Islam… rendered successful by Islam'.[29]

There have been many terrorist attacks, some involving the suicide of the attackers, before. But none has been watched live by tens if not hundreds of millions of people. This is the spectacular in its most extreme, mediatised form. This was grasped by the German contemporary composer, Karl Heinz Stockhausen, and the British artist, Damien Hirst, both of whom, to almost universal opprobrium, have described the attack on the Twin Towers as works of art. As Jean Baudrillard pointed out weeks after September 11th: 'we are far beyond ideology and politics now... the aim is... to radicalise the world by sacrifice'.[30] Bin Laden made this point explicitly in a videotaped conversation he held with supporters in November 2001 in Afghanistan. 'Those young men [the hijackers]... said in deeds... speeches that overshadowed all other speeches made everywhere else in the world. The speeches are understood by Arabs and non-Arabs – even by Chinese.'

The aim is to solve the practical problem posed to the vanguard by hijra and the power of the security forces (or the apathy and reason of the masses) through massive spectacular theatrical violence. This is jihad, the sacrifice for God, the testament of martyrdom, the stunning, impressive horror of the power of faith for the witnesses, and the cataclysmic, millenarian violence that will, through the sheer creative power of destruction, instigate the Muslim world to rise up. It is both the alarum, the call to arms in the cosmic struggle, and the cleansing violence of the battle itself, the unleashing of apocalyptic power which will cause cataclysmic change. From the ashes will rise a new world order. Like theatre, the effect of the attack would have been lost if no one had seen it.

There is no mention of 'al-Qaeda' in a British newspaper before 1998. Now it is impossible that anywhere with an internet connection, a satellite dish or a newspaper is untouched in some way by the phenomenon and discourse that bin Laden 'personifies'. From eastern Indonesia to western Morocco, conflicts are described as 'jihads', casualties as shahid, the enemy is *kufr* (unbelief). Why?

The discourse associated with al-Qaeda is very contemporary. It is accessible, demotic and needs no great erudition or literacy to understand. Like the propaganda campaigns waged during the Iran-Iraq war, it evokes events and personalities, many dating back to the seventh century, in the knowledge that they will be understood by the target audience, a large proportion of whom are illiterate.[31] The symbolism is powerful but easy to grasp. It offers instant gratification, instant empowerment. Any group or individual can find elements that are useful within it. Local groups can pick and choose from its parts like local country franchises designing their McDonalds with a maharaja burger in New Delhi and chips with mayonnaise in Holland. Its symbols have even spread outside the Islamic context. Thai Hells Angels now sport portraits of bin Laden on their bikes and helmets. Bin Laden has become a counter-cultural symbol, representative of a discourse of dissent.

Before satellite TV, phones and the internet, bin Laden might have been nothing more than a Messianic *mahdi* for a thousand tribesmen. But modern communications technology has allowed exiled radicals to broadcast their views to target populations free from state interference or retribution. Bin Laden's gripping and powerful pre-recorded video clip, delivered before the US air raids on Afghanistan and shown by al-Jazeera within hours of their inception, epitomised the inadequacy of the response the most powerful state in the world could muster in the face of basic modern telecommunications used well. Concomitants of modern communications technology have also been important. There is now a far greater sense of community among the world's Muslims, a far more profound sense of the umma than at any time since the Western colonial powers broke up the remains of the Islamic Empire 80 years ago. That has meant a far greater audience for bin Laden's brand of radicalism too.

The huge variety of local articulations of modern Islamic militancy will become clear over the following chapters. It poses a problem of nomenclature. One of the problems of writing about modern Islamic extremists such as bin Laden is that a vocabulary to describe their ideas has yet to be successfully constructed. Various different terms are used with varying degrees of utility and general comprehension. The label 'fundamentalism' was once commonly applied to describe Islamic religious radicals until its obvious limitations (all devout Muslims are in a sense 'fundamentalists', in that they believe in the 'fundamentals' of their religion and consult the holy texts, seen as authentic and revealed, for guidance) resulted in its widespread rejection. It is now returning to vogue. Islamic radicals (such as Kharijites, the Assassins, or the Wahhabis) are sometimes referred to as 'reformist' because they hope to promote reform, *islah*, of their religion. However, the term can also be used to refer to those moderate Muslims who have reacted to the challenges of modernity by adapting Islam to minimise clashes with the politics and culture of the West. 'Revivalist' usually refers to Islamic activists who have hoped to recreate something of the Islamic world's former glory, often through 'reformism' or through Millenarian or Messianic movements, usually led by one charismatic individual. Wahhabis and most reformist movements are *salafis* or *salafist*, another broad term describing those Muslims who believe that society should emulate that of Mohammed and the early believers, the *salaf*, as literally described by the Qur'an and the hadith, with great precision. A useful term, often wrongly used, is Islamist, which describes those Muslims who aim to establish a pure (i.e. reformed) Islamic society by means of the appropriation through activism of modern state structures. Salafism, with its rejection of modernity, theoretically runs counter to Islamism, with its exploitation of the modern state, though the end result might be virtually indistinguishable. Some modern Salafist movements have been termed 'neo-traditional' as a result.

Bin Laden and his fellow extremists are Millenarian, fundamentalist, reformist, revivalist, Wahhabi/Salafi and, at least in their rootedness in modernity if not their programme, Islamist. A key element of the success of their discourse is that it combines so many elements of preceding ideologies. No single term exists to describe their thought or the broad movement of which they are part. However, a detailed look at bin Laden, his career and his operations, situated within the context of modern Islamic militancy, provides an insight that a label cannot.

CHAPTER THREE

RADICALS

It was late October 2001. Across the border, the Pentagon said, the jets were running out of targets. In the frontier city of Peshawar news filtered in through refugees, through snatched conversations on satellite phones with scared Afghan aid-workers, through the Taliban officials who slipped across into Pakistan to rally support and to rest. When I was in the city, between trips out into tribal territory, I spent most of my evenings in the bazaars, in the bar at Pearl Intercontinental, sitting amid mounds of cushions, rugs, meat, rice and grapes at the house of Ekram, my Afghan friend and colleague, or with Mr Khaled.

Mr Khaled, a local journalist who had been deeply involved with the more radical Afghan resistance groups during the war against the Soviets, was well placed to find out what was happening. He also, as he disclosed one evening as we strolled back through University Town from a cheap Afghan restaurant on the Khyber road, had been, for a while, a close friend of 'Mr Osama'.

We were walking along Syed Jamal al-Din Afghani road, a pleasant, quiet street close to the canal that marks off University Town, with its villas for retired Pashtun bureaucrats and senior soldiers, from the more crowded streets in Afghan Colony where the wealthier Afghan refugees have made their homes. It is named after the nineteenth-century Muslim thinker who first started talking about the Islamic world and 'the West' as two discrete entities. The tarmac of the road is perpetually covered in a thick layer of dust and gravel and bright bougainvilleas hang down the whitewashed walls of the houses, most of which are set back from the road behind large well-tended lawns. At the road's eastern end there is a small mosque, built in the classical Mughal style, with complex patterned screens, *chattris* and curling arches, overlooked by tall, mature eucalyptus trees. As we passed it, Khaled told me that he and 'Mr Osama' used to pray there together in the mid 1980s. Mr Osama had been such a sweet man, such a good and honest friend, Khaled said. He could not understand how what had happened in New York could have been done by him. Khaled speaks quietly and with unfailing and elaborate courtesy.

Mr Osama's story starts in the remote, poor and fiercely conservative Hadramawt province of the Yemen. The legend has it that in around 1930 Mohammed bin Awad bin Laden, a powerfully built labourer, six foot tall and with one dead eye, packed a bag and bought a place on a camel caravan that was heading north. It stopped, a thousand miles later, in the port of Jeddah where Osama's father started work as a labourer, putting away a few coins each day as capital for the day when he could set up a company of his own. In fact, Osama's father is more likely to have been a minor Hadramawti sheikh or a master-builder who did little physical work himself.[1] Either way, he had arrived in Jeddah, the southern Arabian port city, at a critical time. Nearly 200 years before, chieftains of the al-Saud clan had given refuge to a militant Islamic preacher and theologian called Mohammed ibn Abd al-Wahhab. Now their alliance was finally bearing fruit. Al-Wahhab's radical doctrines were known as Wahhabism, the latest in a succession of revivalist and reformist movements that swept through the Islamic world in the eighteenth century.

Like ibn Taimiya, to whom he often explicitly referred, and many other reformers, al-Wahhab believed that the original perfection of Allah's message as transmitted by Mohammed had become obscured by centuries of *bida*, or innovation, and called for a fresh interpretation of Islam that returned to its sources. Al-Wahhab said all Muslims must rigorously observe all the laws of Islam if a true and just Islamic society was to become a reality. He was particularly exercised by the sort of intercessionary practices – the use of shrines, talismans and saints – that were common on the Arabian peninsular. These, he believed, constituted *shirk*, or polytheism of the sort practiced by local tribes before the Prophet Mohammed had enlightened them more than 1,100 years previously. Other elements he believed contravened the principles followed by the first and best generation of Muslims included dancing, wearing jewellery and playing music.

The followers of al-Wahhab, known later as the *ikhwan* or brothers, believed that, as they were fighting a 'jihad', death for the cause would gain them entry to heaven as martyrs. This made them extremely effective fighters. Persecuted in his hometown, al-Wahhab was given shelter in a town called Diriya by a local tribal leader from the al-Saud clan. The leader and his successors were to use the ikhwan to great effect against the ramshackle, hierarchical and fractious tribes of the Arabian peninsular. In a series of campaigns, the ikhwan carried the rule of the al-Saud and their own Wahhabi faith to much of central and eastern Arabia, before being rebuffed at the end of the eighteenth century by the Egyptian clients of the Ottomans. The wars, with the al-Saud tribes providing political leadership and the ikhwan providing the muscle, recommenced in the twentieth century. This time the Ottoman Empire, who, as caliphs, were theoretically the successors of the Prophet as political rulers of the Islamic world, were unable to resist their onslaught. The Ottomans had sided with the Germans in the First World War and had been defeated and seriously weakened. A young army officer called Kemal Ataturk took power, launched a brutal and radical programme of secularisation and abolished the caliphate in 1924.

The British, the major power in the region in that post-war period, were happy for the House of al-Saud to consolidate their hold on Arabia. In return for British recognition of his rule, Abdul Aziz al-Saud, the clan's leader, pledged to rein in the ikhwan, who had begun threatening key strategic British outposts along the Gulf.[2] With most of Arabia, including the Holy places of Mecca and Medina, already in al-Saud's control, the ikhwan had outlived their usefulness to the new dominant power in the peninsular and were disbanded in 1929. The more moderate among them were incorporated into the national guard. The more extreme were gunned down at the Battle of Sabilah in March 1929. The state of Saudi Arabia was declared three years later, about the time Mohammed bin Awad bin Laden was getting his construction business off the ground.

Having destroyed the Wahhabi warriors as an independent force, Abdul Aziz took a different tack with the Wahhabi ulema, co-opting them into the new state to provide it with much-needed religious legitimacy. The Saudi Arabian ulema could usually be relied upon by the rulers to issue supportive fatwas when necessary, but the al-Saud dynasty had to pay a substantial price. The Wahhabi ulema were allowed to run state-sponsored schools, universities, government bureaucracies (especially the ministries of Justice and Haj) and were permitted to direct the growing number of international non-governmental organisations established to promote Wahhabism, or its affiliates, overseas. This compact was to be of critical importance, particularly after 1979.

Mohammed bin Laden worked hard to set himself up as a

construction contractor. The discovery of oil in the peninsular in the early 1930s meant that Abdul Aziz, the new king, had huge resources at his disposal, much of which he spent on palaces for the ruling elite, foreign guests and the royal court (as well as funnelling substantial amounts to the religious establishment).[3] By the early 1950s, Mohammed bin Laden was running a successful small firm. By heavily undercutting local firms he expanded quickly. His big break came when a foreign contractor withdrew from a deal to build the Medina-Jeddah highway and he took on the job.[4] By the early 1960s, business was flooding in, bin Laden was a very rich man and the bin Laden group was a huge and growing construction conglomerate.[5]

Mohammed bin Laden, who died illiterate, was born near the holy city of Tarim in Britain's South Arabian Protectorate, a stronghold of traditional 'Shaf'ism'. In Saudi Arabia, he appears to have adopted the rigorous Wahabbi Islam of his adopted land. He hosted large groups of ulema and Islamic leaders from throughout the world at his homes in Jeddah, Mecca and Riyadh, often funding their travel to, and around, the Arabian peninsular. He donated substantial sums to Islamic charities and activists and boasted that, using his private helicopter, he could pray in the three holiest locations in Islam – Mecca, Medina and the al-Aqsa mosque in Jerusalem – in a single day. Visiting the former two sites must have been especially satisfying, for it was the contract to restore and expand the facilities serving pilgrims and worshippers there that had established the reputation of his company across the Middle East, confirmed its status as the in-house builders of the House of al-Saud and made him fabulously wealthy. Quite how wealthy became clear when, in 1964, a royal succession battle was won by Crown Prince al-Faisal. When it was found that the state's finances had been so badly mismanaged that the new king was unable to pay his civil servants' salaries, Mohammed bin Laden stepped in, and for six months he paid their wages instead.[6]

Osama bin Laden's mother, Hamida Alia Ghanoum, was neither Saudi nor Wahhabi, but the beautiful, cosmopolitan, educated 22-year-old daughter of a Syrian trader. She shunned the traditional Saudi veil in favour of Chanel trouser suits and this, coupled with the fact that she was foreign and Mohammed bin Laden's tenth or 11th spouse, diminished her status within the family.[7] Hamida was still married to the millionaire magnate when he died and, as Mohammed bin Laden allowed even his former wives to live at his palace at Jeddah, it was there, amid a huge family and the solid gold statues, the ancient tapestries and the Venetian chandeliers, that Mohammed's 17th son, Osama, grew up. Stories of Hamida, or her son, being rejected by the family appear exaggerated.[8]

Osama bin Laden was born in Riyadh on 10 March 1957 and was ten when his father, of whom he had seen little, died in a helicopter crash.[9] A flavour of the bin Laden household comes from an anonymous document provided to an American PBS television programme in 1998 by 'an anonymous source close to bin Laden'. It offers good, if awkwardly phrased, insights into Osama's childhood. 'The father had very dominating personality. He insisted to keep all his children in one premises,' it reads. 'He had a tough discipline and observed all the children with strict religious and social code... At the same time, the father was entertaining with trips to the sea and desert,' the document goes on. 'He dealt with his children as big men and demanded them to show confidence at young age.'[10]

Teachers at the al-Thagh school, an elite Western-style Saudi school in Jeddah where Osama bin Laden received four one-hour English lessons a week during 1968 and 1969, describe a 'shy, retiring, gracious and courteous' boy who was 'very, neat, precise and conscientious' in his work.[11] In bin Laden's early teens there was little indication of excessive religiosity but the stories of youthful excesses in the nightclubs of Beirut, of drinking and of fights over barmaids are almost certainly false. All authoritative accounts indicate a quiet, rather intense young man unlikely to be out whoring in Beirut's Crazy Horse nightclub, as sometimes alleged.

Quite how much of a personal fortune bin Laden had inherited on his father's death is uncertain. Though high figures are often quoted, it is likely to be far less than the $300m sometimes estimated. Saudi families do not tend to divide their wealth. On the death of the father, the eldest son usually manages it on behalf of the whole family. In bin Laden's case, there was little in the way of cash distributed. Most of the sprawling bin Laden group's assets were simply not realisable, being held in shares, equipment, buildings and land. At most, bin Laden may have had access to a reserve of several million dollars that was his to spend.[12]

Not that the young bin Laden was interested in money. In fact, the very things that had made the father huge riches were troubling the son. The early 1970s was a time of huge cultural change in Saudi Arabia. In 1973, King Faisal brought the country to the attention of the world when he declared an oil embargo following the Arab-Israeli war, trebling the price of a barrel of oil to around $12 per barrel.[13] But the vast bulk of the growing population of his state saw little benefit from the massively enhanced incomes brought to the kingdom. For many, increasing contact with the West and burgeoning links with Muslim countries throughout the world were forcing instead a profound re-examination of old certainties. For most of Mohammed bin Laden's children, the answer lay in greater Westernisation and the elder members of the family set off for Victoria College in Alexandria in Egypt, Harvard, London or Miami.

Osama bin Laden finished high school in Jeddah in 1974 and decided against joining his siblings overseas.[14] He was one of only three bin Laden children not to have been educated abroad. One elder brother, Salim, had been educated at Millfield, the British boarding school. Another, Yeslam, went to university in Sweden and California.[15] Instead, Osama entered the management and economics faculty at Abdul Aziz University in Jeddah. It appears that he married his first wife, a Syrian related to his mother, at this time. He was 17 but a marriage at such a young age would not have been seen as unusual. There is no evidence that in this period, or any other for that matter, Osama bin Laden travelled to the West, despite reports to the contrary.[16]

Salim, the elder brother who had run the bin Laden corporation after their father's death, hoped Osama would take up a useful role in the family business and ensured that a key element of his university course was civil engineering.[17] Osama preferred the (compulsory) Islamic studies component of his course.[18] He graduated in 1979. At university, Osama, already a devout young man, was exposed to the radical fringe of contemporary Islam. Jeddah itself, and Abdul Aziz University in particular, was a centre for Islamic dissidents from all over the Muslim world.

Lecturing at Jeddah were Abdallah Azzam, the Palestinian academic who was to go on to be the primary ideologue of the 'Afghan Arabs', and Mohammed Qutb, the brother of Syed Qutb, the Egyptian Islamist executed in Egypt in 1966, who, posthumously, had become one of the most influential writers and thinkers of modern radical Islam. Both were among the hundreds of radical Islamic activists given sanctuary by the Saudi Arabians as part of their campaign to counter the atheistic socialism that was the dominant ideology in the Middle East at the time. Many lived and worked in Jeddah.

Among those activists every strand within contemporary Islamic thought was represented. There were rigorous Wahhabis and Salafis. There were men whose hope for reform was based on ideas formulated by the moderate reformist thinkers of the late nineteenth century. Many, including Azzam, Syed and Mohammed Qutb, were members of the Muslim Brotherhood, a social and religious reforming movement founded by Hassan al-Banna in Egypt in 1928. Al-Banna himself was drawing on older ideologies, primarily that of Jamal al-Din Afghani. With Syed Abdul A'la Maududi, a Pakistani thinker who lived at roughly the same time, al-Banna is considered the father of what is known as modern political Islamism. Bin Laden and other Islamic militants active today have travelled an enormous ideological distance from the theories and practices of such men. Their thinking is barely recognisable in the nihilistic, anti-rational, millenarian rhetoric and worldview of today's extremists.

As al-Wahhab, ibn Taimiya and the Kharijites had been searching for an answer to the problems that faced them in the eighteenth, fourteenth and seventh centuries respectively in the original texts of Islam, so the major Islamic revivalist thinkers of the mid twentieth century sought solutions for their own set of problems. Others, including bin Laden, were to do the same towards the end of the century. At the time when al-Banna and Maududi were becoming active, it was the end of the caliphate, the parcelling up of almost all the Muslim lands by the Western colonial powers and the clear technological and material supremacy of the West, coupled with the iniquity and social failures of Islamic society, that were felt as a profound humiliation and threat by many Muslims. Al-Banna, who was born in 1906, was a schoolteacher who lived in the Egyptian town of Isma'iliyya on the Suez Canal. He saw Islam as a perfect, total and all-encompassing system, regulating every part of the social, political, personal and religious life of the believer. Like so many reformers before him, he believed that the Qur'an, the hadith and the example of the early Muslim community provided the model for every Muslim's every action and the *Shariat*, which he saw as the totality of a Muslim's practice of his faith, was the ideal blueprint for a modern Muslim society. He deduced, like ibn Taimiya and others, that the current problems faced by Islam were the result of the failure of Muslims to follow the 'straight path'.[19] Given the social injustice that existed everywhere around him, al-Banna concluded that the ulema had failed in their primary duty of regulating the exercise of temporal power to promote a fair and just society and that others now had to take up the struggle. This struggle was, of course, jihad. But al-Banna was not an unthinking reactionary. He believed that a jihad against colonial or neo-colonial domination and for Islamic reform and regeneration should be married to a jihad for literacy, education, social services and justice. *Da'wa*, or preaching, should be directed both at reforming the state and at making existing Muslims better Muslims. This was to be a gradual process; al-Banna did not expect quick results. He started preaching himself and in 1928 founded the Muslim Brotherhood. It was, he said, 'a Salafiya message, a Sunni way, a Sufi truth, a political organisation, an athletic group, a scientific and cultural union, an economic enterprise and a social idea'. In the 1930s, al-Banna expressed admiration for the Nazi Brownshirts.[20]

Like all Islamic revivalists, al-Banna was working in the space between the holy texts and their interpretation. Physically, he was working in the space between the establishment mosques, with their loyal ulema, and the domestic home. It is clear that al-Banna was reacting to the experience of British colonialism and contact with the West. 'Until recently,' he wrote, 'writers, intellectuals, scholars and governments glorified in the principles of European civilization, gave themselves a Western tint, and adopted a European style and manner; today... the wind has changed, and reserve and distrust have taken their place. Voices are raised proclaiming the necessity for a return to the principles, teaching and ways of Islam... for initiating the reconciliation of modern life with these principles as a prelude to final "Islamization".'[21]

Al-Banna, like Syed Abdul A'la Maududi in Pakistan, aimed to transform his society in an immediate and real way. He had begun the process, which, like Maududi, he knew would be gradual, of creating a mass political movement that eventually would, he hoped, establish a truly Islamic state. It is important to remember that he was thinking and working in the 1930s and was interested in mass movements in Soviet Russia and the West. Al-Banna recruited from every sector of society though particularly among the rural, or recently urbanised, petty bourgeoisie. The Muslim Brotherhood built schools and tutorial colleges for poor Muslims and founded clinics and hospitals. Within 20 years his organisation, which became increasingly explicitly political with time, had recruited millions of members in Egypt and dozens of branches overseas. The Brotherhood began to develop violent strands, particularly after groups of activists had fought in the 1948–49 war in Israel-Palestine, and the Egyptian government, which had at times tried to use the movement to counter radical leftwing thought, dissolved it amid widespread disturbances. Al-Banna was assassinated by Egyptian secret police in 1949 in retaliation for the murder of the Egyptian prime minister, allegedly by a member of the Brotherhood's 'secret organisation', a year earlier.

Syed Abdul A'la Maududi, the other great early ideologue of political Islamism and a major influence on al-Banna, was born on 25 September 1903 in Aurangabad, in the princely state of Hyderabad in India. As a *syed*, his ancestry on the paternal side is theoretically traceable back to the Prophet Mohammed. His father, a lawyer, was a devoutly religious man and his family had a long tradition of spiritual leadership.

Maududi went to a relatively progressive high school where modern Western and traditional Islamic styles of education were combined. His undergraduate studies were disrupted by the illness and eventual death of his father and he had no further formal education, Islamic or otherwise. Thus, despite fluency in Urdu, Persian, Arabic and English, he had no credentials as an alim, something that undoubtedly contributed to his view of the ulema as corrupt, conservative and self-serving.[22]

To earn a living, Maududi turned to journalism and in his many writings sought to evolve a coherent body of thought that would equip Muslims, primarily those in India, to face, practically and ideologically, the challenge that the obvious dominance of the West presented. In India in the 1930s that confrontation was particularly acutely felt.

Maududi felt strongly that the *de facto* split that had emerged in Muslim societies between the functions of secular leaders and the religious leadership, the ulema, must end. The idea that the ulema's task was to ensure the ruler governed in accordance with the Shariat, was wrong.[23] In fact, the ulema hindered the implementation of the Shariat. Instead, sovereignty should be exercised in the name of Allah by a small elite, trained in classical Islamic subjects and modern sciences.

To create such a state, Maududi argued that a huge effort, a jihad, was required. In this he was drawing on existing traditions of opposition to oppression in south Asia going back several centuries. His first book, an analysis of the concept of jihad in Islam, was published in 1930 and argued that jihad was the central tenet of the religion. Its aim should be political: to establish an Islamic state. For Maududi, Islam was not just a religion but a political programme that needed to be implemented through practical action. Maududi turned religion into an ideology of political struggle. As with al-Banna, it is important to remember that Maududi was writing at a time when political debate, even in the Third World, was increasingly dominated by the two newly emergent totalitarian ideologies of Fascism and Communism. Islamism, with its own totalising ideology and techniques of mass organisation aimed at seizing and controlling the state, bears comparison with both.

This radical development is reinforced by the clear influence of Western political thinkers in Maududi's writing. His relationship with European thought is far more complex than mere reaction or rejection. According to Malise Ruthven, Maududi was 'strongly influenced by the intellectual climate of the 1930s, particularly the writings of Alexis Carrel, a popular

French writer who would later be discredited for his support for the Vichy government'. Ruthven suggests that Carrel's denunciations of the 'corruptions' of modern living found their way into Maududi's denunciations of the West as a 'sewer of vice and wickedness'.[24]

More obvious, however, is Maududi's borrowing of revolutionary methodology. Maududi founded his Jamaat Islami in 1941 explicitly to create motivated and trained cadres who he hoped would be the 'vanguard' of the Islamic revolution.[25] The name Jamaat Islami is significant and has been used again and again by radical groups. 'The Islamic society' implied is both the aim of the movement, i.e. to Islamicise all society and societies, and the means, i.e. a small self-contained community which practises correct Islam within the broader un-Islamic society and who, by their example, spread the faith. Maududi found useful material in Islamic history to dress what are basically Leninist tactics in more locally acceptable clothes. The earliest Muslims who accompanied Mohammed during the hijra to Medina were deliberately and explicitly redesignated a 'vanguard'. Maududi also used, for the first time, the term *jahillyya* in a modern context. Previously it had been used to describe the state of anarchy, barbarism and lawlessness that the pre-Islamic tribes of Arabia had lived in. Now Maududi used it to describe 'modern society'.[26] This proximity in conception to radical leftwing thought is key, showing the roots of both ideologies in attempts to address genuine social, economic, cultural and political problems.

However, unlike the Bolsheviks, Maududi was committed to staying within the law. Although he initially opposed the creation of Pakistan on the grounds that it was to be dominated by secular nationalists, from 1947, when Pakistan came into existence, his Jamaat Islami cadres – largely recruited from the Urdu-speaking prosperous and educated middle classes – worked hard and without violence (and without much success) to Islamicise the new state.

Indeed it is important to remember that both al-Banna and Maududi were gradualists who looked to appropriate the apparatus of the state to implement their own, admittedly reactionary, aims. As such they were political Islamists and differed greatly from the dogmatically puritan Wahhabis for whom any state differing from that prescribed by the Qur'an, and any Western influence at all, was anathema. However, whereas Maududi and al-Banna believed in a peaceful jihad through social activism and example, the fiery Syed Qutb, the third great ideologue of Sunni political Islamism and the bridge to the more radical contemporary strains prevalent today, did not.

Qutb, a school inspector, joined al-Banna's Muslim Brotherhood in 1953 when he was 47. He came from a poor if well-educated family in Musha, a small village near Asyut in Upper Egypt. His father had been an active member of the secular National Party and involved in rioting against the British colonial administration. Qutb had been an intelligent, sensitive, highly articulate and devout boy whose fragile health persisted all his life. He read European literature widely in translation and was a well-regarded critic. One of his discoveries was the young Egyptian writer Naguib Mahfouz.

Coming from a rural background in Upper Egypt, Qutb was shocked by the unveiled women he met when he moved to Cairo to take up a job as an inspector of schools. Unwilling to marry a 'dishonourable' woman but unable, for lack of family connections, to meet women of 'sufficient moral purity and discretion', he remained celibate for the rest of his life (like Jamal al-Din Afghani, who threatened to castrate himself when it was suggested he should marry, and Mohammed Atta). Profound and unresolved sexual issues are evident in much of his writings. A short story about disappointment in love is called *Ashwak* ('Thorns'). In other work, his fastidious disgust for anything that smacks of overt sexuality is clear. Women are described as 'flirtatious', 'provocative', with 'thirsty lips and bulging breasts'. Frequently they try, without success, to seduce him.[27] In 1948, Qutb was sent to America on a government grant. He returned, three years later, convinced that Western society was decadent, sexually depraved, empty, materialistic, superficial, pagan and ignorant. In America, his darker skin had attracted racist abuse and discrimination and his writing about the country is bilious and bitter.[28] 'Look at this capitalism with its monopolies, its usury and so many other injustices in it,' Qutb wrote later.

> Behold this individual freedom, devoid of human sympathy and responsibility for relatives except under force of law, at this materialistic attitude which deadens the spirit; at this behaviour, like animals, which you call 'free mixing of the sexes'; at this vulgarity which you call 'emancipation of women' ... at this evil and fanatic racial discrimination.[29]

In 1954, two years after the coup in Egypt which brought the charismatic secularist Colonel Gamal Abdul Nasser to power, the Muslim Brotherhood was banned again and Qutb imprisoned. He was released in 1964, arrested again in 1965 and hanged in 1966. His most influential work, *Milestones*, was written in prison. Written in lucid, accessible language it drew together previous trends in radical political Islam and, by looking backwards, took them forward. It is a howl of rage and pain as much as a political tract.

Milestones starts with a simple warning. 'Mankind today is on the brink of a precipice,' Qutb says; the human race is in danger of annihihilation. 'Even Western scholars realize that their civilization is unable to present healthy values for the guidance of mankind and does not possess anything to satisfy its own conscience or justify its own existence.' Nor, Qutb goes on to say, was Marxism, of which the Egyptian government represented the diluted pan-Arabist version, any alternative. 'Marxist theory conflicts with man's natures and needs; it prospers only in a degenerate society or in a society which is tyrannized over.'[30] Qutb did not reject the West entirely. What was needed, he said, was a system which would 'preserve and develop the material fruits of the creative genius of Europe and... provide mankind with the high ideals and values previously unknown in the West that can restore harmony with human nature.' That system, he said, was Islam.

According to Qutb, the reason for Islam's decline relative to the West, the Communist powers and its former glory was straightforward, if, given the pronouncements of his ideological avatars over the centuries, relatively predictable:

> The Muslim community must be restored to its original form... [it is] now buried under the debris of the man-made traditions of several generations and is crushed under the weight of those false laws and customs that are not... related to the Islamic teachings.[31]

The 'pure source' of the Qur'an has become corrupted.[32] The result is a return to the days of jahillyya, barbarism, ignorance and unbelief. 'Jahillyya,' says Qutb 'is based on rebellion against the sovereignty of Allah on earth', and its result is 'the oppression of his creatures' leading to 'the humiliation of the common man under the Communist system and the exploitation of individual and nations due to the greed for wealth and imperialism under capitalist systems.'[33] Here, the influence of contemporary political ideologies is clear. Only under true Islam, said Qutb, do 'all men become free from the servitude of some men to others.'[34] This, Qutb recognises, was 'a revolutionary message' in the days of Mohammed and still is in Egypt in the 1960s. 'The call "there is no god but Allah" is abhorrent to those in power at any age and place.'[35] In the days of the first generation of Muslims, Qutb says:

> The banner of social justice was raised in the name of tauhid... and the name of the banner was Islam... Morals were elevated, hearts and souls purified and... there was no need even to enforce the limits and punishments that Allah has prescribed because now... the hope of Divine reward and the fear of Allah's anger took the place of police and law enforcement agencies.[36]

It is not for nothing that some commentators have called *Milestones* political Islam's Communist Manifesto.

To initiate the revival of Islam, Qutb said, 'a vanguard must set out... marching through the vast ocean of *jahillyyah* which encompasses the whole world'.[37] Unless they separate themselves from the influence of the jahillyyah they too will be contaminated and unable to follow the true path followed by the salaf. 'We must free ourselves from the clutches of the jahili society... [It] is not a worthy partner for compromise. Our aim is first to change ourselves so we may later change society.'[38]

Aware of the timescale of the 'cosmic struggle', Qutb says that though 'the distance between the revival of Islam and the attainment of world leadership may be vast... the first step must be taken towards [it]'.[39]

The sight of Muslim Brotherhood activists being tortured and killed in prison had convinced Qutb that Jahillyya was not limited to non-Muslim societies as Maududi had thought but was also to be found in contemporary Muslim society as well. Drawing on ibn Taimiya, Qutb said that those Muslims, such as President Nasser, who did not strive to live according to the Shariat were unbelievers and thus *takfir*, or excommunicable. Like many other supposedly Islamic rulers in the Islamic world, Qutb said, Nasser may have claimed to be a Muslim but his actions showed that he was not. Instead he was a hypocrite, a *munafiq*.[40]

For the young Osama bin Laden, already steeped in traditional Wahhabism, much of Qutb's message made sense. All his life, bin Laden had listened to impassioned sermons full of references to the past glories of the Arab kingdoms. His teachers had told him that the salaf were those that he, and all Muslims, should struggle to emulate. Mohammed Qutb, Abdallah Azzam and his fellow preachers at Abdul Aziz University offered comprehensible and radical solutions to complex contemporary political and social issues couched in the language of Salafi-Wahhabi traditionalism with which bin Laden had grown up.

One bin Laden family member remembers Osama reading and praying all the time during this period.[41] Bin Laden certainly became deeply involved in religious activities at university after taking part in theological debates and Qur'anic study. He also made useful contacts with young royal princes. As the son of a loyal servitor of the Saudi regime, Osama bin Laden was still far from considering, as Syed Qutb might have done, the rulers in Riyadh as 'apostate' or 'hypocrite'. That was to come much later.

CHAPTER FOUR

MUJAHIDEEN

In 1979, the year bin Laden left university, several massive events shook the Muslim world: a peace deal between Israel and Egypt, the Islamic Revolution in Iran, the Soviet invasion of Afghanistan and the occupation of the grand mosque at Mecca by a radical Wahhabi group. Each event had enormous implications for men like bin Laden. Sadat's peace deal with the Jewish state epitomised the backsliding of the Arab nationalist regimes (particularly given the shaming defeats of 1967 and 1973), the deposition of the Shah, Mohammed Reza Pahlavi, was a clear example of what could be done about such regimes, the Soviet invasion emphasised the imminent threat from the atheistic West and, for Saudis in particular, the occupation of Islam's holiest shrine by Juhaiman ibn Said al-Utaiba, a hardline preacher, and 400 radicals in November cast the royal family in Riyadh in an entirely new light.

Juhaiman was a former national guardsman, a graduate of the Islamic University of Medina and the grandson of one of the Wahhabi Ikhwan killed by the al-Saud regime in 1929. He applied the teachings of the Saudi ulema to their patrons. To Juhaiman and his followers it was thus clear that the House of al-Saud had deviated from the true path of Islam. The rulers of Saudi Arabia were to them little better than tribal warlords. Juhaiman seized control of the grand mosque, the most holy site in Islam, and issued a call to the Saudi nation to overthrow their apostate rulers, their Western backers and establish a rule of 'justice and equality'. His followers were not just Saudis but also included Egyptians, Kuwaitis, Bangladeshis, Yemenis and Iraqis. The response was as international as the attackers. It took 10,000 Saudi security personnel, thousands of Pakistani troops and a contingent of French anti-terrorist experts who, as non-believers, needed special permission from the kingdom's ulema to enter Mecca, to crush the revolt. Though it failed to win the sympathy of the Saudi masses, Juhaiman's rebellion stunned the Saudi monarchy. As the custodians of Islam's most holy places, they had expected threats from Communism or secular Arab nationalism, not from within orthodox Islam, the very discourse that gave the House of al-Saud its legitimacy. In 1962, the *Rabitat al-Alam al-Islami*, or Muslim World League, had been set up by Riyadh to fund an international effort to counter the spread of secular ideologies in the Islamic world through da'wa. When, in 1971, King Faisal had offered Sheikh Abdel Halim Mahmoud, the then rector of al-Azhar University in Cairo, the premier academic institution of the Islamic world, $100m to finance a new campaign in the Muslim world it had been against Communists and atheists, not Islamic radicals.[1]

Bin Laden was deeply impressed by the strength of the rebels' faith. Five years later, he sat on the end of his bed in a communal dormitory on the upstairs floor of the offices of a newspaper run by an Afghan mujahideen faction, at number 40 on Peshawar's Jamal al-Din Afghani Road, talking late into the night with his young friend Khaled.

'I had long arguments and discussions with him about political issues in particular,' Khaled told me.

> I was critical of the role of Wahhabis in breaking up the Ottoman Empire after the First World War. Mr Osama said that Abdul Aziz ibn Saud was not a religious leader at all but just a tribal chieftain. He used to say that Wahhabism was exploited and used as a cover so the House of al-Saud could fight against the Ottomans and win land and wealth. We talked often about the promise of the British to give the Arabs a homeland if they rose against the Ottoman Empire and how they were betrayed. We talked about Palestine and current Middle East issues and about the seizure of the grand Mosque. Mr Osama said the men who seized Mecca were true Muslims and that they were innocent of any crime and that they were killed ruthlessly.

Bin Laden had arrived in Peshawar in early 1980. He has told interviewers that he 'was enraged and went there at once'.[2] In fact, it took several weeks to contact the Afghan and Pakistani religious leaders (whom he had met at the clerical convocations hosted by his father in Saudi Arabia) to make arrangements for travel to Pakistan. The most prominent among his contacts were the leading Afghan Islamic activists Burhanuddin Rabbani and Abd al-Rab al-Rasul Sayyaf.[3]

Bin Laden's first trip to Peshawar lasted little more than a month. He returned to Saudi Arabia and started lobbying his brothers, relatives and old school friends to support the fight against the Soviets. For the next four years, bin Laden split his time between his homeland and Pakistan. It is unclear whether he ventured over the border into Afghanistan during this time. Instead his focus was on fundraising and raising the profile of the Afghan jihad in the Middle East.

By 1984, he was spending the majority of his time in Peshawar, renting a villa at 61 Syed Jamal al-Din Afghani Road to act as a guesthouse and transit point for the growing numbers of Arab volunteers on their way into Afghanistan and as an office. He called it the *Beit ul Ansar*, or house of the supporters, the *ansar* being the original group of converts made by the Prophet Mohammed in Medina after the hijra.[4] He spent much of his time helping out at the offices of *al-Jihad*, Abdallah Azzam's Arabic-language newspaper, which reported the war in Afghanistan throughout the Islamic world. *Al-Jihad* stood out among the 20 or so newspapers and magazines published in Peshawar. It was free, properly funded by its wealthy Arab patrons, appeared regularly and was staffed almost entirely by Arabs.[5] Bin Laden helped the publication with some money and often stayed in the dormitories on the first floor. Journalists in the region began hearing stories of a man known as 'the Good Samaritan' who, it was said, would arrive unannounced at hospitals where wounded Afghan and Arab fighters had been brought. According to the stories, he went from bed to bed handing out cashews and chocolates to the wounded and carefully noting each man's name and address. Weeks later, the man's family would receive a generous cheque.[6]

This picture of the young bin Laden is convincing. Such generosity, perhaps learned from his father who always carried wads of notes to give to the poor, is something that almost all who have fought for or alongside bin Laden mention. Though in the Middle East the distribution of substantial sums would be expected from someone of his status and background, former associates all refer to bin Laden's munificence. Some speak of $1,500 donations for marriages,[7] others talk of cash doled out for shoes or for watches or needy relatives.[8] Bin Laden found time during his intermittent stays in Peshawar to teach at least one Afghan mujahid some Arabic.[9] Many former fighters talk of group discussions during which bin Laden would narrate religious stories or sing religious songs. Most say that, at least in the early 1980s, he was still the quiet shy young man noted by his teachers ten years previously.[10] There were some clues to a burgeoning sense of mission, however. Bin Laden repeatedly referred in conversations to Salah ad Din , the twelfth-century Kurdish general who united the Islamic factions of the Middle East to defeat the Crusaders and spoke often about *sura ya sin*, the 36th verse often referred to as the heart of the Qur'an and devoted to the problem of human moral responsibility and the certainty of resurrection and judgement.[11]

It is often said that bin Laden was funded by the CIA. This is not true and, indeed, would have been impossible given the structure of funding that General Zia ul-Haq, who had taken power in Pakistan in 1977, had set up. A condition of Zia's cooperation with the American plan to turn Afghanistan into the Soviets' 'Vietnam' was that all American funding to the Afghan resistance had to be channelled through the Pakistani government, which in effect meant the Afghan bureau of the Inter Services Intelligence (ISI), the military spy agency. The American funding, which went exclusively to the Afghan mujahideen groups, not the Arab volunteers, was supplemented by Saudi government money and huge funds raised from mosques, non-governmental charitable institutions and private donors throughout the Islamic world. Most of the major Gulf-based charities operating today were founded at this time to raise money or channel government funds to the Afghans, civilians and fighters. In fact, as little as 25 per cent of the money for the Afghan jihad was actually supplied directly by states.[12]

For Riyadh, the financial effort had a clear logic. In 1980, the Saudi government, shaken by Juhaiman's attack on Mecca and the Iranian Revolution, perceived two clear threats to their position. One was internal, from the Islamic extremists who saw them as apostate rulers. The second was external. The events in Tehran had turned the minority Shia strand of Islam into the Islamic world's most radical and inspiring example of modern Muslim activism. Whereas Riyadh had always invoked Islam to uphold the political status quo, Iran's new rulers presented the religion as a revolutionary ideology by which the rule of tyrannical kings could be ended and an egalitarian social and economic order created. Muslims everywhere, Sunnis and Shias alike, were celebrating the events in Tehran.[13] The increased influence of the Shias could clearly damage the interests of the Saudis, and thus the interests of the majority Sunni, of which the House of al-Saud felt themselves to be the pre-eminent guardians, throughout the umma. Pouring their new oil-based wealth into the Afghan jihad and funding a massive campaign to increase the penetration of Saudi-style Sunni Islam overseas would, the House of al-Saud hoped, both roll back the Shia tide while simultaneously bolstering their Islamic credentials at home and abroad.

The result was the exporting on an industrial scale of Wahhabi, Salafi, neo-traditionalist or 'hard' Islam, as some scholars characterise it, with its almost obsessive emphasis on the outward details of Islamic practice, Qur'anic literalism and profound hostility to all other forms of Islamic worship, let alone other religions. The Saudi campaign was bolstered by governments and private donors in Kuwait, the United Arab Emirates and elsewhere in the Gulf. It was to have an enormous effect on the course of the Afghan war and on modern Islamic radicalism.

Prince Turki al-Faisal was, as head of the Saudi intelligence service, responsible for overseeing the distribution of the huge sums of money being collected for the Afghan jihad both from public and private sources. Official Saudi Arabian aid matched that from the USA, which went from $30m in 1980 to $250m in 1985. Unofficial Saudi aid involved similar, if not larger, sums.[14] Though organisations such as the Muslim World League and its subsidiaries the International Islamic Relief Organisation (IIRO) and the Islamic Relief Agency played their part, al-Faisal needed reliable and honest men on the ground to manage the flow of funds to their recipients. Bin Laden was one. A number of other Saudis performed similar roles.

It is a mistake to overestimate the contribution made to the war in Afghanistan by the Arabs. Many Afghan mujahideen fighters, of whom there were somewhere between 150,000 and 250,000 fighting at any one time, saw the volunteers who came to join them from the Middle East as a liability. There were only a few hundred fighting at any one time and their contribution to the 'jihad' in military terms was negligible. The Afghan Arabs rarely fought in discrete groups and were usually deployed as small detachments attached to the various mujahideen factions. There was never an 'Arab' or 'International' brigade as such. Many volunteers merely turned up in Peshawar, made their way over the border and attached themselves to a commander.[15] Estimates of how many Arabs took part in the ten-year combat vary. Some are ludicrous. Former CIA officials stationed in Pakistan at the time say it was a maximum of 25,000.[16] It is likely that less than half of the volunteers actually saw combat, spending their time instead in support activities away from the frontlines. Many married local women and settled into desk jobs based in Peshawar or elsewhere in Pakistan.[17] Though their fighting spirit was not doubted by the Afghans, the Arabs were generally disliked. Indeed, the profound gulf between the Salafi Islam of the majority of the Arab volunteers and the very different Islam of the vast majority of Afghans often caused problems and, on occasion, violence.

The Arab fighters' practice of taking local girls in 'temporary marriages' was particularly provocative.[18] Yet it was the Afghan factions whose beliefs were closest to those of the Arabs and who were marginal at the beginning of the war that were dominant by its end.

The rise of political Islam in Afghanistan during the 1980s might seem to be a, slightly belated, part of the broad trend throughout the Islamic world in this period. The similarities with the rise of other political Islamist movements elsewhere, however, should not be allowed to give radical Islam's eventual domination, ideologically and practically, of the war against the Soviets a sense of inevitability. Though there are strong coincidences with groups overseas, such as in the social backgrounds of key cadres, there are also differences. In 1979, in Egypt, Iran and elsewhere, Islamic radicalism was drawing most of its recruits from the recently urbanised and often impoverished lower-middle classes that had resulted from massive population growth and economic development. In Afghanistan, particularly outside Kabul, nothing even approximating a genuine middle class, let alone alienated, disappointed and struggling urban masses ripe for radicalisation, existed. The Marxist People's Democratic Party of Afghanistan (PDPA) had discovered this very rapidly when it took power in 1978. The PDPA cadres railed against the 'superstition' and 'ignorance' of the rural areas. What they had come up against was the solidity of a genuinely profound, deeply traditional faith.

That religion was, and to an extent still is, so deeply part of the personal identity and worldview of Afghans that it is hard for a secular, atheist Westerner to comprehend. I can remember standing in the early evening by the side of the road between Kabul and Kandahar in the summer of 1998. The road is so bad that, for long sections, the drivers of the ancient coaches, trucks and the newer, if as battered, taxis often prefer to drive along dry riverbeds rather than the linked potholes and craters that pass for a road surface. Traffic was, unsurprisingly, minimal. We had stopped at the crest of a hill and could see for miles in every direction. To the west lay the first ridges of the central Afghan highlands. To the east lay the mountains of the Pakistani frontier. Bands of *koochi* nomads were driving their herds of camels across the thin grass. Buses had halted at intervals along the raised road and by every one I could see the passengers casting their *pattus* (traditional blankets) down in the fine dirt to kneel in prayer. The koochis too were facing Mecca beside their livestock. That night we slept on the floor of a *chaikhanna*, a basic roadside inn. In the morning, 50 men took their blankets and lined up for dawn prayers in the road outside. The equivalent in the West would be the guests of a motorway motel congregating for an outdoor service at 5am.

Such purely visual manifestations of faith reveal little of how Islam textures the lives of most Afghans. In the early 1970s, one Western writer likened 'coming into Afghanistan' to entering 'some sort of temple'. 'Waiting for customers, the shopkeepers counted their prayer beads with half-closed eyes, whispering the attributes of God,' he wrote.

> The dervishes, their head dresses tied… with chord, held out their begging bowls to pious passers-by in the bazaars. Friends greeted each other with hand on the heart, heads bowed, praising the Lord for his gift of good health. The peasants did not ride a horse, an ass, a camel, or a taxi without first murmuring the name of God. The meals began with a divine invocation, the right hand silently kneading the grains of rice or the piece of bread because thus had the Prophet done… Every gesture was dictated by ritual and impregnated with the sacred.[19]

Little, at least in rural areas, has changed today. This was not, and is not, an academic, rarefied faith. It is a very real and practical part of everyday life. 'The Islam practised in Afghan villages, nomad camps and most urban areas (the ninety to ninety-five percent non-literates) would be almost unrecognisable to a sophisticated Muslim scholar.'[20] It was, and is, a tolerant, flexible religion, similar to that practised throughout much of south and southwest Asia, east and north Africa and in many parts of the Middle East, full of mysticism, shrines, saints and tokens. It shares little with 'hard' Salafi and Wahhabi Islam or the political ideologies of Islam.

For the average Afghan villager, the two main religious figures in his life are the mullahs and the ulema. The mullahs are religious functionaries, leading the Friday service in a village mosque, administering the religious buildings, performing the small daily rituals that articulate daily life. Their upkeep is the responsibility of the village or its khan, the most powerful individual there. Though in some places they are respected, there is a strong culture of contempt for the usually unlettered, unsophisticated and parochial mullah. The ulema, however, distinguished by the titles of *maulvi* or *maulana*, are treated with profound respect. Unlike the mullahs, who were attached to an individual community, the ulema are a pan-Islamic body and were thus well placed to mediate between the villagers and the outside world, seen as the umma or the world Muslim community.

The first revolts against the Marxist regime in Kabul in 1978 and then, after December 1979, against the Soviets too, can be seen as part of a long-established tradition of local uprising against zulm, or oppression, reaching back to the days of King Amanullah, who reigned from 1919 to 1929, the wars against the British in the mid and late-nineteenth century and well beyond. Such campaigns were primarily led by local religious leaders, both ulema and Sufi *pirs*.[21] The revolts of 1978–80 were as much against increasing state, and urban, interference in rural life, as against the Soviet invasion. Those areas with the weakest links to Kabul and the regime rebelled first. The tribal areas in the east and south, dominated by the Pashtun tribes which, as the majority ethnic group, have the strongest history of benefiting from and participating in the state, rebelled last. As the ulema and the leaders of the Sufi sects had been intentionally marginalised by the state over the previous century they were a natural rallying point for any resentment against central authority, appearing untainted by contact with power. So in the first year of the jihad it was the *Harakat-e-Inqilab-e-Islami* movement of Mohammed Nabi Mohammedi, an alim, whose powerbase lay among the village mullahs and local ulema in the east of the country, as well as the students they taught, that received most popular support.[22]

In the revolt against the PDPA regime and the early years of the jihad against the Soviets, the aim of the rebels was reactionary: to expel the foreign intruders, but also to roll back the intrusive modern state with its intellectuals, bureaucrats and ideologues. This was a very different aim to that of the Afghan political Islamists who, drawing on the inspiration of Afghani, al-Banna, Maududi and Qutb, wanted not to roll back the state, but to appropriate and Islamicise it. Rural resentment was articulated, as it had been against the British in the nineteenth and early twentieth centuries, in religious terms. Though the offence of the Marxists or the Soviets may not have been specifically directed against Islam, it was seen as such. The fight against it was thus a jihad. But a jihad that was very different from that of Qutb and his acolytes.

The roots of Afghan political Islam lie, like the roots of Afghan Marxism, in the new educational institutions set up by King Zahir Shah's government in the 1950s. When Zahir Shah took power in 1933, the basic structural problems of the nearly 200-year-old Afghan state remained unsolved. Afghanistan was still desperately poor and still lacked an effective system of taxation. The rulers were perpetually short of cash. The power of the ruling clique, still drawn largely from one clan within the Pashtun tribes, still primarily depended on patronage. With no resources at home, Afghan rulers had to get funds from outside the country, much as a rural khan has to find resources from beyond his tribe's immediate neighbourhood. Once, raiding other nations for loot would have been the solution. Instead, Afghanistan's leaders in the post-Second World War period returned to the tactics that had been employed by their nineteenth-century predecessors and traded on the country's strategic position, its biggest asset, to secure the diplomatic and financial advantages that would enable them to keep power. As long as the resources flowed in from overseas the fundamental weakness of the state could be, at least temporarily, covered up. From 1956 to 1978, the Soviets were to give $1.26bn in military and $1.25bn in economic aid to Afghanistan.[23] In 1965 alone, the Americans gave $7.7m and the Soviets $11.1m towards infra-structure projects.[24] The money allowed the regime to buy off all the various interest groups whose support they needed and postpone the serious reform that might have developed the economy, bridged the profound urban-rural divide and co-opted other ethnic and tribal elements beyond the Pashtuns into central government.

There was, however, limited success in one area of modernisation. Opportunities for education were rapidly increased, albeit from a fairly low base. In 1932 there had been 1,350 students in state schooling and no state universities. By 1961 there were 233,809 state schoolchildren and nearly 2,000 in further education. Within a decade the number of graduates would almost treble.[25] American money built most of the schools. The Soviets ran a polytechnic, the French a lycée. At the same time, the bureaucracy and the army were also expanded, to provide jobs for the products of the new education system, to increase the regime's opportunity for patronage and because the centralised, statist style of management learned from the Soviets needed lots of officials.

Ideally, this new educated elite would have become the civil servants, technicians and entrepreneurs who could together have developed their country into an appropriate local version of a consensual, accountable, modern state. Instead, nepotism, corruption, tribal chauvinism and mismanagement meant that the new educated elite merely formed a self-contained, discontented and expensive layer sandwiched between the exclusive royal elite and their cronies, who maintained a monopoly on genuine executive power, and the rest of the country. A liberal constitution, introduced in 1964, failed to fulfil anyone's aspirations. As opportunities for foreign travel, the penetration of international media, tourists and the presence of foreign advisers increased, many became rapidly aware for the first time of their country's backwardness. Their profound frustration at their inability to do anything about it or to better their own positions, provoked a questioning of the established order and a search for new solutions.

Discontent was strongest among the new social element created by the new education system.[26] These educated, or sometimes semi-educated, Afghan youths of rural backgrounds had developed outlooks that were radically different to those of their parents. A survey in 1967 found that 62 per cent of graduates of Kabul University, which was founded in 1947 and became co-educational in 1960, had fathers with no formal education.[27] These phenomena, and their consequences, were common across the Islamic world. Interest in leftwing social theories was one result. The growth of political Islam was another.

As ever, the Kabul regime was short of cash, so Cairo's al-Azhar University sponsored Kabul University's new faculty of Islamic jurisprudence. Many Afghan students and lecturers travelled to Egypt, Egyptians came to Kabul, and the ideas of the Muslim Brotherhood gained wide circulation. The social and political injustices that had inspired al-Banna were, many Afghans felt, evident in their own country too. The works of Maududi and Qutb were widely read. Afghan Islamists also maintained close contact with the Pakistani Jamaat Islami. By 1965, in the year that the Marxists formed the PDPA, Islamists on the Kabul University campus were distributing a leaflet entitled 'A Tract of Jihad', clearly influenced by Maududi, and had formed a Muslim Youth Organisation, popularly known as the Ikhwan, which won the student elections in 1972. The Islamists had learned lessons in organisation from the radical Leninist left. The organisation of groups was very similar: a secretary general, in the case of the leftwing groups, an 'emir' for the Islamists, a central committee for the Marxists or a *shura* (a consultative council) for their opponents.

The leader of the Afghan Islamists was Burhanuddin Rabbani, a Tajik who was a junior professor at the University's faculty of Shariat. Rabbani had a close relationship with senior Egyptian Muslim Brotherhood figures, had studied at al-Azhar during the 1950s and had been one of the first Afghans to translate Qutb into Dari, the dialect spoken in Kabul and by many of Afghanistan's non-Pashtun minorities.[28] Abd al-Rab al-Rasul Sayyaf, also a Kabul University lecturer, and a Pashtun from Paghman province, was elected his deputy. Gulbuddin Hekmatyar, a young Pashtun civil engineering graduate who had turned to radical Islam after flirting with revolutionary Marxism, was placed in charge of political activities, though he could not take up his post at the time because he was in prison for ordering the killing of a Maoist student.

The background of the Kabul Islamists is revealing. They were all from the provinces. Not one was a Kabuli.[29] Most were from relatively wealthy backgrounds (otherwise they would have been unable to complete their education) and they included virtually no representatives of the traditional Afghan ulema. They were almost all university educated, mainly in technical faculties. Comparison with leaders in Pakistan, Egypt, Algeria and Iran shows how typical they were of Islamists elsewhere. Such men were also to provide the bulk of the 20 or 30 senior activists who joined bin Laden in Afghanistan after 1996, further evidencing the essentially political roots, and aims, of the 'al-Qaeda hardcore'.

In 1973, Sardar Daoud Khan, the king's cousin and a former prime minister, led a military coup and established a pro-Soviet government with the help of the PDPA. One of his first acts was to move against the Islamists. Several, including Sayyaf, were jailed. Rabbani and Ahmed Shah Massoud, a Tajik engineering student from the Panjshir valley, fled to Pakistan where Prime Minister Zulfikar Ali Bhutto, irritated by the Afghan government's attempts to foment trouble among Pashtuns in Pakistan, gave them a refuge in Peshawar where they were cared for by a young Pakistani Pashtun Islamist called Hussein Ahmed, a former geography lecturer at Peshawar's Islamia University and the future leader of Pakistan's Jamaat Islami party.[30] Bhutto's adviser on Afghan Affairs was General Naseerullah Babar, a Pashtun himself, who gave the ISI the role of watching over the new arrivals. Hekmatyar was appointed the 'contact' in Pakistan for any Afghan Islamists, boosting his prestige immeasurably.[31] Rabbani received donations from private donors in Saudi Arabia and in 1975, with Pakistani help and training, the Afghan Islamists organised a rebellion from exile. They had hoped they would be the vanguard that would spark an Islamist movement across the country. Massoud, the best military mind among them, was heavily influenced by Mao. He hoped that, by seizing islands of territory, which could be Islamicised, the rebels would inspire, radicalise and mobilise the whole population. Such tactics were to become standard for domestic Islamic radical groups across the Islamic world over the coming decades and would heavily inform bin Laden's later strategic decisions. In 1975, the Afghan Islamists' rebellion, despite Islamabad's assistance, failed utterly to garner any sympathy at all and did nothing but reveal the complete lack of support for modern political Islam in the rural areas.[32] Despite this setback, however, the process that would eventually lead to the weak and marginalised Afghan Islamists running their country had begun.

So how did Hekmatyar, Rabbani, Massoud (who, despite his moderate reputation in the West, remained broadly committed to political Islam all his life) and the other Afghan Islamists manage to gain primacy in the mujahideen resistance movement? The traditional structure of Afghan society, and the continuing weakness of its state, led communities, whether refugees, villagers or mujahideen groups, to turn to those who were most likely to be able to provide resources. The ideological sympathy and mutual political reliance of General Zia and Pakistani Islamists meant that the ISI directed by far the greatest proportion of funds towards those who shared their politics and beliefs. The greatest beneficiary was Hekmatyar's Hizb-e-Islami group.

Zia and his close advisers were acting on two main impulses: the desire to see a compliant and pro-Pakistan group win the war and take power in Kabul; and a genuine ideological and personal sympathy built up over several years between the Pakistani Islamists, especially Jamaat Islami, and their Afghan counterparts. The question of cross-border Pashtun nationalism, a legacy of colonial days, also played its part. Islamabad never recognised Pashtun nationalist parties, or allowed King Zahir Shah, the only figure recognisable to all Afghans, to contact the resistance in Pakistan. An ethnic element also came into play. The Pakistanis favoured the Pashtuns, but only from the Ghilzai branch of the Pashtun tribes. Not one leader of a recognised resistance party was from the broadly pro-Royalist Durrani Pashtun tribes who had held power for centuries and had historically entertained ambitions to enlarge their dominions towards the Indus.[33] Nobody, Pakistanis, Gulf Arabs or Americans, was particularly interested in the 'moderate' parties, which were far more pro-Western and had little sympathy for the hardline political Islamists' project. Four of the seven mujahideen groups allowed to operate by Pakistan were hardline Islamist, the other three could be characterised as moderate Islamists or Islamist/traditionalist.

Hizb-e-Islami, the most radical of the groups in Peshawar in 1979, was, with its better organisation, state sanction and larger resources, best placed to exploit the new and swiftly changing circumstances of 1979–80.[34] In Pakistan, the three million Afghans who poured into the new refugee camps along the country's northwest frontier effectively provided the urban masses that Afghanistan had previously lacked.[35] Stripped of their traditional leadership and their tribal identities and thrown together in the crowded shanty towns of the camps, the refugees provided the political Islamists with a constituency for the first time. They were far more receptive to the messages of Rabbani, Massoud and particularly

Hekmatyar than the pre-war rural populace had been. Zia gave Hekmatyar's cadres privileged access to camps. They made many recruits.

The other Islamist resistance groups, Rabbani's Jamaat Islami and the Hizb-e-Islami faction led by Maulvi Younis Khalis, represented differing strains within Afghan political Islam. Khalis, an alim himself, brought together more radical elements among the ulema of the tribes of his native Paktia province and in Nangahar. There, Jalaluddin Haqqani, another alim, established himself as a highly competent military commander. Rabbani, a Persian-speaking Tajik, largely drew non-Pashtun Islamists to his banner. Though his military commander in the field, Ahmed Shah Massoud, was by far the most effective opponent of the Soviets, his Jamaat-e-Islami group received far less aid than Hekmatyar's faction.

It is important to remember that, as stressed earlier, much of the aid came from the Gulf, not Washington. The Saudi government matched the Americans dollar for dollar and private donors from throughout the Middle East, like those solicited by bin Laden, also sent very considerable sums. Those leaders close to Riyadh received Saudi passports. Most were frequent visitors to the kingdom. The Saudis were not alone in their support. Sheikhs, emirs, princes and devout businessmen throughout the Gulf made huge donations, developing a complex network of personal associations and channels for funding, often through specially created charities, that were to be of critical importance during the 1990s.[36]

Just how important the Gulf funds were is shown by the success of Sayyaf, the Arabic-speaking Afghan Wahhabi. In 1981, two years after escaping to Pakistan, his Ittehad-e-Islami faction was recognised by the ISI. He had managed, purely through his access to Saudi cash and support from the Saudi religious establishment, to build up a mujahideen group from nothing. The American political scientist and Afghan expert Barnett Rubin describes Sayyaf's group as having 'virtually no social networks in Afghanistan… [His fighters] were a heterogeneous group of individuals who affiliated themselves… because of the money and arms he could supply'.[37]

There is no better indication of the influence the Saudis had than Sayyaf's name change from Ghulam Rasul (servant or slave of the Prophet), as he was born, to Abd al-Rab al-Rasul (servant of God and the Prophet), the former, with its implication of the worship of a human, not Allah, being unacceptable to strict Wahhabis. Sayyaf attracted commanders who had no previous claim to authority. Haji Zargoun, a koochi nomad of no distinction at all, started the war with Hizb-e-Islami but then left even Hekmatyar's well-funded group to join Sayyaf. Said Mohammed Pahlwan, a shepherd before the war, left the moderate traditionalist NIPA party for Ittehad-e-Islami in 1984.[38] Gulf funds allowed the creation of 'Sayyafabad', a well-provided refugee camp and complex of warehouses, military bases, mosques and medressas at Pabbi, east of Peshawar, that was to become a crucial location for Islamic militants after the Soviet war.[39] Ittehad-e-Islami was the favourite among the foreign volunteers, many of whom shared Sayyaf's Wahhabi-influenced beliefs. Others were merely drawn by his group's sophisticated overseas publicity machine. When bin Laden first ventured into battle, he did it with Sayyaf.

CHAPTER FIVE

HEROES

For the first five years of the war against the Soviets, few Arabs actually did any fighting; most worked in humanitarian organisations, in political or media offices or as medics. Ayman al-Zawahiri made several trips to Peshawar in 1980 and 1981 with the Red Crescent organisation to look after wounded mujahideen.[1] On the whole, the hundreds of Arabs living and working in Peshawar saw their role as supporting the Afghans. Only later did they start to appropriate the Afghans' jihad for radical Islam.

One of those most instrumental in effecting that change was Abdallah Azzam, the charismatic, erudite, polished preacher whose sermons had made such an impression on bin Laden when he had been at university. Within weeks of his arrival in Pakistan, bin Laden had been introduced to Azzam. The pair got on well. The energy, administrative talent and contacts of the young Saudi complemented the profound Islamic knowledge, confidence, charisma and commitment of the older man.

Azzam, who was a huge influence on bin Laden, became the chief ideologue of the 'Afghan Arabs'. Azzam was not an original thinker like Qutb, Maududi or al-Banna, but he was a powerful orator who fused the historic and the contemporary to create something of unprecedented power. Azzam quoted ibn Taimiya, the Qur'an and the hadith, but spoke about Palestine and the Russians. Moreover, unlike even Qutb, Azzam was preaching to an army that was waiting and ready to fight in a battle that was already underway.

Azzam was born in a village in Palestine in 1941 and joined the Muslim Brotherhood at 18. He studied Islamic Jurisprudence at Damascus University and fought the Israelis in the 1967 war. While studying for his doctorate at al-Azhar in 1973, he befriended the family of Qutb and also spent time with Sheikh Abdel Omar Rahman, the blind Egyptian preacher who was to become the spiritual leader of the violent Egyptian al-Gamaa al-Islamiyya. In 1978, Azzam travelled to Saudi Arabia to teach in Jeddah. He was there in 1980 when, after meeting mujahideen leaders soliciting support from the Gulf for the Afghan jihad, he decided to devote himself to their cause. Well liked by the Saudi establishment, Azzam settled in Islamabad and took a job lecturing at the International Islamic University, built with Saudi funds as part of their global proselytisation drive and opened by General Zia only a year previously. In 1984, Azzam moved to Peshawar where he set up the *Maktab al-Khidamat* (MAK) to receive, supervise and organise the increasing numbers of volunteers and the growing flow of funds from the Middle East.[2]

For Azzam, the jihad in Afghanistan was a moral obligation for all Muslims, the sixth pillar of faith. It was an individual decision to enter the jihad not, as traditionally held, the decision of the senior alim or caliph. 'Right now fighting is compulsory on each and every Muslim on earth,' he said in his 'Last will' written in 1986.[3] His best-known book was entitled *Defending the land of the Muslims is each man's most important duty*. Azzam, a Palestinian, made clear that the jihad in Afghanistan was just a beginning:

> This duty will not end with victory in Afghanistan; jihad will remain an individual obligation until all other lands that were Muslim are returned to us so that Islam will reign again: before us lie Palestine, Bokhara, Lebanon, Chad, Eritrea, Somalia, the Philippines, Burma, southern Yemen, Tashkent and Andalusia.[4]

Bin Laden would specifically refer to Andalusia in his first broadcast after the US air-strikes on Afghanistan commenced in October 2001.

Azzam saw the veterans of the Afghan war as a mobile strike force operating throughout the Islamic world. He stressed again and again the humiliation that the umma had suffered when it had been dismembered into nation-states by the West. Azzam's internationalism was a critical new development and reflected the diversity in the backgrounds of the volunteers answering his call.

As well as rallying recruits, Azzam worked hard to inculcate volunteers with a desire for martyrdom, repeatedly stressing its rewards and quoting the single hadith in which the Prophet assures the shahid absolution from all sins, 72 beautiful virgins and permission to bring 70 members of their household into Paradise with them. Such ideas were to become a key part of the radical Islamist discourse. Azzam's most popular books included a compilation of 'a hundred eyewitness accounts of miracles experienced by the Mujahideen in the Soviet-Afghan Jihad, from perfumed bodies of martyrs to accounts of angels helping the Mujahideen' and 'Lovers of the Paradise Maidens', which 'contains the biographies and stories of over 150 martyred mujahideen'.[5] Both works are widely available, and widely read, today.

One text in particular bears closer examination (and comparison with documents written by the September 11th hijackers and the bulk of modern contemporary radical Islamic literature). In September 1985, the first Saudi Arab, a 20-year-old called Yayha Senyor from Jeddah, was killed in combat in Afghanistan. Azzam wrote an address to the dead man:

> Everything in your soul used to speak that you were the next to be a martyr. There were your brothers who shared with you the pains of the path of sacrifice, the sweat and blood, under the shower of bullets and the thunder of cannons, to awaken an umma whose depths was filled by weakness. I sensed in my depths that you would be a shahid.
>
> O Yahya! Your fragrant blood began to flow and not a single person that touched your body or perfumed themselves with drops of your blood remained without the smell of musk filling their noses.
>
> You refused to let the Muslims' honour be violated, their support reduced or their victory be trampled on. You did not sit by patiently while the Muslims were being humiliated... rather you advanced to Allah, steadfast.

Azzam quoted what he said was Senyor's last letter to his family:

> 'Despite the airplanes, the tanks, and the shelling day and night, and the intense cold and the hunger, I am happy and peaceful, because I feel that I am doing the most beloved of acts to Allah, and Allah rewards those who act. This Jihad is the only way that man can present to Allah acts which please Him and to return to this Umma its full honour.'

It was Azzam's epic, mythic, fantastical language that was to become the standard mode of expression for 'jihadi' radicals over the next decade.

By the time of Senyor's death, Arab volunteers were arriving in significant numbers. The years between 1985 and 1987 marked a turning point in the Afghan war. Existing trends – the growing numbers and radicalism of the Arab volunteers, the increasing dominance of the

Afghan political Islamists, the burgeoning warlordism, factionalism and corruption of the mujahideen commanders – all began to accelerate. In 1986, American and Saudi funding reached record levels and American Stinger shoulder-launched surface-to-air missiles were distributed by the ISI to favoured commanders. The mujahideen, though they still found it difficult to counter Soviet airpower, now had the weapons and munitions necessary to inflict significant damage on their enemies.

The efforts made by Azzam, bin Laden and others to build a network of recruiting offices throughout the Middle East were also paying off. Branches of the MAK had even been opened in Brooklyn, New York. In many places the organisation relied on the existing structure of the Muslim Brotherhood. So many recruits were arriving that in Peshawar the system of guesthouses had to be reorganised. There were now at least a dozen in the city, some in the University Town and some in the western suburb of Hayatabad, one for each nation's recruits.[6]

Though the bulk of the volunteers came from Saudi Arabia, the Yemen, Egypt and Algeria, there were Sudanese fighters, a small number of Indonesians, Filipinos, Malaysians, Chechens, Iraqi Kurds and Bosnian Muslims. Almost every Islamic nation was represented, if only by a few individuals.[7]

However, though the Muslim Brotherhood and other similar organisations played key roles in recruiting and fundraising, an increasing number of the volunteers themselves often had little previous involvement with Islamist politics. Many were very young and few had any profound understanding of Islamism and its antecedents. They were very different from the Islamist cadres of Hizb or Jamaat Islami. Some were attracted by the handsome subsidies provided by Saudi donors. Others flew in for a few weeks over a summer before returning to wealthy homes in the Gulf. Though the leaders of the Arab Afghans were largely middle-class graduates from technical disciplines and thus still fitted the classic activist's profile the rank and file were increasingly filled with far less educated men who were profoundly ignorant both of the cultural, political and intellectual heritage and context of contemporary radical Islam and of the ethnic and political reality on the ground in Afghanistan. The fact that they were still committed to fighting in the war there is good evidence of the conception of jihad as without earthly ends and as a continuing struggle and sacrifice, as outlined in Chapter Two.[8]

The volunteers' lack of political sophistication, and in some cases lack of literacy, made them susceptible to the less coherent, more millenarian message of Azzam. Though Azzam was clearly building on the legacy of al-Banna, Maududi, Qutb and Khomeini, his thought was far less polished and ideological than the earlier thinkers. Its ideological weaknesses were obscured by its rousing call to jihad and martyrdom and broad-brushed depictions of a cosmic struggle between the umma and its enemies, between good and evil. This was a significant step towards the hardening of the dominant discourse within Islamic militancy. As the war progressed the trend was to accelerate. So too was the social shift discernible among the 'Arab Afghans'.

The new radicalism was bolstered by the arrival in Pakistan of a small number of hardened activists from all over the Islamic world, though especially from Egypt, who moved swiftly into leadership positions. Many of the Egyptians had been imprisoned following the assassination of President Anwar Sadat in October 1981. These included several Egyptian Islamic militants, such as Mohammed Shawky al-Islambouli – the brother of the army lieutenant, Khalid al-Islambouli, who had killed the Egyptian leader – and Mohammed Atef, a 6ft 4inch former policeman who was to become one of bin Laden's closest aides. Many already had contacts with Hekmatyar, Sayyaf and other Afghan Islamists.[9] In 1985, Abdel Omar Rahman, the 'blind sheikh', accompanied Hekmatyar on a trip 'inside' Afghanistan and wept when he heard the sounds of combat that he could not see.[10] Al-Zawahiri took up a medical position at a hospital funded by the Kuwaiti government in Peshawar and delivered firebrand sermons each Friday that were popular with the city's growing Arab community.[11] A contingent of Egyptian fighters maintained a strong presence in Nangahar, fighting alongside Hekmatyar's Hizb groups and building a reputation for tenacity and courage.[12]

The Egyptians were known as 'thinkers and the brains' among the Arab Afghans. According to Essam Deraz, the Egyptian filmmaker who spent years with both bin Laden and the Egyptian radicals:

> bin Laden had followers but they weren't organized. The people with Zawahiri had extraordinary capabilities – doctors, engineers, soldiers. They had experience in secret work. They knew how to organize themselves and create cells. And they became the leaders.[13]

Several hundred fought themselves, usually alongside Sayyaf.

However, the vast bulk of the volunteers arriving in Afghanistan were without any military training. At first, most were sent to one of the many mujahideen bases to be taught the rudiments of small arms and heavy weapons use. Each mujahideen group had a main headquarters base with substantial stores and facilities and a varying number of smaller bases out in the field. The latter, which became more numerous in the later stages of the war as local field commanders became increasingly independent of even those local communities that had survived sustained and targeted Soviet bombing, often comprised little more than a dozen or so men in a couple of stone huts or caves. The main bases were sometimes far more elaborate affairs.

One of the biggest was at Zhawar Khili, a dry gully in the mountains southwest of Khost, about four miles over the border from Pakistan.[14] It was constructed in 1985 by mujahideen loyal to Jalaluddin Haqqani, the alim and local warlord, on the orders of the ISI and with Saudi funds.

It was a massive complex. Bulldozers and explosives were used to dig seven tunnels into the side of a mountain valley. The tunnels had brick entrances with iron doors and were big enough to shelter a mosque, a garage, an armourer's shop, a small first aid post equipped with American medical equipment including ultrasound apparatus, a radio station, a library with English and local books, a kitchen, a 'Hotel' and stores. A generator provided power for the aid post, mosque and guests' tunnel and a video recorder.[15]

A similar base, only marginally less extensive, was constructed, again with Saudi money and under the direction of the ISI (the CIA were not allowed to enter Afghanistan) in a natural cave complex called Tora Bora, 30 miles south of Jalalabad, by Engineer Machmud, one of Younis Khalis' commanders. Hekmatyar's Hizb-e-Islami constructed a large complex at Jaji, just over the border from the Pakistani town of Parachinar. In addition to the military training base (the 'seekers of martyrdom' camp) and the 'University of Da'wa and Jihad' he had built at Pabbi, near Peshawar, Sayyaf constructed another large training facility at Khaldan in the no man's land where Pakistan's Kurram tribal agency ends and before Afghanistan begins. In all camps, particularly Sayyaf's, small groups of Arabs trained alongside the mujahideen. These camps were to be the basis for the infrastructure developed by the 'al-Qaeda hardcore' in the late 1990s. At no point between their construction and their demolition in autumn 2001 by American bombs were they empty.[16]

But by 1989, though bin Laden had helped build other camps and shipped in equipment from his family's firm in Saudi Arabia to assist the work, he had built only one base for his own exclusive use.[17] It was known as *al-Ma'asada*, the 'Lion's Den', and had been constructed near Jaji. The exact date of its construction is unclear, though work on it may have started as soon as late 1986.[18] It was one of only two camps used exclusively by Arabs. The other was constructed by an Egyptian group near Khost and was known as Khalid bin Waleed camp, named after the Prophet Mohammed's most effective general. Most Arabs continued training and fighting alongside Sayyaf, Hekmatyar and even Massoud as individuals, not in coherent groups.[19] Bin Laden himself continued his support for the Afghans, as well as the Arabs, appearing regularly in rear areas around Khost to hand out food, shoes and coats to fighters.[20]

It was among the slate-brown hills of Jaji that bin Laden first saw real combat. The village had been the focus of concerted efforts by Soviet troops to cut the mujahideen supply lines from Pakistan for several years. By early 1986, the ISI had become concerned that their effort to keep Soviets away from border areas was failing and that the enemy had gained the initiative. Their operations had been hampered by infighting, the frequent absence of senior Afghan commanders and Soviet air superiority.[21] In a change of strategy, ISI officers issued instructions to dig in to fight around three fortified points in a line set just forward from the border, Jaji, the base at Zhawar Khili and a third site, the hill village of Ali Khel.[22]

The battles through the summer of 1986 were fierce, with both the mujahideen and the Soviets and their Afghan conscript support suffering heavy casualties. Bin Laden and a group of several hundred Arabs were involved in the fighting. Mujahideen remember the 29-year-old Saudi, Kalashnikov in hand, under heavy bombardment.[23] Over the next three years, contrary to claims by his detractors, bin Laden fought hard, often exposing himself to extreme physical danger during combat around Khost, Jalalabad and elsewhere. Though the stories bin Laden tells of seizing weapons from Soviet generals may be exaggerated there is no doubt that he did take part in a large number of operations.[24]

Soon bin Laden was spending up to eight months of the year in Afghanistan, visiting fronts all along the Pakistani border, from Kandahar to Kunar. He used the *nom de guerre* Abu Abdullah, the father of Abdullah, his oldest son, then aged about 11.[25] Bin Laden built up his contacts among the mujahideen, developing close relations with a number of commanders including Sayyaf, Haqqani, Younis Khalis and Engineer Machmud. These connections were to prove of crucial importance in the future. There is also an indication that his political thinking was maturing too. By 1987, he was lecturing the Arabs in Peshawar that American goods should be boycotted in support of the first Palestinian *intifada,* which had started that year.[26]

Bin Laden's reputation among the mujahideen remained mixed. His attitude towards local Islamic practices had hardened during his time in Afghanistan and, whereas once he had been happy to follow local rituals of prayer when in local mosques, by 1988 he was telling Mohammed Said Pahlwan, a senior mujahideen commander in Nangahar province, that he would not cooperate with him on military operations because Pahlwan was clean-shaven and smoked.[27] Bin Laden's shift to a more cohesive, more aggressive ideology was typical of the Arab volunteers. In the last years of the Afghan war, clashes between the 'Arab Afghans' and locals became more common, particularly in the northeastern Afghan border province of Kunar, where hardline Wahhabis had declared an independent state. Nor did bin Laden's willingness to rough it make him particularly popular among the Afghans. It attracted the scorn of senior Afghan commanders used to a degree of luxury in their big University Town villas and the incomprehension of the Afghan fighting men, to whom a display of luxury and consumption was an essential part of the authority of a leader.

However, the image of the rich boy living the life of the fighting soldier played well in the Middle East among potential donors and recruits. Bin Laden carefully managed documentaries filmed of him to show him in his best light, eating poor food and living in caves or rudimentary shelters in the Afghan hills. He continued to fund newspapers in University Town and was careful to cultivate influential journalists. His asceticism was not faked, however. Former associates remembered that bin Laden would eat only yoghurt, vegetables, a little meat and flat Afghan bread when in Peshawar though far better food was available. Though aware of his growing status and fame, he went out of his way to be accessible and informal. 'We used to sit down and eat together like old friends. You would never know how rich he was unless someone told you,' said one former fighter.[28]

In early 1989, the Soviets completed their withdrawal from Afghanistan, leaving a puppet regime behind them in Kabul, propped up by cash subsidies and weapons shipments. It was run by Dr Mohammed Najibullah, a senior PDPA cadre and former head of the hated Khad secret police. Though General Zia had been killed in an air crash two years previously, his Afghan policy had outlived him in Islamabad. The ISI were still committed to installing a pro-Pakistan, Islamist government in Kabul. The collapse of Najibullah's administration within months was predicted and the ISI were anxious to force a successful outcome to the war they had run for ten years.[29]

In February 1989 they convened a shura of the mujahideen groups in Pakistan. With the help of $25m in Saudi funds, they got Sayyaf accepted as the prime minister of a putative Afghan government. The next stage, the ISI believed, was to seize a city that could act as a seat for the new administration. Once the mujahideen were installed on Afghan soil, they hoped, the resistance of the Kabul regime would collapse. In March 1989, massed fighters from almost every faction attacked Jalalabad. The ISI, however, had made a catastrophic miscalculation.

Bin Laden's war climaxed at the battle of Jalalabad. Though the mujahideen made early gains, poor organisation, factional infighting, a lack of supplies and tactical inadequacy meant that they were swiftly forced onto the defensive. More than 1,000 Afghan fighters were killed, several thousand more injured and the Kabul regime received a huge boost.

Bin Laden was mainly involved in combat around the town of Chaprihar, southeast of Jalalabad. Mujahideen leaders remember bin Laden holding a position under heavy bombardment after being surrounded by Soviet soldiers. Many mention bin Laden's lack of concern for his own safety.[30]

His fanaticism was shared by his men. 'I took three Afghans and three Arabs and told them to hold a position,' one mujahideen leader remembered.

> They fought all day then when I went to relieve them in the evening the Arabs were crying because they wanted to be martyred. They were saying, 'I must have committed some sin for Allah has not chosen me to go to heaven.' I told them that if they wanted to stay... and fight then I wasn't going to stop them. The next day they were killed. Osama said later that he had told them that the trench was their gate to heaven.[31]

Shortly after the battle of Jalalabad, the differences between the mujahideen factions flared again. Bin Laden, like many Arabs, was deeply frustrated by the infighting. It was *fitna*, or division and faction, which the Prophet Mohammed had expressly forbidden. Though ideologically closer to Hekmatyar and Sayyaf, bin Laden was also an admirer of Massoud and for the last nine years had devoted considerable effort to reconciling the factions, even paying the rent for a building at 38 Syed Jamal al-Din Afghani road in Peshawar which acted as a neutral venue for discussions between the groups.[32] Bin Laden told the mujahideen commanders that they had defeated the Soviet empire alone because they were united and Allah had blessed them. If they did not join together, he said, they could not do Allah's will.[33]

But the failure to capture Jalalabad, and Pakistan's role in running the fighting, had depressed him greatly. Through the autumn of 1989, bin Laden, now aged 32, split his time between Saudi Arabia and Pakistan. In November 1989, Abdallah Azzam was killed by a car bomb in Peshawar, an attack that is often blamed on bin Laden. Though he made no secret of his irritation at Azzam's placement of relatives in key jobs in MAK, there is little evidence to implicate him in the assassination and a host of more likely suspects. Among the Arabs themselves there was further fitna. One consequence of rejecting the authority of the ulema was that anyone, usually someone educated in the new Saudi-funded Islamic centres that had sprung up separately from the traditional medressas and the universities all over the Islamic world, could claim leadership of a group and a degree of religious authority. Now, with the Soviets gone, the Arab Afghans, never a homogeneous body, split into scores of different groups each focused on the problems of their own homeland.[34] For bin Laden, the jihad in Afghanistan was over by the first months of 1990.

For the Afghans, of course, the struggle was far from finished. Their country was in ruins, warlords were running riot and the most radical elements in Afghan Islam, marginalised before the war, were now in a position to make a serious push for power. For the next five years it would be the fighting amongst the Islamist groups, once peripheral to Afghan politics, that would dominate the political scene.

For the Pakistanis too the jihad continued. In broad terms Islamabad's policy aim was unchanged: to secure a pliable government in Kabul. But Pakistan itself had been altered irrevocably by ten years of the Afghan war. The hardliners of the ISI and the army were in as strong a position as they had ever been. Over the next years, as attempts to re-establish democracy and the rule of law in Pakistan foundered, the war's pernicious effects on Pakistan itself would be revealed.

And for Abdallah Azzam's foreign legion the jihad also went on. The last years of the war had seen the creation of something entirely new. The hardened Arab veterans of the war against the Soviets had evolved an ideology themselves. Afghani, the Muslim Brotherhood, Maududi, even Qutb, had been left far behind. Instead, the new worldview was constructed from the rigorous Salafi reformism of the Wahhabis, from Azzam's call for martyrdom in a pan-Islamic international jihad against oppression, from the very real experience of the brutal violence and chaos of modern warfare and from the empowering confidence founded in the belief, however wrong, that Islam alone had defeated the Soviets and their munafiq stooges among the Afghans. The gradualism of

Maududi, the social reformism of al-Banna, even Qutb's political and ideological focus had gone.

In its place was a radical and violent utopianism. Azzam's writings are not political tracts, or even arguments, but exhortations to violence. Anything but jihad as armed struggle is rejected. The war had reinforced the radicals' sense of cosmic struggle. The battles with the Russians had shown that it was not merely the failure of Muslims to adhere to the true path that had brought suffering upon the umma but also the machinations of the non-believers as well. The Russian assault on Muslim Afghanistan had convinced them that the forces of Kufr, led by the Christians and the Zionists, were plotting continually against Muslims as they had done ever since the Jewish tribes of Medina betrayed the Prophet's pact. As there had never been a pure and just Islamic state since the time of the Prophet and his four successors, the last 1,300 years, far from being the ameliorative evolution seen in the West, were, to the 'Arab Afghan' veterans, a dark age of suffering and perdition. The culture and sophistication of the Ummayads and the Abbasids, the architecture and poetry, the philosophy and the lore of the Muslim world were rejected as tainted by weakness and corrupted by failure. More than a thousand years of history was relegated to little more than a collection of paradigms and anecdotes.[35]

Some of the veterans went home. The role of many of them in the emergence of violent radical movements in Egypt, Algeria and elsewhere is explored further in chapters to come. In the short term, the radical effect of the new ideology was disguised by the seeming strength of the more moderate political Islamism. The late 1980s are seen by many scholars as the highpoint of the political Islamist project. In Palestine, the secular Palestine Liberation Organization's dominance of the intifada was being threatened by the Islamic HAMAS group, founded in 1988 by Shaikh Ahmed Yasin, a member of the Muslim Brotherhood. In 1990, in Algeria, the Front Islamique du Salut, relatively moderate activists who had engaged with the democratic process, made huge gains in the first free elections since independence. In Sudan, a military *coup d'état* allowed one of the key ideologues of contemporary political Islam, Hassan al-Turabi, to come to power. Nor did the Iranian Revolution appear to have run out of energy. A fatwa pronounced by Ayatollah Khomeini on the British author Salman Rushdie ambitiously extended the authority of the Iranian Islamist state and, by implication, 'true' Islamic practice throughout the West.[36] The Communist system was collapsing. Political Islam everywhere appeared in the ascendant.

One critical element of this burgeoning and radical movement is often forgotten: the recruits had not stopped flowing into Pakistan and Afghanistan, even after the Soviets were defeated. In 1989 and 1990 more were arriving in Pakistan than ever before. One was Jamal al-Fadl, then a 26-year-old from the Sudan who had been working at a mosque in Brooklyn, New York that was a branch of Azzam's Maktab al-Khidamat, before travelling to join the jihad himself. After a short time in a guesthouse in Peshawar, al-Fadl had transferred to Khalid bin Waleed camp near Khost where he had received basic training on Kalashnikovs and rocket launchers. He then moved up to another guesthouse, probably the 'lion's den' complex close to the Jaji front. There, after being lectured on his duty to fight the jihad by bin Laden himself, he went into combat.[37]

Al-Fadl told his story, after receiving a substantial amount of American taxpayer's money, in New York during the trial in 2001 of the men who bombed the east African embassies three years earlier. He told the court he had spent most of 1989 fighting, in Peshawar or at a number of different training camps. At al-Farooq camp, another camp near Khost, he was lectured on Islamic jurisprudence and the principle of jihad for two weeks. At the Abu Bakr al-Sadeek camp he was trained in administration. At the Jihad Wal camp, also near Khost, an Egyptian instructor taught him about explosives and bomb-making. Though al-Fadl did not say so in court, al-Farooq was run at the time by Sayyaf and staffed by Egyptian instructors. Nor did al-Fadl mention that Jihad Wal was run by Hizb-e-Islami. Though the instructors and administrators of these camps were Arab, largely because their Gulf patrons did not trust Afghans with substantial sums of money, local mujahideen trained there alongside foreigners. These were not 'bin Laden' camps as is commonly alleged.[38]

Towards the end of 1989, al-Fadl said he was back at al-Farooq camp when an Iraqi volunteer, Abu Ayoub, approached him and asked him if he would be interested in joining a group which, al-Fadl said, was calling itself 'al-Qaeda'. It aimed to train people to continue the jihad outside Afghanistan. The group, which al-Fadl said he joined by signing an oath of allegiance, a bayat, to its leader in triplicate, comprised only around a dozen people, mainly Egyptians such as Ayman al-Zawahiri and Mohammed Atef.[39] The leader or 'emir' was to be bin Laden. As the war in Afghanistan waned, bin Laden hoped to start fresh campaigns to bring an Islamic revolution to the countries of the umma. The main target of his activities was not yet America or 'the West' (in fact it was

Hekmatyar who was the most virulently anti-American activist at the time), but the 'corrupt and hypocritical' regimes in the Muslim world. All around him the volunteers who had fought one enemy during the Afghan war were squabbling. Most of them saw their primary objective as returning to their homelands to struggle against their own governments. Bin Laden's aims have to be seen against their background. He wanted to prevent the fragile international alliance created during the war against the Soviets falling apart. By uniting the various militant movements, split on national lines at the time, bin Laden hoped to concentrate their power.

But a close examination shows that the group that hoped to be 'al-Qaeda', the base for the new international vanguard, were a fairly mixed bunch. Al-Qaeda comprised a dozen or so people at best, mainly recruited from within al-Zawahiri's Egyptian Islamic Jihad faction. Whether the bayat sworn to bin Laden superseded allegiance to local groups was a matter of some discussion. So were the group's aims. Their ideology was unsure and their practical capabilities were almost non-existent.

Indeed, bin Laden was far from the most prominent or the most influential of the many militants active in southwest Asia, and elsewhere in the Islamic world, in the late 1980s. In fact it was Omar Abdel Rahman, the Egyptian 'blind sheikh', who was considered Abdallah Azzam's successor as the spiritual leader of the radical Islamic movement. In the years after bin Laden's departure from southwest Asia, Islamic extremist activism in Pakistan and Afghanistan intensified rather than diminished. As pointed out in Chapter One, in the seven years he was absent from southwest Asia, tens of thousands, possibly hundreds of thousands, of militants trained for terrorism and combat in the scores of training camps in Afghanistan and Pakistan and many of these activists went on to launch an unprecedented wave of terrorist attacks in the Middle East, south Asia, Europe and America. The movements that flourished and grew during that short time, particularly Pakistani militant groups, were to be of critical importance in the late 1990s. Bin Laden's involvement in their activities, as with the camps, was negligible.

CHAPTER SIX

MILITANTS

I had left the domes and minarets of the great Mughal mosque well behind me. A short ride in a rickshaw and a long walk through filthy alleys finally brought me to a door behind a carpet weaver's workshop. The only mark identifying the door as that of the Lahore office of Harkat-ul-Mujahideen (HUM), the militant Islamic group, was a small sticker depicting two crossed Kalashnikovs above an open Qur'an on the doorjamb. I was buzzed in and was met by 'Mohammed', a young HUM cadre I had met in Kashmir a month or so earlier. The office comprised two large rooms and a small kitchen. At night dozens of young volunteers passing through the city on their way to the training camps or combat in Kashmir slept on thin, stained mats on the floor. When we had met previously, Mohammed had offered to introduce me to six HUM fighters who he said had recently arrived from the UK. The British fighters never showed up but, as we spoke about the group's recruitment overseas, Mohammed mentioned a young British-Pakistani who was in prison in India on terrorist charges. I was intrigued and over the next few months was able to piece together much of the story of Omar Saeed Sheikh.

Sheikh fits the profile of the classic politically aware Islamic activist. He was young, the son of a relatively wealthy self-made immigrant (from Pakistan to the UK, rather than from the country to the town), intelligent, literate and a graduate in a technical discipline at university. His passage from an interest in Islamic political issues while a student to the HUM, kidnappings in India and on to an eventual death sentence in a Pakistani court for his role in the murder of Daniel Pearl, an American journalist, in January 2002, tracks exactly the shift in the broader movement of Islamic activism from the political and ideological activism of early

Islamic radical thinkers such as al-Banna to the current debased, millenarian and nihilistic strand of Islamic radicalism that has become so dominant today. It also demonstrates the role of states, in this case Pakistan, in the radicalisation process, shows how bin Laden's influence on such developments and involvement with militant activities in the early 1990s was marginal and is evidence of how the training camps in Afghanistan and Pakistan thrived in the period. More than anything it shows the diversity of the modern Islamic radical movement.

In 1968, Sheikh's father, a wealthy Pakistani businessman, left his village near the eastern Pakistani city of Lahore and, with his wife, travelled to Britain. They settled in Wanstead, a genteel suburb on the eastern outskirts of London, where their first son, Omar, was born in 1973. At the age of nine he was sent to The Forest, a nearby fee-paying school. Schoolfriends and teachers agree that he was a physically and mentally powerful individual. In 1987, his father sold his business in London and decided to move his family back to Pakistan. One reason may have been a wish to raise his children in a more devout environment than could be found in the UK.[1]

Back in Lahore, Sheikh was sent to the prestigious and elitist Aitchison College, known as Pakistan's Eton. Omar lasted two years there before being expelled for fighting. He was either a habitual bully or a principled and brave young man unafraid of physical violence. Accounts of the incidents leading to the expulsions differ.[2]

In 1989, Sheikh's father's business in Pakistan failed and the family returned to London. By December 1990, Sheikh was back at The Forest, working for exams which eventually gained him admission to the London School of Economics, where he studied applied mathematics, statistics, economics and social psychology. He also joined the Islamic society and, during 'Bosnia week' in late 1992, watched a series of documentary films about the oppression of Muslims following the break-up of the former Yugoslavia. In the wars in the Balkans in the early 1990s, tens of thousands of Muslims were brutally put to death in scenes of violence unseen in Europe since the Second World War. Those who killed them, particularly the Christian Serbs, were often projected in the Islamic world as agents of the West, or kufr. Before his time at the LSE, Sheikh had demonstrated little interest in religion or politics. Six months later, however, when he visited Pakistan with his father, Sheikh distributed films of the war in Bosnia and made contact with Islamic militants in Lahore. Within weeks of his return to the UK, he had joined a relief convoy organised by a London-based charity travelling from the UK to Bosnia. Sheikh fell ill at the Bosnian border and, while convalescing in Split, met a Pakistani veteran of the war against the Soviets who was a member of Harkat-ul-Mujahideen. The Pakistani was on his way to join the other Afghan veterans who, reinforced by volunteers from all over the Muslim world, were travelling to fight alongside local Muslims. He encouraged Sheikh to take up arms.[3] The younger man was impressed and sometime in the late summer arrived at the HUM offices in Lahore from where, after a few days in the city, he was sent on to Miram Shah, the dusty town close to the Afghan-Pakistan border area used as a staging post for recruits heading to the training camps around Khost. After a brief stay there Sheikh joined a group of recruits on their way to Khalid bin Waleed camp.

When the Soviet Union collapsed, so too did the flow of funds and material to Dr Najibullah's administration in Kabul. The regime was left unable to buy crucial support outside the narrow groups who were loyal to it, its authority and military capability swiftly disintegrated and the mujahideen factions were able to take control of the capital. Najibullah made a half-hearted bid to escape to India, was stopped at the airport and effectively imprisoned.

When Sheikh arrived in the region in late1993, about 18 months after Kabul had fallen, the camps around Khost and Jalalabad were as full as ever. And though many thousands of militants from all over the Islamic world trained in them in this period the majority of terrorist recruits learning how to fire Kalashnikovs and plant explosives were Pakistani.

Pakistani militancy in this period splits into two broad strands: sectarian militants, who were almost exclusively focused on killing within their own country and showed little interest in any globalised jihad, and a 'Kashmiri' strain composed, paradoxically but for reasons that will become clear, largely of non-Kashmiris who fought Indian security forces in the disputed Himalayan state. Both strands were, at times, supported and exploited by agents of the Pakistani state and funded by states and private donors in Saudi Arabia, Kuwait, Qatar, the United Arab Emirates and elsewhere. Both, until late 2001, remained relatively distinct. Both also, again until quite recently, remained apart from the 'Arab Afghans' who had remained in Pakistan in numbers after the end of the war against the Soviets. The reasons why Pakistan, a supposedly democratic state that was a nominal ally of America and the West, was actively encouraging the training and deployment of thousands of extremist militants, and thus sustaining and perpetuating an infrastructure that would be enormously useful to bin Laden and his allies later on, lie in the structural flaws of the Pakistani state and the degree to which those weaknesses were exploited both by groups within the country and by external actors.

When Pakistan came into being in 1947, it was unclear whether it was an Islamic state, to be constructed entirely on principles laid down in holy texts, or merely a state for Muslims, somewhere where the religion and society of the subcontinent's Muslim population would be safe from the threat of Hindu demographic, cultural and political dominance. The latter does not necessarily imply the former. Indeed, many of Pakistan's founders looked to Western democracies as a model, not the examples of the early Muslims. This lack of definition made the country vulnerable to periodic attempts by domestic religious radicals to enforce a greater degree of 'Islamicisation'.

Pakistan is rarely considered to be part of the Middle East and is often ignored by those analysing that region. However, when the recent histories of Pakistan and of those to its west are compared many illuminating parallels emerge. After a short and unstable period of democracy, in which an inexperienced and fractious elite completely failed to deal with the profound problems bequeathed by British colonial rule, the military took power. For the best part of the 1950s and 1960s Pakistan was governed, like so many countries in the Islamic world, by a secular, Westernising, economically liberal, post-colonial elite composed of senior generals and the civilians who were successfully co-opted by the regime. Pakistan's military rulers also failed to cope with their country's growing social and economic problems caused, as elsewhere, by, among other factors, rapid population increase, migration from rural areas to the cities and their own clumsy attempts at reform.[4]

New cultural influences and a vastly expanded educational sector, as in Afghanistan, also raised aspirations which could not be fulfilled. In 1971, the Pakistani army failed to stop the eastern half of the country peeling off to form Bangladesh. Like the 1967 Six Day War in much of the Arab world, the defeat destroyed the legitimacy of the first generation of post-colonial rulers in Pakistan and opened the way to power for the brilliant, opportunistic Zulfikar Ali Bhutto with his quasi-Socialist slogans. Like President Anwar Sadat in Egypt, Bhutto was a deeply cynical if charismatic politician and unable to deal with the profound problems he faced. Social, economic and cultural tensions were exacerbated by the impact of the oil boom in the Gulf. Much as the political Islamists were to do in Egypt and elsewhere, Maududi's Jamaat Islami party, committed to a gradual but comprehensive Islamicisation of society, was able to capitalise on growing discontent in Pakistan. As in so many countries in the region, both nationalism and socialism had been found wanting, traditional rural Islamic practices were no longer relevant and the certainties of political Islam, with its promise of a just social order attainable through non-violent activism that would not threaten a social revolution, were profoundly attractive to the new middle classes. By 1973, Jamaat Islami had 100,000 members.[5] The huge wealth and cultural dominance of the Gulf states seemed evidence enough that greater Islamicisation was the answer to Pakistan's problems. When Bhutto finally moved to co-opt Pakistan's growing numbers of political Islamists it was too late and the violence surrounding rigged elections in 1977 gave the army, under General Zia ul-Haq, the chance to step in. Zia had Bhutto hanged in April 1979, two months after the Shah had been deposed in Iran.

Zia took power by military means but quickly co-opted the new force that had so weakened Bhutto, inducting several senior Jamaat Islami figures into his cabinet and announcing that Pakistani law would be based on the Shariat. Zia also established Shariat courts to try cases under Islamic law and ordered Islamic punishments for drinking alcohol, theft, prostitution, fornication, adultery and bearing false witness. Tens of thousands of Jamaat Islami activists were given jobs in the judiciary, the civil service and the education system. Many more, from the urban middle classes who provided Jamaat Islami's core constituency, were recruited into the army, fundamentally changing its nature. Externally, Zia, whose own faith was both pragmatic and profound, turned to the Saudis and other Gulf states as natural allies, lending troops to Riyadh to quell Juhaiman's revolt of 1979 and receiving significant financial assistance by way of recompense. The $50m Shah Faisal mosque in Islamabad and the new International Islamic University beside it were the most visible manifestations of Pakistan's new orientation. This shift from secular nationalism to political Islamism, via demagogic socialism, was by no means unique to Pakistan.

However, despite the apparent strength of the political Islamists of Jamaat Islami in the late 1980s, radical neo-conservative trends had already begun to undermine them. During the 1980s, when Jamaat Islami dominated Islamic activism in Pakistan, Deobandism was growing exponentially.

It is easy to confuse political Islamism and the strand of Islamic thought derived from the early Deobandis, yet the two are very different. Where political Islamism is focused on the Islamicisation of the state through what are effectively political channels, the Deobandis reject politics altogether. The emphasis placed by the Deobandis on a rigid observance of a literal reading of Qur'anic injunctions is very different to the relative flexibility of the political Islamists. And where political Islamists like Maududi or Hekmatyar reject the authority of the ulema, the Deobandis venerate the clergy and recognise their monopoly on textual interpretation.

The Deobandis were formed in the mid nineteenth century in reaction to the challenge posed by British power and Hindu demographic superiority to Indian Muslims. In this they follow the pattern of revivalist and reformist movements within Islam reacting to external threats. Though they believed that Indian Muslims could preserve their separate identity by carefully following the exact ritual and personal behaviour prescribed in the Qur'an and the hadith, the early Deobandis learned from the threat they confronted. Medressas, or religious schools, were reorganised in imitation of European educational institutions. They were staffed by a paid faculty who ran classes offering a sequential curriculum.[6] The medressas, and the ulema who taught in them and were charged with interpreting the external world by the texts, thus became the central focus of the Deobandi movement. Though their early attempt to learn from the West was genuine, over time the Deobandi ulema became increasingly reactionary with their fatwas encouraging a retreat from, rather than an adaptation of, the innovations of their colonial rulers. The medressas became an isolated 'Islamicised space' and their inhabitants became an idealised 'Islamic society', islands in a sea of kufr and barbarism. The students at the medressas were known as *taliban*, a Persianised plural of an Arabic word meaning seekers of knowledge or students. It was these students who were to form the foot soldiers of the eponymous movement in Afghanistan in the mid 1990s.

In 1879, there were 12 Deobandi medressas. By 1967 there were 9,000 across south Asia including nearly a thousand in Pakistan.[7] Many had been established in the more conservative Pashtun areas of the North West Frontier Province and attracted a considerable number of Afghan students. Their growth accelerated during the 1980s and by 1988 nearly 400,000 boys and young men were being educated by Deobandis in Pakistan.[8] The key to the growth was the huge funds that had flowed into the Deobandi medressas from the Gulf when governments and donors there had decided that the Deobandis were the closest local equivalent to the Wahhabis and thus should be sponsored as part of the global push to encourage the spread of hardline Salafi strands of Islam. The Deobandis' limited involvement in the war in Afghanistan had also allowed them to concentrate on building up their school system. For the millions of destitute Afghan refugee children, as well as poor Pakistanis, the free education, board and lodging offered by the Deobandi medressas was very attractive. With Pakistani government schools lacking funds, teachers and often buildings, the medressas effectively became a parallel, and very popular, education system catering particularly for the impoverished rural classes. Significantly, most of the graduates from Deobandi seminaries in the NWFP came from villages with less than 10,000 inhabitants.[9]

This rural stress reinforced the crucial ideological differences between the Deobandis and south Asian political Islamists who tended, as we have seen, to come from urban backgrounds. There is a strong sense here of a wider shift too. The medressa boys and their teachers were drawn from the huge swathe of Pakistani society that had been marginalised by the economic growth since independence. They are not the sons and daughters of lower middle-class intellectuals denied what they see as a fair share of the profits of the nation's steady, if deeply uneven, economic growth, but those entirely failed by the modern Pakistani state. Over the next decade the recruits to the broad movement of Islamic militancy throughout the Muslim world would be drawn from increasingly poorer social groups. Increasingly too, militants would subscribe to the anti-rational, millenarian worldview already prevalent by the early 1990s among many 'Arab Afghans'.

The huge volume of young men educated in the medressas had a rapid and obvious impact, playing an important part in creating and propagating the narrow, dogmatic worldview that is a mark of the modern militant. Through the Deobandis, that ideology broke out from its ghetto among the foreign 'Arab Afgans' in Peshawar or attached to certain Afghan mujahideen groups and began to spread among the Pakistani population more generally. Teaching methods in the medressas were basic, relying largely on rote learning, and discipline was often poor. In a fascinating study of language in the medressas, Tariq Rahman, an Associate Professor of Linguistics at Quaid-i-Azam University, Islamabad, demonstrates how language teaching was a part of the process of indoctrination, supporting, reproducing and reinforcing the philosophical import of other doctrinaire subjects.[10] The worldview it created is entirely religious. The true believer is defined against the 'other', the non-Muslim, the heretic, the blasphemer or even the follower of another sect or a Westernised non-practising Muslim. The emir must be obeyed. Rahman points out that many of the texts used in medressas date back to the fifteenth century and that even the more recent textbooks include exercises involving sentences like: 'These girls have been ordered to put on the veil and they have been stopped from going to the *bazaar*', 'You women are really ungrateful to your husbands,' 'Tariq bin Ziyad conquered Andalusia' or 'The English were always the enemies of Islam.'

The medressas provided the foot soldiers for both the sectarian terrorists and the more international, Kashmir-focused Harkat-ul-Mujahideen. At first, fighters were trained in the medressas themselves. Many were taught basic skills in the huge religious complexes, such as that at Akora Khattak, 40 miles east of Peshawar. By the early 1990s, the sheer number of recruits from Deobandi schools meant that most military instruction of sectarian terrorists had to be done in the camps or at other specialised locations within Pakistan. One of the biggest such facilities was at Khalid bin Waleed camp in Afghanistan, where Omar Saeed Sheikh arrived in late 1993.[11]

Khalid bin Waleed consisted of several low stonewalled, wood and mud-roofed single-storey barracks-like buildings, where instructors and administrators lived, and a series of large tents for recruits, stores and ammunition. The camp is off the main road between Khost and the big complex at Zhawar Khili.[12]

Sheikh was put on the standard six-week basic training course in rudimentary military skills. Recruits would be woken before dawn to pray and then would exercise until the sun rose. After a breakfast of tea, bread and yoghurt, there would be instruction in basic infantry tactics, movement on the battlefield, unarmed combat and some weapons training. Occasionally the recruits would get to fire their guns but ammunition was short. The afternoon and often much of the evening would be spent on religious studies.[13] The training corresponds closely to that described in exercise books I found in camps run by bin Laden and his aides in the late 1990s, right down to the lack of live rounds, and to that described by mujahideen who were trained by Pakistani instructors during the mid to late 1980s.[14]

Having done well at the basic skills, Sheikh was selected by his instructors for more specialised training. The syllabus of the special course was exactly the same as had been taught in the mujahideen camps for nearly a decade. This was not surprising. Many of Sheikh's instructors were from the Pakistani Army's elite Special Services Group, the same unit that had trained Hekmatyar, Massoud and Rabbani for their abortive uprising in 1975. The specialised course taught the recruits the techniques needed for irregular warfare. They learned about mines, sabotage, covert surveillance techniques and secret communications.[15]

Alongside the Pakistani cadres in the camps were HUM volunteers from the Maghreb, Saudi Arabia and even the Philippines. When KK Muhamed, who was involved in the bombing of the American embassy in Dar es Salaam in 1998, was asked by the FBI where he had trained, he told them, according to the FBI agent who repeated his testimony in court, that he had been taught bomb-making in 1994 and 1995 in a camp run by 'Har Qatar', meaning 'Harkat-ul-Ansar', the name HUM were using at the time.[16]

In February 1994, as Sheikh was finishing his training at Khalid bin Waleed, Maulana Massoud Azhar, a charismatic Punjab-born Deobandi cleric and a senior figure in Harkat-ul-Mujahideen, was arrested by Indian security forces while travelling by rickshaw on a fake Portuguese passport in southern Kashmir. Sheikh was approached by the HUM leadership and asked to travel to India to seize hostages to force New Delhi to let Azhar go.

Pakistan and India fought their first war over Kashmir in late 1947. The Pakistanis, aware of their own military weakness, had tried to use irregular tribal fighters to force out the Hindu maharaja of the state during the partition of the British south Asian dominions. They had failed and, with New Delhi committed to holding on to India's only Muslim majority state, clashes between regular forces had followed. When, on 1 January 1949, a ceasefire was declared the Pakistanis controlled the western third of the former states of Jammu and Kashmir, and the Indians controlled the rest, including the Muslim-dominated valley of Srinagar.

In 1965, the Pakistanis tried again. Hundreds of infiltrators were sent across the Line of Control (LoC, the *de facto* boundary that separates Indian and Pakistani-held parts of Kashmir) in a failed bid to spark a revolt. Once again, the regular army troops were committed without success. More fighting in 1971 was similarly inconclusive.

The debacle of the war in Bangladesh of 1971 confirmed Islamabad's preference for proxy warfare. Along with the Afghan Islamists who had arrived in 1974, Pakistan also supported Sikh terrorists in western India, albeit intermittently, and sundry other south Asian insurgencies. A factor in Zia's enthusiasm for the war against the Soviets was the Pakistani military's long-term reliance on such proxies. The tactics in Afghanistan were seen as so successful that their application elsewhere, particularly in Kashmir against Pakistan's 'auld enemy', became an inevitability.

The Pakistanis first turned to the Jammu and Kashmir Liberation Front (JKLF), a small group of Kashmiri academics and intellectuals who wanted independence from both Pakistan and India and were more influenced by Frantz Fanon's radical leftist Third Worldism than by Qutb. In 1983, the ISI approached the JKLF and offered logistical support and training in return for control over military operations. By late 1987, a deal had been done and sometime in early 1988 a group of JKLF activists travelled into 'Azad' Jammu and Kashmir, as the semi-autonomous Pakistani parts of Kashmir are known to Islamabad, for training. The results of the ISI involvement were clear almost immediately. On 31 July 1988, a series of powerful explosions rocked Srinagar and Jammu.[17]

These blasts are usually taken to mark the start of the 'Kashmir insurgency'. But there were other factors beyond Pakistani interference that precipitated the surge of anger and violence that consumed Kashmir in the late 1980s. The 1987 provincial elections in the state had been thoroughly rigged by New Delhi. Many activists were inspired by the impending Soviet withdrawal from Afghanistan, the Palestinian intifada and the fall of the Communist regimes in Eastern Europe. The Indian government responded to the agitation with vicious repression.

Because the JKLF favoured independence rather than Pakistani rule, the ISI swiftly began looking for more pro-Islamabad alternatives. During the 1980s a Kashmiri version of Jamaat Islami had begun to emerge in the Indian-controlled areas of Kashmir. Its support came from largely the same social groups as its Pakistani parent body: the urban, educated middle classes, who were frustrated at the negligible economic development in the state, the lack of opportunities for social advancement for Muslims and the limited democracy.

By 1990, with peaceful demonstrators being gunned down by Indian forces in the streets, Jamaat Islami activists in Kashmir were rapidly becoming disillusioned with the traditional non-violent stance of the movement. Jamaat Islami in Kashmir formed an armed wing, known as Hizb-ul-Mujahideen, which, with its pro-Islamabad stance and obvious links to Zia's allies in JI in Pakistan, was a natural focus for the ambitions of the ISI and the senior Pakistani military command. Supplies and training for the JKLF were cut off. Gulbuddin Hekmatyar, who continued to be the favourite of the ISI, provided training facilities for the new group at his camps in Afghanistan. One particularly large camp, known as the Markaz Faiz Mohammed Shaheed, was set up with ISI trainers and administrators on the road between Zhawar Khili and Khost in late 1991.[18] Other militants were trained in camps set up around

Muzzafarabad in 'Azad Kashmir', in NWFP and in the Punjab. Trainers were borrowed from Hekmatyar and the syllabus was based on that taught by the ISI to the Afghan mujahideen.

After Zia died in 1988, Pakistan returned to civilian rule, first under Benazir Bhutto, then under Nawaz Sharif. Bhutto's party, the Pakistan People's Party had developed alliances with the Jamaat-e-Ulema-e-Islami, an organisation established by the Deobandi movement as a lobby group rather than as a political party. Sharif, with his Punjabi commercial and industrial support base, was far closer to the urban political Islamism personified by Zia, Hekmatyar's Hizb and Jamaat Islami than the feudal and rural Bhutto. By 1993, when Bhutto returned to power for a second time, she felt strong enough to try to overturn Zia's legacy and break the political Islamist nexus of the ISI, Hizb-e-Islami and Hizb-ul-Mujahideen. The political Islamist project in Pakistan was, as elsewhere in the Islamic world, beginning to weaken.

Certainly Pakistan's Zia-inspired foreign policy was failing. Much favour had been lost in the Gulf when JI had come out in noisy support of Saddam Hussein against the Saudi government in 1990. In Afghanistan, the ISI remained set on backing Hekmatyar against the Tajik-dominated faction led by Rabbani and Massoud and the Shia groups, despite his increasingly rabid anti-Americanism and willingness to kill civilians.[19] Between 1989 and 1992, the internecine conflicts among the factions had been disguised by their campaign against the Moscow-backed regime in Kabul. Once in control of the capital the failure of the various political Islamist factions to successfully govern their country was manifest.

Neither could the ISI or the senior army staff point to much success in Kashmir. There, though casualties among their security personnel were high, the Indians showed no sign of weakening. Despite hundreds of militants, and civilians, dying it was clear that any concessions from New Delhi were unlikely.

So when the Pakistani military wanted a new army of proxies to revitalise the flagging guerrilla campaign in Kashmir and replenish the cadres that the Indian military had decimated, there was an obvious place to look.[20] Two new groups, both Deobandi, were formed, trained and sent over the LoC.[21] The two groups were Harkat-ul-Mujahideen and Lashkar-e-Toiba (LeT, 'the army of the pure'). The LeT had its roots in the Ahl-e-Hadith movement, a relatively small Wahhabi group that had existed in Pakistan since partition but had grown swiftly, largely thanks to Saudi private funds, during the 1980s. LeT were smaller than the HUM and focused more closely on Kashmir. By 1994, both groups had established bases in Muzzafarabad and were running overt recruiting offices throughout Pakistan, such as the one I, and Omar Saeed Sheikh, had visited in Lahore. HUM also received considerable funds from Pakistani emigrant communities and from the private and governmental sources in the Gulf.

The Harkat-ul-Mujahideen and the LeT subscribed to the new Jihadi doctrine that had evolved during the latter stages of the Afghan war. They had little in common with Hizb-ul-Mujahideen's cadres, who saw themselves as fighting an Islamist political struggle for the Kashmiri people. The Harkat-ul-Mujahideen and the LeT were also considerably more violent and indiscriminate in their attacks and targeted the moderate and Sufi-influenced Kashmiri Muslims, berating them for their lax practices, attacking religious shrines, demanding that videos and TVs be banned and even, in the case of some cadres from an LeT splinter group, throwing acid in the faces of unveiled women.

Tragically for the people of Kashmir, the insurgency they had started in the late 1980s had gone through a rapid process of radicalisation that was largely out of their control. When the first demonstrations had started back in 1987, the Kashmiri grievances were largely articulated within a contemporary Western human rights discourse, albeit with a religious and economic undercurrent. The only Islamic activists seriously involved believed in a gradualist political Islam. Seven years later the insurgency had become dominated by the most violent fringe of modern Islamic activism.

By the time Sheikh arrived in New Delhi in the autumn of 1994 he was very much part of that fringe. He started looking for foreigners, preferably British or American, among backpackers in the city's Parganj quarter, attempting to strike up friendships.[22] With several accomplices, he eventually managed to kidnap three Britons and an American, holding them in safe houses well away from Delhi. It was an amateurish operation with, at one point, Sheikh himself forced to deliver a ransom note to a BBC office. Police stumbled across the kidnappers close to one of the safe houses and in the gunfight that followed Sheikh was shot in the shoulder. All the hostages were freed unharmed. Sheikh was sent to prison and largely forgotten. Eight years later he would make a spectacular return to the world of international Islamic militancy when he kidnapped Daniel Pearl of the *Wall Street Journal* in Karachi. Pearl was less lucky than the Delhi hostages and was brutally killed.

CHAPTER SEVEN

TERROR

At 12.17 and 37 seconds on 26 February 1993, a bomb exploded under the World Trade Center in New York, killing six people, injuring more than a thousand and causing $300m damage. The device, 1,200lbs of explosives, several heavy tanks of hydrogen, a detonator of nitroglycerine and two 20-foot fuses, had been hidden in a rented yellow Ryder Econoline van that had been parked in a public car park beneath the Twin Towers 12 minutes earlier. The bomb, on level B-2 of the complex, had smashed a hole through the foyer of the Vista hotel, two floors above it, and penetrated three floors down. A 3,000lb steel joist was ripped from its mountings and thrown 35 feet inside Tower One. That evening Ramzi Ahmed Yousef, a 25-year-old Pakistani, took a $30 cab ride to JFK airport, boarded a Pakistan International Airlines plane to Karachi and disappeared.

Ramzi had arrived in America nearly six months earlier. He had been detained on arrival but released because immigration officials were too busy to deal with him. Within days he had started gathering a team around him. A group of disaffected and alienated young Muslims had congregated around the al-Farouq mosque in Brooklyn, once the Maktab al-Khidamat's favourite recruiting ground for the Afghan jihad in New York, and there Ramzi found his first volunteers. For the next two months Ramzi recruited, surveyed his target and planned. Then he bought 1,500lbs of urea and 130 gallons of nitric acid and, in a rented apartment, mixed them to form urea nitrate, an explosive hardly known in the USA at the time. He added aluminium azide and ferric oxide to increase its force and is said to have considered using some kind of cyanide to produce a poison gas as well as an explosion. The preparation of the device took nearly two months. Ramzi wanted to build a bigger bomb but lacked funds. He had aimed, he later said, to topple one tower into another. He had wanted to kill 250,000 people.[1]

This chapter examines the careers of Ramzi, currently incarcerated in an American high-security prison, and of Khalid Shaikh Mohammed, another Islamic militant who was one of the key planners of the September 11th attacks. Shaikh, who was captured in late February 2003, was considered the most dangerous of all those who escaped with bin Laden and al-Zawahiri from the American dragnet in Afghanistan.

The stories of both men are important. In addition to showing how militancy continued to flourish in Pakistan and Afghanistan between 1989 and 1996 (without bin Laden's assistance), their activities reveal how modern Islamic militancy worked before bin Laden and his close aides were able to construct their base in Afghanistan in the latter half of the decade. They thus give a very good idea of how Islamic terrorism has been working since that base was demolished in the autumn of 2001.

What we can see clearly is how both men were able to put together the constituent elements for a terrorist attack again and again without at any stage being affiliated to any one individual or organisation. Both Khalid Shaikh Mohammed and Ramzi Yousef were committed to wreaking havoc on the West. For that they needed people, money, expertise and equipment. They both had, or at least swiftly developed, the contacts, the drive and the experience to be able to find those resources. They were 'operational hubs'. Like a professional party organiser, an infelicitous but useful analogy, or an international businessman brokering deals, they drew on their contacts books, filled with numbers picked up during time in the jihad or in training camps or through family or tribal connections, to gather what they needed. Ramzi, in his short career, was involved with Arab veterans of the Afghan war of a dozen different nationalities, bankers from half the countries in the Gulf, a series of different Islamic militants, several former Afghan mujahideen leaders, Pakistani sectarian terrorists and a whole range of recruits he found in Bangkok, Manila, New York, Peshawar, Quetta and Karachi. Bin Laden's involvement in any of this was tangential at best.

From 1989 to 1995, Pakistan, with its own raging sectarian militancy, its proxies in Afghanistan and its state sponsorship of radical Islam in Kashmir, remained the first port of call for any aspiring Islamic terrorist. Pakistan was also home to a thriving community of foreign 'jihadis'. Many were militants who had remained in Pakistan or Afghanistan after 1989 simply because they could not return to their own countries for fear of arrest, incarceration and execution by the governments of their various homelands. Others had married Afghan women and now had families and would not have returned even if it had been possible. Several lived in Gulbuddin Hekmatyar's compound in Peshawar's University Town. Several hundred more, including many senior figures, lived in cheap accommodation provided by Abd al-Rab al-Rasul Sayyaf in his extensive complex at Pabbi. Other Arabs were living in Jalalabad or its environs or around Khost. Not many were actually fighting. Only a few hundred actually took part in the campaigns between 1989 and 1992 against the Afghan Communist regime left in place by the Soviets. Only around 250 Arabs were involved in the successful capture of Khost in 1991.[2] Most foreigners trained for jihad elsewhere or plotted attacks in their own countries, in Kashmir, Chechnya or Bosnia, against the munafiq regimes and, increasingly, against America.

Some of the Arabs who stayed in Pakistan were thoroughly domesticated, working in the scores of Arab NGOs that maintained a presence in the city. The exact role of these charities is often difficult to determine. Many were involved in perfectly legitimate relief work. Others acted as conduits for funds for the training camps or other military activities. Some did both. Azzam's Maktab al-Khidamat kept several offices open in Peshawar and opened an 'office of information' in Jalalabad in 1992.[3] Though bin Laden's *beit al-ansar* was shut down in 1992 he continued to fund the maintenance of several guesthouses for itinerant militants in Peshawar. They included a *beit al-shuhada* (house of martyrs), *beit al-salaam* (house of peace) and *beit al-momineen* (house of the faithful) and a fourth guesthouse in Hayatabad, the suburb in the west of the city.[4] Of course, there were scores of other groups all running their own guesthouses too. The groups were broadly divided along national lines, as they had been during the war against the Soviets. Each had their own lines of funding, ideologies, tactics and ambitions. Many individual activists, including those acting as instructors in the training camps, were not directly linked to any organisation but were effectively freelance. They worked for whoever had sufficient funds to support them. One such man was an Egyptian-American called Ali Mohammed who, in Peshawar in 1992, taught surveillance to a number of men who were close to bin Laden. Ali Mohammed, a former American special forces supply sergeant, had made contact with Islamic Jihad around 1985 and through them had been introduced to bin Laden in 1991. Ali Mohammed, like a number of other individuals and groups, appears to have been hired by bin Laden for short periods for specific tasks.[5]

The camps opened by the Pakistanis supplemented rather than supplanted the training camps that had been built during the war against the Soviets. Camps such as Khaldan and those around Zhawar Khili remained open and full. Indeed, several new camps, funded by donations from Egypt, Saudi Arabia and the Gulf, were opened to cater for a surge in volunteers making their way to Pakistan from all over the Islamic world for training. Though Sayyaf and Hekmatyar's vocal attacks on Riyadh during the Gulf War crisis of 1990 and 1991 had ended the flow of official Saudi funds there was no shortage of funds from wealthy private individuals.

Various groups ran the camps. Harkat ul-Mujahideen and the Pakistani secret services were, of course, involved in the administration of several. As both Hekmatyar and Maulvi Younis Khalis had maintained their links to the ISI and to wealthy patrons in the Gulf they were able to access the necessary funds for their respective Hizb-e-Islami factions to continue running facilities. As they had found during the Afghan war, running camps was essential to sustained political and military success. Recruits, whatever their original background, naturally felt some allegiance to the group that trained them. An element of credit from the trainees' subsequent activities was reflected on their patrons. That credit in turn attracted more recruits and more funds and so created a virtuous circle. Outside Jalalabad, Hekmatyar abandoned an attempt to set up a radio station in an old Soviet army base called Darunta and turned it into a camp where Arabs could train alongside his Afghan fighters. Khalis evacuated the cold and uncomfortable caves of Tora Bora and moved the Arabs who had been training there down to camps just south of Jalalabad, near an old Soviet collective farm called Hadda.[6]

As Hekmatyar had nurtured and sustained his links in Pakistan so Sayyaf had kept his longstanding connections in Saudi Arabia. His Khaldan camp was still running, under a Palestinian or Algerian 'emir' and Middle Eastern Arab instructors. An overflow camp, the 'al-Aqsa' camp, was built in Afghanistan, near Torkham on the Pakistani border.[7] These two facilities were perhaps the most international of all the camps at the time with volunteers from the Balkans, southwest China, the former USSR and the Philippines all training alongside the Pakistanis pouring out of the new religious schools of the Punjab and NWFP. Khaldan in particular crops up repeatedly in the testimony of captured terrorists and militants. As early as 1990 it appears to have been acting as a 'clearing camp' for foreign volunteers providing basic training to those with no experience of military activities and allowing instructors to select the best recruits for further training in more advanced techniques elsewhere.

This is not to say that bin Laden was completely without representation in Pakistan and Afghanistan at this time. He was primarily involved with the logistics of processing recruits through Peshawar. This was why he had kept the four guesthouses open in the city. A young Palestinian called Zein al-Abideen Mohammed Hassan, known as Abu Zubaydah, handled many of the young men who arrived in Peshawar, assigning them to different camps. Abu Zubaydah, who had been wounded in fighting in Afghanistan, was later to become a key member of the al-Qaeda 'hardcore' though his exact relationship with bin Laden and al-Zawahiri at this time is unclear. It appears he was working for a rump Maktab al-Khidamat rather than al-Qaeda. Many other key figures who were later to emerge as significant were also in Peshawar at this time.

Bin Laden also had connections at al-Farooq , a camp run largely by Egyptians near Khost and under the nominal authority of Sayyaf. Trainers in al-Farooq included L'Hossaine Khertchou, who was to become key in later years in the Sudan, an Egyptian called Abu Rahman Abu Hajer and a Palestinian called Mohammed Sadeeq Odeh. The latter two were both to be involved in the 1998 African embassy bombings.[8] Another instructor at al-Farooq was Abu Ubaidah al-Banshiri, bin Laden's Egyptian-born military coordinator who was a key member of the al-Qaeda hardcore until he was killed in 1996 in a boat accident in Africa. Abu Ubaidah was a former Cairo police officer who had been dismissed for Islamic activism and who had made his name fighting alongside Ahmed Shah Massoud against the Soviets; he was one of those who had joined bin Laden's al-Qaeda in 1989 and was in touch with bin Laden during this period. It is possible that bin Laden made a contribution to the cost of the camp. Bin Laden's relations with Sayyaf were good. This does not, however, make it a 'bin Laden' camp.

Khertchou, like al-Fadl, was a prosecution witness in the trial of those responsible for the 1998 bombings and may have been tempted to fit his evidence to the FBI's mode of thinking. In his testimony he said men like al-Banshiri and Odeh had declared their loyalty to bin Laden and al-Qaeda by the early 1990s. Even if this is the case they were only a few among many thousands of militants training in the camps at any one time. There were so many foreign militants in the region at the time that moderate Afghan commanders wrote to the American and Saudi Arabian ambassadors to warn them.[9] A CIA memo dating from around 1996, declassified and released in 1998, claims that bin Laden funded the 'Kunar camp', presumably located in Kunar province north of Jalalabad, in this period. Kunar camp, the memo says, 'provides training to Islamic Jihad and al-Gamaa al-Islamiyya members'. The memo mentions no other camps connected to the Saudi and extensive interviews with former mujahideen, Hezb i Islami and Sayyaf activists have confirmed that bin Laden's involvement was marginal in the Afghan training camps at this time.[10] Bin Laden did, however, leave one important legacy. Some time between 1990 and 1992, the 11-volume 'Encyclopedia of the Jihad', codifying the teaching in the camps, was compiled with his financial assistance.

Of all the terrorists learning and planning in the guesthouses, religious schools and camps in western Pakistan and eastern Afghanistan from 1989 to 1995, perhaps the most effective, and certainly the most high profile, was Ramzi Yousef.

Ramzi, who called himself 'Pakistani by birth, Palestinian by choice', was born in a working-class suburb of Kuwait on 27 April 1968. His real name is probably Abdul Karim Basit. He is the son of a tribesman from the southwestern Pakistani province of Baluchistan who had moved to Kuwait during the boom years of the oil industry in the early 1970s. In Kuwait, Ramzi's father, an engineer, became influenced by a group of local religious conservatives.[11] When Ramzi was 18, the family moved back to Baluchistan but were able to arrange a visa for their son to travel to Britain to study 'computer-aided electrical engineering' at a college in Swansea. In the summer of 1989, Ramzi travelled back to Pakistan and put his newly acquired skills to use by spending his summer vacation teaching electronic bomb-making skills in the training camps around Peshawar.[12]

Ramzi returned to Pakistan in 1991. Within months he was back in the training camps. During this time he is believed to have met Abdurajak Abu Bakr Janjalani, the Muslim militant born on the island of Basilan in the southern Philippines. Janjalani had studied *fiqh*, Islamic jurisprudence, in Saudi Arabia in the early 1980s before taking part in the war against the Soviets. Since 1989 he had been travelling between Pakistan, Afghanistan and his native Philippines, where he had set up the Abu Sayyaf group, named after the man in whose mujahideen faction he had fought and the Prophet Mohammed's sword-bearer. He asked Ramzi to go with him to the Philippines to train militants. Yousef spent several months with Janjalani but by mid 1992 was back in Pakistan. According to Simon Reeve's excellent book *The New Jackals*, Ramzi was teaching electronics and bomb-making to militants at 'the University of Da'wa and Jihad' in Pabbi. The university was part of the complex run by Sayyaf and so extensive that it was dubbed 'Sayyafabad'. It was, contrary to many reports, primarily a religious school.[13] Its extensive air-conditioning, funded by Sayyaf's Arab patrons, contributed to its popularity. However, Sayyaf did run occasional training camps for students at the university who wanted to learn about more than the Holy texts, and it is certainly possible that Ramzi was teaching bomb-making skills in one of its classrooms at some stage. At least one activist who visited the university at the time said that many militants ran such courses in the guesthouses nearby where many of the volunteers lived. So as not to attract the attention of nearby Pakistani military personnel, light bulbs were used instead of explosives when testing a bomb's circuits.[14]

Ramzi also appears to have spent some time as a tutor in Sayyaf's Khaldan, where he trained alongside Pakistani sectarian militants.[15] It was in Khaldan that he met Ahmed Mohammed Ajaj, his accomplice in the World Trade Center bombing.[16] Ajaj was a former pizza delivery man in Texas who left his job and travelled to Pakistan via Saudi Arabia, where he had picked up an introduction letter to Khaldan camp. He may well have spent time in Sayyaf's compound at Pabbi too.[17] Ajaj and Ramzi flew first class from Karachi to New York together on 31 August 1992. Ajaj was detained when his poorly forged passport was spotted as a fake and bomb manuals were found in his luggage. Ramzi, travelling on a fake Iraqi passport, scraped through.

Ramzi's movements after the attack on the World Trade Center are as revealing as those preceding it. He left New York on the night of the blast and went straight to Quetta, the provincial capital of Baluchistan. When his home there was raided by Pakistani investigators he moved north to Peshawar, staying for some time, according to Pakistani investigators, in bin Laden's beit-al-shuhada.[18] He appears to have received some funding from wealthy Pakistani or Gulf businessmen and picked up old associations with the Pakistani sectarian militants with whom he had trained in Khaldan and elsewhere. In July 1993, he was asked by unidentified Pakistani militants to assassinate Benazir Bhutto, then starting her second term as Pakistani prime minister, but the bomb he was planting outside her home in Karachi detonated prematurely, injuring his face. The sources Ramzi had drawn on to bring together the elements he needed for the attack are interesting. One of his accomplices in the attack had been trained in al-Farooq camp (run by Sayyaf) a year previously, the *materiel* required for the bomb was purchased with money from a mysterious Saudi donor passed to Yousef by a Middle Eastern businessman known as 'Khaled' and was picked up from a refugee camp in Pabbi. The camp is also unidentified but, being in Pabbi, was almost certainly run by Sayyaf too. Ramzi was actually visited in hospital by senior figures in the radical Pakistani terrorist group, the Sipa-e-Sahaba Pakistan (SSP).[19]

The SSP were one of the biggest and most brutal of the various sectarian groups that had sprung up in Pakistan in the late 1980s and early 1990s. Though there had been outbreaks of sectarian violence before, the roots of the wave of attacks that swept across Pakistan lay in the policies of General Zia, the effects of the war in Afghanistan, the meddling of overseas states and the willingness of private donors in the Islamic world to provide funds to killers. All these factors compounded the fundamental weaknesses of the Pakistani state outlined in the previous chapter.

In the early 1980s Pakistan's previously unpoliticised Shia groups had formed a union against what they saw as Zia's (Saudi-backed) Sunni hegemony. They had obtained financial support from Tehran and had organised a series of demonstrations, some of which turned violent. The leaders of Pakistan's Sunni religious parties had decided to fight this new threat. Debates over how this should be done were overtaken by events in the hot, dusty southern Punjabi city of Jhang. In September 1985, Haq Nawaz Jhangvi, a local radical religious leader known for his hardline speeches, had announced the formation of a group called Sipa-e-Sahaba. Jhangvi was acting as a frontman for a group of local Sunni businessmen who hoped to exploit sectarian resentment among Sunni landless labourers and urban poor of the hugely wealthy Shia 'feudals' who dominated politics in the area.[20] Over the next five years, Iran helped set up a series of increasingly violent Shia groups in Pakistan. Perhaps predictably, Saudi Arabian and Gulf funds were channelled, sometimes through the Pakistani government, sometimes independently, to the growing raft of hardline Sunni organisations set up to counter them. Soon hundreds were dying in bombings, grenade attacks on mosques and assassinations.[21] The parallels with the proxy war contemporaneously being fought between clients of Pakistan, Saudi Arabia and Iran in Afghanistan are obvious. Perhaps unsurprisingly, Haq Nawaz Jhangvi was an alim of the Deobandi school, as were the vast majority of the recruits to the new Sunni sectarian groups.

In 1994, Ramzi flew to Thailand and swiftly recruited a group of devout young Muslims in Bangkok for an attack on the Israeli embassy there. When that failed, Ramzi fled back to Pakistan and then flew to the Philippines.[22] There he set about implementing the so-called 'Bojinka Plot', a plan to simultaneously destroy as many as 12 passenger jets in the air and, possibly, hijack a plane and fly it into an American target. The plotters also wanted to assassinate the Pope when he visited Manila. Ramzi managed to place a small, if technically sophisticated, bomb on a Japanese plane in December 1994, killing a passenger. A fire in his safe house and laboratory in Manila in early January forced him to flee back to Pakistan where he was betrayed by a new recruit and arrested by a joint FBI and Pakistani team in the Su-Casa guesthouse in Islamabad on 7 February 1995.[23]

Ramzi is often described as an 'al-Qaeda' agent. Bin Laden himself has said that 'he did not know' Ramzi.[24] A close examination reveals broad associative links, mainly through mutual acquaintances, but little more.

There are several alleged links between the two men. The first is through Mohammad Jafal Khalifa, the husband of one of bin Laden's half-sisters, who, in 1988, flew from Jeddah to Manila, the Philippines' capital, to establish a branch of the Saudi-based International Islamic Relief Organisation (IIRO). The charity, as well as running a rattan furniture business, is alleged to have channelled bin Laden's funds to Islamic militants in the region. Again, it is certainly possible that the IIRO, or even Khalifa, provided resources to Janjalani's group, and even Ramzi, but there is nothing to indicate that those monies included funds from bin Laden himself. There would have been no need for Khalifa to be in touch with bin Laden. His own connections were broad-ranging. In 1994, Khalifa was accused by Jordan of involvement in plots to bomb public places, including cinemas, in the country. According to the FBI, two of the alleged bombers had spent time with Khalifa in the Philippines. At his trial in Jordan, Khalifa was acquitted but admitted he had known the bombers and had sent them money, though he said the cash was for past services.[25] Furthermore, the IIRO is a huge organisation that receives donations from a variety of sources, private and governmental, and has been implicated in the funding of terrorism all over the world. Khalifa denies the charge of supporting terrorism, has since returned to Saudi Arabia and has publicly criticised bin Laden's activities.[26] It is worth remembering that Khalifa's family link with bin Laden is less close than it may first seem. Bin Laden has at least 50 siblings, many of whom have lived separately from him since childhood.[27]

Ramzi is also meant to have stayed in one of bin Laden's guesthouses in Peshawar. Again, this is plausible but hardly a solid link to the Saudi. Many hundreds of young militants stayed at bin Laden's guesthouses during this period. That is what they were for. Bin Laden himself was in the Sudan at the time of Ramzi's alleged stay and it is hardly likely that he knew all of the guests at the various establishments he funded in Pakistan personally.

Also militating against a bin Laden link is the difference between Ramzi's beliefs and lifestyle and those of most followers of bin Laden. Ramzi prided himself on his womanising, did not fast during Ramadan and was anything but ascetic. His worldview was modern and he used none of the references to early Islamic history that bin Laden is so fond of. The myth and eschatology of Abdallah Azzam and his ideological heirs is almost entirely absent from Ramzi's statements. Instead, as the demands his group issued after his World Trade Center attack show, his language was far closer to that of the leftwing terrorists of the 1970s than that of the followers of modern militant Salafi Islam:

> We, the fifth battalion in the Liberation Army, declare our responsibility for the explosion on the mentioned building. This action was done in response for the American political, economical, and military support to Israel, the state of terrorism, and to the rest of the dictator countries in the region.
>
> Our demands are: 1) stop all military, economical and political aids to Israel 2) All diplomatic relations with Israel must stop 3) Not to interfere with any of the Middle East countries' interior affairs.
>
> We invite all of the people from all countries and all of the revolutionaries in the world to participate in this action with us.

It is significant that many American analysts have alleged that Ramzi, far from being linked to bin Laden, was actually an Iraqi agent. There is no space to examine this fairly esoteric debate here but it is interesting that the evidence of a link to bin Laden is seen to be so thin that a link to another backer, a state, is supposed. There is, of course, a more straightforward answer. Ramzi was connected to neither bin Laden nor the Iraqis. All that he needed in terms of expertise, training, funding and logistical assistance was available through the myriad individuals and groups of which the broad movement of Islamic militancy was composed at the time. Ramzi was a highly motivated man who, like any successful political campaigner, was able to bring together a series of different backers, activists and specialists at different times in order to complete different projects. To look for a single line of command or resource is to totally misunderstand the nature of what Ramzi, and thousands of other men, were doing then and are doing now.

One particular link is worth pursuing: Ramzi's dealings with his uncle by marriage, Khalid Shaikh Mohammed. At the time of his involvement with Ramzi, Shaikh cannot be considered an associate of bin Laden, though he would go on to play an important role in bin Laden's group towards the end of the 1990s and in the September 11th attacks. Since the war in Afghanistan of 2001, Shaikh's importance has been recognised. He was dubbed 'the new bin Laden' or 'the new leader of al-Qaeda'. This is, of course, to fundamentally misconceive the nature of both 'al-Qaeda' and Shaikh's activities before his capture. He was merely one of the many hundreds of men who, after the war against the Soviets ended, had followed Azzam's instructions and had turned his attention to a new series of targets. With the destruction of his secure base in Afghanistan, and the resources that his relationship with bin Laden and others gave him, Shaikh merely returned to doing what he did before, albeit in slightly altered circumstances.

Shaikh was born in Kuwait in 1964 or 1965,[28] three years before Ramzi, and raised in Fahaheel, a booming and cosmopolitan oil town south of Kuwait City packed with foreign workers. His family appears to have been devout, though details of his sister, Ramzi's mother, are scant. Nor is it known whether Shaikh or other members of Ramzi's extended family were close to the same group of religious conservatives who influenced Ramzi's father. However, Shaikh's older brother, Zahed, was the leader of the Kuwait University branch of the Muslim Brotherhood in the 1980s.[29] Shaikh's background shows many of the elements typical in those of political Islamists: devout parents, rapid social and economic change around the family, exposure to new environments, a university education in technical disciplines.

Shaikh went to a modern and relatively secular school where teachers remember him as a studious boy who concentrated on science. His family were clearly wealthy for, like many other rich Middle Eastern men, he travelled to the USA for his further education. After a year improving his English at a college in North Carolina, Shaikh enrolled on an engineering course at a state university. In 1986 he graduated but, instead of returning to Kuwait, headed to Peshawar where his brother, Zahed, was running a large aid agency, the Kuwaiti charity, *Lajnat al-Da'wa al-Islamia*, the Committee for the Call to Islam. The charity had more than

1,000 employees and was spending $4m each year in Pakistan. By 1989, Shaikh was in Peshawar, teaching engineering at Sayyaf's University of Da'wa and Jihad in Pabbi. The Shaikh brothers were very much part of the local 'Arab Afghan' community, worshipping at the mosque on Arbat road where Ayman al-Zawahiri and Sayyaf occasionally preached.

In 1992, Shaikh moved to Karachi, posing as a businessman. His activities are unclear but he appears to have been acting as a fundraiser and intermediary between wealthy jihadi sympathisers in the Gulf and the young men who were prepared to act but lacked funds. One of these young men was Ramzi. Quite who approached whom is unclear but it is likely that Shaikh was the mysterious 'Khaled' (which is the usual Pakistani rendering of Khalid) named by Pakistani investigators as the man who supplied the finance for Ramzi's 1993 attempt, in conjunction with the Sipa-e-Sahaba, to kill Benazir Bhutto. The involvement of Shaikh completes the jigsaw. The attack on Bhutto was paid for by wealthy Gulf donors. The money was delivered by Shaikh to Ramzi who had been temporarily recruited by the SSP. The equipment for the attack, as mentioned above, was provided by Sayyaf. This is how modern Islamic militancy works. Benazir Bhutto likes to claim that it was bin Laden who was trying to kill her.[30] The truth, as ever, is a lot more complicated.

Indeed there is the intriguing possibility that Ramzi and his uncle may have collaborated earlier. Both men had been in Sayyaf's university in Pabbi, one as a student, one as a teacher, in 1989 and, according to Reeve, as early as 1991 Yousef was linked to a mysterious Karachi-based Saudi businessman who used the import of holy water from Mecca as a cover for more nefarious activities. The businessman, Reeve says, was keen to congratulate Ramzi on his return from New York after the WTC attack.[31] An authoritative report in the *Los Angeles Times* mentions that while in Karachi, Shaikh 'told people he was a holy water salesman, an electronics importer and a Saudi oil sheikh'. If Shaikh is Reeve's mysterious Saudi then he may have had some involvement with the WTC attack itself.[32]

Shaikh next surfaced in the Philippines. According to Philippine intelligence, Shaikh was in Manila at the same time as Ramzi, who was there planning the Bojinka Plot. The exact relationship between the two is unclear though it was clearly close. When Ramzi was forced to flee, Shaikh left too.[33] It is possible that Shaikh, like Ramzi, returned to Pakistan. A close inspection of the register at the Su-Casa guesthouse reveals that one of the guests present when Ramzi was seized by the FBI was a Karachi-based businessman who had signed in under the name of Khaled Sheikh. No one paid him any attention.[34]

Ramzi's arrest in 1995 came at a good time for the Pakistani government. Bhutto's second administration was under massive international pressure to crack down on the foreign militants in Peshawar. In the aftermath of the World Trade Center attack, Egypt, the USA and Saudi Arabia had all given Islamabad lists of radicals and suspected terrorists who were living in Pakistan. The Egyptians were particularly incensed at what they saw as the Pakistanis' reluctance to act against the numerous Islamic Jihad activists in Pakistan or in Afghanistan. They included Mohammed Shawky al-Islambouli, who had been sentenced to death *in absentia* in 1992 for plotting to overthrow the government of Sadat's successor, Hosni Mubarak. Another wanted man was Saif al-Adel, a former special forces officer who was a trainer at al-Farooq.[35] When the Pakistani government finally set about registering the 'Arabs' they gathered more than 5,000 names, including 1,142 Egyptians, 981 Saudis, 946 Algerians, 771 Jordanians, 326 Iraqis, 292 Syrians, 234 Sudanese, 199 Libyans, 117 Tunisians and 102 Moroccans.[36]

By 1995, Pakistan's three strands of Islamic militancy all appeared to be completely out of control. In Kashmir, the Deobandi Harkat ul-Mujahideen and Lashkar-e-Toiba cadres had pushed the level of violence to an unprecedented level. A series of murders of Westerners there had drawn international outrage. Pakistan itself was convulsed with sectarian violence.

In June 1995, Islamic activists based in the Sudan and linked to Egyptians in Peshawar, nearly killed Hosni Mubarak, the Egyptian president, in Addis Ababa, Ethiopia. Then, on the morning of 19 November, the calm of Islamabad's diplomatic quarter, several square miles of leafy roads and high-walled compounds, was shattered by a huge explosion. An enormous bomb had reduced the Egyptian embassy to a smoking pile of rubble, killing 16 people and injuring 60. Windows several miles away were splintered by the blast. The attack was claimed by both Islamic Jihad and their rival, al-Gamaa al-Islamiyya. In fact, it was a faction of the former, led by al-Zawahiri, which was responsible. Over the next month, dozens of foreign extremists were arrested in Karachi and in Peshawar. One of the biggest raids was on Sayyaf's compound in Pabbi. Benazir Bhutto told the world that her government had a grip on the problem. Few believed her.

CHAPTER EIGHT

SEEKERS

Long lines of men were striding through the weak sunlight of an Afghan autumn afternoon. From the main bazaar, from the ruins of the west of Kabul, from the wealthier suburbs to the north and east the crowd flowed swiftly over the bridge in the centre of the city and on to the old football stadium with its rotting concrete terraces and rusting Olympic rings. Toyota pick-up trucks, packed with heavily armed Taliban fighters, pitched and swerved on the potholed roads. The dark blankets the fighters had wrapped around their shoulders against the cold and the tails of their black turbans fluttered like pennants.

The crowds, thicker than normal for an execution, filed into the stadium slowly. That afternoon's entertainment was special. A woman, a self-confessed murderer, was to be killed. Behind the spectators on the top row of the terraces was a clear blue sky and the brown, craggy mountains that ring Kabul which, it being November, were topped with snow and very beautiful.

A microphone had been set up on the edge of the football pitch and a mullah, wearing a white turban and wrapped in a cream cloak, was standing before it. A little over a year earlier, I had heard the same man addressing a similar crowd in the same place. It had been a hot day in August and the atmosphere was very different. Then the spectators had cheered as a male murderer was shot and two thieves had a hand and a foot amputated. As I left the stadium, I had watched a Taliban fighter holding the men's severed hands above his head to keep them out of the reach of the young children scampering around him. The children were leaping up to try and touch them, broad grins on their filthy faces. Blood ran from the severed wrists down the talib's own.

Now the mullah's tone was almost plaintive. There was none of the confidence and triumph of a year before. He knew, and the spectators knew, that there had to be a very good reason for shooting dead a middle-aged woman in the centre of a stadium. He was trying to give them one:

> Where once there was crime and anarchy there is now order. There is no thieving and your women are now safe. It is only because of the implementation of justice according to the Shariat that there is this security. Life is given by Allah and so is His mercy.

A red pick-up truck bounced into the middle of the pitch with three women sitting in the back in light-blue *burqa*. A group of soldiers fanned out around the truck as the condemned woman was helped down. She walked unsteadily and, though actually only 35, seemed very old. She was led to the edge of the penalty box and knelt down and then started to rise again but seemed to change her mind and knelt once more. Then, like a shy, unsure child on stage in a school play looking for her teacher, she glanced over her shoulder uncertainly.

The mullah read from a page of notes over the microphone:

> This woman is Zarmina, daughter of Ghulam Haznat of Paghman province of the Islamic Emirate of Afghanistan. She is a mother of seven children and has confessed to killing her husband with a heavy hammer five months ago. The sentence of death has been upheld by three courts.

The mechanical rasp of the breech being worked on the Kalashnikov could be heard clearly from where I was sitting around 20 metres away. It seemed extremely loud and was followed by a long moment of utter silence during which I watched the breeze gently ruffling the pleated hem of the woman's burqa. Then three sharp shots cracked out through the still air and though they were less than a second apart I saw the dust spurt each time from the ground in front of the woman's crumpling body and then, on the third shot, saw white shards of skull fly out through the air and hit the grass. Then the blue burqa, darkening quickly, fell heavily across the spattered stain on the ground and hid it. This time there was no triumphal cheer but just a low muttering of 'Allahu Akbar' that rose, almost imperceptibly, like an oath or an excuse or a muttered blessing or imprecation, into the still, cold air.

It was November 1999, just over three years since the Taliban had captured Kabul, more than five years since they had first emerged in the southeast of Afghanistan. At the time they exercised nominal control over around 80 per cent of the country. The exact reasons for their extraordinarily swift rise to power are still unclear. The Taliban themselves, and supporters in Pakistan, say that in the spring of 1994 a Deobandi mullah in the dirt-poor village of Singesar to the east of Kandahar became so incensed at the depredations inflicted on local people by the warlords who had carved out fiefdoms there after the end of the war against the Soviets that he had gathered a group of men around him to act. Thousands spontaneously joined him in a bid to clean up their neighbourhood, and then their country. Because everyone was sick of violence and chaos, the Taliban had been welcomed everywhere.[1]

Many contested this story, and still do. It does indeed have all the hallmarks of a foundational myth. Instead, political opponents within Afghanistan claim, the Taliban were little more than proxies of Pakistan and Saudi Arabia, their success entirely due to the support of foreigners. Others, particularly non-Pashtuns, alleged the Taliban were simply a product of Pashtun tribal chauvinism and arrogance. Observers have pointed out, correctly, that much of Afghanistan was relatively peaceful in 1994 and that the Taliban often had to fight hard to conquer territory.[2] To the millions of people across the world who suddenly found themselves focusing on Afghanistan for the first time in the immediate aftermath of the September 11th attacks, the movement appeared indistinguishable from the al-Qaeda leadership and fighters they harboured. None of these views is entirely right, or entirely wrong.

The narrative sweep of the rise and fall of the Taliban movement is covered by a number of excellent books and I have no wish, or ability, to duplicate that here. I hope instead to explain the phenomenon of the Taliban and to examine their relationship with bin Laden and the other Islamic militants who gathered in Afghanistan during the Taliban's rule. The changing nature of that relationship shows clearly that extant groups, rooted in a specific conjunction of local and broader factors, developed links with bin Laden and were influenced by his ideology at a relatively late stage in their history. It is important to remember both that the Taliban had established themselves as a major force in Afghanistan long before bin Laden arrived there and that they did not invite bin Laden or his aides to their country. It is also important to understand that the ideology and worldview of the Taliban and that of the militants around bin Laden were, at least to start with, very different. The Taliban were a local movement with limited knowledge of the world, Islamic or otherwise, and profoundly parochial ambitions. The defining element of bin Laden's discourse was its burgeoning internationalism.

Both the Taliban and the new wave of internationalist Islamic militants of the early and mid 1990s can be seen as part of a broad reaction across the Islamic world to the inability of the political Islamism that emerged in the mid to late-1980s to achieve its goals. In earlier chapters, I traced the shift from early post-colonial ideologies including nationalism, socialism and pan-Arabism to political Islamism as the dominant discourse articulating aspirations for change in the Islamic world. The early 1990s saw another shift. Scholars such as Olivier Roy, Giles Keppel and Malise Ruthven all detect the retreat (even 'the failure' in Roy's case) of political Islamism at this time. Its apparent strength in the late 1980s and early 1990s was, they say, an illusion.[3] As a result the angry and the alienated turned towards more violent, nihilistic and mythic discourses instead. These are the ideologies, if such a word befits such essentially anti-political ways of thinking, that predominate today.

Certainly by the mid 1990s it was becoming very clear that the various political Islamist groups that had emerged in the previous two decades across the Islamic world were further away than ever from seizing power and Islamicising their respective states. The Iranian Revolution had once seemed the natural candidate to lead a wave of Islamist revolts but had failed to inspire similar developments in other Muslim countries except among some Shi'ite minorities. By the early 1990s, Iran had implicitly acknowledged its failure to export the revolution and was, despite radical rhetoric, simply using radical groups abroad as a tool of its nationalist foreign policy.[4] The dissatisfaction bred by the reign of the mullahs among the vast bulk of Iran's young population was clear. In Pakistan, as we saw in Chapter Six, the years when the government was at its most Islamist saw the emergence of sectarian conflict, not its end. There were few genuine Islamic measures on the part of the post-Zia governments. In fact, political Islamism was being marginalised as the army, Jamaat Islami and Nawaz Sharif, Zia's protégé, lost ground to the Deobandis.

The situation in Algeria, where the relatively moderate political Islamists of the Front Islamique de Salvation lost its battle to Islamicise the Algerian state and was swiftly supplanted by a new wave of violent extremists led by Afghan veterans, gave a glimpse of the future. The same situation prevailed elsewhere. Most mainstream Islamist bodies, such as Refah in Turkey or the Muslim Brotherhood in Jordan, were caught between repression and radical splinter groups and opted for a lower profile.

In Afghanistan, this shift from political Islamism to more radical strains of Islamic activism can be seen very clearly. By 1993, the men who had failed to mount an Islamist rebellion in the country in 1975 were in power. Yet they proved completely incapable of effecting radical change or bringing about a significant improvement in the living standards of the Afghan people. Certainly social justice, the key aspiration behind political Islamism, was as far off as ever. Political Islamism had always been hampered by the lack of a coherent idea of what to do after seizing power. Though an effective ideology for opposition, it had little to offer in the way of practical guidance for governing a modern state. In Kabul that failure was particularly obvious.

It was this failure to bring justice that motivated the early leaders of the Taliban. Almost to a man, they adhered to the narrow Deobandi salafism they had been taught in their medressas in Pakistan and Afghanistan. Though their salafism is superficially similar to that of bin Laden, al-Zawahiri et al, it stems from a very different source. The Taliban movement can be placed squarely in a tradition of religious (or religio-political) revivalist movements in southwest Asia going back several centuries. Such movements in Afghanistan have already been detailed. More broadly, one could include the long series of uprisings against the British on the northwest frontier in the nineteenth century (including the campaign of Syyed Ahmed Barelvi around the Peshawar frontier in the late 1820s), the Indian 'Mutiny' of 1857 and even the fatwas of Shah Waliullah, the Indian Muslim cleric, against the threatening Hindu Marathas before that. The Taliban can also be seen as part of Islamic revivalist movements elsewhere in the Islamic world going back to the Sudanese Mahdi, the Wahhabis and beyond. In all these cases, anger and a sense of injustice compounded by continued social and economic crisis resulted in movements coalescing around charismatic, religious figures who used the language of Islam to articulate a variety of diverse grievances and to suggest a solution. The solution almost always relied on a rejection of current Islamic practice and political structures and actors in favour of a reversion to a pure and unpolluted 'truth'. However, these movements are not purely 'fundamentalists'. Though their frame of reference may be Islamic, their aim, though often indistinct, is to create, or return to, some kind of imagined 'just' traditional society. Revivalism is underpinned by a desire for a 'revolution' in its original, inherently conservative sense, as in a reversion to a previous, more just time. For the Taliban this was imagined as a nostalgic, idealised, mythic vision of rural Pashtun village life. This has been nicely characterised as neo-Traditionalism and adequately sums up the early aims of the Taliban.

Where the Taliban were close to both the more extreme political Islamists and men like bin Laden was in their salafism, their rigorous insistence on the practical implementation of the behavioural injunctions contained in the holy texts. For the Taliban, the Shariat was 'the way'. 'Shariat' derives from the old Bedouin word used to describe a well-worn route across hazardous territory to an oasis or similar destination. Deviation from the path could, of course, be fatal. For the Taliban it was clear that if all Muslims followed the way then the destination, an almost mystical transformation to a just and perfect world, imagined, in their case, as a Pashtun rural idyll, would be achieved. Outside Mullah Omar's office in Kandahar a slogan had been painted on a huge board. 'Success springs from Allah,' it said. 'The hour of complete victory is at hand.' This is an almost millenarian conception that at some defined moment, when God is ready or sufficiently appeased, all will be set right, and it is shared by bin Laden and his associates.

The Taliban's beliefs were avowedly and unashamedly anti-rational and thus anti-modernist. They did not attempt to engage, in the tradition of Afghani, al-Banna, Maududi and even Qutb, with the contemporary world but shunned it. This is not surprising, given that the experience of the modern world for many of the Taliban involved Soviet helicopter gun-ships, Communist edicts, refugee camps, poverty and exile. A slogan painted on the wall of the Ministry for the Prevention of Vice and the Promotion of Virtue in Kabul, the base of the Taliban's 'religious police', in 1998 read: 'Throw reason to the dogs. It stinks of corruption.' 'In every breath there is a taste of death. Nothing is permanent,' said another. Again, this violent, anti-rational millenarianism was also shared by the new wave of Islamic militants who had emerged in the wake of the war against the Soviets.

However, the Taliban were rooted very specifically in the context of late twentieth-century Afghanistan. Even the failure of political Islamism, something occurring on a broad stage, was felt by the men who made up the early leadership of the Taliban in a powerfully local way. Of all Afghanistan, Kandahar and its immediate surroundings were the most violent and chaotic in the years following the fall of Najibullah's Communist regime. The southeast was also one of the poorest regions of Afghanistan, largely because its agricultural infrastructure had been destroyed by the Soviets' 'scorched earth' tactics in the 1980s.[5] A consequence of this was that the hundreds of thousands of refugees from the area were unable to return to their homes. Political Islamists like Hekmatyar and Sayyaf had, as Ghilzai Pashtuns with urban, literate and relatively educated support bases, never had much support in the rural, largely illiterate, Durrani-Pashtun dominated southeast anyway. The situation in and around Kandahar five years after the Soviets had left was enough to discredit most of those senior leaders who had emerged during the war.

The Taliban did not just reject political Islamist figures but the more traditional leadership as well. As the traditional khans had eventually been rejected in the changed environment after the Soviet invasion, so the men who had replaced them as leaders of local communities were rejected in the circumstances that followed the Soviets' withdrawal. In March 1996, Mullah Omar called a meeting of 1,200 religious figures in Kandahar to decide the future direction of the Taliban movement and to appoint a leader. He did not invite the local military commanders, the traditional tribal and clan leaders or political figures.[6] Even among the ulema who attended the meeting those who were seen as tainted were rejected. The candidacy of Maulvi Mohammed Nabi Mohammedi, who had led many of those present during the war against the Soviets and was a distinguished scholar in his own right, was refused because he, like most mujahideen leaders, was felt to have sown fitna among the Afghans after the war. Only people without previous involvement in politics were acceptable. Mullah Omar was voted *amir-ul momineen*, leader of the faithful, and marked his appointment by taking a relic believed to be the cloak of Mohammed from its shrine in Kandahar and publicly wrapping it around his body.[7]

The rejection of the traditional leadership went further. Those ulema who came to fill leadership roles in the Taliban had rarely been more than sub-commanders in the war against the Soviets. Indeed their emir, Omar, was a simple mullah, albeit one with a distinguished war record. This was a radical break. In traditional Pashtun rural society the mullah was seen as far further down the social order than the alim. Even though villagers might respect them for their role in leading prayer and teaching children the fundamentals of piety and Islamic knowledge, any intervention in public affairs would be resented.[8] Yet after the khans, the traditional religious leaders and the political Islamists had all failed, it was the mullahs who became the latest vehicle for the aspirations of southeastern Afghanistan's suffering population.

A final point is that the Taliban were rooted very much in the ethnic and tribal struggle for dominance within Afghanistan. Since Ahmed Shah Durrani, a Pashtun warrior king, had first seized Kabul more than 200 years before, Pashtuns – and largely Durrani Pashtuns from subtribes that had substantial representations in the Taliban leadership – had run the country, with only one short break between 1929 and 1931. In 1994, the Jamaat-e-Islami of Professor Burhanuddin Rabbani, dominated by Tajiks, was in power. For the Taliban, leadership and foot soldiers alike, any return to an imagined pre-war ideal society would necessarily involve a Pashtun in power in Kabul.[9]

Taken together, these factors show the Taliban's deep local roots. The movement should not be conflated with other strands of Islamic militancy. But although these elements go some way to explaining the appeal of the Taliban movement in a relatively restricted area around Kandahar, they do little to explain their astonishing success further afield.

When Mullah Omar and his band began their quest for power in the spring of 1994, they had 16 weapons between 30 men. By October 1994, when the Taliban launched an attack on the Hizb-e-Islami base at Spin Boldak near the border with Pakistan, they numbered 200. By December they were 12,000 strong.[10] By the middle of the next year, when they launched an attack on the western (and non-Pashtun) city of Herat, they had nearly twice as many fighters. To understand how this astonishing growth was possible, one has to look across the porous, haphazard and artificial border with Pakistan.

The Taliban were a political, tribal and religious movement. The Pashtun tribes have never recognised the Afghan-Pakistan border and the war against the Soviets had created a massive Pashtun refugee population within Pakistan. Many refugees were studying in the newly constructed medressas in Pakistan and this allowed the leaders of the Deobandi school to amass an unquestioningly loyal cross-border following that gave them considerable political power. They did not hesitate to deploy that resource when they felt fit and a substantial number of the 12,000 fighters, and many of the leaders, who had gathered in Kandahar under the white flags of the Taliban in the autumn of 1994 were either current students or recent alumni of the Deobandi medressas of Baluchistan and the North West Frontier Province. Over the next five years, tens of thousands of boys from the medressas in Pakistan would cross to fight for the movement, providing a critical reserve of manpower. On some occasions, such as in August 1996, the schools would even be shut to allow reinforcements to be drafted for specific operations or offensives. Senior Taliban leaders often returned to their alma maters to speak to students.[11]

The Pashtun chauvinism of the Deobandis reinforced that of the (overwhelmingly Pashtun) Taliban leadership and plugged the Taliban into a whole series of Pashtun-run networks within Pakistan, which were crucial in accessing assistance. That aid came both from actors within the Pakistani state and outside it.

The Pakistani state is not monolithic and did not relate to the Taliban in a uniform way. Until late 1995, for example, the ISI remained loyal to their (political Islamist) Hizb-e-Islami favourites. However, a number of factors compelled a variety of Pakistani interest groups to become involved with the Taliban once they became aware of the existence of Mullah Omar's little band during early and mid 1994.

Much has been made of the potentially hugely lucrative trade routes that elements within the Pakistani administration hoped to open between their country and the new central Asian republics. Benazir Bhutto and her minister of the interior, Naseerullah Babar, certainly hoped that a route running from Quetta through Kandahar and Herat to Turkmenistan could be made safe. This was the same route that another project with huge potential to make money, an oil and natural gas pipeline, was planned to follow. Two rivals were interested in the construction of the pipeline: an Argentinian firm and an American-Saudi consortium.

But the key factor was not Pakistani pipe dreams but the addiction of key Pakistani officials and politicians to proxy warfare. One of the main aims of all Pakistani involvement in Afghanistan had been to secure 'strategic depth', which was understood to mean enough space west of the Indus for the Pakistani army to reform and rebuild if forced back behind the river by an Indian invasion. With Hindu nationalism on the rise this was felt to be of special importance. Babar, who effectively ran Islamabad's Afghan policy, was the man who had, with the consent of Zulfikar Ali Bhutto, trained, equipped and launched the very same Afghan Islamists who were now squabbling violently over Kabul on their failed bid to instigate an Islamic revolution in Afghanistan. Babar was not motivated by any religious fervour then, and had not obviously become any more devout in the intervening 18 years. He saw the Taliban as a perfect tool for the execution of Pakistani, rather than God's policy. The Afghans' own interests did not enter into the equation.

Babar was doing more than just clearing trading routes and securing Pakistan's strategic position. He was deliberately undercutting the ISI and much of the military, which, still full of Zia-era senior personnel, was supporting Zia's protégés and allies like Nawaz Sharif, the Hizb-e-Islami (Hekmatyar) and the Pakistani Jamaat Islami. Benazir Bhutto, Babar's political patron, had already cosied up to the Jamaat-e-Ulema-e-Islami, the political wing of the Deobandis, in order to outflank Sharif.

Babar was doing the same within the Pakistani executive. His Afghan operations were run out of a special cell within the Ministry of the Interior and funded from the civilian budget. The ISI, who had recently been revealed to have bankrolled Sharif's political campaigns, were cut out of the loop. The Foreign Ministry, as ever in Pakistani Afghan policy, was barely involved.

Such domestic considerations are important. Ethnic competition within Pakistan also played its part in securing Islamabad's support for the Taliban. Babar was a Pashtun and a degree of chauvinism undoubtedly influenced his calculations. Again, this ethnic consideration fitted the political strategy: the powerbase of Sharif, the ISI, the army and the Jamaat Islami was the Punjab. In the two crucial provinces of Baluchistan and the North West Frontier, Pashtuns far outnumbered Punjabis in the local administrations. Their support was critical to Bhutto's second administration avoiding the fate of the first. The shifting axes of power in Pakistan, each movement of which was projected into Afghanistan and Kashmir and further afield, thus had ethnic, political *and* religious dimensions.

Yet the links between the Pakistani state and the Taliban went beyond the Deobandis, proxy warfare, ethnic prejudice and political manoeuvring. The Taliban leadership had strong tribal and often personal ties to some of the key figures in the shadowy world of smuggling. Smuggling in Afghanistan involves more than a few extra bottles of duty free. In 1995, Afghanistan was producing 2,400 tonnes of opium and refined heroin each year. It was the biggest single producing country of the drug.[12] Smuggling consumer goods to Pakistan from Dubai and the Gulf was worth, according to a World Bank study, around $2.5bn each year.[13] The huge sums involved bred corruption everywhere, from the predominantly Pashtun transport mafia who provided the trucks to move the goods around the region, to the officials who allowed its passage. The Taliban were as keen to profit as anyone. In 1994, their income from dues raised on smuggling reached $100m.[14] Drug smugglers paid a set ten per cent tax on the value of any shipment of opium. The money, around $20 million each year between 1995 and 1997, was crucial for the Taliban's ongoing war effort.[15] The Taliban also helped arrange heavily armed convoys which took the drugs from Kandahar across to the Dasht-e-Margo desert and into Iran. Major drug smugglers lived openly in Kandahar, Quetta and Karachi and maintained good social relations with senior Taliban and senior Pakistani soldiers, politicians and civil servants.[16]

The Taliban also showed themselves adept at playing their various allies off against each other when it suited them. In a sense they were doing what Afghans vying for power have always done. The continued weakness of the Afghan state has always made it vulnerable to intervention from overseas. This has been a two-way process with elements within Afghanistan keen to procure resources, material or symbolic, from outside the country and external actors keen to exploit the situation for their own ends. The situation in 1994 demonstrates many of these characteristics. The Taliban needed resources but could provide strategic, economic and political advantage in return. With the range and depth of cross-border contacts outlined above, plus many more that we look at below, Pakistan's involvement in the Taliban was, if not inevitable, then certainly always likely.

The aid they received, albeit from a variety of different sources within Pakistan, was substantial. The medressa boys who travelled to Kandahar in the autumn of 1994 crossed the border in buses, something that would have needed the assent of the border authorities; the sudden development of relative tactical and organisational sophistication of the Taliban fighting forces reveals the hand of Pakistani army advisers; there is evidence for the provision of shells and other ammunition for the Taliban during their successful push on Herat in 1995, the Pakistanis have admitted construction of radio and telephone systems and other logistical equipment for the nascent Taliban administration (they could hardly fail to given that the dialling code for Kandahar was the same as Quetta); in late 1995, Pakistani paramilitaries, acting on orders of the ISI, led the Taliban to huge former arms depots on the Afghan border; the substantial sums of money despatched to Kabul at regular intervals throughout 1997 and 1998 to help the Taliban pay the bureaucrats' wages was an open secret among Islamabad diplomats at the time. The fact that Pakistan was the first country to diplomatically recognise the Taliban, prematurely as it turned out, after their near-capture of the northern city of Mazar-e-Sharif in 1997, was another clear indicator of Islamabad's position. So was the pressure they exerted on other nations' diplomats in the city to follow suit.[17] It was only with great reluctance, in the weeks and months after September 11th, that Islamabad abandoned the men they had been helping for so long and, with them, its interventionist Afghan policy.

The Taliban's involvement with other countries beyond Pakistan was more straightforward. Regional powers formed three main axes in and around Afghanistan. One could loosely be characterised as Sunni Muslim and relatively hardline in religion. It included Saudi Arabia, the United Arab Emirates and Pakistan. These three nations recognised the Taliban diplomatically and provided moral, diplomatic and material support. It is a mistake to see state actors as necessarily primary in all these manoeuvres.[18] There were also, as during the war against the Soviets, significant flows of funds from devout private donors in the Gulf and in Saudi Arabia prepared to support the Deobandi Taliban to promote their Wahhabi-style Islam and fight against the Shias.

Opposing the Sunni states was a second axis comprising Iran and their Shia proxies among the Hazara factions within Afghanistan. A third axis comprised the Turkic and Tajik-descended ethnic groups in Afghanistan and their backers, Tajikistan, Uzbekistan, Russia and even, on the basis that anything or anyone opposing Pakistan must be good, India. Turkmenistan was largely neutral but tilted towards the Taliban.

Further afield, the attitude of the USA (and to an extent the United Nations) could be characterised as uninterested rather than disinterested. The State Department was distracted by the Gulf War of 1991 and then by crises in east Africa and the Balkans and was simply not that concerned by events in Afghanistan. This abandonment, particularly given the intense involvement during the 1980s, must go down as one of the most ruthless and shortsighted policies of recent times.

The attitude of the British was much the same. Though junior British diplomats had contacts with the Taliban from relatively early on, the High Commission in Islamabad and the Foreign Office in London saw the movement as 'just another fundamentalism', little different from Hekmatyar or Sayyaf in views, intent and capability.[19]

Few in the West had heard of the Taliban before they seized Kabul in late September 1996. It was the measures they took immediately after taking power that brought the movement global attention. Within hours, President Najibullah and his brother had been killed and strung up from a lamppost with cigarettes shoved in their mouths and money pushed into their pockets. Radio Kabul became Radio Shariat, broadcasting Qur'anic readings and music without instrumentation. Women were banned from work, from schools and from the streets unless accompanied by a male relative; the burqa was made compulsory. Kite-flying, pigeon-racing, make-up and photographs were banned. Men's beards had to be of a specific length. Suits and ties were forbidden in favour of Afghan dress.

These measures were widely reported and provoked international outrage. However, there was little attempt made to comprehend the motivations of the men behind them.

Every time I visited Kabul, I would drive up to the frontlines north of the city to report on the fighting. It was always a good opportunity to talk to the Taliban foot soldiers. In the small village of Guldara, a collection of bullet-pocked and mud-walled homes around a huge mulberry tree under which the Taliban had parked an anti-aircraft gun, I found Nazar Gul, a 30-year-old commander, and his men. They were all from Kandahar, though few had lived in their native city for several years. Nazar Gul told me he had left his medressa near Quetta in 1995, where he had been nearing the end of an eight-year course in Islamic Studies, to join the Taliban. 'When I heard about them I put down my books,' he said as we crouched in the basement of a farmhouse during a bout of shelling. 'These men we are fighting are criminals and thieves. They have corrupted our homeland. We will fight them for as long as it takes.' He said he had already qualified as a *Qadi*, or Islamic judge, and hoped one day to resume his studies.

For men like Nazar Gul, the source of much of the corruption that needed to be purged from Afghanistan was Kabul. The roots of this view lie in the profound gulf between the rulers and the ruled, the urban and the rural, the cosmopolitan metropolis and the reactionary provinces, that has developed over centuries in Afghanistan and underlies so many of the country's problems. During the 1970s, Kabul had been a favourite holiday destination in the region, with top jazz singers entertaining drunken partygoers beside the rooftop pool of the recently constructed Intercontinental Hotel.[20] The contrast with the conservative, undeveloped provinces could not have been greater. The gulf widened during the war against the Soviets. Then Kabul was seen by those in the rural areas as a city that had collaborated. Soviet subsidies transformed the city, which, unlike the ravaged countryside, did not suffer any physical damage. The Soviets also provided substantial salaries and unprecedented sports and cultural facilities to those among the middle-class urban elite who cooperated with the regime. Local dress in the city was frowned upon and the burqa banished. Though President Najibullah's Khad secret police killed and tortured tens of thousands in the city, this suffering was forgotten by those from rural areas who had seen their villages destroyed or who had grown up in exile.[21]

The Taliban saw Kabul as a direct threat. The logic was clear. The transformation to a just and perfect society would be jeopardised by any un-Islamic behaviour by anyone. Afghanistan had to be purged. If the country was to be transformed then the Afghans, or at least those living in their homeland, would have to behave exactly as laid down in the Shariat. Only then would the community of the first generation of Muslims, imagined with a Pashtun rural twist, be recreated and Allah would help His faithful. The name of the ministry of Prevention of Vice and the Promotion of Virtue is not, as so many commentators said, Orwellian, but Qur'anic. The first converts to Islam were told: 'You are the best community raised for the good of mankind. You promote what is good and forbid what is evil and you believe in Allah.' Senior Taliban figures always admitted that their rules in Kabul were obeyed through fear. It was unfortunate, they said, but necessary. People were addicted to sin. All threats were to be eradicated. Thus anything smacking of Westernisation, such as leather jackets or American or British hairstyles, was forbidden.

This is 'orthopraxy' of an extreme nature. It is enforced salafism on Saudi Arabian Wahhabi lines. The name given by the Taliban for the religious police, *Amr bil-Maroof wa nahi An il-Munkir*, was derived, indirectly, from the excerpt of the Qur'an quoted above, and directly from Riyadh. Yet the local specificity of what was happening should not be forgotten. In justifying the execution of Zarmina that November afternoon, the mullah had referred to the Shariat that he said was compulsory for all Muslims to implement. But he had also been at pains to stress the benefits of observing the word of God. 'Have we not brought security?' he had asked.

Kabul, in the Taliban worldview, was Babylon and, like the biblical city, was full of whores. The Taliban attitude to women was, until 1998 and bin Laden's sudden rise to global prominence, their most controversial quality. Yet it too was rooted in experiences and cultures specific to Afghanistan.

The burqa was not a Taliban invention but had been worn by Afghan women, as a form of portable *purdah*, whenever they moved into an environment where there were substantial numbers of men who were not related to them or were not part of their immediate social grouping, for many years. In the fields or around their villages, rural Afghan women would wear a headscarf, often highly decorated and individual. As mobility increased with modern communications and social relationships, so Afghan women found themselves surrounded more and more often by strange men. As a result, the burqa was increasingly worn. Nor is it just Pashtuns, or even just Afghans, who wear burqas. They are worn by women from non-Afghan ethnic groups in southern Sindh in Pakistan and, in various versions, across India and much of the Middle East. A similar situation prevails with *maharams*, or the male family member who accompanies women, by law in Taliban-run Afghanistan and in current Saudi Arabia, outside their homes.

As William Maley points out, in traditional Afghan society women have always performed strictly circumscribed social roles based on the economy of the household. Within certain bounds, however, Afghan women have historically shown an ability to assert their interests within networks of kinship. But, though Afghan popular tradition has venerated certain women as moral leaders (particularly Mallalai, who challenged the British, and more recently Nihad, a Kabul schoolgirl killed while demonstrating against the Soviet invasion), it was only in the urban areas, and then only recently, that women had much opportunity to move beyond the realm of the household and into the public sphere.[22]

This has reinforced the gulf between the rural populace and the urban communities who have historically supplied the ruling elite and has focused mutual resentment and misunderstanding of the issue of gender roles and relations. This tension goes back at least to the 1920s. Indeed, the revolts against King Amanullah, and those against the PDPA hardliners 70 years later, were provoked by ill-judged attempts by the centre to impose change in gender relations on the regions by force.

There are echoes of this all over the Islamic world where, throughout the twentieth century, different regimes have battled conservatives over women's bodies in attempts to prove their modern orientation and identity. Reza Shah Pahlavi in Iran, Kemal Ataturk in Turkey and Habib Bourguiba in Tunisia all banned or discouraged veiling and encouraged Western dress as a sign of modernity. The abolition of the veil in 1936 by Reza Shah Pahlavi has often been celebrated as a major step towards women's emancipation. The reform chiefly benefited upper-class elite women, traumatised many less Westernised women and did little to counter the established patriarchal practices throughout the rest of the state.[23]

Even in 1959, when the Afghan government made the veil voluntary, there was little change outside the capital. Only the western city of Herat developed anything like the substantial body of middle-class, relatively wealthy, educated and politically conscious women that could be found in Kabul. It was these women, who were teachers, lecturers, journalists and doctors under the Communists and the mujahideen, who suffered most under the Taliban. They were also articulate and sympathetic enough to command substantial representation in Western media reports from the country. Their memories of professional life, well-stocked libraries, mini-dresses and sidewalk cafes in Communist Kabul struck a chord with Western journalists (predominantly middle-class graduates themselves).[24] For the Taliban, however, these women were the living, talking and walking embodiment of what had ruined their homeland.

Throughout the Islamic world, radical Islamic activists have found that the actual practice of formulating and implementing an Islamic state or a return to the use of Islamic law in politics, business and economics is in fact very difficult and have found it easier to focus on women and the family instead.[25] In Iran, members of the Iranian Revolution's own version of the religious police, the Komiteh, who were recruited largely from the working class, focused their attacks on unveiled, secular, middle-class women. These recruits saw themselves as the guardians of the values of an Islamic republic and thus felt a duty to persecute any remaining members of the middle class who had somehow managed to hang on to their social status and cultural capital.

In Algeria, the victories of the Front Islamique du Salut in local elections resulted in moral prohibitions that 'pointed a finger' at the Europeanised secular middle class, whose members were more or less emancipated from traditional taboos. Gilles Kepel sees sexual politics as an important factor:

> [This] allowed impoverished young men, humiliated and forced into abstinence or sexual misery by the crowded family conditions in which they lived, to become heroes of chastity who sternly condemned the pleasures of which they had been so wretchedly deprived.[26]

This has an immediate parallel in the experiences of the vast bulk of largely unmarried Taliban cadres whose experience of sexual relations had been warped by warfare, life in the refugee camps and the strict codes of Pashtunwali.[27]

The gender issue is another point of significant difference between traditionalists like the Taliban and political Islamists, who on the whole consider women essential to education and society. Islamists are largely opposed to dowries and divorces of convenience and Islamist organisations often include entire women's sections like 'the Muslim Sisterhood', *al-Akhwat al-Muslimat,* created in Egypt in 1944. Though Islamists often exclude women from posts as judges and heads of state, their obsession is with segregation, not exclusion. In Iran, this involved the invention of a new kind of dress, comprising a scarf, raincoat and gloves that allowed women to achieve two contradictory objectives, to come out of purdah and to maintain modesty. Islamists may still be deeply sexist, convinced of the weakness of women and their 'overly emotional sensibilities', but in Iran women vote and drive cars.[28] In Saudi Arabia they do not.

But again, though differences from political Islamists must be stressed, this does not mean that the Taliban were part of the militant Islamic movement of bin Laden, the Algerian 'barbus' or the foreign militants fighting in Kashmir. The Taliban's attitude to women was rooted in their own Pashtun culture. It is here that the Islamic tradition of revivalism and Pashtunwali, the cultural code of the Pashtuns, coincide to generate such force. Pashtunwali was born to counter a violent and insecure environment. Women are thus seen as the repository of the honour of a male individual and the family. Any threat of dishonour – the theft of cattle, defeat in battle and the rape of a sister being roughly equivalent – is to be defended against at all costs. Pashtun, and to a great extent Afghan, women are also expected to uphold family honour by conforming to accepted behavioural norms.[29] In Pashtun society, there has always been a complex interplay between Pashtunwali, the 'honour code', and various understandings of Islam. Both provide useful resources to articulate a range of concerns or grievances. The Taliban were thus genuinely bewildered and aggrieved by the international reaction to their treatment of women. They felt that they were merely fulfilling their duty as Muslims, Pashtuns and men to protect the honour of women and that the best way to do this, in an environment of insecurity, was to get them, by force if necessary, to behave in a particular way. As the self-possessed and confident women of Kabul were unwilling to voluntarily do what they should for their own good, and the good of all Afghans, they would have to be compelled to comply.[30]

The Taliban, with few exceptions, had no conception of how footage of young men lashing out at women in burqas with leather straps or lengths of rubber hose was viewed in the West. That inability to imagine the effect on politicians or the public elsewhere is indicative of the narrowness of the Taliban's worldview. On one occasion, in December 1998, I was waiting to interview Maulvi Qamaluddin, the minister in charge of the Prevention of Vice and the Promotion of Virtue, outside his residence in Kabul. A group of young religious policemen was standing nearby. I began talking to them in Urdu which, as most were educated or had lived in Pakistan, they understood. I asked them if I could join the religious police. They conferred for a few moments and then told me they could see no reason to prevent me. Did it matter that I was not a Muslim, I asked. There was some consternation at this unexpected news, more conferring and then an answer. It did not matter, I could come with them to the mosque for dawn prayers the next morning, become a Muslim and all would be fine.

These were, of course, foot soldiers. But the vision of more senior men was as narrow and parochial. The jihad that they believed themselves to be engaged in was conceived of being within the bounds of Afghanistan only. Even some ministers had shaky ideas about the exact geography of Asia, let alone the location of Europe or the USA. Some, such as the worldly Taliban ambassador to the United Nations, Hakeem Mujahed, were relatively well travelled. But they were a minority. Mullah Omar had certainly never been outside the immediate environs of Quetta and Kandahar. In seven years as the head of the Taliban, he visited Kabul twice. Bin Laden and the other 'Jihadi Salafis' in the new Islamic militant movements saw their internationalism as a fundamental tenet prescribed by the Qur'an. They were committed to overcoming national and tribal borders and reuniting the umma. For the first four years of the movement's existence, senior Taliban rarely referred to the umma or indeed to any events overseas. Even their anti-Americanism was muted. The issue of Kashmir, let alone Chechnya, Iraq or Palestine, was never raised. Long after their capture of Kabul in 1996, senior Taliban officials were plaintively asking visiting journalists why their movement was yet to be recognised as the legitimate government of Afghanistan by the United Nations. This was all to change dramatically.

CHAPTER NINE

HOME

Prince Sultan stood up, walked across the sumptuously decorated room and stood next to Osama bin Laden. He touched bin Laden on the shoulder and turned to face the guests who had been admitted into his home in Riyadh an hour previously. In his hand he held the five-page document bin Laden had handed him a few minutes earlier. 'The bin Laden family have always been loyal friends of our family,' the Crown Prince said emolliently. 'I look forward to many more years of that friendship.' Bin Laden's face was black with anger.[1]

It was September 1990. The 33-year-old had approached Prince Sultan, the Saudi minister for defence, with an offer. Accompanied by a group of senior Afghan mujahideen leaders and prominent veterans of the war in Afghanistan, he had submitted a detailed proposal of how he could raise a force of Islamic militants who could protect the kingdom. That the kingdom needed protecting was indubitable. On 2 August, Saddam Hussein had invaded Kuwait and appeared to be threatening Saudi Arabia itself. A week after the invasion, the Saudi Arabian government had accepted an American offer of assistance. Within days, the first US military forces had begun to arrive in the land of the two holy places. Bin Laden's plan for an Islamic army was a non-starter. His interview with Sultan was short. His scheme was summarily rejected.

When bin Laden had returned to Saudi Arabia in late 1989, he was feted in Islamic activist circles as a brave mujahid. His pious ascetism during the war against the Soviets was well known and had won him substantial support. He continued to shun the luxurious lifestyle of the Saudi elite and moved into a house in Jeddah which was barely furnished.[2] But, though he maintained his contacts with Afghanistan, talking regularly to commanders from both Hizb-e-Islami factions and Abd al-Rab al-Rasul Sayyaf's group and paying for many Afghan leaders to travel to Saudi Arabia for haj or religious conferences, his relations with the Saudi government were cordial.[3] His family had welcomed him back, even making arrangements for him to take up a managerial position in the bin Laden group. During his first months back in Saudi Arabia, his political activities were limited to promoting a boycott of American goods because the profits were used to 'repress Palestine'.

It was never likely though that bin Laden was going to spend the rest of his life organising the construction of motorways or airports. He had returned to his homeland full of confidence and zeal. With him were several of the most experienced and committed of the militants he had known in Afghanistan. They included Mohammed al-Zawahiri, the brother of Ayman, and several other senior Egyptian activists. These men, and those of the 'al-Qaeda hardcore' who had sworn allegiance to bin Laden in Peshawar in late 1989, had done so in order to access the funds that they knew bin Laden could raise. They had no intention of allowing the blandishments of his family or the state to divert their new patron from the course he had pledged to follow.

Yet if there was ever a chance that bin Laden might have succumbed to the temptations of life as a super-rich Saudi businessman, it was gone when Iraq invaded Kuwait. Bin Laden had warned that Saddam, the very incarnation of a secular 'hypocrite' leader, might threaten the land of the two holy places. When the Iraqi tanks moved into Kuwait City, he saw it as the first opportunity to put Azzam's idea of an international army of militants, exactly what he had hoped to create through the foundation of al-Qaeda a year previously, into action. When his own government refused his assistance it came as a profound shock.

The events of late 1990 had jolted many Saudis and many Muslims. They are comparable in their seismic effect to the Soviet invasion of Afghanistan, the Iranian Revolution or Juhaiman's seizure of the grand mosque in Mecca. The Saudi Arabian regime had always based its legitimacy as rulers on its religious credentials. This involved sponsoring the export of Sunni Wahhabi strands of Islam throughout the world, bankrolling much of the jihad in Afghanistan and protecting and maintaining *al-Haramain*, the holy places of Mecca and Medina. The acceptance of the American offer of military aid, and the subsequent stationing of hundreds of thousands of men and women in their country, stunned many Saudi Arabians. The Prophet Mohammed himself, according to an oft-quoted hadith, had ordered that 'there be no two religions in Arabia'. The construction of synagogues or churches was banned as a result. Now the defence of the kingdom, of the *ka'aba* itself, was in the hands of the Americans. This was a savage indictment of the regime's competence, particularly given the vast funds lavished on military equipment. Economic factors played a significant part in the discontent of the general populace. After years of boom, the oil price had crashed in 1986 and the massive and sudden drop in income had exposed gross mismanagement of the economy. Attempts to remove many of the benefits Saudi citizens had come to expect to be free in the years running up to the Gulf War had been deeply unpopular, particularly while the thousands of royal princes continued to live lives of lavish decadence. This resulted in unprecedented discussions in Saudi Arabia of many issues that had previously been confined to the private domain. The Saudi political system and the legitimacy of the regime had never been questioned in such a way before. When, in January 1991, Sheikh Abdelaziz bin Baz, the most senior alim in the kingdom, delivered a fatwa authorising jihad against Saddam even if it involved the assistance of non-believers, anger turned on the establishment ulema as well.[4] Many were disgusted at what they saw as the pathetic compliance of the government-funded clergy.

The growing aggression of the Islamist opposition was part of this general ferment. The strongest criticism came from the 'rank and file' of young religious ulema. They used their *khutba*, or Friday sermon, to attack the regime's decision to allow in American troops. In September 1990, Dr Safar al-Hawali, dean of the Islamic college of Umm al-Qura University in Mecca, released a tape claiming that the real enemy was not Iraq but the West. 'We have asked the help of our real enemies in defending us,' he said. 'The point is that we need an internal change. The first war should be against the infidels inside and then we will be strong enough to face our external enemy. Brothers, you have a duty to perform. The war will be long. The confrontation is coming.'[5]

Years later, bin Laden said that it was the government's imprisonment of al-Hawali and Salman al-Auda, a faculty member at Imam Mohammed ibn Saud University in Riyadh, that turned him against the royal family as much as their rejection of his proposal for an armed international brigade of Islamic militants. He hinted at some reluctance in opposing the benefactors of his father: 'When the Saudi government transgressed in oppressing all voices of the scholars and the voices of those who call for Islam I found myself forced… to carry out a small part of my duty of enjoining what is right and forbidding what is wrong.'[6]

Bin Laden may have been lacking in scholastic credentials, but his war record and his obvious and public rejection of luxury brought its own authority. His own lectures, reiterating his earlier call for a boycott of American goods in protest at their support for Israel, were popular. By the end of 1990, his tapes had become more radical, calling, in increasingly strident terms, for action against kufr and any regimes that supported, or were supported by, kufr.

In Saudi Arabia, however, bin Laden was not a major figure in the early 1990s. His influence was marginal compared to that of better-known radical clerics. A small group, willing to die for bin Laden and his cause, was dedicated to him as a leader and bound to him by a bayat. Then there were the 'Arab Afghans', the Saudi youths who had been to Afghanistan and had different degrees of allegiance to him but generally saw him as a hero. Finally there were those who were not close to him but saw him as an inspirational force and considered him, however erroneously, 'the godfather' of Islamic activism in Arabia.[7] This tripartite division, into a 'hard core', a network of networks and a broad movement of sympathisers and militants with roughly coincident aims, is repeated again and again, at a national, regional and international level, when one examines bin Laden's position within the broader movement of modern Islamic militancy. It is also interesting to note how almost all the prominent dissidents in Saudi Arabia in this period were somehow socially marginalised. Many suffered under the strict tribal hierarchy of the kingdom. Bin Laden's own Yemeni roots mean that his *deera*, or land, is not considered to be Saudi Arabian and so, in spite of his family's incredible wealth, he is thus not considered truly Saudi. For this alone even the poor of the Najd, the most dominant Saudi province, look down on him.[8]

A key cause of the frustration of bin Laden's supporters in Saudi Arabia was the gulf between the state-sponsored rhetoric of jihad that had taken so many of them to Afghanistan and the total lack of appreciation shown for their efforts when they returned home. They had come back expecting to be lauded as the victors of the war on Communism. Many hoped to be rewarded financially. They felt badly let down by both the Saudi Arabian public and the elite.[9] For thousands of angry young men, bin Laden's rejection by Crown Prince Abdullah in the autumn of 1990 epitomised their betrayal. This sense of humiliation, disappointment and hurt, sublimated into violent hatred, was to be a leitmotif of bin Laden's own statements over the next decade.

There were other clues to what was to come in the future. In May 2001, bin Laden issued a communiqué to 'members of al-Qaeda'. Not only was this one of the very rare instances where bin Laden himself refers to 'al-Qaeda' but in the communiqué, signed 'your brother in Islam', bin Laden also explained the group's project. 'I bring you good news,' he said. 'The moment is right for the formation of a single pure and Muslim army... of 10,000 soldiers who would be ready, at a moment's notice, to march to liberate the land of the two holy places.' This is the realisation of an idea that 'germinated ten years ago', bin Laden said, 'in the earth of the Yemen'.[10]

The reference to the Yemen seems, at first sight, slightly confusing. After all, bin Laden was based in Saudi Arabia between late 1989 and 1991 and, though he may have visited the Yemen, certainly spent no great amount of time there. However, following his interview with Prince Sultan, it seems that the first experiment in organising militancy overseas that he undertook was in the impoverished Arabian coastal state.

Bin Laden did, of course, have a longstanding interest in the Yemen. One of his wives was Yemeni, his father's roots lay in the southern Hadramawt province and he had contacts among the many thousands of Yemenis who had fought the Soviets, particularly with Sayyaf's faction.[11] The Yemenis had been known as fierce fighters and had distinguished themselves at the battle of Jalalabad in 1989. In Afghanistan, they had been led by a major Yemeni tribal chief called Tariq al-Fadhli. Al-Fadhli's father had been stripped of his sultanate by the British and denied restitution by the Moscow-backed Marxist government that succeeded the colonial regime. While in Afghanistan and Pakistan between 1987 and 1989, al-Fadhli had become friendly with bin Laden. On returning to their homeland, the Yemeni veterans, led by al-Fadhli, headed for the remote north, close to the unmarked border with Saudi Arabia, where they set up several training camps.[12]

In May 1990, after talking about it for years, the Yemen Arab Republic and the People's Democratic Republic of the Yemen merged, bringing together the Islamic, conservative and nominally capitalist north and the secular, Marxist south. Events in the Yemen were watched carefully by regional powers. Saudi Arabia felt threatened by the unification and began to work to fragment the country. Wahhabi organisations in the Gulf saw an opportunity to propagate their brand of Islam, which had been introduced to the country by returning Afghan veterans, and began pouring in missionaries.[13] In a sense, bin Laden, just a thousand miles to the northwest in Jeddah, was part of this effort. On at least one occasion in the early 1990s he contacted a Yemeni exile living in Saudi Arabia and offered him a substantial sum of money if he would return home and live as 'a good Muslim' and it is likely that he saw the Yemen as a base from which the peninsular could be 'purified'.[14] He also began sending money and representatives to Yemeni Islamic militants in the north. His contacts with al-Fadhli were invaluable. This pattern, of exploiting personal connections to tap into opportunities provided by local contingencies, was to become well established over the coming decade.

Few in the West took any real interest in the convoluted internal politics of the Yemen until bombs went off outside the two most expensive hotels in Aden in December 1992, killing a tourist and a hotel worker. The attack appeared to be directed at the hundreds of US servicemen transiting the country on their way to launch the ill-fated Operation Restore Hope, part of a United Nations effort to prevent millions of people dying of starvation in Somalia. The blasts focused attention on the small coastal state rather suddenly.

In fact, though bin Laden is often alleged to have been behind the bombs, it is far more likely that Tariq al-Fadhli organised the attacks.[15] Extensive investigations undertaken by the authoritative American author and journalist Peter Bergen indicate that bin Laden's involvement went no further than the supply of funds to al-Fadhli's group around this time. This would fit in with the emerging bin Laden *modus operandi* of instigating and facilitating, rather than directly funding, militancy and terror.

By 1991, bin Laden was under a form of house arrest in Jeddah.[16] He was increasingly unhappy and felt very strongly that his duty was to flee the Arabian peninsular as long as American troops were 'occupying the land of the two holy places'. In this he was following the Mohammedan Paradigm, aiming to retreat so as to better struggle in the future. Bin Laden persuaded a brother to convince the deputy interior minister, Ahmed bin Abdelaziz, to release his passport on the basis that he needed to travel to Pakistan to sort out some financial arrangements in person. He promised to return to Saudi Arabia. This, of course, was a subterfuge. The first thing he did on arriving in Peshawar was write to his brother apologising for misleading him and admitting that he had no intention of going back to his homeland. After around three months in Peshawar, where he appears to have attempted to broker an agreement between Hekmatyar and Massoud, he flew to the Sudan, probably from the airstrip at Jalalabad which was then under the control of Maulvi Younis Khalis, to whom he was close.[17] According to both Jamal Isma'il, a journalist who interviewed bin Laden several times during this period, and a comprehensive investigation undertaken post-September 11th by the respected London newspaper *al-Quds al-Arabi*, bin Laden arrived in the African state in 1992, moving into a large villa in a suburb of Khartoum.[18]

CHAPTER TEN

FLIGHT

The house was a plain, two-storey, stucco villa in a quiet and affluent quarter, well away from the bustle of the centre of Khartoum. It had no fridge, no air-conditioning and nothing but carpets on the floor. There were many visitors and they ate sitting in rows on the hard floors with their host. Five times a day he would lead all of them a few hundred yards down the dusty streets to the nearby mosque.[1]

Bin Laden was not without friends in Khartoum. A large group of associates, primarily from Islamic Jihad, had moved to the city at least a year before he arrived. According to Jamal al-Fadl, the prosecution witness at the African bombings trial, 'al-Qaeda' had begun their shift from Pakistan to the Sudan almost 18 months before bin Laden reached the country. In late 1990, while bin Laden was in Saudi Arabia, Ayman al-Zawahiri, the leader of Islamic Jihad, had given al-Fadl $250,000 and sent him to buy a farm to the north of Khartoum. The advantages of locating in Sudan were obvious. The huge border with Egypt is entirely unguarded and, with Khartoum hostile to Cairo, the regime was considered likely to support militant activities against Mubarak's government. By the time bin Laden arrived, Islamic Jihad were already training in explosives and weapons drills. Hundreds of other Afghan veterans, unaffiliated either to Islamic Jihad or to bin Laden, had preceded him too. Activists in Afghanistan and Pakistan had been in touch with Sudanese Islamists since the mid 1980s. With many facing arrest and incarceration in their own countries, Sudan was a popular destination. Most were not involved in any specific groups but were effectively freelancers.[2]

The new Islamist regime in Khartoum, which had taken power in 1989, had sought out Islamic Jihad and bin Laden to invite them to their country in 1990. Al-Fadl told the court that they were so keen to have bin Laden, al-Zawahiri and their associates that they sent a deputation to Peshawar to convince them to make the move.[3] This is an early example of how bin Laden and other radicals profited from developments within the Islamic movement that were entirely independent of their own activities. In the Yemen, bin Laden had been able to exploit the existence of radical groups to further his own anti-Saudi agenda. In Afghanistan, he was able to do the same with the Taliban. It is important to recognise that the groups in the Yemen and Afghanistan, and the regime in the Sudan, have roots in local contingencies that pre-date bin Laden and, should he be removed from the scene, will still need to be dealt with if radical Islam is to be countered.

Indeed, political Islamism in the Sudan dates back to when a branch of Hassan al-Banna's Muslim Brotherhood was founded there in 1944.[4] As in Egypt, Pakistan and elsewhere, though the Brotherhood was quick to gain a foothold in the middle classes, their brand of Islam remained confined to the limited educated and intellectual circles in the country until the 1960s. Islam in the Sudan was instead dominated by mystical brotherhoods led by local religious figures with the supernatural gift of blessing, called *baraka*, who bear comparison with the pirs and *syeds* of Afghanistan. In the Sudan, as elsewhere, Leftists and Nasserites in universities and trade unions hindered the Brotherhood's expansion.[5]

Hassan al-Turabi, the leading figure of modern Sudanese Islam, is the quintessential self-made political Islamist. He has a traditional Qur'anic education, a degree in law from the University of Khartoum, a masters from the University of London and a doctorate from the Sorbonne, Paris. Like Islamists in Afghanistan he copied the organisation for his own party from his main leftist rival, the Sudanese Communist Party, and focused his efforts on students, the product of a burgeoning educational sector. By 1965, his party was winning 40 per cent of votes in student elections against the leftists' 45 per cent. Al-Turabi's appeal to undergraduates was boosted by his promise to allow women, suitably veiled, to play a full role in public life. He was also assisted by the Saudis and the other Gulf states. As elsewhere in Africa, huge amounts of Gulf money were poured into the training of local preachers in conservative Wahhabi-Salafist strands of Islam in a bid to counter the appeal of both Christian missionaries and the mystic brotherhoods in Sudan. Al-Turabi's focus on young students in the universities meant that successive administrations, desperate for trained, educated people, were forced to rely more and more on al-Turabi's cadres. Consequently, by the late 1980s, many senior positions in the bureaucracy and the military were occupied by people loyal to or at least heavily influenced by him. In June 1989, a *coup d'état* mounted by General Omar Hassan al-Bashir was supported by Islamist army officers and the ulema who had been promised the introduction of Shariat law.[6] Al-Turabi was the power behind the throne and was keen to develop Sudan as a rival to Riyadh as leader of the Sunni Islamic world. He thus supported Saddam Hussein in 1990, organised a series of international conferences of Islamic militant activists in Khartoum and invited the veterans of the Afghan war to set up bases in his country. Al-Turabi appears to have hoped that bin Laden, in addition to being able to subsidise major development projects in Sudan, would also put up the funds for the 23 new training camps for militants and government militia that he wanted to build.[7] Bin Laden, possibly naïvely, obliged and, within two years of his arrival in the country, had spent tens of millions of dollars building a highway across the desert from Khartoum to Port Sudan, contributing to a new airport for Khartoum and keeping al-Turabi's administration financially afloat during a series of foreign exchange crises that threatened to leave the country without fuel.[8]

Most of bin Laden's time in the Sudan appears to have been devoted to setting up and running a sprawling and less than successful business empire. He took visiting businessmen to see his experiments with different types of tree, ran dozens of trading companies and a million-acre farm where the military instruction of Arab Afghan veterans and the cultivation of peanuts took place simultaneously. Other firms produced honey and sweets. There was an investment company, a tannery, a bakery and a furniture-making firm.[9] There were also plenty of committees, lots of ludicrous schemes that went nowhere and frequent disputes among bin Laden's staff over pay. A barely serviceable plane was bought for $230,000 and then written off.[10] Scores of bank accounts were set up across the world. Several were in bin Laden's own name. This can be seen as either an astonishing lapse of security or an indication that bin Laden genuinely saw himself as nothing more than a devout and legitimate businessman who financed Islamic activism. Many such men existed in his homeland and elsewhere in the Gulf. Another clue to bin Laden's thinking, perhaps hinting at a more militant position, might be in the name of the construction company that he set up as a joint venture with the Sudanese government: 'al-Hijra'.[11]

Amongst the sesame seed farms and the experimental arboriculture one can also begin to make out the very indistinct form of what would later become bin Laden's primary role in modern Islamic militancy: using the resources at his disposal to help realise the 'jihadi' ambitions of young men throughout the Islamic world. There is substantial trial testimony from (prosecution) witnesses that corroborates reports that large numbers of militants were training in Sudan at this time. Many, though by no means all, were under the aegis of bin Laden and Islamic Jihad. Algerian GIA, Lebanese Hizbollah and Palestinian Hamas also had a presence in Sudan in the early 1990s along with Eritrean, Ethiopian and other African radical dissident groups.[12] Nothing emphasises the sense of a broad and diverse movement, in which bin Laden was nothing more than a marginal player, than the list of guests at one of al-Turabi's 'International Islamic' Conferences. Some of the groups used facilities run by the Sudanese government or 'arms-length' organisations, others used camps run by people like bin Laden.

The number of different groups in Sudan allowed bin Laden and his associates to start building, or often reinforcing, contacts. The Jamaat-e-Jihad of Eritrea and the Abu Ali group in Jordan were both given grants of $100,000. Fighters were also dispatched to Chechnya via an office set up in Azerbaijan. Two men, an Egyptian and a Sudanese, visited training camps run by Hizbollah, a Shia group, in the Lebanon, al-Fadl said he was told, and returned with videos showing how bombs large enough to destroy entire buildings could be constructed. Libyans and Algerians close to bin Laden and al-Zawahiri set up contacts with their own domestic groups. Al-Fadl also said, though he admitted it was only hearsay, that groups of fighters had been sent to Tajikistan and the Philippines. Bin Laden does seem to have been considering attacks on Western interests, even if he appears to have been incapable of actually executing them. In 1993, Ali Mohammed, the Egyptian Jihad activist who had been in Peshawar training militants in surveillance in 1991, turned up in Khartoum. He travelled to Nairobi and took pictures of the US embassy there. He brought them back and showed them to bin Laden, who apparently pointed to where a suicide bomb might go.[13]

Though he had been only tangentially involved in the 1992 hotel bombs in Aden, by 1993 bin Laden's involvement in the Yemen was deepening. Al-Fadl related how he and several others were directed by Abu Ayoub al-Iraqi, one of the founder members of 'al-Qaeda' in Pakistan, to take several crates full of weapons from the farm bought by al-Zawahiri and used by Islamic Jihad in Khartoum to Port Sudan, where they were loaded onto a boat to be ferried across the sea to the Yemen. The operation was supervised by agents from the Sudanese government. Independent sources corroborate al-Fadl's claim that bin

Laden was transferring weapons to groups in the north of the Yemen at this time.[14]

Sudan was not the only state involved in the Yemeni conflict. The fusion, in 1990, of the northern and southern Yemeni regimes in a coalition governement pending multi-party elections had failed to smooth over profound differences.The unification of the armies of north and south Yemen was thus delayed. This meant that when a north-south war broke out in 1994 both sides had armed forces that they could call upon. The Saudi government, worried by the prospect of a populous and united state on its borders, committed substantial resources in secret backing for the southern forces. One underlying factor was Riyadh's desire for a corridor of sovereign territory to allow oil exports to the Arabian Sea. When it actually came to the fighting, the Afghan veterans and Islamic groups supported the north. Their role in securing a northern victory is still debated; it was certainly significant, though probably not decisive.

It was shortly after the 1992 bombs in Aden that bin Laden and the senior Islamic Jihad figures with whom he spent much of his time in Khartoum began to talk about attacking the Americans in Somalia. The continuing argument over bin Laden's supposed involvement in Somalia centres on the question of whether fighters linked to or trained by bin Laden, or his close associates, were involved in the battle of Mogadishu in October 1993, where 18 American servicemen were killed and three helicopters shot down during a botched attempt to seize General Farah Aideed, the Somalian warlord.

An intent to attack the Americans was certainly not lacking. Jamal al-Fadl refers to Mohammed Atef, both a senior figure in Islamic Jihad and nominally loyal to bin Laden, visiting Somalia twice in the months before the battle. Atef, other Islamic Jihad figures and bin Laden sent other Afghan veterans into Somalia to contact local tribes and to offer support and training. One was Mohammed Odeh, a Saudi Arabian-born Palestinian who grew up in Jordan and had been inspired to make his way to Afghanistan after watching a video of Abdallah Azzam. After training in al-Farooq camp and serving as a combat medic near Jalalabad in 1991, he was introduced to Saif al-Adel, the Egyptian former special forces officer, who told him that the war in Afghanistan was over and asked if he would go to Somalia via Kenya. Odeh eventually spent seven months in 1993 training the Um Reham tribe in small arms and battlefield medicine.[15] Another man linked to bin Laden and in Somalia during this period was Harun Fazil. Fazil, like Odeh, would later play an important role in the attacks on the east African embassies in 1998. He was actually in Mogadishu during the battle though appears not to have participated.[16] There is a possibility Fazil was there to survey possible UN or US targets for an attack.

Bin Laden has repeatedly denied involvement in the Mogadishu battle, telling CNN in 1997: 'With Allah's grace, Muslims over there cooperated with some Arab "Mujahideen" who had been in Afghanistan.'[17] Some authors have taken this to be an admission of guilt; however, it seems to me that bin Laden was probably telling the truth. American specialists have made much of the fact that the technique of firing rocket-propelled grenades at the rear rotor of a helicopter was one taught to resistance fighters in Afghanistan. Given the number of Arab Afghan veterans in east Africa at the time, there seems to me to be no particular reason why it would have to be bin Laden's fighters, or even Islamic Jihad's, who transferred their skills to the Somalis.

Certainly journalists who worked in Somalia at the time found little evidence of any 'al-Qaeda' involvement in the 'Black Hawk Down' episode. When asked in 1999, General Mohammed Aideed's aides laughed at the claim that bin Laden helped them and said unanimously that they had never even heard of bin Laden until he began boasting about Somalia years later.[18] Bin Laden's involvement in Somalia was also examined during the African embassy bombing trial in New York. Prosecution evidence linking al-Qaeda to the attacks on the US forces failed to stand up and was struck from the court record. The evidence was largely based on the interception of communications in Arabic during the battle, which suggested to the US government that bin Laden's associates were involved. It was pointed out, however, that Arabic is widely spoken in the region and that those tribes named by witnesses as having been in contact with 'al-Qaeda' were in fact fighting *against* General Aideed not for him. Only after strong protests from the prosecution did the judge agree to rule that no members of 'al-Qaeda' affiliated to defendants in the trial were at the battle, rather than ruling that no 'al-Qaeda' members at all had taken part.[19] Senior American officials at the time called bin Laden's boast of involvement in the Somali deaths 'preposterous'.[20] Madeline Albright, the US Ambassador to the UN, and others briefed reporters that Aideed was getting 'significant' help from Iranian and Sudanese advisors, as well as cash from Libya.[21] US officials told Peter Bergen that 'the skills involved in shooting down those helicopters were not skills that the Somalis could have learned on their own', but it is worth remembering that, after the battle of Little

Big Horn, American press reports blamed the defeat on secret French advisors fighting alongside the native American tribes.[22]

Another interesting point is that the trainers appear to have been sent to Somalia by Mohammed Atef, albeit with bin Laden's assent. Jamal al-Fadl told the court that 'al-Qaeda' had a military committee, headed by Atef with Abu Ubaidah al-Banshiri as his deputy. Both had taken a bayat to bin Laden but were Egyptians and involved with Islamic Jihad long before they met the Saudi. In fact, the more closely one examines the composition of the group said to comprise 'al-Qaeda' in the Sudan, the more one can see that it is dominated by Islamic Jihad. In Peshawar, before the move to the Sudan, the sheer number of Egyptians holding senior positions had prompted complaints of discrimination from other members of the group.[23] In a sense, this dominance is to be expected. Egypt has historically enjoyed a degree of cultural, and often political, supremacy in the Middle East. But the sheer number of Egyptian militants, all of whom had practical experience of Islamic activism that far outweighed bin Laden's own, raises significant questions about who exactly was in charge of whom. Alliance with bin Laden, even nominal obedience to him as emir, brought great benefits to the impoverished Islamic Jihad group. As well as lacking funds, Ayman al-Zawahiri, though an effective organiser and military tactician, also lacked the spiritual authority of his main rival in Egyptian militancy, Sheikh Omar Rahman. Association with bin Laden, who made up for what he lacked in clerical credentials in charisma and reputation, was thus doubly useful. The more one examines the relation between al-Zawahiri and bin Laden in this period, the more obvious it is that the older man was manipulating the younger rather than vice versa. Al-Zawahiri was also the more sophisticated thinker of the two. He was, and is, a huge influence on bin Laden. His story is worth looking at in some detail.

Ayman al-Zawahiri was born in a wealthy Cairo suburb on 19 June 1951. His family had moved from Heliopolis and, though both parents were from prominent families connected among the Egyptian elite, they were not well off. Al-Zawahiri's father was a professor of pharmacology but, with five children to educate, he could not afford a car. Though al-Zawahiri's upbringing was religious it was not overtly pious. He was a bright child, known at school as introverted and intense.[24] Al-Zawahiri's background thus shows many of the elements seen in that of radical political

Islamists in Afghanistan, Pakistan and elsewhere: recent migration from the provinces to the capital, middle-class professional parents, a family full of aspirations and ambitions that were unlikely to be fulfilled.

Though the death of Qutb and the trials of the Egyptian Islamists had elicited little sympathy among the general population, the ignominious failure of Egypt and the Arab powers in the 1967 war with Israel had a huge impact. In 1970, Nasser died and Anwar al-Sadat, his replacement, recognised that his predecessor's ideas had gone to the grave with him. Sadat, who cultivated an image of Islamic piety, hoped to use Islam against the Communists and released many activists from jail.[25] They gravitated towards the fertile political ground of the universities.

During the 1970s, various small militant groups formed, unformed and reformed. Many were instigated or aided by the secret services, which had been ordered by Sadat to counter the left by promoting socially conservative strands of Islam among young Egyptians. In 1977, the banned Muslim Brotherhood, tacitly allowed by the regime to operate under the name of 'al-Gamaa al-Islamiyya' (Islamic societies), won a majority in the Egyptian Student's Union. During the 1970s, the number of Egyptian students had doubled, educational facilities were stretched to breaking point and graduate unemployment was a serious problem.

The students were largely drawn from the rural, petty bourgeois, who had always provided the backbone of the support for the Muslim Brotherhood. Sadat's economic policy, particularly his attempt to woo overseas investment from the West, had led to growing inequality. Between 1964 and 1974, the share of the Egyptian GDP of the politically critical middle 30 per cent of the Egyptian population had halved while the top ten per cent had doubled their income.[26] The Gamaa proposed an Islamic solution of varying degrees of radicalism which was profoundly attractive to many.

Most of those involved with the Gamaa, as befits the Muslim Brotherhood under another name, restricted themselves to providing facilities where the state failed. The agenda was Islamicisation. So women were offered segregated classes (solving the problem of overcrowding) or free public transport (if they wore the veil). Many Egyptian militants looked to the blind sheikh, Abdel Omar Rahman, who lived in Fayoum, two hours drive south of Cairo, for spiritual leadership. Rahman had been influenced by Qutb and Maududi and had taught in Saudi Arabia before returning home in 1980, soon after Sadat signed the Camp David peace treaty with Israel. Within months of his return, his fiery sermons, taped and distributed at mosques, had become notorious. As a qualified and learned scholar with a doctorate from al-Azhar, Rahman was able to take on the Egyptian ulema, who had issued fatwa justifying the peace treaty, on their own ground.

Al-Zawahiri graduated from medical school in 1974. By the end of the decade, a variety of radical groups were emerging on the fringes of the Gamaa. A young electrical engineer called Abdessalam Faraj had the strength of character and ideological sophistication to weld some of the disparate elements of Egyptian Islamic militancy into something useful. On 6 October 1981, President Sadat was assassinated by a group led by Faraj, who justified their act by reference to ibn Taimiya and Qutb. Al-Zawahiri was arrested as he headed to the airport to fly back to Pakistan for another stint tending to wounded mujahideen and refugees in Peshawar. In the clampdown that followed the assassination, al-Zawahiri, like thousands of other militants, was imprisoned and brutally tortured. In jail, the tenuous unity brokered by Faraj fell apart and the Egyptian Islamists split once more into various groups. The two largest were al-Zawahiri's Islamic Jihad and a group led by Abdel Omar Rahman, which re-used the name al-Gamaa al-Islamiyya. Where Islamic Jihad were strong in and around Cairo and Alexandria, reflecting the more urban background of their cadres, al-Gamaa al-Islamiyya were most active further south, particularly in the Nile valley around Aswan, Luxor and Asyut. Both groups believed that a twin approach of da'wa and violent struggle would enable them to achieve the familiar Salafi-Wahhabi aim of 'compelling good and driving out evil'.[27] By 1989, after several brief periods in jail, Abdel Omar Rahman was in America, having somehow obtained a visa in Cairo, and had settled down to teach in Jersey City, where he remained until his arrest in 1993. Al-Zawahiri was released from prison in 1984 and had returned to Pakistan by 1985.

The crackdown of the early 1980s, and the distraction of Afghanistan, kept the militants in Egypt quiet until the middle of the decade. Sadat's assassins had hoped their spectacular act would provoke a huge spontaneous uprising. Though nothing of the sort occurred, the root causes of the appeal of the Islamic radicals had not disappeared. In the mid 1980s, Egypt entered another period of acute economic crisis exacerbated by obvious corruption and ostentation on the part of the elite and government officials. From 1984 to 1994, the proportion of Egyptians living beneath the poverty line increased from 42 to 54 per cent.[28] Despite successive government crackdowns, the Muslim Brotherhood and its various associated splinter groups grew rapidly, particularly on the university campuses. By 1985, the year a young engineering student called Mohammed Atta enrolled at Cairo University, almost all the student unions were dominated by Islamists who were pressing authorities to 'Islamicise' curricula and enforce segregation.

From the late 1980s, the violence in Egypt, particularly in the upper Nile, grew. Al-Gamaa al-Islamiyya had recruited heavily among the unemployed young graduates of the new rural universities of the Nile valley and these new cadres were able to mobilise the rural or recently urbanised poor using, in an echo of contemporaneous anti-Shia agitation in Pakistan, violent rhetoric directed at local Coptic Christians. As in Pakistan, Saudi Arabia, the Yemen and elsewhere, the return of Afghan veterans from 1989 onwards lent a hardened, fanatical edge to an existing conflict. During the first half of the 1990s, Egypt would be plunged into a welter of violence. Terrorist attacks, mostly perpetrated by al-Gamaa al-Islamiyya, killed more than a thousand people.

Quite when al-Zawahiri reached Khartoum is unclear. According to Jamal al-Fadl, Islamic Jihad were training cadres in the Sudan before bin Laden arrived in 1992 so it is likely that al-Zawahiri preceded the Saudi.[29] However, 'the doctor' appears to have travelled widely in the early 1990s, so determining quite how much time he spent in Khartoum is difficult. In addition to the funds that bin Laden could access (on one occasion the Saudi bought two large consignments of Kalashnikovs in Omdurman and gave them to Islamic Jihad to be sent on camel trains across the border into Egypt), the safe haven that the Saudi's good relations with the Sudanese allowed was also crucial to al-Zawahiri's operations.[30] Though the vast bulk of the attacks in Egypt were committed by al-Gamaa al-Islamiyya, Islamic Jihad were soon able to start launching operations, trying, in August 1993, to kill the Egyptian interior minister.

In April 1995, al-Zawahiri chaired a meeting in Khartoum attended by members of both al-Gamaa al-Islamiyya and Islamic Jihad. The continuing violence in Egypt had provoked a massive response from the authorities and the militant groups were suffering heavy losses as tens of thousands of Islamic activists, few of whom were actually connected to terrorists, were rounded up. Despite al-Zawahiri's efforts, the groups failed to reconcile their differences and al-Gamaa al-Islamiyya decided to attempt a spectacular attack on President Mubarak.[31] Mubarak's motorcade was shot up during a state visit to Addis Ababa, the capital of Ethiopia, but the Egyptian premier escaped injury. Islamic Jihad switched their focus. In November, they successfully bombed the Egyptian embassy in Islamabad.

This attack and the attempted assassination of Mubarak are often wrongly blamed on bin Laden. So too are the bomb blasts in 1995 and 1996 in Saudi Arabia that killed a total of 24 Americans. The first of the two Saudi bombings took place on 13 November 1995, when a 220lb car bomb exploded in Riyadh outside a building leased by the Pentagon for American military contractors. It killed five American officers and two Indian civilians and was the first such attack in Saudi Arabia's history. In April 1996, Saudi Television broadcast the confessions of the four men accused of the attack. They all appeared to be Saudis, spoke Saudi Arabic and had Saudi tribal names. Though the confessions could have been beaten out of the four, their statements contradicted Riyadh's previous claims that the blast was the work of 'outside forces', possibly Iraq or Iran, and seem likely to be genuine. Three of the four were 24 years old and had fought in the war in Afghanistan; one, slightly older, was a veteran of combat in Bosnia too. All four came from modest backgrounds and had started their activism with the Jamaat Tablighi, the pacifist missionary group whose membership runs into millions across the Islamic world and whose activities are not only legal in Saudi Arabia but positively encouraged. The experience of the Afghan jihad had clearly radicalised all four. Each of them admitted links to radical Islamic leaders, including Mohammed al-Massari, the British-based chair of the Committee for the Defence of Legitimate Rights, and bin Laden. Their connection to bin Laden comprised of reading his writings after being faxed them from London, along with al-Massari's publications and periodicals of the Egyptian al-Gamaa al-Islamiyya.[32] All four were executed.

The second attack in Saudi Arabia came seven months later, on 25 June 1996, when a bomb in a fuel truck parked outside the Khobar Towers military complex in Dhahran exploded, ripping the front off the building and killing 19 US servicemen. Though suspicion initially focused on Afghan veterans in the country, 600 of whom were arrested, investigations swiftly showed that an Iranian-backed Shia group within Saudi Arabia was responsible. Shias within Saudi Arabia have suffered significant repression and have a long history of active resistance, if not terrorism on the scale of the Dhahran attack. The Americans indicted 13 members of Saudi Hizbollah for the attack and even a cursory look at the extraordinarily detailed indictment, which includes timings of phone calls from senior Iranian officials to the conspirators and long descriptions of the bombers' movements over a period of months and even years, is enough to convince all but the most adamant that neither bin Laden nor any other of the various Sunni radical militants operating in the region at the time were involved in the attack.[33] In his 1997 interview with CNN, bin Laden praised as 'heroes' those behind the bombings but denied responsibility. 'What they did is a big honour that I missed participating in,' he said.[34]

By late 1995, al-Turabi and other senior figures in the Sudanese government were beginning to think that their bid to turn Sudan into a centre for Islamic radicalism was a miscalculation. Their attempt to counter Riyadh's pre-eminence in the Islamic world had failed. Relations with the Saudis, who had stripped bin Laden of his citizenship and frozen his assets in 1994, were at a new nadir. Cairo was incensed at the protection offered to men who had tried to murder the President and were responsible for scores of other attacks. The continuing presence of Algerian GIA, Lebanese Hizbollah, Palestinian Hamas and others had badly damaged Khartoum's overseas image. America had listed Sudan as a state sponsor of terror in 1993 and the big Western oil firms who, it was hoped, would pour money into the country's infrastructure were leery of any investment as a result. It was becoming increasingly clear that the benefits of bin Laden's presence in their country did not outweigh the international opprobrium it brought. The Sudanese were particularly angry when it emerged that men close to bin Laden had murdered a young boy suspected of collaborating with the Egyptian intelligence services. Sudanese intelligence put bin Laden on notice. He was not the only one to be warned that the time had come to leave. Officers went round the various militant groups in their country and told them that if they did not go of their own accord they would be expelled.[35]

There was a deeper problem too. Al-Turabi's brand of Islamism was very different from the radical internationalist Azzam-influenced jihadi salafism evolved by bin Laden, al-Zawahiri and their associates. For al-Turabi, the priority was gaining and retaining political power to allow an Islamic society to be created. Bin Laden's presence jeopardised that project. Early in 1996, informal approaches were made to the US State Department, which responded with demands that included access to the training camps and the provision of details about various individuals associated with terrorism, included bin Laden. There was, apparently, no explicit demand that bin Laden be handed over. The Sudanese said they were prepared to deliver him to Riyadh but the Saudi government, fearful of domestic unrest, refused the offer.[36] At the time, Washington was not inclined to accept custody of bin Laden on the basis that, as he was yet to be indicted, there would be no grounds to hold him in the USA.[37]

Before contacting the Americans, Khartoum had tasked an intelligence official attached to their embassy in Pakistan but based in Peshawar with finding out if Afghanistan might be a feasible destination for bin Laden should he leave Sudan. The official had learned Pashto and built up excellent contacts among Afghan commanders during the war against the Soviets. He focused his efforts on three commanders around Jalalabad. Bin Laden, no doubt aware of his precarious position, had already got in touch with two old friends from his time among the mujahideen, Maulvi Younis Khalis and Jalaluddin Haqqani. On 18 May 1996 he returned to Afghanistan.

CHAPTER ELEVEN

STRUGGLE

Just after eleven o'clock on 7 August 1998, Mohammed Rashid Daoud al-Owhali, a slim-shouldered, bearded 22-year-old from Saudi Arabia, was standing in front of a toilet bowl in the men's lavatories on the ground floor of a private hospital in the suburb of Nairobi called Parklands. He was holding a set of keys and three bullets. His clothes (jeans, a white, patterned shirt, socks and black shoes) were soaked with blood. The keys fitted the lock on the rear doors of a light brown Toyota pick-up truck which, half an hour earlier, had ceased to exist when the huge bomb it had been carrying had exploded, demolishing the American embassy, an adjacent secretarial college and badly damaging a nearby bank. The explosion killed 213, wounded 4,600 and effectively vaporised the driver of the truck, another young Saudi called Azzam. He and al-Owhali had been friends and had sung songs of martyrdom in Arabic as they had driven the truck to the embassy. Azzam was killed when, still sitting in the driver seat, he pressed a detonator button taped to the dashboard. But al-Owhali ran. And so was standing in the toilet holding the keys and the bullets.

One hour and 15 minutes earlier, al-Owhali and Azzam had left a small detached house in a suburb on the outskirts of Nairobi and driven their truck towards its centre. The truck contained several wooden crates containing TNT, aluminium nitrate, aluminium powder and a detonator that was wired to three or four large vehicle batteries which themselves were connected to the dashboard button. Al-Owhali sat in the passenger seat wearing a lightweight jacket in the pocket of which he had placed a 9mm Beretta pistol. He had wedged three homemade stun grenades, made from a quarter finger of TNT, some aluminium powder and black tape, in his belt. As they drove along Haile Selassie Avenue, Azzam suggested that the jacket might make it difficult to reach the stun grenades, so he took it off and put it on the seat beside him. Because neither man knew Nairobi well they were following another jeep driven by a local called Harun. It was mid morning on a Friday and the streets were busy.

The American embassy was a five-storey building set in a compound by a roundabout where Moi Avenue meets Haile Selassie Avenue. Azzam drove the truck to the drop bar at the entrance to the car park at its rear. Harun drove his vehicle past the embassy and disappeared into the heavy traffic. It was 10.38. At the drop bar, Azzam stopped the truck. Al-Owhali opened his door, stepped to the ground and moved towards the guard on the gate. The plan was for him to force the guards to lift the bar by threatening them with his pistol. He was then to follow the truck through the gate into the car park so that if Azzam was for some reason unable to detonate the bomb once in position under the embassy, al-Owhali could do so himself by unlocking the rear of the truck and throwing in a grenade.

But things went wrong. As he approached the guard at the drop bar al-Owhali realised his pistol was in his jacket, which was on the seat in the truck. He hesitated, decided it would take too long to get it and threw a stun grenade instead, shouting in English. The guards scattered and the drop bar stayed down. Azzam rammed the truck up close to the embassy wall. Al-Owhali saw the vehicle against the embassy and decided his job was done and he didn't need to die after all. He turned to his right and started sprinting. Azzam pressed the dashboard button.

The blast knocked al-Owhali to the pavement and cut the centre of his back, his right hand and his forehead. When he picked himself up, Haile Selassie Avenue was a shambles. There were bits of concrete and twisted metal, broken glass and papers everywhere. Acrid smoke filled the air. There was a terrific amount of noise. Several buses lay burning with corpses hanging from the windows.

He walked to a first aid station, noticing when he got there that he still had a stun grenade tucked into his belt, which he dropped in a rubbish bin. After some initial treatment, an ambulance drove him to MP Shah Hospital where his wounds were stitched. Then he went out onto the street and wondered what to do. As he was supposed to die, there had been no escape plan for him. He had left his plane tickets and false passport at the bomb factory.

Standing in front of the hospital, al-Owhali checked his pockets for money. All he found were the keys to the back of the truck and three bullets from the pistol he had left in the jacket. He went back inside the hospital, found the men's toilets and washed the keys and the bullets in a sink to remove fingerprints. Then he tried to flush them down a cistern. When they wouldn't go he fished them out and stood there.

It was just after eleven o'clock in the morning. He had spent the last week preparing for death. Less than a mile away his friend had blown himself up along with an embassy and thousands of people. He was standing in a hospital full of badly injured casualties, casualties of the bomb he had delivered. He had no money and no passport and no one knew he was alive.[1]

Late in the afternoon of 18 May 1996, two planes landed at the airstrip east of Jalalabad. They were carrying Osama bin Laden, his three wives, at least three of his ten children and around 30 male followers. Three local warlords had driven out onto the pitted tarmac in front of the old Soviet-built airport buildings to meet them. All three, Maulvi Saznoor, Fazl Haq Mujahed and Engineer Machmud had been to see bin Laden in Khartoum a month earlier. Each had fought with a different faction in the war against the Soviets. Saznoor was roughly aligned with Abd al-Rab al-Rasul Sayyaf's Ittehad-e-Islami group, the others with Hekmatyar and Maulvi Younis Khalis respectively.[2] Now each commander hoped to use bin Laden, his wealth and his international connections, to gain leverage in the complex manoeuvring for power in post-war Afghanistan. It was the old Afghan game, played by leaders at every level from the village to the palace, of accessing resources from overseas for local advantage.

Bin Laden moved into the Bagh Zahera, a two-storey villa set in gardens close to the river in Jalalabad. It had been built as a royal lodge and had been used as a military headquarters under the Soviets. There was plenty of room for 'the sheikh' and his entourage. Bin Laden spent most of his time there or in one of the houses of the three men who had invited him back to Afghanistan.[3]

There were others, though, who were interested in bin Laden. A few weeks after he had arrived, strangers started approaching the children of commanders who had had contact with bin Laden's own children. They showed them pictures of bin Laden's sons and asked where the boys lived. Bin Laden decided that Jalalabad, a small but busy city, was not safe and in late June he moved his family up to a *qala*, a traditional

Pashtun fortified compound, owned by Younis Khalis near the former Soviet collective farm at Hadda, about five miles south of the city. A month after that they moved further south, up to the Melawa valley in the foothills of the Spin Ghar mountains where Engineer Machmud was using the old mujahideen base at Tora Bora as a supply dump. It was from there, on 23 August, that bin Laden issued an 8,000 word 'message… unto Muslim brethren all over the world generally and in the Arab peninsula specifically'. It was entitled: 'A declaration of war against the Americans occupying the land of the two holy places'.

This lengthy and sometimes rambling document was the first in a series of public statements and interviews over the next nine months that set out bin Laden's objectives and methodology. Bin Laden's short-term aim was immediately clear. Most of the Declaration of War is taken up by a lengthy diatribe against the House of al-Saud. It is in fact largely a re-write of Communiqué 17, 'an open letter to King Fahd', issued almost a year earlier through associates of bin Laden in London. The only difference was that bin Laden excised many of the references in the communiqué to the early Wahhabis to make it more resonant to a wider audience outside Saudi Arabia.

In religious language and with references to early Islamic history, the Qur'an and the hadith, bin Laden voices a series of very specific and very modern grievances. So, within four paragraphs, bin Laden has referred to the battles of the pre-Islamic warlords in Arabia, Somalia in 1993, the suicide bombings directed at American troops in Beirut in 1983 and the battle of Badr of 624. He announces that he has returned to the high Hindu Kush mountains of 'Khorasan', using the name given to modern-day Afghanistan during the great days of Islamic expansion under the Abbasid dynasty where, he says, 'the greatest infidel military force of the world [the Soviets] was destroyed and the myth of the superpower withered in front of the mujahideen cries of Allah u akbar'.

Bin Laden says that the consequence of his homeland straying from the correct Islamic 'way' is 'injustice', which has affected 'civilians, military and security men, government officials… students… as well as… hundreds of thousands of unemployed graduates'. The results of this 'injustice', bin Laden says, include poorly paid, indebted government employees, the devaluation of the Rial, the 'miserable situation of the social services' and 'especially the water service' and the non-payment of bills by the government to 'great merchants and contractors'. The government, bin Laden says, had ignored peaceful means of protest. Now violence is the only alternative. The mixing of complaints about sanitation provision and invoicing problems with accusations of zulm, or tyranny, is utterly unselfconscious. This is a political manifesto, springing from a sense of social injustice that is blamed on bad government and expressed in religious terminology and with reference to religious myths.

Following ibn Taimiya (whom he quotes repeatedly) and Qutb (whom he doesn't, though his influence is clear), bin Laden says that because the House of al-Saud follow a 'pagan' legal code and have not implemented the Shariat they can no longer be considered Muslims and are thus hypocrites and unbelievers, who must be resisted. This resistance, as ibn Taimiya and Abdallah Azzam stressed, is not a collective duty but an individual duty on every Muslim. 'It is a duty on every tribe in the Arab peninsular to fight jihad and cleanse the land from these occupiers,' bin Laden says. This is jihad as resistance and is thus a defensive, and thus just, war. Though there are disagreements among Islamic theorists over when 'pagans' or unbelievers should be attacked, there is consensus over the justification for defensive military actions. Here bin Laden, whose own preference is for the more radical interpretation of jihad found in the sword verses, is at pains to justify his planned campaign in more moderate terms that appeal to the widest possible audience.

If, in the short term, bin Laden is focused on Saudi Arabia, he clearly has a broader aim too: to end the repression of Islamic world by the hypocrite governments and the 'Crusader-Zionist' alliance supporting and manipulating them. That the West and the Jews want to maintain the Islamic world in a state of weakness, division and poverty is taken as a given. Bin Laden ignores the Islamic injunction for tolerance towards the 'people of the book'. In his world (and the world of Azzam, Qutb, al-Zawahiri et al) the Crusades never finished. For bin Laden, the hostility of the Crusader-Zionist alliance is manifested both in their support of munafiq governments and in their own repression of Muslims. 'It should not be hidden from you,' warns bin Laden in his Declaration of War:

> that the people of Islam have suffered from aggression, iniquity and injustice imposed on them by the Zionist-Crusaders alliance and their collaborators... [Muslim] blood was spilled in Palestine and Iraq. The horrifying pictures of the massacre of Qana, in Lebanon, are still fresh in our memory. Massacres in Tajikistan, Burma, Kashmir, Assam, the Philippines... Ogaden, Somalia, Eritrea, Chechnya and Bosnia-Herzegovina... send shivers in the body and shake the conscience.

This is a 'difficult period in the history of the umma', bin Laden points out. The reason for the current tribulations and humiliations suffered by the Muslim community is that they have allowed the holy places (including the al-Aqsa mosque in Jerusalem) to be occupied, in contravention of the will of Allah. The only solution to this humiliating situation, he believes, is a jihad. This is the essence of the creed of aggressive Sunni militant salafism.

In the Declaration, bin Laden also outlines the means by which his aims are to be achieved. After 4,000 words on the current ills of Saudi Arabia and the problems of the umma in general, he turns to address his 'Muslim brothers (particularly those of the Arab peninsular)' who he hopes will 'today have started your jihad in the cause of Allah to expel the occupying enemy out of the country of the two holy places... in order to re-establish the greatness of the umma and to liberate its occupied sanctuaries'. Bin Laden admits that there is an imbalance in forces. The answer is to use 'fastmoving light forces that work under complete secrecy'. These forces will 'hit the aggressor with an iron first... re-establish the normal course and give the people their rights'.

Most of the Declaration is explicitly directed at 'the youth' of Saudi Arabia. Bin Laden calls for a vanguard, who will martyr themselves. Despite his complete lack of scholarly credentials, bin Laden makes the controversial assertion that those who die in such a way will go 'to the highest levels of paradise'. That so few have so far come forward as volunteers is easily explained. It is the 'corrupt media' who have been used to 'trick' many Muslims into loving 'this materialistic world'. Many of the ulema in Saudi Arabia have been fed falsehoods, which they have passed on to the faithful. Others have been wilfully misleading to further their own interests. Predictably, bin Laden says, this is the work of the 'Zionist-Crusader alliance' which:

> moves quickly to contain and abort any corrective movement appearing in Islamic countries. Different means and methods are used... Sometimes officials from the Ministry of the interior who are also graduates of the colleges of the shari'at are [sent] to... confuse the nation and the umma... and to circulate false information.

Little of bin Laden's thought is original. Most of his ideas can be found repeated in thousands of similar 'Salafi' tracts distributed over the last decade. His lack of a clear political programme is a feature of most modern Islamic extremist ideology too. In a revealing moment in an interview with CNN early in 1997, bin Laden was asked what kind of society would be created if the Islamic movement takes over Arabia. Though he had viewed the questions in advance he still failed to articulate any vision of the practical instrumentalities of his Islamic state and merely referred once more to the primary Islamic texts and the example of the earliest Islamic community:

> We are confident, with the permission of God, praise and glory be to Him, that… God's religion, praise and glory be to Him, will prevail in this peninsula. It is a great pride and a big hope that the revelation received by Mohammed, peace be upon him, will be resorted to for ruling. When we used to follow Mohammed's revelation, peace be upon him, we were in great happiness and in great dignity.[4]

What is new in bin Laden's thought, however, is the shift in target. The Declaration makes clear that the priority for bin Laden is to attack the Crusader-Zionist alliance, even if the focus on Saudi Arabia in most of the document makes it clear that such an attack is merely, in his mind, the means to a specific and local end. Previously, Islamic groups had largely targeted their own governments, the hypocrites and the apostates, directly, not their supporters. Bin Laden may have been interested in forming an international group of militants that would restore Islam to its rightful superiority in the world, but hitherto this was to be effected by targeting the regimes that ruled Muslim countries, not the USA or other representatives of global kufr. This shift in strategy was radical and controversial and there is evidence that it was opposed by al-Zawahiri and senior figures in Islamic Jihad who feared a diversion of attention from their campaign against the Egyptian government. In his statement, bin Laden argues that the 'greater enemy' must be overcome before 'the lesser enemy'. The focus on the USA, a common foe, is a useful way of overcoming the particularism that had hobbled extremist, and less radical, Islamic reformist movements over the preceding three decades. It would also bind together the disparate groups and individuals that comprised the Islamic militant movement at the time. In the Declaration, he goes to great lengths to justify the shift, even employing an uncharacteristic bit of analogical reasoning:

> The situation cannot be rectified, as the shadow cannot be straightened when its source, the rod, is not straight either, unless the root of the problem is tackled. Hence it is essential to hit the main enemy who divided the umma into small and little countries and pushed it for the last few decades into a state of confusion.

Here he had hit upon one of the key elements that would allow the rapid spread of the 'al-Qaeda' message in the next few years. In an interview published in October 1996 in a radical Islamic magazine, *Nida'ul Islam,* bin Laden is more explicit: 'It is crucial to overlook many of the issues of bickering to unite our ranks so we can repel the greater Kufr.'[5] Bin Laden realised that tapping the profound and widespread resentment in the Islamic world of Western supremacy and policy would enable him to overcome fitna and unite radical Islamists under his banner. The failure of the more moderate political Islamists to move beyond parochial local interests had left a huge gap that bin Laden with his explicitly supranational message, which was left vague enough not to clash with any group's local agenda, was able to exploit. This internationalisation was to become progressively more marked in the coming years.

However, bin Laden still needed to find an effective way to mobilise the vanguard he had so often talked about. Al-Banna, Maududi and Qutb had all faced similar problems. They had decided to patiently build popular networks and organisational structures that would allow them to achieve their aims, albeit over a long period. Bin Laden, hunted by a dozen security services and stuck in a mountainside cave complex without electricity or running water in a country without a proper telephone network, did not have that luxury. The hugely enhanced capacity of the modern media could help, but words have to be backed by deeds to be effective. Bin Laden's associates in Islamic Jihad had learned the power of a single, stunning strike with the assassination of Sadat. Such a strike would get massive publicity, bring in more recruits and inspire more attacks. Bin Laden was aware of the difficulties facing him, telling Abdul Bari Atwan, the London-based editor of *al-Quds al-Arabi,* during an interview at Tora Bora in November 1996 that:

> Preparations for major operations take a certain amount of time, unlike minor operations. If we wanted small actions, the matter would have easily been carried out immediately after the [August 1996] statement. [But] the nature of the battle calls for operations of a specific type that will make an impact on the enemy and this calls for excellent preparations.[6]

The initial attacks needed people and a secure base. Bin Laden had neither. The Taliban, who viewed bin Laden with a significant degree of suspicion, had seized Jalalabad three weeks after the declaration was issued.

But though bin Laden lacked manpower and security, there were several groups in Afghanistan which did not. In Chapters Five, Six and

Seven, I examined the training camps and the militant organisations, some backed by governments in the Gulf, some by the Pakistanis, others by private donors throughout the Islamic world, which had been able to thrive in Afghanistan and Pakistan after the end of the war against the Soviets. It was on bin Laden's arrival in the region in 1996 that the true consequences of this became apparent. Bin Laden arrived back in Afghanistan with an ideology but no way of prosecuting it. In the camps he found his weapon. Within five years, he, al-Zawahiri, Mohammed Atef and others would together be able to build an astonishingly sophisticated infrastructure for terrorist training.

Bin Laden was not entirely devoid of resources on his return. Though his bank accounts were depleted, they still existed and funds from wealthy private backers in the Gulf were still flowing in. He had the core group of militants who had returned with him from the Sudan. He also had his own contacts in Peshawar and tribal belt. Abu Zubaydah, the young Palestinian who had helped funnel recruits for the jihad into training camps in the late 1980s, had been able to hang on in Peshawar where he had been looking after an office-cum-guesthouse funded by bin Laden in Hayatabad. There were others too. Al-Gamaa al-Islamiyya, the Egyptian group, had an estimated 200 fighters training or billeted in and around Jalalabad. Islamic Jihad, their rivals, also had volunteers undergoing training. Sayyaf was still running camps for militants from all over the Islamic world in Kunar. His Khaldan camp on the border of Pakistan and Afghanistan was also still functioning. Hekmatyar's Hizb-e-Islami had facilities at Darunta, outside Jalalabad, and in what had become a huge complex of different camps on the road between Khost and the border with Pakistan. High on a ridge, in six camps known collectively as the al-Badr complex, Hekmatyar, assisted by instructors from the Pakistani ISI, continued to train Pakistani sectarian militants from a variety of groups including Harkat-ul-Mujahideen, Hizb-ul-Mujahideen, Lashkar-e-Toiba and the Sipa-e-Sahaba Pakistan.[7] Hizb-ul-Mujahideen ran 'Salman al-Farsi' camp alone, though most camps tended to be divided into Pakistani, Afghan and Arab sections. The latter category included Saudis, Yemenis, Filipinos, Uighurs, Kurds, Jordanians, Tajiks and Uzbeks among many other nationalities. Khalid bin Waleed camp, where Omar Saeed Sheikh had trained before heading off to New Delhi on his first kidnapping mission, was still pumping out militants. There were so many Pakistanis that the camps were known locally as the 'Punjabi ghund [camp]'.[8]

Relations between Hekmatyar's men and the Taliban were poor. The two groups were ideologically opposed and had fought for control of several provinces. So when the Taliban seized the provinces around Khost in the summer of 1996 they immediately shut down two of six al-Badr camps and handed the rest over to the Harkat-ul-Mujahideen (HUM), who were fellow Deobandis. The HUM had their own political links within Pakistan and were very close to the Jamaat-e-Ulema-e-Islami (JUI), the Pakistani Deobandi political party which had been inducted into government by Benazir Bhutto three years previously and whose medressas in the North West Frontier Province, Baluchistan and elsewhere had supplied much of the manpower for the Taliban. The JUI in turn were close to Jalaluddin Haqqani, the Deobandi cleric and veteran mujahideen commander who had originally built and run the Zhawar Khili base. Haqqani, the main powerbroker in the Khost area, had joined the Taliban in August 1996 and was very happy to expel Hekmatyar's cadres and bring in his allies. Haqqani also had strong connections to the Pakistani military and to the Gulf, allowing him access to financial and political resources, publicly and privately from Islamabad, Dubai and Riyadh.

This shift in the administration of the camps, from the political Islamists linked to Jamaat Islami, the party founded by Maududi, to the neo-traditionalist Deobandi Taliban, is more than just a local detail. It is representative of what was happening more broadly in Afghanistan, in Pakistan and across much of the Islamic world as well. Political Islamism, riven by particularism and ideological weakness, had simply failed to achieve many of its declared aims by the mid 1990s. Alternatives, such as the harsh brand of Islam practiced by the Taliban or the salafi radicalism of bin Laden and his associates, were emerging as the dominant discourse for articulating radical dissidence in its place.

Bin Laden never took over the administration of these camps. He did not need to. None of the other groups training in Afghanistan at the time were focused on attacking America. By advertising his intention to launch strikes against US interests, bin Laden was able to cream off the most talented and the most motivated volunteers. If they wanted to fight in Kashmir, against Shias in Pakistan or for the Taliban then there were organisations able to help them. If they wanted a 'martyrdom' operation against the forces of kufr, then there was only one group to go to. This was where bin Laden's close relationship with Egyptian Islamic Jihad was critical. Egyptians had historically filled many of the more senior or specialised positions in the camps and comprised a significant proportion of the trainers and administrators. Two camps in particular, al-Farooq and Abu Jindal, had been run by Egyptians with Gulf funds (some channelled through Sayyaf) for nearly a decade. With al-Zawahiri and others back in Afghanistan it was a relatively easy process to appropriate them for the exclusive use of bin Laden and his associates. They became the specialist camps for those selected to receive the intensive training necessary to take part in terrorist operations against the 'Zionist-Crusader alliance'. Camps like Khaldan acted as clearing camps where volunteers received basic military training, as they had been doing for the best part of a decade. Most went on to fight for the Taliban, or returned to their own countries. Only the best went on to al-Farooq or Abu Jindal. Mohammed Rashid Daoud al-Owhali was one.

Al-Owhali had reached Afghanistan shortly after bin Laden. He was coming up to his 20th birthday. There is no evidence that it was bin Laden's presence in Afghanistan that attracted the young Saudi. He had grown up in a wealthy, prominent and devout family in Riyadh. During his teenage years he had become drawn to the radical fringe, listening to the tapes produced by Saudi Arabia's dissident Islamic activists and reading magazines and tracts produced by the Arab mujahideen. Abdallah Azzam's works, the *al-Jihad* magazine and books such as *The Love and Hour of the Martyrs* were particularly influential. He then spent two years at a religious university. In mid 1996, a friend returned from fighting in Bosnia and inspired al-Owhali and several others. They discussed going to Bosnia themselves, or to Chechnya but, al-Owhali told his FBI interrogators, could not find anyone who could get them there. Instead they decided to go to Afghanistan. Al-Owhali arrived in Khaldan camp, then under the command of a man known as Sayyid al-Kurdi, late in the summer. Five years later, with American bombers in the skies overhead, I was able to reach the city of Khost days are the Arabs had withdrawn.[9] In a compound known simply as 'the Arab camp' on the northern outskirts of the city, I found a small packet of letters. They were from volunteers who had been trained in Khaldan camp between 1996 and 1998. Each had written to thank his tutor and to complain or offer suggestions about the instruction they had received.

The letters provided a fantastic insight to life in Khaldan camp at the time that al-Owhali was there. Al-Owhali only briefly sketched out his time in Khaldan, describing it to the FBI as 'a basic military training camp' where he was instructed in 'light weapons, some demolition, some artillery, some communication'. The syllabus had remained unchanged since the days of Pakistani instruction for mujahideen guerrillas in the late 1980s and was identical to that being taught in the HUM camps. Al-Owhali also spoke of religious training. Most extremist religious movements and cults try to create discrete spaces away from the broader social and cultural environment where their normative systems can prevail and any uncertainty on the part of recruits can be progressively eliminated. As we have already noted, Islamic groups in particular have an interest in creating 'Islamicized spaces' where they can attempt, on a necessarily small scale, to create their utopian vision of the 'Islamic society' based on their reading of the texts and early history of Islam. This is justified by reference to the Qur'anic injunction for true believers to withdraw from the community, physically as well as mentally, so as to be able to better follow the true path of the Shariat. In contemporary terms, this has led to a profound interest in creating physical areas set apart from kufr or unbelief.[10]

However, it is important not to see the Afghan camps as instruments of 'brainwashing'. Those who travelled to Afghanistan in this period were highly motivated individuals who had made significant sacrifices and overcome significant obstacles to reach their goal of participating in jihad. Of course, once in Afghanistan there is no doubt that, especially if they were selected for 'elite' training, there was an important process, as in any military organisation, of building a particular identity based in a certain sense of group solidarity. Al-Owhali told the FBI that, at Khaldan, he had received religious instruction including 'fatwas which called for violence'. He had explained to his interrogator that 'if a ruler changed something in contradiction to Islam that particular ruler had blasphemed and therefore it was your right and duty to kill him'. The statements he had heard from bin Laden, who addressed the recruits on rare occasions, 'further solidified his religious feelings', he had said.[11] Sayyid al-Kurdi's letters reinforce this point. 'I learned so much about how to become strong internally,' Said Ahmed, a Pakistani volunteer told his tutor.[12]

The letters also reveal the sheer internationalism of the camp. Abu Ziad, a Kurd, asks his tutor to send his regards to other tutors, including Faris al-Bosni (Bosnian), Abu Omar al-Yemeni, Zaid al-Najdi (from the Saudi province of Najd). Another letter mentions Abu Omar al-Jazairi (Algerian), Omar al-Tajiki, (Tajik) and Jalib al-Afghani. Yet such diversity, as bin Laden was aware and so often spoke out against, was a problem. 'The Algerians keep to themselves, so do the Turks and everyone keeps to their own groups. They should mix more,' moaned Abu Zubeir al-Makki. Their chief instructor himself was the cause of various complaints. According to Abu Ziad al-Yemeni, 'Abu Sayyid never really joked or socialised outside training. He was always very serious with those undergoing training both inside and outside the camp'.[13] Interestingly, many of the letters are poorly written and ungrammatical, even by those for whom Arabic is their first language. This hints at a shift in the type of recruit to radical Islam from those drawn from the more educated political Islamist cadre, such as Khalid Shaikh Mohammed, Omar Saeed Sheikh, al-Zawahiri or bin Laden himself, to those drawn from poorer, less educated social groups.

One important feature to note is how the structure of the camps mirrors the tripartite division of the phenomenon of 'al-Qaeda' and modern Islamic militancy described in Chapter One. There is the hardcore, a small number of committed activists, many of whom are veterans of the Afghan war, who have coalesced around bin Laden and who fill senior administrative positions in the most specialised camps or perform command roles for those who graduate from them; there is the next group of those connected with the 'network of networks', men belonging to or recruited by individual groups in their own countries and sent to Afghanistan for training. Many of these men have previous experience in conflicts in Bosnia or elsewhere. Some of them are selected by the first group for 'martyrdom' operations. Others merely sent home. Thirdly, there is the broad mass of volunteers who fill camps like Khaldan. Predominantly young men, increasingly drawn from more deprived social groups, these are the cannon fodder who, inspired by the literature of Azzam, the sermons of local firebrand clerics or the message of bin Laden himself, find their way to the camps, 'ardent for some desperate glory'.

Bin Laden, usually referred to as 'the sheikh' or 'the emir', is mentioned infrequently. There are occasional requests to send 'salaams' to him or mentions of lectures that clearly inspired the young recruits, but little else. Far more frequent are complaints that the training was not appropriate to the war the volunteers were expecting to fight. The basic military skills imparted at Khaldan are not useful in 'striking the tyrants in the cities where they live', one recruit complained. Many request training in 'assassination and bombing' techniques. One recruit complained about a lack of ammunition to allow live firing exercises. There are, predictably, many references to martyrdom in the letters. 'We are grateful to God for this training and the chance to die as a martyr,' says one of Sayyid al-Kurdi's former students.[14]

Al-Owhali told the FBI that he had met bin Laden for the first time in mid September 1996. Along with several others, he had been nominated by Sayyid al-Kurdi for an audience with 'the emir' because he had done well in training. Bin Laden spoke to the group and, according to al-Owhali, had 'impressed upon them the need to fight the Americans and cast them out of the Arabian peninsular'. Bin Laden had also recommended that they get further training. Al-Owhali spent the next six months in three different camps, including al-Farooq, where he received training in 'security and intelligence, how to gather information, how to protect information from being divulged, how to conduct hijackings on buses or planes, how to do kidnappings and how to seize and hold buildings'. Al-Owhali had done well. Such training was highly sought after. In a letter addressed to Faidullah al-Turkestani, Abu Hadaifa al-Jazairi explains his absence at Khaldan camp: 'I promised to return in three days but came across some guys I know from al-Farooq camp who were in Kabul and through their contacts I managed to get onto this training session.'

Towards the end of his time in al-Farooq, al-Owhali met bin Laden several times and asked him for a mission. Al-Owhali said he was asked, as Jamal al-Fadl said he had been back in 1989, to take an oath of allegiance to bin Laden and to al-Qaeda. Al-Owhali refused, on the basis that he wanted the liberty to be able to refuse any non-military mission that bin Laden or his aides might assign him. This is evidence of the strong personal authority bin Laden could exert over those who swore an oath to him but also shows that he and his associates were quite happy to use people who had not sworn allegiance to them. As ever, the exact meaning of 'al-Qaeda' remains elusive. The FBI asked al-Owhali to explain, through an interpreter, what 'al-Qaeda' was. According to the FBI, he said: '[It] is not a particular place but it's a group and it stands for the base of God's support, and that bin Laden is in overall charge of al-Qaeda.'[15] With no military mission forthcoming, despite his repeated requests, al-Owhali decided to look elsewhere for his jihad.

In the summer of 1997, the Taliban met with their first serious reverse. In confused battles in and around the northern city of Mazar-e-Sharif, somewhere between 700 and 2,000 of their fighters had been killed in ultimately fruitless combat. After three years of war, the original Afghan recruits to the movement were either dead or had grown tired of the constant campaigning. There was also a limit to the number of fighters who could be produced by the medressas in Pakistan. Early batches had included youths from a range of school years and many who had long left. That resource had been exhausted.

Shortly after the Taliban had seized Jalalabad in September 1997, two of bin Laden's main protectors, Engineer Machmud and Maulvi Saznoor, had been killed in an ambush almost certainly organised by the Taliban. Bin Laden swiftly set about building a relationship with the movement. This was not as straightforward as many have made it seem and will be dealt with in greater detail in later chapters. However, it is important to stress again that, though superficially there appear to be many similarities between the hardline Islamic ideology of the Taliban and that of bin Laden and his associates, in fact in 1996 there was little beyond a literalist interpretation of Islam's core texts, an extreme orthopractic tendency and a paranoiac worldview to unite them.

In the summer of 1997, after persistent requests, bin Laden gave permission for al-Owhali to go and fight for the Taliban. After a bout of tuberculosis, during which he was cared for by a fellow Saudi called Azzam, he was posted, as most of the non-Afghan fighters were, to the frontlines north of Kabul. Al-Owhali, despite his relative lack of experience, found himself caught up in fierce combat. In one firefight, which became known as the 'C-Formation' battle, he and five other men held off much larger forces. The battle established his reputation as a soldier and shortly afterwards al-Owhali and Azzam were taken to a camp outside Kabul and, with four others, underwent a month of intensive instruction in how to run a covert terrorist cell. Their trainer was an Egyptian who had been trained by another Egyptian, probably Ali Mohammed, the former US special forces sergeant. The camp they were at is impossible to identify but appears to be one of the newer bases that bin Laden and his associates were establishing around Kabul by early 1998 to cope with an influx of volunteers. Shortly after completing his training, al-Owhali was given a false Iraqi passport in the name of Abdul Ali Latif and told to travel to the Yemen. He arrived in April 1998 and stayed in Sana'a with Ahmed al-Hazza, one of the men who fought with him in the C-Formation battle. Al-Owhali must have already known what his 'mission' was likely to entail because, for the first time in two years, he called his parents in Saudi Arabia. On 18 May, he flew back to Pakistan. In Peshawar a man called Khalid, possibly Khalid Shaikh Mohammed, briefed him on his mission. Al-Owhali was told he was to die driving a truck full of explosives into an American target in East Africa. He recorded a video claiming the strike in the name of the 'First Squad of the El Bara bin Malik division of the Liberation Army of the Army of Liberating the Islamic Holy Lands'.

On 28 May, bin Laden held a press conference at one of the Khost camps. It was the culmination of a series of press statements and interviews. Over the previous 18 months, bin Laden had seen several prominent British and American journalists, ensuring coverage on US networks and local media worldwide. Since the days of the war against the Soviets, bin Laden had always been acutely aware of the importance of the media. In 1994, he had been involved in the creation of the Advice and Reformation Committee, based in London, which appears to have been, at least in part, one of a long series of attempts to improve his image overseas. Bin Laden sent audiotapes of his lectures to be played at meetings of radicals in Pakistan. In early 1998, he sent a signed letter to an associate in Pakistan telling them to increase payments to selected journalists. He wanted to see an increase in coverage of his statements and activities, he told his correspondent.[16] Bin Laden has always been careful to tailor his statements carefully for the intended audience. Only a few days before the May 1998 press conference, he issued a signed communiqué aimed at the Pakistanis. India had just tested a nuclear device in the Rajasthani desert and the Pakistani government of Nawaz Sharif was under enormous international pressure not to respond. This, bin Laden said, should be rejected. The Muslim nations should strive to build a nuclear weapon to counter the unbelievers. Bin Laden exploited every local sensitivity with some precision, mentioning the 'hundreds of millions' of Indian Muslims threatened by the Hindu nationalist government as well as the alleged long-term hostility of New Delhi to Islamabad. He also made a rare reference to 'occupied Kashmir'.[17] Sometimes bin Laden seemed to show an incredible instinctive grasp of modern marketing techniques. Shortly after the security scare in Jalalabad forced him to move to Tora Bora, bin Laden organised the circulation of hundreds of genuine 100 Pakistani rupee notes stamped with his face and a parody of a Saudi or American request for information about him.

In February 1998, bin Laden had announced the formation of the 'World Islamic Front' and had issued a statement promising a 'Jihad against Jews and Crusaders'. In its call for the defeat of factionalism, its selective Qur'anic references, its description of the 'nations attacking Muslims like people fighting over a plate of food', there was little that was new. The focus on the US was, however, stronger. A quotation from the sword verses of the Qur'an, 'Fight and slay the pagans wherever you find them', stressed the international dimension of the cosmic struggle between good and evil that bin Laden felt was occurring.[18] The statement also included a fatwa that:

> to kill Americans and their allies – civilians and military – is an individual duty for every Muslim who can do it in any country in which it is possible to do it, in order to liberate the al-Aqsa mosque and the Holy Mosque [in Mecca] and in order for their armies to move out of all the lands of Islam, defeated and unable to threaten any Muslim.

The declaration was signed by bin Laden, al-Zawahiri in his capacity of 'emir' of Egyptian Islamic Jihad, Abu Yasir Rifa'I Ahmad Taha of the Egyptian al-Gamaa al-Islamiyya and Fazlur Rahman, 'emir' of the Jihad Movement in Bangladesh.

The press conference was theatrical. A party of journalists was brought from Pakistan over the high passes along the border and driven in circles through the hills before reaching the camp. There, local mujahideen fighters, especially recruited and armed for the occasion, put on a noisy display of firing.[19] Bin Laden sat flanked by al-Zawahiri and Mohammed Atef and reiterated his fatwa of February. Around the same time, he gave an interview to John Miller of ABC, the American news network. He explained that:

> any American who pays taxes to his government is our target because he is helping the American war machine against the Muslim nation... Terrorising oppressors and criminals and thieves and robbers is necessary for the safety of people and for the protection of their property.

He denied being a 'terrorist', saying: '[They have] compromised our honour and our dignity and dare we utter a single word of protest against the injustice, we are called terrorists.' The World Islamic Front had been formed, he said, as 'a higher council to coordinate rousing the Muslim nation to carry out jihad against the Jews and the Crusaders'. Bin Laden said that 'Westerners were under the impression that [Muslims] are butchers'. History proved that this was not the case, as the peace and protection offered to Christians living under the Ottomans in 'eastern Europe, Turkey and Albania' proved. The misapprehension was because 'the Western masses have fallen under the effect of the Jewish media', bin Laden said, emphasising once again his interest in modern communications, 'who do not broadcast on Muslims except that we butcher, and without showing that the number of us who were butchered it is the biggest number'. 'It is our duty to lead people to light,' bin Laden said and promised ABC news of a major action soon.[20]

In the early 1990s, a basic structure had been laid down by Islamic Jihad in east Africa. Several veterans of the war against the Soviets or volunteers who had been trained in the camps between 1989 and 1995 had been sent there or returned to homes in the region. They included Mohammed Odeh and Harun Fazil, who had both travelled to Somalia in 1993 and 1994. By 1996, Ubaidah al-Banshiri, the Egyptian military specialist, was at work in Africa, dealing in tanzanite and gold as well as setting up and recruiting cells.[21] Though Ubaidah was killed in a boat accident, progress was being made in setting up networks capable of major terrorist attacks. The work was not easy and was made harder by the absence of local groups who could be co-opted. Eventually, most of the bomb team 'talent' came in on direct orders of senior, and still unidentified, associates of bin Laden in Afghanistan. Khalid Shaikh Mohammed and Mohammed Atef are the prime suspects.

Al-Owhali arrived in Nairobi on 2 August. He went by taxi to a small suburban hotel, took a room and rang Pakistan. He was told he would be contacted and within an hour Harun Fazil, whose jeep he would follow less than a week later as he drove with the bomb to the embassy, arrived. Harun paid the hotel bill and the pair then drove to a house on the outskirts of the city. The next day, two men arrived. One was Azzam, the young Saudi alongside whom al-Owhali had fought in Afghanistan and alongside whom he was now supposed to die. The other was an Egyptian known as Saleh. This was Abdullah Ahmed Abdullah, the operational commander running both the Nairobi operation and the simultaneous attack planned in Dar es Salaam. He had been associated with bin Laden and Islamic Jihad since the late 1980s. The bomb had been ready for two weeks. On 4 August, al-Owhali, with Mohammed Odeh and at least one other man, drove to the embassy and videoed it. On 5 August, a fax was sent to the Cairo office of the *al-Hayat* newspaper from Egyptian Islamic Jihad, threatening that American interests would soon be attacked.[22]

On the evening of 6 August, Abdel Rahman, an Egyptian that al-Owhali had met in the al-Qaeda training camps, came to the house and readied the bomb. Then the two men who would deliver it were left alone. There was little need to discuss an escape plan or what they would do after the bombing. Telephone records obtained by the FBI show a flurry of calls towards the end of the week. At 8.44pm on 6 August, al-Owhali rang 00 967 1 200578, the former comrade in Sana'a, and spoke for a little over seven minutes. At 9.20 on the morning of 7 August, he called the Yemen again, speaking this time for three and a half minutes. Azzam called his family in Saudi Arabia. At 9.45am, the pair drove the truck away from the house and, tailing Harun in his jeep, headed into Nairobi. The bomb went off 54 minutes later. The bomb in Dar es Salaam exploded ten minutes after that. Five days later, al-Owhali was arrested at the cheap hotel he had stayed in when he had first come to Kenya, not quite four weeks previously.[23]

CHAPTER TWELVE

GLOBAL JIHAD

We drove into Kandahar around noon, just over 40 hours after leaving Kabul. It had been a long, hard, if very beautiful, journey. I had dust in my nostrils, eyes, hair and throat. I paid off my taxi and checked in to the United Nations guesthouse then, after lunch and a shower, walked the few blocks through the dusty streets, past Mullah Omar's new residence, to the foreign ministry office. The Taliban leader's home was set in a high-walled compound with painted gateposts with multi-coloured tiles set into them. It was hot and very dry; the sun was directly overhead and the shadows hardly stretched across the melting tarmac of the road, the only metalled surface anywhere south of Kabul, in front of its high gates. It was 20 August 1998, 13 days after the bombings in Nairobi and Dar es Salaam.

Saeed Rahmatullah, a young assistant at the Ministry of Foreign Affairs, spoke almost flawless English. He said he had trained as a computer programmer in Denmark. We talked about the Afghan economy. 'We are hoping to encourage private sector investment and privatisation and to utilise overseas investment to rebuild our economic infrastructure,' he said. His taste for Western management-talk did not fit his black Taliban turban and dark grey shalwar kameez. After tea, sugared almonds and mulberries, he took me across to see the governor of Kandahar, Mullah Hassan Akhund, one of the founders of the Taliban and known as a hardliner with a fiery temper. The governor was in a conciliatory mood. We discussed bin Laden. I suggested that he was unpopular with many senior Taliban figures. The governor, tapping his wooden leg against a table, was diplomatic. There was no proof of the involvement of bin Laden, who was a guest in his country, in the attacks on the two embassies, he said. No one should leap to conclusions. On the other hand, the governor said, the Taliban desired good relations with all nations. As we left, Rahmatullah asked me if I thought the Americans would bomb Afghanistan. I was genuinely surprised at the suggestion. No, I answered, they wouldn't do anything so clumsy. Reassured, Rahmatullah returned to his office and I went off to buy some fruit in the bazaar. I was, of course, completely wrong. Even as I spoke, American warships were readying themselves in the Persian Gulf. At 10.30 local time, they launched around 80 Tomahawk cruise missiles. Three destroyed a medicine factory in the Sudan, the rest struck six training camps that US intelligence had linked to bin Laden in the al-Badr complex in and around Zhawar Khili near Khost.

I was in Kandahar to see a man who was to take me, after a long vetting process, to meet bin Laden. After the strikes, the meeting, which I had set up from Pakistan weeks earlier, was obviously unlikely to happen. For the next two days, with ten other UN employees, I waited to be evacuated. In Kabul, an Italian soldier on attachment to the UN was shot dead by incensed gunmen. Elsewhere, UN offices were attacked. Though the UN, inevitably, was well equipped with large, new land-cruisers, the roads were considered too dangerous to drive even though the Pakistani border, and thus safety, was a mere 50 miles away. At Friday prayers at the main mosque in Kandahar, the governor told an excited and angry crowd that according to Pashtunwali we were, though Westerners, their guests and thus must be protected. The Taliban suggested that we only travel at prayer time when the people most likely to harm us would be otherwise occupied. And so at noon prayer on the Saturday we drove at speed through the half-empty streets, through the checkpoints and out to the airport. There was a tense wait before we saw the slim white lines of the UN plane through the heat haze that hovered greasily over the desert. A Taliban helicopter gunship wheeled overhead as we boarded and took off.

Operation 'Infinite Reach', as the missile strikes were known, was meant to send a signal. That signal was received differently by different people. The intended audiences, in rough order of priority, were the domestic public in America, bin Laden and his associates, militants worldwide and any who wanted to join their ranks. The effect on the broader Islamic world was not a major consideration. Domestically, the impact of the missile strikes was marred by their coincidence with the climax of the Monica Lewinsky affair, leading to the obvious charge that President Clinton was attempting to distract attention from his personal affairs. If the strikes were meant to intimidate bin Laden and his close associates, they failed. The attack merely confirmed to them, and others with similar views worldwide, that their conception of the world as a cosmic struggle between good and evil was the right one. For bin Laden and his followers it was clear that they had struck at *Hubal*, the grand idol that had been smashed by Mohammed at Mecca. Hubal, wounded, had tried to strike back but Allah had protected His followers from harm.

For bin Laden himself, the strikes were confirmation that his controversial decision to start targeting America before the munafiq rulers in power in the Middle East was the right one. To Islamic activists around the world, the bombings showed that bin Laden was not, as many had previously thought, merely a dilettante showboating rich kid who lived in safety in Afghanistan far from the tough struggle against the states' security apparatus in Saudi Arabia or Egypt or Jordan or Algeria. For aspirant activists all over the Islamic world, bin Laden, of whom many had not heard previously, became the focus of their ambitions. This conversion to cult status dramatically emphasised to local groups the symbolic and material advantages that alliance with him could bring. In the Islamic world more generally, shock and disgust at the terrorists' violence in east Africa was tempered with a genuine respect, admiration and identification with an undoubtedly charismatic individual who appeared to be standing up against America, a state that was widely seen as overbearing, exploitative and, at the very least, uninterested in the suffering of Muslims worldwide, if not indeed directly responsible for it. In Pakistan, Egypt and elsewhere, large demonstrations of angry young men protested against the missile strikes. Posters and stickers of bin Laden, portrayed with all the traditional iconography of an Islamic *ghazi* (holy warrior), appeared on coffee shop walls and taxi drivers' dashboards from Malaysia to the Maghreb. Donations to bin Laden, which had been falling off for several years, increased markedly. Frustrated American intelligence officers revealed that government audits in Saudi Arabia had shown that businessmen there had transferred millions of dollars through Islamic charities to bank accounts linked to bin Laden in late 1998.[1]

When he had arrived back in Afghanistan, bin Laden had realised he need to create a virtuous circle. Successful attacks would bring in recruits, money and prestige and mobilise and radicalise the 'Arab street'. His enhanced capability would then allow more successful attacks, which would accelerate the process. His aim had always been to instigate. When the situation had become sufficiently radicalised, his own interventions would be unnecessary. The Muslim youth would have cast off their illusions, embraced the true Islamic path and launched their own attacks against the tyrannical oppressors. In late 1998, that process appeared to be unfolding according to plan.

The missile strikes also helped realise the second of the objectives he had formulated back in May 1996. Then, fresh from successive expulsions from Saudi Arabia and Sudan, bin Laden had wanted a secure base. The need for a safe haven was something that men like al-Zawahiri and Mohammed Atef, with their greater experience of the practicalities of Islamic militancy, had known all along.[2] The attacks on the embassies had been a tremendous, if calculated, risk, gravely threatening bin Laden's relationship with his Taliban hosts and thus his security in Afghanistan. The missiles, however, had assured that security.

Bin Laden's relationship with the Taliban had never been easy. His Arab followers tended to look down on the Afghans as unlettered and uncivil, without the necessary experience, education and intelligence to understand contemporary politics. In a letter recovered from a computer used by senior 'al-Qaeda' figures, one complained that the Afghans 'change their ideas and positions all the time' and 'would do anything for money'.[3] For their part, Afghans, even Islamic activists, were generally resentful of the foreigners who had come to their country. Many senior Taliban figures were angry at the unwanted attention bin Laden was bringing them.[4] Among the junior ranks of the Taliban, few fighters knew who bin Laden was. A few days after the bombs in east Africa, I asked the commander of the security detail at the Ministry of Defence in Kabul for his view on the Saudi 'master terrorist'. He had no idea who I was talking about.

Shortly after the Taliban captured Kabul, bin Laden sent a deputation to Mullah Omar in Kandahar. It received a cool reception. Several months later, in early 1997, Mullah Omar asked bin Laden to move from Jalalabad to Kandahar 'for his own safety'. On the long drive down to the southeastern desert city, bin Laden spent two nights in Kabul with Mullah Mohammed Rabbani, the Taliban mayor of Kabul and the movement's deputy leader. Rabbani met bin Laden in the *hujra*, or guestroom, of his requisitioned villa in the middle-class suburb of Wazir Akbar Khan. Ignoring the huge doctrinal and cultural gulf between them, bin Laden praised the movement's achievements and offered his unconditional financial, and military, support. Bin Laden told his hosts that if they wanted him to leave so they could get international recognition then he was prepared to go. Mullah Mohammed Rabbani, head of the Kabul shura, agreed that recognition was unlikely if bin Laden remained but told his guest he should stay. 'Allah will thank us,' Rabbani said. Rabbani was 'pleased and flattered' by bin Laden, witnesses of the meeting say, and sent a relatively favourable report about the Saudi to Mullah Omar. Omar, however, remained unconvinced.[5]

Over the next months and years, bin Laden tried to repeat the tactics that had allowed him to develop a close relationship with al-Turabi in the Sudan and to build links with militant groups elsewhere. He made several large donations to the Taliban treasury and promised to fund a series of public works in and around Kandahar (including the renovation of a large residence for Mullah Omar). He organised the import of several hundred second-hand Toyota estates from Dubai to be given to the families of casualties in the ongoing fighting against the forces of Dostum, Massoud, Rabbani and the Iranian-backed Shia groups.[6] But the gifts, though gratefully accepted, failed to overcome the fundamental differences between the worldviews of the worldly bin Laden and the parochial backwoods mullahs who led the Taliban. Mullah Omar was particularly irritated by bin Laden issuing fatwas.

Omar's anger over bin Laden's fatwas reveals key differences between the radical international jihadi Salafism of bin Laden, with its fusion of Wahhabism and elements of contemporary political Islamism, and the parochial neo-traditionalism of the Taliban. For the Taliban, only the Deobandi ulema had the authority to give opinions on religious problems. For the political Islamists, most ulema are seen as stooges of corrupt and un-Islamic governments and thus can no longer be considered the guardians and interpreters of the Islamic tradition. The political Islamists, themselves largely educated in secular institutions, have adopted a far more flexible attitude to exactly who has the authority to practice ijtihad, or interpretative reasoning. Maududi, a journalist who viewed the Indian clergy as entirely corrupted by their links to the British Raj, said, 'whosoever devotes his time and energy to the study of the Qoran and the sunnah and becomes well-versed in Islamic learning is entitled to speak as an expert in matter pertaining to Islam'.[7] Hassan al-Turabi, the Sudanese ideologue whose own Islamic credentials could qualify him as a traditional alim, has said something similar: 'Because all knowledge is divine and religious, a chemist, an engineer, an economist, or a jurist are all ulema.'[8] Al-Turabi is listing the professional groups from which many political Islamists are drawn.

Though autodidacts like bin Laden can issue a fatwa, he and his audience are well aware that it will lack authority. It is better, if at all possible, to find a fully qualified alim, untainted by connections with the state, who can provide the requisite opinion or endorsement. So, when, in the summer of 2001, bin Laden was criticised by the extremists of the Takfir wal Hijra strand within militant salafism, he asked Omar Abu Omar, the Jordanian Palestinian scholar better known as Abu Qutada for a definitive fatwa. Qutada has impeccable traditional and modern salafist credentials and had acted as the in-house alim to radical groups, particularly in Algeria, from his base in northwest London since 1994. The basis for the Takfiris' criticism was that bin Laden supported, and was protected by, the Taliban who themselves were 'apostate' because they wanted to be recognised by the United Nations, a kufr organisation. Abu Qutada decided that the Takfiris were in error. His fatwa, running to 68 pages of closely written Arabic, was widely circulated in Afghanistan, Pakistan and elsewhere. It pointed out that the Takfiris were declaring 'very senior and important movements include Hamas, the Taliban, the Muslim Brotherhood in Syria and Islamic Movement in Kurdistan' as kufr. 'Not just anyone can make such a decision, only Islamic scholars,' Abu Qutada said, with no detectable irony. He then proceeded to bury the Takfiri position under an avalanche of textual references from the Qur'an, the hadith, their interpreters and sundry Islamic thinkers.[9] Qutada himself had become famous after issuing an opinion on an Algerian cleric's fatwa in 1994, in which he backed the view that the killing of women and children by militants in Algeria was justified.

Extreme literalism, and a consequently fierce demand for fatwas, is typical of many modern Islamic activists. Every group needs its own ulema. Most set up their own fatwa committee, staffed by senior members of the organisation whose task is to pronounce on the legality or otherwise of any projected action. Often the committee, its members not usually particularly learned themselves, refers to a particular authority for definitive answers. For the al-Gamaa al-Islamiyya, that authority was Sheikh Abdel Omar Rahman. He was able to counter the slew of fatwas issued against the militants by ulema from the al-Azhar establishment in Egypt in the 1980s. According to French intelligence, telephone monitoring of Islamic militant cells in 1999 and 2000 revealed that more calls were made about minor points of Islamic observance than the terrorist activity the cell members were supposed to be engaged in. Chechen fighters have requested fatwas on the legality of telling hostages they were to be released and then killing them, even after the actual murders.[10] In March 2000, the Lashkar Jihad group in Indonesia applied to Sheikh Moqbul al-Wadai'l at the al-Dammaj school in the Yemen to justify a campaign, backed by the Indonesian military, of ethnic cleansing. 'The Christians have fanned the fires of conflict,' the 70 year-old sheikh told them. 'They have massacred more than 5,000 Muslims. That is why you, honourable people of one faith, must call all to total jihad and expel all the enemies of Allah.'[11]

In April 1998, the Taliban received a high-level American delegation in Kabul. In retrospect, this was the highpoint of relations between Washington and the movement. Two months later Mullah Omar met Prince Turki al-Faisal, the veteran head of Saudi intelligence, and agreed a secret deal to hand over bin Laden for trial in Saudi Arabia for treason, a crime punishable by death. Mullah Omar asked only that a joint commission of Afghan and Saudi Arabian ulema be set up to formulate a correct legal justification for the expulsion.[12] The press conference a month earlier, during which bin Laden publicised his World Islamic Front against Jews and Crusaders, had particularly annoyed Mullah Omar, not least because he only learned of it from a report on the BBC pashto-language service.[13] In July, the Taliban leaders sent an envoy to Saudi Arabia to reaffirm the deal and replaced bin Laden's team of Arab bodyguards with Afghans loyal to Mullah Omar.[14]

But Operation 'Infinite Reach' changed everything. Three weeks after the missile strikes, two Saudi Arabian jets landed on the Kandahar airstrip. One carried Prince Turki, the other, full of commandos, was there to carry bin Laden back. In a stormy meeting, Mullah Omar reneged on his promise to hand over the Saudi dissident. Prince Turki asked Omar to remember the substantial financial assistance Riyadh had given his movement, enraging the Taliban leader, who accused the prince of doing the the Americans' dirty work for them. Though Turki returned to Saudi Arabia empty handed, Omar was still profoundly aggrieved with bin Laden too.[15] The ambivalence of the Taliban's position is amply demonstrated by a news item in their magazine, *Nida-ul-Momineen* ('The Call of the Faithful'), published from Karachi, which described yet another press conference held by bin Laden in September 1998. The headline for the article was 'bin Laden calls Mullah Mohammed Omar Leader of the Faithful and says that he will obey him as a religious duty'. The author, Maulvi Obaid-ur-Rahman, repeatedly stressed that 'the guest Mujahid' denied having any link to the east African bombings. The magazine also reproduced what it called

'Osama bin Laden's written pledge to [the] Amir-ul-Momineen'. It took the form of a traditional bayat, similar to that Jamal al-Fadl and others have said they swore to bin Laden:

> Hazrat Amir-ul-Momineen, Mujahid Mullah Mohammed Omar (May Allah protect you and keep you safe). As Salaam-o-'Alaikum.
>
> Hazrat Amir-ul-Momineen! Allah has blessed you with fresh glorious victories in... Afghanistan. This is an auspicious moment for us, to heartily congratulate you and pledge ourselves anew [to] stand by you, to render all possible assistance to you for the supremacy of Islam, for the stability of the Islamic government, for the enforcement of the law of Allah till the time that all dissension, conflicts come to an end and Allah's religion reigns supreme.
>
> On this occasion we renew our pledge too that we consider you to be our noble Amir and that obedience, allegiance and assistance to you is as compulsory upon us as it to an Amir appointed by Shariat. We invite all Muslims to render assistance and co-operation to you, in every possible way they can.
>
> Wasallam-o-'Alaikum,
>
> Your brother, Osama bin Muhammad bin Laden, 15/09/1998.[16]

The show of loyalty did little to pacify Mullah Omar. According to *al-Quds al-Arabi,* Omar made bin Laden wait several hours before seeing him when the Saudi came to offer his respects at *eid* celebrations to mark the end of Ramadan.[17]

The Taliban's solution to the problem was to have bin Laden 'disappear' and claim, fairly implausibly, they did not know where he was. Given that I was able to locate him at Farm Hadda, the former Soviet collective farm, in June 1999,[18] it is likely that US and other intelligence agencies were not fooled either. The Taliban then issued a series of announcements claiming that they had taken away bin Laden's satellite phones and that he had promised not to involve himself in any overseas activities. Bin Laden's tactics had been impeccable. The missile strikes meant that the Taliban could not expel him without appearing to be either frightened of America or stooges of the Saudi Arabians. His base, though uncomfortable, was secure. The next step would be to turn the Taliban from reluctant hosts into allies and partners.

There were other dynamics forcing the Taliban and bin Laden closer together. Towards the end of the decade, Pakistani support for their chosen proxies in Afghanistan began to wane. By 1998, there was increasing concern in Islamabad about the effect the example set by the Taliban in Afghanistan was having on Pakistan's volatile and lawless border areas and the haven they were offering to violent Pakistani groups that had begun targeting the Pakistani state. Taliban-style militias were springing up in towns and villages throughout the tribal areas and attacking video stalls and cinemas, smashing televisions, harassing 'immodest' women and teachers and pledging jihad against the government. Islamabad's involvement in Afghanistan was causing problems elsewhere too. Pakistani intelligence agencies attributed a fresh wave of sectarian violence in the Punjab to the ongoing tension between Iran and Saudi Arabia over the latter's support for the Taliban. Both states had released fresh funds to Shia and Sunni militias within Pakistan to extend the proxy war being fought in Afghanistan to Karachi and the cities of eastern Pakistan. A crackdown by Pakistan's new civilian government, Nawaz Sharif's Pakistan Muslim League, complete with new anti-terrorist courts and a government-approved policy of targeted assassination of militants, foundered on the simple fact that key individuals could flee to Afghanistan whenever they wanted.[19] The problems caused by the welcome extended by the Taliban to the Pakistani radical groups, most of whom had offices and camps in Kabul and elsewhere, was evident. It was Pakistani Sipa-e-Sahaba (SSP) militants who shot dead the Italian colonel in Kabul in August 1998 while I was waiting for evacuation from Kandahar. Conspirators involved in the January 1999 attempt by the newly formed Lashkar-e-Jhangvi group to blow up the prime minister, included a bomb-making instructor at an HUM camp in eastern Afghanistan.[20] In June 2000, the Pakistani military government gave the Taliban a list of 18 camps where sectarian militants were believed to be training. In response, the Taliban closed three.[21] Three months later, Islamabad unsuccessfully demanded the extradition of 15 militants.[22]

That Pakistanis were training in the Afghan camps was an open secret. The exact number of casualties inflicted by Operation 'Infinite Reach' is still unclear, but it appears that around 20 people were killed. The dead included three Yemenis, two Egyptians, a Saudi and around 20 Pakistanis. At an HUM press conference soon after the bombing, it was claimed that another 40 Pakistani volunteers were injured.[23] Only two of the camps hit by the missiles, Abu Jindal and al-Farooq, were exclusively used by Arabs. The rest were, to a greater or lesser extent, run by HUM.[24] But even while Islamabad was complaining vociferously to the Taliban about the sanctuary senior SSP cadres had found in Kabul and about the training camps, HUM fighters were being deployed into Kashmir along with militants from Lashkar-e-Toiba. The ISI, the Pakistani military senior command and the politicians were all keen to keep their supply of paramilitary proxies to use to destabilise India in Kashmir. In the summer of 1999, hundreds of HUM fighters were used as auxiliaries in the Kargil operation, Pakistan's most audacious border incursion for decades, which involved hundreds of Pakistani troops seizing and holding a series of key ridges well over the Line of Control and deep inside Indian-held territory.[25] The positions were only relinquished after fierce fighting and under massive international pressure. I spent several weeks on the frontlines during the conflict, saw the militants running supplies under shellfire up to the Pakistani soldiers in the forward positions and later spoke to many HUM fighters who had been deployed alongside the Pakistani Northern Light Infantry on the high peaks. Many had been trained in Afghanistan. Several had fought alongside the Taliban before being redeployed to the Indian border.

And so the Pakistani policy began to fall apart. Different groups within the country continued to relate to the Taliban in different ways. Though the civilian politicians began to move away from the increasingly radical movement, the ISI, and the Deobandi religious and political groups with whom they were now aligned, maintained their support. The result was to bring the most radical elements on all sides closer together.

For the Pakistani militants were as useful to the Taliban as they were to the hardliners in Islamabad. By the summer of 1999, the supply of fighters from the Deobandi medressas in the NWFP and Baluchistan had been exhausted and even powerful Afghan commanders with tribal authority, longstanding reputations and deep pockets, like Jalaluddin Haqqani, were finding it hard to mobilise troops. As the politicians began to get leery of the Taliban, the logistical support offered by Islamabad diminished and the HUM cadres, and others who were less directly linked to the Pakistani government, became increasingly important to the Taliban. The medressas of the Punjab, which had closer links to the harder-line sectarian groups, became prime sources of cannon fodder. In the summer of 1999, I watched scores of teenage Pakistani boys doing star jumps in clean, new white and blue shalwar kameez at a base a mile or so behind the frontlines north of Kabul. HUM, SSP and LeT cadres were increasingly used as shock troops. The close relation between the Pakistani radicals and the Taliban that had developed as a result was most obvious when an Air India jet was hijacked by HUM militants on its way out of Kathmandu and flown to Kandahar in December 1999. The hijackers demanded the release of Maulana Massoud Azhar, the cleric and founder member of the group, from prison. Five years after the first attempts to free Azhar, the HUM was trying again. This time the aim was to liberate all those who had tried to free him previously but failed. Among them was Omar Saeed Sheikh. After the Indian government had met the hijackers' demands, the Taliban helped them flee to Pakistan. Sheikh and Azhar disappeared into Pakistan too. The Taliban were swiftly being inexorably sucked into the broad international movement of international militancy, whether they liked it or not.

Along with HUM, Arabs also began to play an increasingly important role in the fighting. In the summer of 1998, it had been a group of Arabs who had forced their way up the strategic Ghorband valley, opening the way into central Bamiyan. On occasion, if required, bin Laden or Mohammed Atef would deploy, for short periods, brigades composed of highly skilled, highly motivated men drawn from the specialised training camps that they ran. The Arabs were very effective, fighting in a way that was entirely at odds with the ritualised, and largely casualty-free traditional mode of Afghan combat and the Taliban became increasingly reliant on them.

But the Arabs, whether or not connected to bin Laden, and the HUM were far from the only source of auxiliaries for the Taliban. As previously mentioned, thousands of young men from all over the Islamic world came to fight for them. One major source of troops was the Islamic Movement of Uzbekistan (IMU). The IMU had established itself in Mazar-e-Sharif and the north of Afghanistan. Like the HUM, the IMU supplied the Taliban with fighters in return for sanctuary. From around 1997, the IMU, under its charismatic leader Juma Namangani, provided around 600 fighters for each campaigning season. Their total strength was somewhere between three and four thousand.

There is no space to examine the roots of the IMU in detail here but several elements are worth noting. Many are familiar from the development of radical Islamist groups elsewhere. Central Asia's Sufi-influenced and tolerant Islam was repressed by the Soviets for ideological reasons. The Bolsheviks were well aware that a series of anti-Imperialist revolts over the previous century had taken a religious form. They themselves faced major uprisings, which were, at least in part, religious. Islam continued to be a discourse of dissent throughout central Asia under Soviet rule. On the break-up of the Soviet Union, Islam Karimov, a party apparatchik, maintained his grip on power in Uzbekistan by brutally repressing any free speech or practice of religion. He failed to deal with the appalling economic and environmental problems bequeathed by the Soviets. In the early 1990s, Salafi literature and hardline Wahhabi preachers from Saudi Arabia, Kuwait, the UAE and Pakistan flooded central Asia and easily swamped indigenous forms of worship that had been weakened by decades of repression. There had been Central Asian Muslims fighting on both sides during the Soviet war in Afghanistan. Many had been radicalised as a result. During the early 1990s, more militants were trained in Pakistan and Afghanistan, some with the help of the ISI, and their return also fuelled the radical movement in Uzbekistan and elsewhere. The IMU emerged in 1992 in one of the most deprived, and most heavily proselytised, regions of central Asia, the Ferghana valley. Its leaders publicly challenged the secular government on a religious platform. The government in Tajikistan, at odds with Karimov, gave sanctuary to the IMU allowing it critical time to grow until international pressure forced the movement to leave its bases in the anarchic northern part of the country, which the poverty-stricken Dushanbe government was unable to rule, and set up new bases in the north of Afghanistan which the Taliban had just conquered. I was given a taste of quite how incapable the Tajik leadership was of running its own country when I was held up and robbed at gunpoint by bandits three times in six hours on a road only a few miles north of the capital in 1999. Namangani first met bin Laden sometime in 1997, though it is unclear whether the IMU leader requested or was granted any aid. Namangani has his own lines of funding from the Gulf and elsewhere and may not have needed bin Laden's assistance. The IMU's cadres, who were to play a key part in the war in autumn 2001, were largely drawn from Uzbeks, Tajiks, Chechens and southwestern Chinese Uighurs but included some Arabs as well. The bulk of their strength was deployed in a series of increasingly audacious military attacks in Uzbekistan and Kyrgyzystan though, as mentioned, a sizeable force was lent to the Taliban, sometimes commanded by Namangani in person.[26]

Several factors in the rise of militancy in Uzbekistan are worth swiftly highlighting, as they are shared by so many other radical movements. These include a history of anti-imperialist religious revivalism, the influence of hardline Islamic propaganda from Saudi Arabia and other Gulf nations, simultaneous repression and severe economic problems and support for local militancy by outside powers for short-term, pragmatic reasons.

The Taliban were also pushed further towards bin Laden by the attitudes and actions of the international community. Only Pakistan, the UAE and Saudi Arabia ever recognised the Taliban as the legitimate government of Afghanistan and the country's United Nations seat remained in the hands of the shifting opposition elements that comprised Burhanuddin Rabbani's 'Northern Alliance'. This was an issue that was frequently raised by Taliban ministers in conversation and throughout the seven-year existence of the Taliban it was the question of relations with the outside world, whether represented by the USA, the UN, NGOs, Prince Turki or bin Laden, that most divided senior Talibs.[27] A faction of relative moderates, led by Mullah Mohammed Rabbani before he died of cancer in the spring of 2001, wanted a pragmatic engagement with the international community and favoured the expulsion of bin Laden. Their hope was that recognition would bring public and private international finance in its wake, allowing the development of the country and the consolidation of Taliban rule. However, their position was consistently undercut by the attitude, particularly after 1998, of the West, which made little genuine attempt at diplomatic engagement. The US Assistant Secretary of State for South Asia, Karl Inderfurth, met frequently with Taliban representatives but opted to hector them rather than actually talk to them. By February 1999, Inderfurth was telling senior Taliban ministers that they would be held responsible for bin Laden's actions. In July 1999, the US imposed unilateral sanctions to punish the Taliban for their refusal to hand over the Saudi.[28]

The critical moment for the moderates came in the autumn of 1999, when Mullah Omar agreed to ban opium. Omar had been deeply ambivalent about the move, not least because a very substantial proportion of the Taliban's revenues depended on the drugs trade, but was convinced by more moderate elements that it would gain the Islamic Emirate of Afghanistan international recognition. The ban was duly promulgated and was effectively enforced. Some Taliban leaders profited by some clever insider trading, but on the whole the ban was a genuine measure and opium production dropped from around 4,000 tonnes in 1998–9, two thirds of the world's total annual production, to a negligible amount in Taliban-held territories. However, the West ignored the move and 'security sources' briefed journalists that it was a sham, despite clear satellite evidence to the contrary. Critics pointed to the stockpiles of opium that remained, forgetting that in rural areas the storage of opium acts as an informal banking sector. To have destroyed stored opium would have meant wiping out the savings of millions of farmers with devastating results in a land already suffering under a severe drought. Instead of recognition, as the moderates had hoped, the United Nations, despite the advice of their own expert agency, the United Nations Drugs Control Programme, imposed their own sanctions to punish the Taliban for refusing to give up bin Laden.[29] Car-bomb attacks on Mullah Omar and his close aides increased their sense of isolation.

I was in Kabul when the UN sanctions came into force (a month after the opium ban was announced) and can remember the mood of sadness and disappointment among ordinary Afghans. A small demonstration was organised by the Taliban, a UN office was attacked, but overall the mood was one of resignation and resentment, not anger. Ironically, after three years of rule in Kabul, the Taliban appeared at the time to have marginally relaxed their regime. Though women outdoors still had to wear the burqa, the laws which had made it an offence to travel anywhere without a close relative were widely flouted. Children played with kites (once banned) and men had begun to wear their beards far shorter than regulation length. In Jalalabad, hundreds of covert girls' schools had opened with the tacit assent of the governor of the city.[30]

But the sanctions effectively destroyed the credibility of the moderates and the increasingly combative rhetoric on both sides allowed bin Laden to increase his influence on Mullah Omar. From the beginning of 2000, the Taliban became heavily influenced by the new ideology of which bin Laden was the most prominent, but by no means the only, proponent in Afghanistan. Having been rejected by one international community, the Taliban turned to an alternative international community, the Islamic international radical fringe, which was far more welcoming. In an interview with visiting Pakistani clerics in early 1996, Mullah Omar had described the Taliban as 'that part of the Afghan mujahideen whose purpose right from the start has been to enforce the commands of the Shariat *in the country of Afghanistan* and to banish evil and atheism *from this country*' (my emphasis).[31] The contrast with a second document, the first (and only) issue of *Islamic Emirate Magazine*, published in July 2000 in English from Kandahar, is stark. 'The real issue,' Mullah Omar says, 'is not terrorism but Islam.'

> We ourselves are victims of terrorism. Sometimes we are harassed by Russia, sometimes hit by American cruise missiles and sometimes devastated by car bombs and sabotage. Other countries constantly interfere in our internal affairs and we are subjected to international sanctions. In regards to Osama bin Laden, he was once championed

as a mujahed but now he has become a 'terrorist'. The issue is… Islam. There is a power struggle in progress between Islam and kufr.[32]

Omar goes on to explain that 'the ongoing competition for global domination is destabilizing the world, leading to persecution of entire peoples and violation of their rights to self-determination'.

In language and tone the magazine is a classic text of modern Islamic militancy. Its rhetoric is almost identical to bin Laden's own. Bin Laden had said that the 'American bombardment has only shown that the world is governed by the law of the jungle'.[33] The magazine's editorial announces that 'Afghanistan's real problem' is the United States, 'creator, director and star of its own dramatic production, known as The New World Order'. The UN, according to the editorial (and to bin Laden), is 'a pawn'. In Iraq, the magazine stresses, 'millions' have died 'due to American-sponsored policies'. Echoing bin Laden's call for radical action by a vanguard, it calls on 'the Muslims' to 'awaken from their slumber and assume their rightful position as leaders of humanity'.[34]

Increasingly, as bin Laden had hoped, the various groups in Afghanistan were beginning to unite under the very broad banner of jihadi Salafism. In January 2001, Arif Ayub, the Pakistani ambassador to Kabul, listed, in a paper that he was preparing for a conference, the various groups of 'militants' in Afghanistan. They included 500 Arabs left over from the war against the Soviets, 500 Chechens, 100 Uighurs, 100 Tajiks, 100 Bengalis, 100 Filipinos and 5,000 Pakistanis. Significantly, Ayub noted that distinguishing the different groups in Afghanistan was increasingly hard.[35] The story of John Walker Lindh, the 'American Taliban', gives an insight into the increasingly symbiotic relationship of bin Laden's group, the Taliban and Harkat-ul-Mujahideen.

Lindh grew up in Marin County, an affluent area about 20 miles north of San Francisco, California, though his family were not wealthy. Lindh suffered from an embarrassing intestinal disorder and moved from school to school. For several years he was taught at home, studying with a tutor and rarely venturing outside to play. Family life was strained with his parents' marriage in difficulties. Lindh left school at 16, developing an interest in conspiracy theories and religion and spending hours researching both on the internet. By his late teens, the tall, awkward, teenager was wearing Islamic dress and, in late 1997, converted to Islam at a small Salafi mosque near his home.[36]

Lindh became more deeply involved in Islamic activism after meeting followers of Jamaat Tablighi. In 1997, Lindh travelled to the Yemen to learn Arabic at a secular language centre but dropped out to study at a Salafi university. Though Lindh's lawyers deny that he travelled there, it is possible that he found his way to Sheikh Moqbul al-Wadai'I's medressa at al-Dammaj in the north of the country. By December 2000, Lindh was in Pakistan, at the Saudi-funded Iltimas' Madrasah al-Arabia in the North West Frontier Province.[37] By May 2001, he was in a HUM training camp in northwestern Pakistan where, according to his US indictment, he asked to fight for the Taliban. He was sent across the border to Kabul where he presented himself at the HUM office with a letter of introduction.[38] Lindh spoke Arabic and no Urdu and had no combat experience, so the HUM passed him on to the Arabs. He travelled to a guesthouse in Kandahar and was sent to a training camp west of the city, described as an 'al-Qaeda facility' in the indictment. There he underwent the standard basic battlefield course and in June or July met bin Laden personally who thanked him and other volunteers for 'taking part in the jihad'. Obviously taking an interest in an American with an American passport, Mohammed Atef approached Lindh shortly afterwards and asked if he was interested in travelling outside Afghanistan 'to conduct operations against the USA and Israel'. Given the timing, it is possible that Atef was considering him for some role in the September 11th attacks. Lindh declined in favour of going to the frontlines with the Taliban, which he did, sometime in August 2001, travelling with a group of around 150 'non-Afghan' fighters to Takhar in the northeast, where his group was placed under the control of Abdul Hady, an Iraqi.[39]

Bin Laden, as always, was doing everything he could to encourage the growing symbiosis between the groups. By March 2001, Mullah Abdul Jalil, the Taliban's deputy foreign minister, was buying boxes of antacids for him when in Dubai.[40] Mullah Omar's decision to destroy the huge statues of the Buddhas of Bamiyan, built in the third and fourth centuries, appears to have been taken after a concerted lobbying campaign by foreign militants inside Afghanistan supported by a series of fatwas from Wahhabi clerics in Saudi Arabia.[41] Pakistani diplomats, in confidential memos to Islamabad found after the fall of Kabul, lamented that the Taliban seemed addicted to 'international jihad'.[42] For his part, bin Laden had embarked on a massive programme of arms buying. Dealers in Landi Kotal, the rough and scruffy town at the top of the Khyber Pass, began receiving large orders for guns and ammunition, which were then trucked (with ISI consent) into Afghanistan. In June, with stocks in the tribal areas exhausted, further purchases were made from dealers in Peshawar. According to one dealer, men linked to bin Laden were offering 200,000 Pakistani rupees for Stinger missiles. One dealer sold $800,000-worth of weapons, mainly AK47s, which were sent over the border and dumped at a site near Jalalabad.[43]

Bin Laden and his associates had one final sweetener for the Taliban. Sometime in May 2001, a polite letter in bad French was typed, probably by al-Zawahiri, on a computer later found in an office in Kabul by looters during the fall of the city. It was addressed to Ahmed Shah Massoud, the military leader of the Afghan opposition. The writer had worked for 97 minutes, according to the computer's internal record, then printed out his work. It was a request on behalf of 'one of our best journalists, Mr. Karim Touzani' for an interview.[44]

On 9 September, Massoud agreed to see two French-speaking Arabs who had come to interview him. Both were in fact Tunisian, not Moroccan as they claimed. They were carrying stolen Belgian passports, one in the name of 'Karim Touzani'. The cameraman was wearing a belt full of explosives. He and his target died almost instantly, though Massoud's aides only confirmed their commander's death later in the week.[45]

CHAPTER THIRTEEN

THE MILLENNIUM PLOT

It was 6pm on 14 December 1999 and the last car, a rented Chrysler 300, had just driven off the Coho ferry from Victoria, British Columbia, Canada and drawn up at the customs checkpoint at Port Angeles, Washington, United States of America. As Diana Dean, an American customs official, questioned the driver, a young Algerian who gave his name as Benni Norris, she noticed that he was sweating despite the chill and that his hands were shaking. When Dean and her colleagues opened the boot of the car they found out why. Where the spare wheel should have been were four timing devices, 118 pounds of urea crystals, 14 pounds of sulphate powder and 48 ounces of nitroglycerine. The driver's real name was Ahmed Ressam, he was 33 and he was on his way to plant a bomb in Los Angeles International airport.[1]

Following Ressam's arrest, thousands of FBI agents were assigned to the 'Borderbom' investigation. With less than two weeks until the Millennium, with millions worldwide planning to attend events that would be easy targets for terrorists, the pressure to roll up any broader network linked to Ressam was huge. In fact, Ressam was not the first arrest to be made of conspirators in the so-called 'Millennium plot', a series of attacks linked to 'al-Qaeda' and bin Laden timed to coincide with the end of 1999. On 30 November, police and paramilitary security forces in Amman, Jordan had raided several addresses around the city and on its outskirts and arrested 16 people who, officials said, had hoped to machine-gun tourists at biblical sites in the Middle East and to blow up a huge hotel in central Amman full of Jewish and American tourists and pilgrims. Ressam himself had hoped, evidence indicated, to kill hundreds with a large bomb on the crowded concourse of Los Angeles airport. Later it would become clear that other attacks too had been planned by Islamic militants around the world to coincide with the end of 1999. One, an attempted attack on the USS *The Sullivans* on 3 January off the coast of the Yemen, failed when the bombers loaded the speedboat they hoped to ram into the ship with so many explosives that it sank.

The details of the 'Millennium plot' show, as American investigators said at the time, 'the modern face of global Islamic terrorism and how it functions'.[2] In their conception, planning and execution the attacks were very different from the bombings of the eastern African embassies. The attacks in Nairobi and Dar es Salaam were directly organised by bin Laden's close aides using a small number of long-term associates of the group and teams of specialists flown in for the occasion. The 'hands-on' involvement of men like Mohammed Atef in Afghanistan and the careful grooming of key individuals like al-Owhali was made necessary by the lack of an operational structure on the ground in east Africa and by the lack of trained volunteers. But the Millennium attacks in Jordan and California reveal a different, and far more dangerous, pattern of operation. Understanding the genesis of the plot and its attempted execution is of enormous importance in understanding the threat posed by modern Islamic terrorist violence today.

Those involved with the plot were acting on their own initiative. They were not even part of established and known local Islamic militant groups. Most importantly, they had initiated the contact with 'al-Qaeda hardcore', deciding to approach them for help with training, funding and, as their plans moved towards completion, to ask permission to claim the bombings in bin Laden's name. Indeed, it appears unlikely that any of the plotters in the American or Jordanian cells ever met bin Laden. They were not acting on the orders of bin Laden or his associates, they were merely using the facilities he was able to provide to execute the plans and projects they themselves had conceived.

Ahmed Ressam was born on 19 May 1967 in the small town of Bou Ismail, on the Mediterranean coast west of Algiers. His father, Belkacem Ressam, had fought in the war of independence against the French from 1954 to 1962 and, as something of a war hero, had been rewarded with a job as a government driver. The family were not wealthy but did not live in hardship. There was always food on the table, even if they only ate meat once a week.[3]

Though Belkacem Ressam prayed five times a day and went to mosque on Friday, he did not demand that his five sons did likewise. His wife and two daughters wore the *hijab* outside the home, but the family's Islam was cultural and unpoliticised. Belkacem Ressam had seen his fight against the French colonial regime in typical anti-imperialist, Third-Worldist, leftwing terms. The war had involved bombings, assassinations and the systematic terrorising of civilians by all involved.[4] 'We are a revolutionary family,' said one of Ressam's brothers when asked by a reporter to explain Ahmed's involvement in terrorism.[5]

Belkacem Ressam hoped that his son would be able to take the tough qualifying examinations that would get him a free university education. A college degree would mean entry to Algeria's small middle class. However, though Ressam was a lively and intelligent boy with a talent for mathematics, ill health held him back at school. He was sent for treatment in Paris, where he read the French books that were banned at home describing how the Algerian military had seized power in the years immediately after independence. On his return, he struggled to catch up at school and failed the university entrance exam. Applications to the police and military security were refused on account of Ressam's lack of qualifications.[6]

It was a bad time to be a young man out of a job in Algeria, possibly the worst for 40 years. Since gaining independence in 1962, the leaders of the Front de Libération Nationale and the senior Algerian military command had relied on oil revenues to prop up a Soviet-style one-party state. For the first 15 years, socialist and nationalist rhetoric, combined with the legitimacy earned by key regime figures during the war against the French, kept resentment at the lack of democracy and real development in the country in check. The spike in oil prices in the early 1970s allowed the Algerian government, struggling with a centrally planned economy, to buy cheap commodities from overseas. These, and substantial Soviet aid, bolstered the regime. Fierce state repression also helped. Though a group of Algerian ulema had set up a salafist group in 1934, Islamic radicalism or revivalism had played only a small role in the war against the French.[7]

By the mid 1980s, this construct was beginning to fall apart. The collapse of the price of oil in 1986 had a devastating effect on the government's budget. The profound economic problems of the country, caused and compounded by population increase, a massive influx to the cities, unplanned and inadequate urban development, corruption and unemployment, particularly among the graduates of the newly expanded education system, undercut any faith in the nationalist, socialist ideology of the regime.[8] In 1988, Algeria was wracked by huge street protests, which forced the regime to call the first elections since independence. The original impulse of the demonstrators was anger at the manifest failings of the regime and was not articulated in Islamic terms. However, the Front Islamique du Salut (FIS), formed in 1989 to unite Algeria's disparate Islamist groups, assumed the leadership of the protestors on the streets.[9] Ahmed Ressam had not been out throwing rocks though. His father had used his savings to open a small coffee shop next to the main mosque in Bou Ismail, and Ahmed worked there, getting up at 4.30am, working through to noon and spending his small earnings on designer jeans and visits to nightclubs. He drank, smoked hashish and went to bars and nightclubs. He had long since stopped praying.[10]

The whole range of modern political Islamic thought was represented in the FIS leadership. There were members from hardline groups who followed Qutb and had waged a desultory terrorist campaign against the regime between 1982 and 1987 alongside moderate political Islamist groups, closer to Maududi, whose aim was to Islamicise the state gradually and without violence. Until the late 1980s, the numbers of Algerian Islamists had been small, the groups had been wracked by infighting and their role in political and cultural life had been limited. However, the internal weaknesses of the FIS were obscured by the huge wave of support they were able to ride. Though the government had copied Egypt, Saudi Arabia, Afghanistan and other states and attempted to build itself a tame, state-sponsored ulema by creating an Islamic university (complete with imported scholars from Egypt's al-Azhar) in 1985, the Islamists, with a message that was 'simple, demagogic and powerful', easily outflanked the regime's religious leaders. In 1990, the FIS swept to power in a majority of the country's local authorities. They were helped by excellent organisation and substantial funds from Saudi Arabia.[11] The new mayors and municipal councillors were largely Islamist intellectuals, teachers and professors, but they were backed by, in addition to the urban poor who had turned out to vote in unprecedented numbers, shopkeepers and small businessmen.[12]

But in the aftermath of their victory at the polls, moderate elements with FIS found it difficult to resist the demands of the more radical elements. Thousands of Algerians had fought alongside the mujahideen in Afghanistan and, with the war against the Soviets over, by 1989 had begun to return to their own countries.[13] Suddenly, groups of Afghan veterans in combat fatigues, beards and *pakols*, the round woollen hats favoured by some mujahideen groups, began appearing at the head of demonstrations.[14] Soon FIS councils had ordered female municipal employees to wear the veil, had shut shops selling alcohol or videos and cafes that allowed gambling, banned the hugely popular *rai* music which fused local traditions with Western pop and had segregated public bathing. Moves were also made to boost the prestige of Arabic at the expense of French, seen as the language both of colonialism, the disgraced regime and its elite stooges, and of Western cultural and economic neo-imperialism. In Bou Ismail the moderate imam of the main mosque was forced out. Growing confrontations, sparked by the government's attempts to gerrymander electoral constituencies in the run-up to national elections, led to the army declaring a state of emergency and arresting the senior FIS leadership. The movement was virtually decapitated. In fact, the army had merely opened the field for the real militants. The army's actions had convinced moderate Islamists the electoral process was a farce. The Afghan veterans, some of whose travel to Algeria had been paid for by bin Laden, had been against any concession to the kufr regime at all. In November 1991, a group of army conscripts at a remote border post were brutally killed by Afghan veterans. Despite the background of rising violence and their own lack of direction, the FIS won the first round of elections to the national legislative assembly (though with markedly reduced support from a year previously) a month later and looked set to do well in the crucial second round too. The army promptly cancelled the second round of the ballot and dissolved the FIS entirely. Thousands of militants, activists and elected FIS officials were interned in camps in the Sahara. Over the next five years 100,000 people would die in a civil war of horrific savagery. This was not a war in which neutrality was an option. As bombings, strikes on defence installations and attacks on civilians, journalists and intellectuals multiplied, the security forces retaliated with detentions, executions and widespread torture. On 5 September 1992, 25-year-old Ressam got up at dawn, said goodbye to his brother, sleeping nearby in the room they shared, took a bus to Algiers and then a ferry to Marseilles.[15]

For the next 18 months, Ressam drifted among the illegal expatriate community in France. When the French authorities caught up with him he fled, with a fake passport, to Canada where he claimed political asylum on the (false) basis that he had been tortured by the Algerian military.[16] Though issued with a deportation order, Ressam was able to stay in Canada, supporting himself through petty theft, credit card fraud and welfare payments. Targeting foreigners proved especially lucrative, not least because certain men in the Algerian community in Montreal were willing to pay hundreds of dollars for stolen passports.

One was a 35-year-old shop owner called Fateh Kamel, who was among a group of Algerian immigrants that congregated at the Assuna Annabawiyah mosque in Montreal. The mosque had been built in 1993 with money raised in the local community and from wealthy donors in the Gulf. Though Algerian Islamic tradition is tolerant and pacifistic, the mosque, owing to the origin of the funds for its construction, tended towards a strongly Salafist brand of Islam. The mosque runs a website which has links to fatwas by senior Saudi clerics and is typical of the tens, if not hundreds, of thousands of mosques built with Saudi money around the world.[17] Its bookstore, like that of many similar establishments, sold tapes and videos of fighting by 'mujahideen' and atrocities against Muslims in Bosnia, Chechnya and in other theatres of 'jihad'. Fateh Kamel regularly attended the mosque, and so did an older man in his mid forties called Abderraouf Hannachi. Both Kamel and Hannachi had spent time in Afghanistan. Hannachi told the younger men in the group about fighting the Soviets and described how he had been trained, at Khaldan camp, in light and heavy weapons and demolition techniques. Kamel had his own stories to tell.

Kamel's and Hannachi's relationship with Ressam is archetypal. A brief survey of the process of the induction of young disaffected men into violent Islamic militancy shows that often, though not always, contact with a more senior man at a critical point has acted as a catalyst, turning a vague aspiration towards 'jihad' into a definitive course of action. Typically such men are in their late thirties or forties and are veterans of the war against the Soviets. Some established themselves, often by gaining political asylum, in the West in the years after the end of that conflict, fleeing the repression of Islamic movements in their own lands, such as Algeria and Egypt, in the early 1990s. Others managed to hold on in their homelands despite the attention of domestic security services. Many went on to be involved in the conflicts in Bosnia or Chechnya. Often such men hold positions of respect within the social groupings centred on the more radical mosques that exist to cater for a minority of expatriate Muslims.

The exact mechanics of the role such men play varies. In some instances the older men simply acted as facilitators for people who were already highly motivated. Often it was the stories told by other young men, friends or acquaintances or fellow-worshippers at a particular mosque who had themselves returned from 'jihad' that were the inspiration, as in the case of Mohammed Rashid Daoud al-Owhali. Sometimes, though more rarely than imagined, a far more proactive recruitment was carried out and young, impressionable individuals, often with significant personal problems, were, if not indoctrinated, then certainly steered, gradually and carefully, towards a particular course of action. Usually the older man who did this had connections, sometimes directly, sometimes through a third party, with senior figures who were close to the leadership of either national or, in the case of bin Laden, transnational, radical Islamic groups. These contacts were forged in the Afghan war, in the camps in Pakistan, Afghanistan and, to a lesser extent, Sudan, or in Bosnia earlier in the 1990s.

Abderraouf Hannachi and Fateh Kamel were both connected to the Groupe Islamique Armée (GIA), though exactly how closely is unclear. The emergence of the GIA as the dominant group in Algeria was far from inevitable. A lengthy hiatus followed the banning of the FIS in 1992 as those moderates who were not interned in the Saharan camps or in prisons tried to organise themselves. It took nearly two years, but by 1994 the Armée Islamique de Salvation (AIS) had been formed. Though led by the middle-class intellectuals who had provided the bulk of the FIS's senior ranks, many fighters were simply shopkeepers or labourers told by their leaders that if they remained at home they would be arrested. The AIS hoped that a discriminate use of violence in the short term would force the regime to make radical changes and allow the FIS back into the political process. At first they were unarmed but as weapons, many seized or sold from army stores, became available, violence became endemic and there was no way they could return to their homes.[18] The GIA, by contrast, was composed of scores of 'groupuscules' of Afghan Arabs and a number of long-term radical Islamic activists who, following Azzam and Qutb, believed in total war against a kufr and munafiq government. They had been active since 1989 or 1990 and were sufficiently well organised and equipped to exploit the gap left when the FIS cadres were rounded up. The GIA, who were more of an alliance of different factions than a coherent group, were popular among poor, young, urban and rural men and swiftly established themselves in and around Algiers. Led by a series of 'emirs', all in their twenties and all killed in swift succession, the GIA's tactics were horrendously brutal and the group swiftly eclipsed the AIS in efficacy, violence and notoriety. Events in Algeria thus fitted the pattern emerging elsewhere of the more moderate, domestically orientated political Islamism (older both ideologically and in the actual age of its cadres) being supplanted by the newer, younger (in both senses), internationalised, more violent jihadi Salafism.

Between 1994 and 1995, their campaign was exported to France with a series of bombings on the Paris Metro and the hijacking of an Air France airbus, possibly with the intention of flying it into the Eiffel Tower. The former colonial power was a target both according to the new internationalist doctrine and for local domestic reasons, as the French were widely felt to be propping up the corrupt and hated military regime.

There is little evidence that bin Laden was involved in any meaningful way in any of the GIA's activities. The GIA had an office in Khartoum and were in contact with bin Laden and his Islamic Jihad associates while in the Sudan.[19] Algerian security services insist that bin Laden was instrumental in arming the GIA in its early days. However, this conflicts with accounts from former GIA fighters who say that the GIA leadership asked bin Laden if financial assistance would be possible in 1994 but were unhappy with the degree of ideological and operational control that the Saudi demanded as a condition for any aid.[20] One activist in Khartoum at the time says that bin Laden dispatched an emissary to talk to groups within the GIA about a possible alliance at the time. He got a very hostile reception and barely escaped with his life. The activist subsequently witnessed a GIA deputation, led by a Libyan called Abu Basir, arriving at bin Laden's house and threatening to kill the Saudi if he contacted any of their cadres again.[21] However, it is certainly possible that individual activists within individual GIA groups made their own contacts with bin Laden himself or his associates. Tracts published and videos circulated by the GIA or their mouthpieces in London show the similarity of their language and ideas.[22]

Fateh Kamel appears to have liaised with several significant GIA figures within Algeria. In France, Kamel led a small group of Muslim militants, many of them white French converts who had been radicalised during visits to Bosnia, in a series of violent robberies, used to finance arms purchases and to create false ID documents.[23] The documents were needed to facilitate the movement of Islamic militants transiting France and to send new recruits to Afghanistan and Pakistan for training.[24] The group's activities culminated in a bomb plot that was discovered by police in 1996. Kamel, who fled to Canada, had himself fought in Bosnia and had been trained in Afghanistan in the early 1990s, when he met Abu Zubaydah, the young Palestinian aide of bin Laden who had been acting as coordinator and gatekeeper for several of the training camps from a base in Peshawar.[25] Abderraouf Hannachi also knew Abu

Zubaydah and was close to senior GIA figures in Algeria. Ressam appears to have been one of those recruits who needed little persuasion. The example of 'friends' coming back from Afghanistan with tales of Khaldan motivated him to travel himself, he later told a court. Hannachi contacted Abu Zubaydah and made the necessary arrangements. Ressam, with several other Canadian recruits, arrived in Peshawar in March 1998 and was sent to Khaldan camp.[26]

Ressam spent six months in the camp, with around 30 other Algerians as well as Yemenis, Saudis, Swedes, Frenchmen, Turks and Chechens. Each nationality formed its own group, led by an emir, and stuck together for tuition in light weapons, infantry tactics, sabotage, urban warfare, assassination and explosives, all based on the now-familiar syllabus. A fatwa from Abdel Omar Rahman, the Egyptian blind sheikh imprisoned in America, was circulated but bin Laden did not appear. Over the six months of the training, Ressam and his Canadian Algerian friends discussed possible plans. Their 'emir' was Haider Abu Doha, an experienced and committed Algerian activist in his mid thirties whose real name is probably Amar Mahklulif. Ressam, his friends and Abu Doha talked about launching an operation in America, possibly against an airport, timed for the turn of the Millennium. Other groups in Khaldan discussed launching operations in Europe, the Gulf and Israel. Funds were a problem and Ressam suggested robbing banks. Abu Doha told him that finances could be arranged.[27]

In September 1998, Ressam was told by the camp administrator that he had been selected to go to Darunta, the former Hizb-e-Islami camp just east of Jalalabad, for more specialised training. There, in a six-week course, Ressam learned about bomb-making. An exercise book I saw in Darunta and dated 1998 gives an idea of what Ressam learned in the camp. The 100-page book is full of lecture notes by a Turkish recruit and describes various modes of assassination, the use of different types of bullets and silencers, buying and selling arms, injunctions on 'listening to teachers', car bombs and truck bombs, intelligence gathering and surveillance discipline. At one point the student had scribbled down 'important advice':

> 1. help each other 2. during lessons listen carefully 3. give the right answer. If we don't know we say we don't know 4. don't be afraid of making mistakes 5. be patient when things get difficult 6. if one person makes a mistake the whole group pays for it.[28]

Darunta was also known as the base where chemical weapons research was carried out. Ressam watched as one of the instructors, almost certainly an Egyptian called Midhat Mursi, *aka* Abu Khabab, experimented with a crude form of cyanide gas, killing a dog in a box.[29] In December 1999, talking to the Pakistani journalist Rahimullah Yusufzai, bin Laden would say: 'Acquiring weapons for the defence of Muslims is a religious duty. If I have acquired these weapons I am carrying out a duty. It would be a sin for Muslims not to try and possess weapons that would prevent the infidel front inflicting harm on Muslims.'[30] There is no evidence that bin Laden or any of his associates were successful, though their interest in developing chemical, biological and even nuclear weapons is clear and was genuine. In a camp in Khost in November 2001, I found a stack of photocopied manuals on chemical and biological 'nasties' that had been downloaded from American rightwing websites. Many other journalists found similar material, some indicating an interest in nuclear armaments. A series of contacts between bin Laden and his aides, particularly Abu Khabab, and Pakistani scientists with nuclear know-how also indicates an effort to develop a capability in radiological devices or 'dirty bombs'.

In December 1998, as their training neared an end, the Algerian students began discussing how to get back to Canada to put their plan to attack the US into action. Their supervisor, Abu Doha travelled to Kandahar to meet bin Laden and, in the words of the US government complaint against him, to 'discuss co-operation and coordination between bin Laden's terrorist network... and a group of Algerian terrorists whose activities he coordinated and oversaw'.[31] The wording here is critical. Abu Doha was seeking out bin Laden to obtain funds or other resources for the plan that the Algerian students had concocted. Though Abu Zubaydah was running the administration of the camps, the plan for the bombing did not originate with him, with bin Laden or with any of bin Laden's close associates. It was the volunteers' own. In early 1999, Ressam went to see Abu Zubaydah again and asked him to arrange his return to Canada. Abu Doha, true to his word, had sourced some funds, though hardly a huge sum, probably from bin Laden. Ressam was given $12,000 by an Algerian instructor in Darunta, a sample of a hexamine booster for explosives, his Western clothes and a ticket home.[32]

The Jordanian part of the Millennium plot demonstrates many of the same elements as the Canadian component. Neither group was aware of the other's plans. Indeed, the only people who were aware of the various groups' attacks were bin Laden and a small number of his close associates. Testimony from a variety of sources makes clear that Abu Zubaydah knew of the schemes. It is reasonable to surmise that Mohammed Atef, who ran bin Laden's 'military operations', and Ayman al-Zawahiri knew too.

In part this was due to the nature of the attacks. Of the thousands of volunteers making their way to Khaldan camp, only a few were selected by the camp emir for further training at sites such as Darunta or al-Farooq. Of these 'graduate students', even fewer would have their requests for logistical support for the plans they had formulated granted by bin Laden or Atef. As each group made their requests separately, only a handful of individuals were in a position to see the larger picture.

The Jordanian cell's plans dated back to May 1996, when two Palestinian Islamic activists, both veterans of Afghan training camps, met in a Palestinian refugee camp in Syria. One, 33-year-old Khadar Abu Hoshar, had fought against the Soviets. He impressed the younger, Raeed Hijazi, then 26, who, though born in California in relative privilege, had grown up in Saudi Arabia. Hijazi later told prosecutors that he had become involved in radical Islam while attending a mosque and cultural body, funded with Gulf money, called the Islamic Assistance Organisation, while studying at university in Sacramento, California. Through the mosque he had made contacts that had allowed him to travel to Khaldan camp around 1994, where he had had basic training. At the time of their meeting, Abu Hoshar was trying to raise a group of militants in Jordan, where there had been a series of attacks by Islamic radicals since the beginning of the 1990s, who might be willing to carry out attacks on Israeli and American interests in the country. Hijazi had been inducted into the group. However, the pair's plans hit an early snag. At the end of 1996, Abu Hoshar returned to Jordan and was promptly arrested and jailed for 18 months. Hijazi fled back to America where he picked up work as a taxi driver in New York. When Abu Hoshar was released, he contacted Hijazi; the pair resurrected their plan and set off through Jordan, Syria and the Lebanon looking for recruits. They found several people willing to take part, including some previous associates from Afghanistan. Many of the new recruits, however, needed tuition. Abu Hoshar asked one of them, an Algerian militant, if he knew anyone who could arrange training for them. The man contacted Abu Zubaydah in Peshawar. This was the first contact between the group and anyone close to bin Laden. Abu Zubaydah responded with a fax outlining his conditions for assisting the Jordanians. Contacts had to be through one person who could vouch for the people being sent, he said, and nobody should be coerced into missions.[33]

No one travelled to Afghanistan immediately. For the first six months of 1999, Hijazi worked at accumulating the material he needed for several huge bombs. The group rented a house in a poor suburb of Amman, enlarged a basement to act as a makeshift laboratory and began experimenting with different explosives. They followed instructions contained in the 'Encyclopedia of Jihad', the 11-volume document compiled in Peshawar with bin Laden's financial assistance in the early 1990s. It had subsequently been carefully transferred to a computer disk by a Jordanian-American activist based in Pakistan called Khalil Deek and by 1999 was circulating widely in radical Islamic circles. In June 1999, Abu Hoshar called Abu Zubaydah in Pakistan to tell him that he was sending Hijazi and three other men for training. Hijazi, who was coming to Afghanistan for a specific purpose and had no time to waste bolstering the Taliban, skipped the basic infantry training in Khaldan and went straight to al-Farooq camp where he was taught advanced explosive techniques. On his way out of Afghanistan, after several weeks of tuition, he met Abu Zubaydah again and took a bayat of loyalty to bin Laden, which he was told authorised him to act 'anywhere in jihad territories' in the name of his 'emir'.

As Raeed Hijazi was undergoing his specialist bomb-making training in Afghanistan, Ahmed Ressam was trying to sort out the details of the scheme which bin Laden, in very general terms, had authorised six months previously. Buying the electrical components for a bomb was easy enough, but he needed manpower. Of the five-man team who had been in Darunta with him only he had made it back to Canada. The rest had either been arrested and detained or were missing; even Fateh Kamel had been arrested, in Jordan in April. In their place, he recruited three of his friends who had expressed an interest in going to Afghanistan or fighting in Chechnya.[34] Then he called Pakistan and spoke to a senior figure he knew had access to bin Laden.[35] Ressam wanted him to get bin Laden's blessing for the attack he was planning. He wanted to credit it to 'the sheikh'. Then, on 8 November, he called Abu Doha in London, asking for arrangements to be made to fly him out to Algeria after the bombing.[36] On 19 November, Ressam hired a motel bungalow on the southern outskirts of Vancouver and began mixing explosives. Just over three weeks later, he loaded the timers, the urea and the nitroglycerine into the back of a hire car and headed towards the ferry to America.

In Jordan, events were moving fast too. On 30 November, Abu Zubaydah called Abu Hoshar in Amman and told him that 'the time for waiting was over'. Acting on a tip-off, the Jordanian security services intercepted the call. The tip-off came from Khalil Deek, the computer expert who was close to Abu Zubaydah. He was in fact a Jordanian agent. Within hours of the call, the Jordanians had raided a series of addresses in the capital and on its outskirts and had 16 people in custody. They found the explosives on 5 December.[37] Hijazi had been arrested by Syrian authorities a month earlier. He was later sentenced to death but cleared of 'membership of al-Qaeda'. Khalil Deek was arrested in Pakistan, extradited to Jordan, was released and disappeared.

On the day of Ahmed Ressam's arrest at the Coho ferry, Michael Sheehan, the US State Department Coordinator for Counter-Terrorism, called Wakil Ahmed Muttawakil, the Taliban foreign minister, in Kandahar. Through an Arabic translator, Sheehan told Muttawakil that America would hold the Taliban responsible for the acts of bin Laden. 'If there's a criminal in your basement and you are aware that he has been conducting criminal activities from your house, even if you are not involved in the crimes you are responsible for them,' Sheehan said. 'In fact, your willingness to give him refuge makes you complicit in his actions, past and present.'[38]

CHAPTER FOURTEEN

THE HOLY WAR FOUNDATION

They had gathered in the shade of the plane trees to celebrate a wedding. Beyond were the fields of wheat and opium, dusty hills and then the dry wastes of the desert stretching away to the horizon. The bride, a girl of 14, sat demurely with the women. The bridegroom sat with the men. He was Mohammed bin Laden, 19 years old and Osama bin Laden's second son. He was marrying the daughter of Mohammed Atef, Osama bin Laden's military chief and second in command.

The service was short and afterwards the smiling father of the groom said a few words. Then he read out a poem he had composed for the occasion:[1]

> A destroyer, even the brave fear its might,
>
> It inspires horror in the harbour and in the open sea,
>
> She sails into the waves
>
> Flanked by arrogance, haughtiness and false power,
>
> To her doom she moves slowly,
>
> A dinghy awaits her, riding the waves.

The reference was obvious to all who were listening. Only three months earlier, on 12 October 2000, a small powerboat loaded with explosives had rammed the *USS Cole*, an American destroyer, as it waited to refuel off the harbour at Aden in Yemen. Seventeen American sailors and two bombers, who stood upright and saluted as their boat ploughed into the side of the warship, were killed. Within hours, American FBI teams had arrived in Yemen to conduct an investigation.

There were a number of suspects. Even in 2000, after six years of unified government and a presidential election, much of the Yemen, particularly the areas on the Saudi border, remained a violent, anarchic place where authority lay with tribal sheikhs and arms were plentiful. Attempts by the government to force out the Islamic extremists, both the militants training in the camps in the north of the country and the ideologues who ran the Wahhabi schools such as that which had attracted John Walker Lindh, had met with fierce resistance. In 1999, Egyptian Islamic Jihad and al-Gamaa al-Islamiyya, the Algerian GIA, the Libyan Fighting Group and Hamas, all had a presence in the country.[2] Hundreds of Yemenis were making their way each year to Afghanistan to fight with bin Laden, the HUM, the Taliban or other groups.

In December 1998, an armed group calling itself the Islamic Army of Aden-Abyan had kidnapped 16 Western tourists, including 12 Britons, two Australians and two Americans, in southern Yemen. Four of the tourists died during a rescue attempt by security forces. The Yemeni government linked the group, who had been running a training camp in the Yemen for several years, to bin Laden but provided no evidence to substantiate the claim. One link, however, might have been Osama al-Masri, the deputy commander of the kidnappers, who was a member of Egyptian Islamic Jihad. He was, however, killed in the shoot-out. In fact, the man that the leader of the group, Abu Hassan al-Midhar, phoned barely an hour after seizing the tourists to discuss the successful attack was not bin Laden but Abu Hamza al-Masri, a preacher at Finsbury Park mosque in north London.

As well as linking him to the kidnapping, Yemen also accused Abu Hamza of having sent 10 young men from Britain, including his son and a stepson, to attack British and American targets in Aden. (He denies both charges.) Six of the men were arrested in December 1998, before any attacks took place. According to the Yemenis, the Islamic Army then kidnapped the tourists in the hope of securing the men's release.[3] Abu Hassan was executed in late 2000.

Following the *USS Cole* attack, Yemeni police arrested six men, all veterans of the Afghan war. The suspected leader of the cell was Jamal al-Badawi, who reportedly told Yemeni investigators that he was trained in bin Laden's 'Jihad Camp no1' in Afghanistan (possibly Jihad Wal camp in al-Badr or one of the new camps that were built to cater for the influx of recruits after the 1998 embassy bombings and the missile strikes) and had also fought in Bosnia in 1994. Al-Badawi said he was acting on telephone instructions from a man called Mohammed Omar al-Harazi, a Saudi-born Yemeni based in Dubai, whom he hadn't seen for ten years.[4] Al-Harazi, whose real name is Abd al-Rahim al-Nashiri, met bin Laden during the war against the Soviets and is suspected of having recruited 'Azzam', the man who died when he detonated the truck bomb outside the Nairobi embassy and who is thought to have been his nephew. Yemeni investigators believe al-Harazi spent time in Aden between the attempt on the *USS The Sullivans* and the *USS Cole* and then left shortly before the bombing.[5] The departure before the attack by the senior commander, the use of a small cell, the careful surveillance and preparation, are all hallmarks of attacks orchestrated by those experienced militants connected to the 'al-Qaeda hardcore', at least according to the *modus operandi* taught in the Afghan camps.

There is other evidence linking bin Laden to the attack, though much of it is circumstantial. Bin Laden has long had connections with Yemeni militants and a family tie to the country. Mohammed Rashid Daoud al-Owhali stayed in Sana'a before travelling to Nairobi. Phone records from bin Laden's personal satellite phone show hundreds of calls to the Yemen made between 1996 and 1998.[6] Yemeni telephone records from 1998 to 2000 show calls between telephones used by suspects in the *Cole* attack and telephones belonging to suspects who were operating for bin Laden's organisation in East Africa before the 1998 bombings there.[7]

In addition, at about the time of the attempted attack on the *USS Sullivan,* bin Laden appeared in specially filmed recruitment videos with a *jambiya,* the traditional Yemeni dagger, at his waist. And, according to some reports, when the Sana'a government tried to close down the training camps run by the Islamic Army of Aden-Abyan a representative of bin Laden attempted to mediate.[8] In 1997, bin Laden sent an envoy to the Yemen to find out if it would be a suitable base should the Taliban expel him from Afghanistan.[9] The air in Yemen, he told an interviewer, was 'free of humiliation'.[10] And while in Kandahar in 2000, bin Laden, having divorced an earlier wife who remained in Saudi Arabia rather than come to Afghanistan with him in 1996, had married a Yemeni.[11] The presence of men in the Yemen who were, at least theoretically, under the control of bin Laden and his associates is revealed by another of the letters found by the *Wall Street Journal* on the computer picked up in Kabul. Several files show leaders in Kabul trying, with varying degrees of success, to maintain control of militant groups abroad. One lengthy report referred to a cell in the Yemen which was showing too much independence: 'The general management shall be consulted on issues related to joining and firing from the company, the general strategy and the company name,' it said. A member of the cell, the report complained, had been overheard talking 'in an unsuitable way' with a woman on the telephone and had then tried to avoid questions about the relationship by 'pretending to be busy reading the Qur'an'.[12] Yet despite all of this evidence, the exact mechanics of bin Laden's relation with the *USS Cole* bombers is unclear.

In fact, the exact mechanics of bin Laden's involvement, whether with individual terrorist acts or with other groups, are often unclear. Partly that is the consequence of the extreme difficulty of investigating terrorist attacks and the problems of gathering solid intelligence on an amorphous and opaque group of activists. Unfortunately, this means that, rather than try to comprehend the multiplicity of different ways in which bin Laden and other Islamic radicals interact, it is far easier to reduce them to a simple boss-worker, commander-foot soldier relationship. Such an over-simplification is wrong.

Instead it is useful to think of a scale with, at one extreme, an attack like the Nairobi bombing, involving a tight, well-organised cell based on an idea originating within the 'al-Qaeda hardcore', run closely by them and comprising a large number of personnel flown in especially for the purpose who have no previous local links, and, at the other extreme, local groups or even individuals who merely share broadly sympathetic aims with bin Laden but whose links to him or his associates are extremely tenuous. Somewhere in the middle of the scale, there are men like Ahmed Ressam, who conceived and planned an attack himself, selected his own targets and whose dealings with 'al-Qaeda' were limited to contact with Abu Zubaydah, training and a development grant for his idea. The attack on the *USS Cole*, which appears to have been the work of a group of local militants drawn together and organised by a more senior bin Laden associate, would slot in between Ressam and Nairobi.

Between 1996 and 2001, bin Laden was linked to other groups and individuals in a bewildering variety of ways. Every relationship was different. An examination of his dealings with Harkat-ul-Mujahideen and the Taliban has already shown how, in the late 1990s, groups with very different agendas began to converge in terms of ideology, methodology and targets. Bin Laden's relations with the Groupe Salafiste de Prédication et Combat (GSPC) in Algeria and in Europe, Islamic groups in Kurdistan and a particular cell in Malaysia, linked to the Jamaat Islamiyya organisation of Indonesia, are also revealing.

In Hosh el Hadair, a small village about 75 miles to the southwest of Algiers, life is very different from the crowded, cosmopolitan capital. There is no running water, limited electricity and the nearest metalled road is miles away.

Late in July 2001, 12 armed men came silently through the vine fields that surround the village. They shot nine men and cut the throat of a tenth, Djilal Bouaissaoui. Bouaissaoui had spent most of his 62 years working the dusty patch of land that soaked up his blood. The thick dark stain on the sandy soil was still visible two days later. He was the 105th person to die that month. After his funeral, I sat with his son and ate grapes and couscous. My heavily armed government security detachment waited nearby. The massacre barely made the local newspapers.[13]

During the mid 1990s, state repression and flagging support among the middle classes had effectively ended the campaign of the more moderate Armée Islamique de Salvation and had forced the Groupe Islamique Armée (GIA) down a path of ever-increasing radicalism. Soon thousands of people, civilians, militants and security officers were dying each year. The violence reached a peak in 1997 when the GIA, and possibly agent provocateurs from the security services, committed a series of horrendously brutal and seemingly random massacres. GIA cadres were responsible for butchering, literally, entire villages. The GIA leadership justified the acts on the basis that any Algerian who did not join them was 'takfir' and thus an unbeliever and should be killed. Unsurprisingly, this extreme position alienated many in Algeria who had previously supported the Islamic groups and the GIA, stripped of any broad social base, imploded in a maelstrom of violent infighting. In 1998, one of the group's senior cadres, Hassan Hattab, condemned the 'shedding the blood of innocent people in massacres', formed the GSPC and announced that his group would exclusively target security forces. The GSPC rose to prominence after President Abdelaziz Bouteflika announced an amnesty for militants in January 2000. Although some 5,000 AIS militants surrendered their weapons, Hattab's group – the strength of which is estimated at between 500 and 1,500 – refused the amnesty.[14] Several other 'groupuscules', whose motivations are often more criminal than religious, also refused to hand in their weapons. The massacre at Hosh el Hadair was probably committed by one of them.

Typically, hard evidence of links between the GSPC and bin Laden is difficult to find. Algerian and French security service sources insist that bin Laden provided funds for Hattab to allow him to set up the GSPC.[15] It is certainly true that al-Zawahiri condemned the indiscriminate violence of the GIA, issuing a series of statements to that effect. A former GSPC cadre told an Algerian court that he had overheard a series of conversations between Hattab and bin Laden on a satellite phone in 1998. Bin Laden had 'urged' Hattab to set up a group to 'improve the image of jihad', he said.[16] What is also certain is that between 1996 and mid 2002, bin Laden, in an echo of his activities as a self-appointed mediator in Afghanistan in the 1980s and early 1990s, made a series of attempts to unite the fractious groups in Algeria.[17] His motives were not entirely altruistic. Bin Laden, steeped in an archaic and nostalgic sense of Arabic (and Afghan) culture, feels that an ability to solve disputes is an attribute that all 'sheikhs' need to display to maintain the respect of their followers and to attract further support. In addition, in a very practical sense, the brokering of a deal increases his own influence over two parties over whom previously he had no authority. In traditional Middle Eastern society, the two elements are related. In June 2001, bin Laden sent Emad Abdelwahid Ahmed Alwan, alias Abu Mohammed, a trusted 37-year-old Yemeni aide, to Algeria via Ethiopia, the Sudan and the Niger. Alwan had developed contacts in the GIA after helping Algerian Islamic militants establish camps in the Yemen in the early 1990s and was tasked by bin Laden with establishing a more solid link with the Algerian groups.[18]

Bin Laden may also have been motivated by a desire to build a network in Europe. Few militants arrested in Europe in recent years have proved to be simply 'al-Qaeda', as commonly designated. Instead the majority of them, at least until 2001–2, have been linked to the GIA and the GSPC. Indeed, Hattab's group effectively inherited the European network that the GIA had built up throughout the 1990s, when the GIA ceased to exist as an effective force around 1998. A press release appearing in the Algerian *al-Youm* daily soon after the attacks of 11 September 2001, allegedly authored by Hattab, reveals the GSPC's focus. Hattab threatened that the GSPC would 'strike hard' at 'American *and European interests in Algeria* if they implement their threats to attack Arab and Muslim states… [or] if they continue to harass [the] Islamist network in the US, *UK, France, and Belgium*' (my emphasis). The careful emphasis on local, post-colonial and international targets is an interesting example of the fusing of different agendas.[19] That the GSPC are actively recruiting, and have sympathisers in the UK, was amply demonstrated in January 2002, when a contact gave me a video made by the group that was being passed around Islamic militants in London and the Midlands. It featured graphic footage of Algerian soldiers having their throats cut after being captured in an ambush near Algiers in 1999, spliced with calls to 'kill the infidels and sick people' and pictures of the group's everyday life in the Algerian maquis. During 2001, scores of GSPC activists were arrested in Europe and dozens of cells uncovered. In Milan, a group of Tunisians and an Egyptian were linked by Italian prosecutors to the GSPC, another in Madrid was composed of six Algerians who were also alleged to be GSPC members.[20] They were in possession of false passports and sophisticated forgery equipment and were thought to be responsible for sending scores of recruits to Afghanistan and, bizarrely, Indonesia for training. Wiretaps placed by Italian authorities revealed discussions of attacks on American targets being planned in the hope that they might find backers in Afghanistan prepared to fund them.[21] Another well-organised GSPC cell, comprising three Algerians, was discovered plotting to bomb a Christmas market in Strasbourg. Following the techniques taught them in the Afghan camps, they had videoed their target. They raised some funds from drug-dealing but needed more and were caught when a call they made to Abu Doha, the Algerian activist in London who had arranged cash for Ahmed Ressam, was intercepted by MI5, the British domestic intelligence service.[22] In Belgium, two French converts from Catholicism, associates of GIA/GSPC activists, were making up false passports. They provided those carried by the two Tunisians who killed Massoud. Many of these men appear to have considered themselves to be members of the GSPC and were in touch with GSPC leaders. However, as well as GSPC-linked material (such as the recruiting video referred to above), their flats were full of jihadi salafi literature of a more international nature, their conversations included references to 'the sheikh' or 'the emir', presumed to be bin Laden, and to travel to Afghanistan. They saw no conflict of interest or loyalty between the two. Again, this growing convergence is worth noting.

Bin Laden's ability to penetrate and appropriate the networks built up by the Algerian groups was due to his own increasing profile and to the training facilities he could offer. The practice of training volunteers recruited by the GSPC in Afghan camps linked to bin Laden resulted in a subtle form of entryism. By the time the volunteers returned to Algeria or to Europe to join the GIA or GSPC from Afghan camps, they were as much bin Laden's operatives as they were Hattab's or any other group's. Over time, with combat, surrender and infighting killing more senior men, the proportion of 'bin Laden-linked' operatives in any group became higher and his influence increased commensurately. Such relationships were reinforced by the grant of substantial funds to older and more established activists, particularly the men who recruited the new volunteers and arranged their travel and training. These men too developed 'dual loyalties' to bin Laden and to their own domestic groups, the GIA, the GSPC, Egyptian Islamic Jihad or whoever. It is in this context that key international figures like Abu Qutada, the Palestinian-Jordanian cleric living in London, were critical.

The case of Djamal Beghal, an Algerian-born French recruit, arrested at Dubai airport on his way from Afghanistan to France in August 2001, is revealing. Beghal, 36, presented himself to his interrogators as a dupe of bin Laden. He said that he had only ever been involved in moderate political Islamism and some proselytising before going to Afghanistan in 2000. In fact, it appears that Beghal had been involved with Algerian terrorist groups by the beginning of the 1990s and, like so many activists, had made his way to Afghanistan to seek help with projects he had already formulated.

Beghal had come to France in the mid 1980s, married a French woman, gained citizenship and lived in a rundown tower block on the outskirts of Paris for over a decade. Beghal had been active in militant circles since the beginning of the civil war in Algeria and was, in fact, picked up by French police on suspicion of membership of the GIA in or around 1995.

In 1997, Beghal and his family moved to Britain, settling in the nondescript city of Leicester, 100 miles northwest of London. Beghal told his interrogators that his aim was merely to study with Abu Qutada, whose taped lectures he had frequently heard in France. After some time, Abu Qutada encouraged his admirer to commute across the channel to distribute texts and tapes of his speeches in France. 'Abu Qutada never asked me to set up a network for him in France but just to spread his message,' Beghal said in his interrogation. French investigators do not believe this is the truth.

In 1998, Beghal and his spiritual mentor discussed the duty of hijra, the flight of the faithful from impious lands. Afghanistan was mentioned as a possible destination. In the autumn of 2000, after some time in France, Beghal and his family travelled to Afghanistan where he underwent basic training at a camp run by bin Laden's associates near Kabul. This was his first contact with bin Laden's group. In the spring of 2001, he asked to return home. 'I was called in by Abu Zubaydah,' Beghal told his interrogators:

> He told me that the time for action had come and asked me if I was ready. I said I was and he said that the plan was to blow up the US

> embassy in Paris. He gave me three presents: a stick of *niswak*, a bottle of perfume and a prayer cap. He said they were from bin Laden. He told me that 350,000 Francs ($55,000) had been placed in a bank account in Morocco for me.[23]

Beghal told the interrogators that he had been radicalised in the Afghan camps and then been given a mission by the al-Qaeda 'higher command'. Before that, he said, he had shunned violence. However, there is plenty of evidence that he was lying. For one thing, he told his interrogators that he had known the man who had received the $55,000 allocated by the 'al-Qaeda hardcore' for the attack, a Mohammed Raquiq who had had residency status in Spain, since June 2000.[24] In addition, Beghal admitted meeting the man who was to be the suicide bomber in the attack in London during Friday prayers at Abu Qutada's mosque in West London long before coming to Afghanistan. This was a Tunisian called Nizar Trabelsi, a former footballer who had developed a serious drug problem before turning to radical Islam while living in Belgium.[25] In addition, before leaving for Afghanistan, Beghal had shared a flat with another Algerian called Kamel Daoudi, a computer expert who had already been to Afghanistan and is suspected of a long-standing involvement in Islamic militancy.

French and British intelligence believe that Beghal, Daoudi, Trabelsi and others had formulated their plan to attack the US embassy in Paris before travelling to Afghanistan.[26] This would fit with the pattern of individuals such as Ressam or Hijazi, formulating plans and then taking them to al-Qaeda for approval and resources. Under interrogation, Beghal was careful to minimise his own role and to stress that he was 'only following orders'. However, the evidence suggests otherwise.

The shooting began to lessen by the late evening. Our commander had his handgun on the table next to a bottle of cheap Turkish whiskey and the rest of our weapons were piled around us. No one cared about the odd burst of automatic fire a few blocks away. There was supposed to be a truce and the men, who had been fighting all summer, were planning on getting drunk.

It was August 1991 and I was in the northeastern Iraqi city of Sulaimaniya with Peshmerga fighters (the name means 'those who face death') of the Kurdish Democratic Party. I was 21 and had joined the group during a university summer vacation. I was young, idealistic and wanted an adventure and a cause. The Peshmerga taught me how to use a Kalashnikov and took me with them across northern Iraq. The first Gulf War was over and, with belated assistance from allied airpower, the Kurdish tribes were consolidating their control of a sizeable slice of northern Iraq. Burnt-out Iraqi army vehicles littered the roads, Saddam Hussein's jets flew overhead and skirmishes between his troops and the Kurdish fighters were still common. That was the adventure. The national struggle of the Kurds was the cause.

The Peshmerga I had been with had been aggressively secular. They had drunk, smoked, sworn and I had never seen them pray. Their slogans were all about liberation and self-determination, about rights and democracy. When I told them I was studying 'nationalism' at university they were pleased. When I told them I was a student at Oxford, they were even happier. The idea of any of them mentioning a 'jihad' was almost risible. Though angry and resentful at what they felt, with some justification, to be the West's repeated betrayals, they were still vociferously pro-Western. Despite living with them for weeks on end, I had been barely aware that the men I was with were Muslims. Yet by 2001 an aggressive and militant hard-line Islamic movement had emerged in Iraqi Kurdistan with, so Washington claimed, links with bin Laden. They were strongest in the hills east of Sulaimaniyah.

The Islamic Movement of Kurdistan (IMK) has its roots in the Iran-Iraq war and in the Iranian Revolution. Until the 1980s, political Islamic activism in northern Iraq was limited to a small number of members of a local branch of the Muslim Brotherhood that was almost entirely restricted to the major cities. More radical strains of Islam were unheard of among the Kurds, particularly in the rural areas, among whom a tolerant Sufi-infused Sunni Islam similar to that of Afghanistan and rural Pakistan was prevalent. Decades of secular policies and an enormously successful literacy drive in the 1970s had diluted Islamic observance still further. Radical Salafi or Wahhabi-style Islam was extremely rare. During the Iran-Iraq war, Tehran worked to unite and strengthen the various disparate Islamist groups emerging in northern Iraq, with the aim of bolstering the Kurdish opposition forces against Saddam Hussein. The groups eventually united, with prodding from Tehran, under the umbrella of the IMK, between 1989 and 1991. The leader of the IMK was Mullah Uthman Ali Aziz, a senior cleric from an established religious family near the eastern town of Halabja.[27]

Mullah Uthman Ali Aziz's own personal connections with the Iranian mullahs were close. Drawing heavily on Qutb and Khomeini, he believed that a free Kurdish state needed to be run according to the Shariat. He also believed that violent means were justified in attaining that aim. The Kurdish opposition movement to Saddam Hussein was, as it still is, dominated by the Kurdish Democratic Party (KDP) and the Patriotic Union of Kurdistan (PUK). Both were heavily influenced by Soviet ideology – and received Soviet assistance – during the Cold War.

In the late 1980s, several senior Kurdish Islamic activists travelled to Afghanistan to fight the Soviets. They included many of the future leaders of the radical Islamic movement in Kurdistan. Most were graduates from technical faculties in the newly expanded Iraqi universities and came from recently urbanised families and thus fit the classic profile of political Islamic activists in this period. One, Najmuddin Feraj Ahmed, known as Mullah Krekar, established a guesthouse for Kurdish mujahideen in Peshawar and, until 1991, taught modern science at the Islamic University in Islamabad where he became close to Abdallah Azzam.[28]

The uprising against Saddam Hussein's regime in the wake of the Gulf War in 1991 allowed the Kurdish Islamists to come out into the open without fear of repression for the first time. In the elections for a Kurdish government following the uprising, the IMK failed to gain the seven per cent minimum they needed for representation in the new parliament. However, their failure in the polls did not reflect the IMK's growing popularity among young urban Kurds. Between 1991 and 1996, when UN security council resolution 986 allowing Iraqi oil to be traded for food was passed, the economic situation in the Kurdish enclave was appalling. Inhabitants had effectively suffered two sets of sanctions: those imposed on Iraq by the UN and those imposed on the Kurds by Saddam Hussein. The secular parties' lack of funds for basic social services necessitated substantial foreign assistance. As Western NGOs moved in so too did a raft of Islamic relief organisations, funded by the Saudi government, Saudi private donors and other wealthy Gulf patrons. Islamic religious leaders throughout the Middle East had viewed the influx of the Western NGOs as a threat to the Islamic faith of the Kurds and had called for strong measures by Islamic governments and private individuals to counter it. A series of Gulf-based Wahhabi organisations, including the International Islamic Relief Organisation, opened branches in Kurdistan. Their aims were explicit and they were brazen about linking the distribution of aid to proselytisation.[29] Aid to orphans and widows was made contingent on attendance at the mosque and at Qur'anic study groups and the wearing of the veil. For a student to receive a subsidy, free food or a room in a free dormitory, his whole family had to abide by strict rules.[30] In the hundreds of mosques built by the groups, the mullahs were paid according to how many converts to Wahhabism they made.[31] The charities even offered bounties to anyone prepared to give up membership of secular political parties.[32] Subsidised Wahhabi literature was widely disseminated. For many older Kurds and established ulema, the expansion of radical modern Islam was a shock.[33]

The result of the charities' activities, coupled with the continued failure of the warring secular parties to solve Kurdistan's profound social and economic problems, was a surge in recruitment to the IMK. By 1993, the IMK had established offices throughout Kurdistan and was growing in confidence. There were growing tensions within the movement as the men returning from Afghanistan began to steer the Islamic movement in Kurdistan in a more radical direction, as their counterparts had done in Algeria and elsewhere. Krekar returned to Kurdistan in 1991, forming his own independent Islah ('reform') group a year later and explicitly rejecting any accommodation with the secular government.[34] A series of explosions, assassination attempts and attacks on 'immodest' women convinced the new Kurdish administrations (the Kurdish enclave had split into discrete PUK and KDP sectors by 1992) to launch a crackdown. There was widespread fighting until, under pressure from Iran, a truce was brokered under which the IMK would be given the posts of mayor and chief of police in Halabja in return for foregoing the armed struggle.[35]

Despite continuing internecine conflict, the economic situation was vastly ameliorated by the UN's decision to allow Iraq to sell oil for food. A significant proportion of the funds thus amassed went to the government of northern Kurdistan. The impact was immediate and allowed the secular parties to counter the activities of the Islamic charities. Recruitment to the IMK dropped away sharply and moderates within the movement were satisfied when the IMK were given a ministry in 1996.[36]

But a year later the PUK and various breakaway elements from within the IMK clashed again. The fighting was led by a group, commanded by a 35-year-old Islamic activist known as 'Mullah Aso' who had returned from Afghanistan a year previously. Again echoing developments in Algeria, he took the view that everyone other than themselves, including Abdelaziz, was takfir and, with several hundred fighters, occupied a handful of villages in the hills above Halabja.

Between 1998 and 2000, individual militants in Iraqi Kurdistan had made their way to Afghanistan. One of the letters I had picked up in

Khost, addressed to Sayyid al-Kurdi, written in Arabic and dated 27 October 1997, had been sent by 'Abu Yakub' from Kurdistan. It thanked him for his tuition.[37] A second letter to the instructor was undated but had been signed 'Abu Ziad al-Kurdi'. The writer was apologetic. 'We did not set up a group as you asked,' he says.

Early in 2001, three groups within the IMK had broken away to form a separate organisation called the Ansar ul Islam. Ansar ul Islam comprised Mullah Krekar's Islah, a second group called the Markaz-i-Islami (Islamic Centre) and a third known as Hamas al-Tauhid. However, the unity of the groups was an illusion. Shortly after the formation of Ansar ul Islam, two of the three constituent groups separately sent representatives to Afghanistan to contact bin Laden. Krekar, who had had no contact with the Saudi or any of his associates previously, sent a three-man delegation after contacting Kurds who had been in Afghanistan with bin Laden for some years, possibly including Sayyid al-Kurdi. He introduced them to Mohammed Atef who sent the three men to a camp near Jalalabad, probably Darunta, where they received training in the now familiar curriculum. Because the al-Qaeda leaders in Afghanistan knew of Krekar's history during the Afghan war and of his role in the fighting that had been going on in Kurdistan in the previous decade, the delegation from his group was allowed, as Raeed Hijazi had been, to skip the basic infantry training and move straight on to the more advanced terrorist techniques that Krekar had asked them to learn.[38]

Before the three Islah men had returned to Kurdistan, another small group, from Hamas (al-Tauhid), arrived. They had made an approach to bin Laden through Abu Qutada, the London-based cleric. Qutada had wired them money and told them to go to Tehran to meet a man called Abu Jaffar al-Pakistani, an Iranian Kurd who had been in Pakistan for long enough to earn himself his soubriquet. In mid March 2001, Abu Jaffar passed them on to al-Qaeda in Afghanistan where they made their request for training and funds in person to al-Zawahiri.[39]

Once two of the three groups that constituted Ansar ul Islam had visited Afghanistan, bin Laden, or perhaps al-Zawahiri or Atef, saw an opportunity. Within weeks, an Arab veteran of the Afghan war called Abu Abdullah al-Shami had been sent from Jordan to make contact with the third hard-line group in Kurdistan, the Markaz-i-Islami, the only one that had not yet approached the al-Qaeda leadership with a request for training or financial support.[40] The Markaz proved enthusiastic and, following bin Laden's approach and offer, a delegation set off through

Iran to Afghanistan where they met al-Zawahiri. On their return several weeks later, the three men were arrested by the Iranian police with video recordings of the lectures that they, and Mullah Krekar's men, had received in the training camps loaded onto CD-ROMs. The IMK leadership used their contacts in Tehran to secure their release and by June all the various delegations were back in Kurdistan. In late August, Markaz and Hamas (al-Tauhid) joined forces and decided to call themselves Jund-ul-Islam and, on 1 September, issued the call to Jihad. The agreement was brokered by al-Shami, bin Laden's representative, who had returned to Kurdistan with the Markaz group.[41] It took al-Shami until December 2001, however, to convince Krekar to join the group. When he did, the new formation called itself Ansar ul Islam (again) and launched a wave of violent attacks, supervised by al-Shami, on the PUK and other targets. The ferocity of the attacks, which included the ritual butchering of Peshmerga prisoners and suicide bombings against government offices, was unprecedented.

In August 1999, well before any of the Kurds, Mohammed Khalim bin Jaffar, a slight 36-year-old printer from Singapore, arrived in Afghanistan and sought out Mohammed Atef. He had come on behalf of a group of Islamic militants in the island state who were, like so many others, seeking practical help in launching a bomb attack on American interests. Khalim's associates had even gone to the trouble of preparing a video of their projected targets. The video, which was later found in the rubble of Atef's Kabul office after an American airstrike shows images of a regular shuttle service in Singapore conveying US military and diplomatic personnel between two railway stations. A voiceover explains how an attack could work and how much damage it would do. Atef does not appear to have been too impressed with the presentation as there is no evidence that Khalim, who stayed for nine months in Afghanistan, returned to Singapore with any funding.[42]

The history of radical Islamism in Southeast Asia is complex and any attempt to condense its complexities and myriad variations risks oversimplification. However, there are certain elements in the origins of the group that hoped to launch the attacks in Singapore that are worth highlighting. The coincidence with other groups, as far away as Uzbekistan and Algeria, is interesting. Once more the role of states in fomenting or sheltering radicalism for short-term political gain is clear.

Though based in Malaysia, the roots of the plot lie in Indonesia. Indonesia, and Southeast Asia in general, is far from a terrorist hotbed. Of Indonesia's 220 million people, 85 per cent are Muslim and follow a very moderate form of Islam heavily influenced by Sufism and the area's strong Hindu traditions. Islam arrived from the Middle East through the spice trade. Proponents of radical 'modernist Islam', as it is known locally, are a small, if a growing, minority. Those who believe in using violence to achieve their aims of a 'Jemaa Islamiyya' are rarer still.

In Indonesia, the more radical movements have their roots in the struggle for independence against Dutch colonialists. Successive governments have used Islamist groups to counter Communist and democratic opposition. When out of favour, Islamist groups have been viciously repressed. It was one such bout of repression that drove leading Indonesian Islamic activists into exile, a hijra, in Malaysia in 1985. Several of them subsequently travelled to Afghanistan and returned to Malaysia full of jihadi Salafist ideas that they hoped to apply to their own environments.

One such man was Riduan Isamuddin, currently known as 'Hambali'. He was born in 1966 in a small village in rural west Java and attended an Islamic school and college. He became involved in the Islamist movement based on the religious school near the city of Solo that was run by the cleric Abu Bakar Ba'asir. He fled to Malaysia with Ba'asir in 1985 and spent two years in Afghanistan, returning in 1990.[43] By 1991, he was living in a compound with other migrant workers in a small village south of Kuala Lumpur. Hambali told his landlord that he had fled Indonesia to be able to 'practice Islam more freely'. Though virtually destitute on his arrival, he appears to have prospered and in late 1993 or early 1994 opened an export company with one of Ramzi Yousef's co-conspirators which police now say was used to channel funds to the Philippines for the so-called 'Bojinka plot'. He is also reported to have met Khalid Shaikh Mohammed.[44]

During the 1990s, Hambali and Ba'asir preached their brand of radical Islam in prayer meetings, mosques and Qur'anic study groups, focusing, as most political Islamist groups historically had done, on lower middle-class, frustrated white collar workers in medium-sized rural towns.[45] Hambali facilitated the travel of many of his new supporters to Afghanistan. By the late 1990s, he appears to have organised around 20 recruits from Singapore into several cells. They included several full or part-time policemen and at least eight full or part-time servicemen with the Singaporean armed forces. By 1997, they had begun reconnaissance of a variety of American or Western European targets and in 1999 despatched Khalim with his tape to Afghanistan in an attempt to raise funding. As mentioned, Khalim returned from Afghanistan to Singapore in April 2000 empty-handed and the plan to attack the shuttle bus and the railway stations was temporarily shelved.

There was, however, a postscript. Abu Bakar Ba'asir and several other more senior Indonesian Islamists returned to their homeland in 1998. Hambali appears to have remained active in Malaysia, maintaining and strengthening the network of activists he had built up. In January 2000, Yazid Sufaat, a 37-year-old former Malaysian Army captain with an American degree in biochemistry, played host to two young Saudis, Khalid al-Midhar and Nawaf al-Hazmi, in his flat in Kuala Lumpur. The meeting may well have been arranged by Hambali.[46] Sufaat also provided a young Frenchman called Zacarias Moussaoui, allegedly the '20th of the September 11th hijackers', with a letter, identifying him as his company's 'marketing consultant' for the USA, Britain and Europe. Moussaoui stayed with Sufaat while he inquired about flight schools in Malaysia. He found one but he decided against attending because it was more than two hours from the capital and did not provide training on 747s. He decided to try the USA instead. According to the FBI, Sufaat agreed to pay Moussaoui $2,500 a month during his stay in the USA, along with a lump sum of $35,000. Singaporean investigators also alleged that Sufaat had used his clinical pathology company, Green Laboratory Medicine, to obtain four tons of ammonium nitrate, the component for the explosive favoured in truck bombs, which was subsequently used in a series of attacks in the Philippines and Indonesia. According to the statement of Omar al-Faruq, a Kuwaiti-born activist who was picked up in Java in June 2002, $70,000 to buy the explosives was transferred to Sufaat through a Saudi-based charity, al-Haramain, by Mohammed Atef.[47] Hambali has also been linked to a series of church bombings in Indonesia on Christmas Eve 2000.[48]

One further point about militancy in Indonesia is worth making. The most violent and effective Islamic group in the region, in terms of the number of people killed, is Lashkar Jihad (LJ), an Indonesian militia whose formation in early 2000 was substantially helped by officers in the Indonesian security forces hoping to destabilise the new democratic government in Jakarta. Lashkar Jihad has waged a vicious campaign against Christians, killing several thousand in the east of the archipelago. The group has fought alongside official military units on a number of occasions. LJ's leader, Jafar Umar Thalib, has denied having any links to bin Laden, although he admits meeting him in Afghanistan in 1987.

At the time, he has told reporters, bin Laden struck him as a 'jet-setter' whose views were at odds with his own. Thalib has also claimed that bin Laden sent representatives to Indonesia to meet him in 1999. He claims they offered financial assistance in return for a degree of influence and authority over the group. Like the GIA, Thalib felt that the strings attached made the deal unattractive and he rejected it. Like Abu Sayyaf in the Philippines, Lashkar Jihad, which was formed in January 2000, is very much focused on a domestic agenda, confining its activities to Indonesia and aiming to eradicate internal domestic threats to Islam rather than launching offensive terrorist strikes. It attracted a small number of 'foreign' militants from the Middle East, whose travel was often facilitated by the GSPC cell in Madrid discussed above, and elsewhere in the region.[49]

So, what can we say about 'al-Qaeda', its structure, organisation, personnel and operations between 1998 and September 2001? As ever, it is easier to say what it is not. As has become clear over the preceding three chapters, the idea that al-Qaeda is a coherent hierarchical terrorist group, with a single leader, a broadly uniform ideology and an ability to conceive and execute projects globally through well-disciplined cadres, sleepers and activists spread around the world is misplaced. Saying what 'al-Qaeda' was during the period, and thus to a large extent, is now, is far more difficult.

In my introduction, I defined several different al-Qaedas. We have seen all of these al-Qaedas over the last three chapters. There has been the hardcore, to my mind the only entity that warrants the label of 'al-Qaeda', even if they do not use it. In 2001, this was almost exclusively based in Afghanistan. Then there were men like Hambali, Abu Doha in London, Abu Abdul al-Shami in Jordan and northern Iraq and al-Nashiri in the Yemen. All are long-term associates of bin Laden, al-Zawahiri and others, who accept missions from them or act as intermediaries and recruiters for others. They were 'associate members of al-Qaeda'. Along with people like Beghal, Ressam, Abu Hoshar, Khalim and others they act as links between the 'al-Qaeda hardcore' and the rest of the vast, amorphous movement of modern radical Islam, with its myriad cells, domestic groups, 'groupuscules' and splinters, joining the 'network of networks' to the hardcore itself. Sometimes these networks are happy to be brought under bin Laden's umbrella. Often they have no interest in surrendering an element of their autonomy in return for access to funds or training, however much either is needed. Frequently other figures, such as Abu Qutada in London or ibn Khattab, the Jordanian-Saudi militant leader in Chechnya, or indeed the Pakistani or Indonesian government, can provide anything that is needed, whether it be fatwas, weapons or funds, without recourse to bin Laden and his close associates.

One thing that quickly becomes apparent, however, is the willing participation of those that bin Laden managed to co-opt. This mirrors the eagerness of volunteers, like al-Owhali, who overcame significant obstacles to make their way to the training camps where they remained for considerable periods, without compulsion. What is particularly striking is how, particularly when it came to terrorist attacks, it was more often al-Qaeda that was approached with ideas or plans for an attack than groups or individuals approached by al-Qaeda. Indeed, by the end of 2001, volunteers requesting martyrdom operations were being ticked off by senior aides of bin Laden if they did not come up with their own ideas for attacks. When Zuhair Hilal Mohammed al-Tubaiti, a Saudi who had made his way to the training camps in 2000, asked Ahmed al-Moula al-Billal, a member of the 'al-Qaeda hardcore', to be allowed to participate in an operation in which he would die, he was told, fairly abruptly, to go away and formulate a plan and submit it for approval like everyone else.[50] Al-Tubaiti, and the men he recruited himself in Morocco and brought to the camps, are part of the third group of people who are so often lumped in under the label of 'al-Qaeda', those who are part of the huge groundswell of anger and resentment throughout the Islamic world which leads thousands of young men to set out in search of their own personal 'lesser' jihads each day.

Such men, as I have stressed a number of times, cannot be considered 'al-Qaeda'. Something that can be labelled 'al-Qaeda' did exist between 1996 and 2001. It was composed of a small number of experienced militants who were able to access resources of a scale and with an ease that was hitherto unknown in Islamic militancy, largely by virtue of their position in Afghanistan and the sympathy of so many wealthy, and not so wealthy, Muslims across the Islamic world, though particularly in the Gulf. This 'al-Qaeda' acted, as the name suggests, like a wealthy university disbursing research grants and assisting with facilities such as libraries or with teaching that can allow the ambitions of its pupils, particularly those star students who have attracted the attention of the chancellor or the senior lecturers, to be fulfilled. It is the Holy War Foundation. Another model is venture capitalism. Individuals or small groups (companies) would approach the chief executive and board (bin Laden, Atef, et al) with ideas that they believed were worth support. Of hundreds of such proposals, only a few were chosen. Some received a significant investment, others were merely given a small amount of cash. The firm's bank of experts were on hand to assist, sometimes travelling to do so. Other experts were stationed overseas, encouraging local businesses and picking ones that looked capable of turning a profit. A third model, familiar to anyone in the world of media, is of al-Qaeda as a newspaper or TV production or publishing house. Bin Laden and his associates acted as commissioning editors of films, books or newspaper articles. Freelancers approached them with ideas that were sometimes funded and resourced but often rejected. Occasionally, old ideas were rehashed or the editor's own ideas were given to people whose own ideas had been rejected. Equally often, the approaches of the university, venture capitalist or commissioning editor were rejected as inappropriate, unwelcome or simply unnecessary. This is a complex and varied picture. There are, of course, hundreds of different universities, venture capitalists and TV production companies. Some have higher profiles than others and their reputations or media images may not accurately reflect the extent of the work they do. This picture may be less seductive than the image of the James Bond villain fomenting global mayhem from his secret headquarters, but it does have the virtue of being accurate.

CHAPTER FIFTEEN

SEPTEMBER 11TH

At 7.58am on 11 September 2001, United Airlines Flight UA175, a Boeing 767, left Logan International Airport, Boston, Massachusetts, bound for Los Angeles, California. On board were 61 passengers, 11 crew and 26,000 gallons of kerosene fuel. Shortly after take-off, five of the passengers, armed with simple box-cutter knives and led by a young Emirati called Marwan al-Shehhi, took control of the aircraft. A minute later, another 767, American Airlines Flight AA11, followed UA175 along Logan's runway. It too was bound for Los Angeles. AA11 carried 81 passengers and 11crew and was hijacked, 14 minutes into the flight, by five men led by an Egyptian called Mohammed Atta.

At 8.20am, American Airlines AA77, a Boeing 757, took off from Dulles International airport, outside Washington, DC. It too was heading to Los Angeles. AA77 carried 58 passengers and six crew. At 8.50am, the last routine radio contact with the plane was made. Four minutes later, the aircraft began an unauthorised turn to the south and, shortly afterwards, radar contact was lost. At 8.42 United Airlines UA93 took off from Newark. Another 757, it was heading for San Francisco with a crew of seven and 37 passengers.

AA11 crashed into the North Tower of New York's World Trade Center at 8.35am. Half an hour later, watched live by tens of millions of television viewers, UA175 hit the South Tower. At 9.39am, AA77 crashed into the western side of the Pentagon. Finally, UA93, after a struggle between the passengers and the men who hijacked it, crashed into a muddy field near Stoney Creek Township, Pennsylvania at 10.03am, killing everyone on board.[1] Before the end of the day, around 3,000 people would have been killed.[2]

An enormous amount has been written about the September 11th attack. The mechanics of the plot have been examined in infinitesimal detail. The tragic events themselves have been analysed from every conceivable angle. Currently, we are far too close to them to place them in any kind of context. For the moment they remain, for most commentators, unprecedented and unique.

But, though in many ways that assessment is justified, it disguises an important truth. Though the damage done and the reaction they provoked were unlike anything previously seen, in terms of their ambition, the complexity of their execution and their spectacular nature, the September 11th attacks were not so much a radical break with previous developments as a summation of them.

Mainland America had been a target for Islamic militants for some time. In 1993, Ramzi Yousef had attempted to demolish the World Trade Center, and a group led by Sheikh Abdel Omar Rahman had planned attacks on a series of other high-profile targets in New York. Late in 1998, Abu Doha, the London-based Algerian activist, had received the al-Qaeda leadership's backing for Ahmed Ressam's scheme for an attack on airports or similar targets on the American west coast. Indeed, an attempt by bin Laden and others within the broader Islamic militant movement to execute a spectacular attack on a symbolic target in the heartland of America had been recognised as an inevitability by counter-terrorist experts for several years. In the years immediately following the end of the war in Afghanistan most radical activists, including those close to bin Laden, had considered the various Middle Eastern regimes in their respective home countries as their primary target. Throughout the mid 1990s, America, whose support was seen as crucial to the continued existence of those regimes, began to be seen as a target in itself. By the end of the decade, the USA was perceived by many extremists as the primary evil. The American intelligence community was well aware of this.[3] The increasing ambition and scale of 'al-Qaeda' attacks from 1998 onwards is also clear. And any analyst could be fairly confident that, given the utter failure of bin Laden and his associates, after several years of campaigning, to radicalise and mobilise more than a very small minority of the world's 1.2 billion Muslims, any coming attack would be spectacular, carefully designed to appeal to and exploit the capability and sensitivity of modern media.

Nor were the means used in the attack novel. Though by 2001 no one had yet successfully executed an attack using planes as offensive weapons, such a tactic had often been discussed by Islamic militants. In 1994, Ramzi

Yousef and an accomplice had the idea of hijacking a plane and flying it into the CIA headquarters in Langley, Virginia. In the same year, the GIA tried to force the pilots of the Air France jet they had hijacked in Algiers to fly into the Eiffel Tower. In 1996, American intelligence officers received information that a group associated with Sheikh Abdel Omar Rahman was planning to fly a plane from Afghanistan to the USA and crash it into the White House and that an Iranian group was planning to hijack a Japanese plane over Israel and force it to crash into Tel Aviv. Information about similar plans was received by US intelligence agencies throughout 1998 and 1999. They ranged from a Turkish group's scheme to plunge a plane into Kemal Ataturk's tomb during a government ceremony to an Afghan-based Egyptian group who hoped to launch a kamikaze-style attack on the Egyptian presidential palace in a hang-glider packed with explosives. Individuals more closely associated with bin Laden are also thought to have planned similar operations.[4] Even radical ideologues also dreamt of such attacks. In a fatwa published in the summer of 2001, Ahmed Abdallah al-Ali, a leading Kuwaiti Wahhabi cleric, discussed the legality of the death of a 'mujahed' who died 'while crashing an aircraft into an important city'.[5]

So in its means and its intentions the September 11th attack was part of a process that had been underway for well over a decade. Likewise the hijackers, and those who gave them logistic support and directed their operations, are representative of previous trends within al-Qaeda and within Islamic militancy more generally.

Those involved in the September 11th plots can be divided into four separate groups. Three groups comprise the hijackers, who, though they may look like a homogeneous group at first glance, are in fact divisible into three discrete units with very different characteristics, and a fourth comprising the 'hardcore' of 'al-Qaeda' elements in Afghanistan who maintained overall control, albeit at some considerable distance, of the operation. A number of other individuals, in Europe, the Far East and the Arabian Gulf, were instrumental in the formation and execution of the scheme and their stories too are important and illuminating.

To provide anything approaching a comprehensive narrative of the September 11th attacks is difficult. It is an enormously complex story that developed over a decade at least and involved scores of characters and dozens of locations. However, there are certain elements that help make sense of the whole and help place the attacks within the context of broad trends within Islamic militant activity in the 1990s. The three groups of hijackers correspond with the analysis of the structure of the modern Islamic radical movement, and bin Laden's role within it, that I have developed over the preceding chapters. There is the 'al-Qaeda hardcore' and its experienced, though independent, 'associate members'; there is the 'network of networks', and then there is a group drawn from the broad mass of jihadi sympathisers.

The 'hardcore' group comprises the senior aides of bin Laden who were involved in the execution of the strikes from their base in Afghanistan and Khalid al-Midhar and Nawaf al-Hazmi, two young Saudi Arabians who died on Flight AA77. Both were veterans of combat in Bosnia, and possibly in Chechnya as well, and were known to bin Laden and his associates after spending time in camps in Afghanistan during the mid to late 1990s. Al-Midhar and al-Hazmi's journey to America involved scores of other hardline activists from the Yemen to Malaysia.

The second group consists of those hijackers usually referred to as the 'Hamburg cell' and include three of the four pilots, Mohammed Atta, Ziad Jarrah and Marwan al-Shehhi. The members of the Hamburg cell all arrived separately in Germany between 1992 and 1996. They came together through mutual friends and social networks, particularly those centring on a particular radical mosque, the al-Quds, in central Hamburg. Atta, the oldest, was the first member of the group to arrive in Germany. They correspond closely to the networked, though independent, groups who allied themselves with bin Laden during the 1990s to access resources to allow them to execute plans that they had developed on their own.

The third group of hijackers had a specific job: to contain passengers while the trained pilots flew the planes to their targets. They have been dubbed 'the Muscle'. Of the 13, 12 were Saudi Arabian.[6] These men had all made their own way to Afghanistan in the hope of receiving training to enable them to go to fight in Chechnya or elsewhere. Some indeed may have done so. Not one ever appears to have entertained any idea of involvement in more sophisticated terrorist operations until it was suggested to them by senior al-Qaeda figures in the training camps in Afghanistan. Indeed, it is far from clear that they had any ambition to be involved in terrorist operations at all until that point. Some were selected by associates of bin Laden in the general camps, such as Khaldan, or from newer establishments set up to deal with the post-1998 influx of volunteers. Others were selected from more specialised camps such as al-Farooq. In this, the senior al-Qaeda men were following a practice nearly 15 years old, often in camps that were as aged. The men they selected for the September 11th operation had volunteered for jihad in a way that tens of thousands of other young Muslims had done over the previous two decades. They may have been diverted by senior al-Qaeda figures to their deaths in America but went without compulsion and without compunction. This group corresponds to the broad mass of radical Islamic activists who, in their mosques, their schools, their homes or their Islamic centres, have their own ambitions to fight in the 'jihad' wherever they can find it.

Mohammed Atta was born in 1968 in the sprawling Nile delta town of Kafr el-Sheikh. His father came from a relatively prosperous provincial agricultural family, had got into Cairo University and trained as a lawyer. He was a domineering man who pushed his son hard, forbidding him from playing with other children and forcing him to study. When Atta was ten, the family moved to Cairo, taking a large apartment in one of the poorer districts. There is little evidence of political or religious activism in Atta's childhood and youth though his father was moderately devout. His two sisters went to university and qualified as a doctor and a zoologist respectively. Like their mother, they dressed fashionably and went unveiled. Atta's father does not appear to have been involved with the Muslim Brotherhood despite fitting the profile – with his provincial background, middle-class profession, disappointed aspirations of social advancement, resentment of the Egyptian elite and university-level education – of the contemporary political Islamist perfectly. He was, however, prone to rants about the Jews, the Zionists, the excesses of the Cairene elite and the plight of the Palestinians. His son, whom schoolmates remember as a shy and effeminate boy, said he wanted to be an engineer and in 1985 began to study architecture at Cairo University.[7] Again, though the Brotherhood and more radical groups, such as al-Gamaa al-Islamiyya and Islamic Jihad, were active on the Cairo campus and especially strong in technical faculties, there is no evidence that father or son was involved in political or religious activism, even during the upsurge of radical Islamic violence in the country that followed the end of the war against the Soviets and the return of Egyptians from Afghanistan.[8]

Atta senior arranged for his son to pursue doctoral studies in Germany. In July 1992, Atta arrived in Hamburg and, lonely and homesick, appears to have begun following a more rigid, literalist and orthopractic interpretation of Islam, praying regularly, refusing to touch food prepared in pots used to cook anything that was not *halal* and avoiding contact with dogs and women. After disagreements with his first host family, largely caused by his uncompromising new stance, Atta moved into student accommodation near the campus of the Hamburg-Harburg technical university where he was enrolled in a graduate course in urban planning. Students and professors there remember him as withdrawn, meticulous and hardworking. Roommates in the student accommodation where Atta lived until 1998 say he was difficult, overbearing and anti-social.[9] The staff of Plankontor, the design company where he started part-time work shortly after arriving in Hamburg, remember an earnest and awkward young man.

In 1994, Atta visited Aleppo in Syria to do fieldwork for his doctoral dissertation on an old neighbourhood that had been ravaged by intrusive modernisation. What he saw made him extremely angry. In 1995, he won a scholarship to return to Cairo and study plans by the Egyptian government to 'restore' an area of the old Islamic city by evicting many of its inhabitants, repairing the old buildings and bringing in troupes of actors in 'traditional dress' to entertain tourists. Again, Atta was incensed, blaming Westernisation and the Egyptian government's closeness to America for the plan to create an 'Islamic Disneyland' in the heart of one of the Muslim world's most celebrated cities.

Atta's profound resentment of such projects is interesting. That they represented, for him at least, the humiliation of what he felt to be his own culture, society and religion is clear. But one of the things that had so angered him in Aleppo was the way taller, newer buildings in the Western style overlooked, and thus invaded, the courtyards of older traditional dwellings.[10] As mentioned before, concepts of space, and more particularly, the idea of 'Islamicised space', are hugely important to many militant Islamic activists and repeatedly feature in their literature and discourse. For many recent immigrants from Muslim countries living in the West, such locations, whether they be mosques, cultural centres, certain quarters of a city or domestic homes, are often of enormous importance. At their most positive, such spaces can contribute hugely to our multicultural societies. For the homesick or for those who find the challenge of life in the West too much they provide havens of cultural familiarity and affirmation. However, some such spaces perform a more pernicious function, allowing a definite physical and psychological separation from mainstream life and promoting a culture that facilitates both a deliberate rejection of assimilation and its almost inevitable corollary, political and religious radicalisation. The Hamburg cell depended on a series of such spaces: the mosque at which the members met, the flat they hired together, the Islamic study room they arranged at their university and finally the discrete Islamicised spaces of the training camps and Afghanistan under the Taliban. Modern Islamic activists have also recognised the importance of establishing religious spaces outside those dominated by establishment ulema or other traditional, and thus often regime-run, places of worship or religious study. Thus the important role that 'Islamic centres', places that are new and neither mosque nor medressa, often play for militant groups.

From Cairo, Atta made a pilgrimage to the ultimate Islamicised space, Mecca. On returning to Egypt, he investigated career options but became swiftly disillusioned. Few of the structural problems that had crippled the Egyptian state over the preceding decades had been addressed by President Hosni Mubarak's government. Without contacts in the elite, Atta, despite his now impressive qualifications, stood little chance of getting a satisfying job anywhere. His newly grown beard, the mark of a devout believer, was a particular problem. He would, he told friends, be 'criminalised' and would be unable to practise his profession without harassment. This, he said, upset him profoundly because it was 'his dream' to work in his own country.[11]

Atta was in Egypt at a time when violence between the Egyptian security forces and the resurgent al-Gamaa al-Islamiyya was reaching a peak. He could not have been oblivious to the brutal struggle taking place around him. The summer of 1995 saw the attempt on Mubarak's life in Addis Abbaba, masterminded from Khartoum, and a major crackdown on the Muslim Brotherhood, which had won control of several major professional unions in Egypt, in which hundreds of militants were arrested.[12] Within two years, the violence was to climax in the massacre of 58 tourists by an al-Gamaa al-Islamiyya splinter-group at Luxor, an act which caused a huge swathe of the Egyptian middle and lower classes to withdraw their support for radical Islam and forced the more moderate elements among the militants to declare a truce, much as had happened in Algeria.

But it was not religious issues that angered Atta most. Acquaintances in Cairo remember him becoming incensed by essentially political concerns that are common among activists of all ideologies throughout the developing world. Underlying them all was, friends said, a powerful sense of 'social justice' that underpinned Atta's anger at the inequities of Egyptian society. He was particularly exercised by the 'complete ignorance of social problems' manifested by Egypt's elite, repeatedly criticising government officials and politicians for focusing on their careers and the enrichment of their families above all else. This he attributed, at least in part, to American political and cultural influence on the Cairene elite. He resented the fact that the rich preferred the American University in the capital to Cairo's own university where he had studied. Those who ran Egypt and who enjoyed comfortable lives were 'alienated' from their own people and culture, Atta told friends. That the Egyptians grew cash crops such as strawberries for the European market but were forced to import wheat angered him too. On another occasion he criticised the Egyptian government for allowing industrial waste from developed countries to be dumped in his own country and made a point of describing to Volker Hauth, a fellow student, the problems that had resulted from President Sadat's neo-liberal financial policies in the 1970s. They had enriched the elite at the expense of the poor, Atta said. The lack of opportunity for young Egyptians was also a constant complaint.[13] Atta also profoundly resented the international community's failure to help Bosnian Muslims and the Palestinians. He contrasted the mobilisation of huge forces against Saddam Hussein with the seeming inability to act elsewhere. This was, he felt, indicative of the West's cynical attitude to the Islamic world.

When Atta returned to Hamburg, he began attending the al-Quds mosque in Steindamm, known locally as a centre for radicalism, and made friends with a number of the young men who worshipped there. In March 1996, two of his new friends witnessed Atta's will, a bizarre mix of Salafi orthopraxy and personal neuroses which specifies that Atta's body should be laid on its side facing Mecca, women should be barred from the burial and anyone who prepared his body should wear gloves and avoid touching his genitals. Atta, as far as anyone knows, died a virgin. There is no evidence for any close relationship with any woman outside his family at any stage of his life.[14] The will confirms the impression that Atta, despite his intense interest in religion, was far less steeped in the culture, tradition and language of Salafi Islam than many of the activists he was associated with. The will lacks the Qur'anic and exegetical references that one would expect from someone who was genuinely familiar with the holy texts.

It was at al-Quds mosque, or possibly Hamburg's Goethe Institute, that Atta met Marwan al-Shehhi, who was to die flying UA175 into the World Trade Center's South Tower. Al-Shehhi had arrived in Germany in 1996, on a military scholarship, worth $10,000 annually, from the United Arab Emirates government. He was the son of an imam in Ras al-Khaimah, one of the poorest and most conservative of the emirates and an area steeped in the Wahhabi tradition. Al-Shehhi was a deeply religious boy who helped his father at the mosque and eventually won a place at a prestigious local religious college, al-Ain University.[15] A family dispute led al-Shehhi to travel to Germany to study. If Atta's background is close to that of the classic political Islamist activist, then al-Shehhi's is that of the radical, neo-traditionalist alim. Al-Shehhi had begun attending the al-Quds mosque in mid 1997.[16]

Ziad Jarrah, who had dreamed of becoming a pilot since childhood, came from a secular, prosperous and prominent family in Lebanon. He had been to a Christian school and had no record of any involvement in any of Lebanon's internecine strife. In the spring of 1996, aged 20, Jarrah moved to Greifswald, in the former East Germany, to begin college and almost immediately started a relationship with a young female Turkish-born medical student. Jarrah appears to have swiftly started behaving in a devout fashion, possibly as a result of the influence of radical Salafi clerics in Greifswald, well before moving to Hamburg in August 1997 to study aircraft construction at the University of Applied Sciences. He met Atta shortly afterwards through another young Muslim, Said Bahaji, a 22-year-old German-Moroccan computer buff who spoke four languages.[17] Jarrah, with his secular background, is different both from Atta, with his relatively devout petit bourgeois upbringing, and al-Shehhi, with his traditional religious credentials. Nonetheless, the apocalyptic, utopian worldview of bin Laden and Azzam made sense to all three.

Atta had been made redundant by Plankontor and, though he continued to work on his doctorate, he spent lengthy periods away from the university. In early 1998, he is thought to have travelled to Afghanistan, probably to Khaldan camp. Al-Shehhi probably went with him along with a 26-year-old Yemeni former banker called Ramzi bin al-Shibh, who had arrived in Germany around two years earlier and was part of the same circle of friends and activists in Hamburg. Atta and the others were in Afghanistan at an important time. In February 1998, bin Laden had issued his fatwa calling on Muslims to kill Americans. The embassy bombings were only a few months away. On their return to Germany, Atta and the others moved into a run-down and anonymous flat in a complex near the university. Atta, acquaintances say, seemed more confident and more purposeful. On 1 November 1998, the group moved again. Atta, Said Bahaji and bin al-Shibh took a flat at 54 Marienstrasse in Harburg; Atta signed the rent payments slips *Dar el Ansar* ('the house of the supporters of the Prophet'). Jarrah became a frequent visitor and friends noticed that his behaviour became more devout. He told his girlfriend to wear a veil and, on a visit home, his parents were surprised and concerned to see that he had grown a beard.

There are differing interpretations of how the Hamburg cell was formed and how its involvement with the September 11th attacks evolved. One particular point of difference is over the question of who had the idea for flying planes into the World Trade Center. German investigators, who have a strong interest in emphasising the agency of the Hamburg cell to help convict those members they have been able to prosecute, maintain that by mid 1998 the cell was fully formed and fully functioning. It comprised, they say, 'seven Muslim students [who made up]... an outwardly isolated, actively conspiring organisation'.[18] This group included Atta, Jarrah, al-Shehhi, Bahaji, Bin al-Shibh and two other young students at Hamburg-Harburg technical university, both Moroccan-born, Munir Motassadeq and Zacarias Essebar. The German investigators note that it was at this time that the group was granted a portacabin on the university campus, to use as a 'prayer room', in which they installed a telephone and a computer.

Over the next year, the Germans say, a steady radicalisation took place as the group socialised, prayed and worked together at odd jobs. In late November 1999, Atta, Jarrah, al-Shehhi and bin al-Shibh followed the well-worn path to the camps in Afghanistan.[19] According to the Germans, the idea 'to commit assassinations by means of aircraft attacks had [already] developed... in October at the latest'. It is here that the Germans depart most radically from the account of events given by their American, British and French counterparts. If the Germans are right, the four young activists made their journey to Afghanistan to get help with plans they had already formulated. The German prosecutors say the cell travelled 'in order to talk about the details with the persons responsible of the international network and to secure financial and logistic support'.[20] The Germans say that their conclusion that the Hamburg cell had the idea of using aircraft for terrorist purposes independently of 'al-Qaeda' is supported by internet records that show that, in addition to hardline jihadi websites, the members of the Hamburg cell had been researching flight simulators prior to travelling to Afghanistan. But the German theory, though it fits patterns of previous militant behaviour, is contradicted by many other investigators. They point out that in fact only a single website, with a page featuring a variety of computer games, was accessed and at a time when most of the cell were out of Germany. They believe that al-Qaeda figures visited Germany and began recruiting there in 1998 or 1999. Some have even claimed that Atta had been a 'sleeper' since the early 1990s or that the group had been formed through the agency of radical activists with links to al-Qaeda and was activated by planners in Afghanistan when they decided the time was right. Indeed, senior al-Qaeda figures themselves have claimed all the credit for thinking up the idea of the attack on the Twin Towers and said that they suggested it to Atta and his group on their arrival at the training camps in Afghanistan at the end of 1999.[21]

Whatever the case, the four men had returned to Hamburg by early spring and set about executing their new mission while Essebar and Motassadeq travelled to Afghanistan themselves. First they obtained fresh passports, thus obscuring the telltale stamps from the Gulf and Pakistan. Then they set about getting American visas. Meanwhile, Atta began researching flying schools, sending e-mails to 31 schools in America during March. On 26 March, Jarrah signed up with a flight school in Venice, Florida. By the end of June 2000, Atta, al-Shehhi and Jarrah had all arrived in America. They were not the first hijackers to arrive in the USA. Al-Midhar and al-Hazmi, the second group I identified above, were already there.

In late 1999, the CIA learned that two militants suspected of links with bin Laden, known only as 'Nawaf' and 'Khalid', were planning to travel to Malaysia.[22] The information came from intercepted telephone conversations between senior al-Qaeda figures in Afghanistan and individuals in the Yemen. The telephone number belonged to Ahmed al-Hazza, the former comrade with whom Mohammed Rashid Daoud al-Owhali had stayed on his journey to Nairobi from Pakistan 18 months previously, and was the number he had called when trying to arrange his own escape from Nairobi after the bombing.[23] In the first days of 2000, 'Khalid' was identified by the CIA as Khalid bin Mohammed bin Abdallah al-Midhar, a father in law of al-Hazza. His travelling companion, Nawaf al-Hazmi, was identified later. Little was known about either man. They appeared to have fought in Bosnia during the mid 1990s and spent a considerable amount of time in Afghan camps. Al-Hazmi is thought to have fought in Chechnya in 1997 and to have taken the bayat to bin Laden in 1998, possibly while in al-Farooq camp. It appears that Nawaf al-Hazmi may have been present at meetings between the first group of hijackers to travel to Afghanistan (led by Atta) and the al-Qaeda leadership in late 1999.[24] The presence of both men in the USA by mid 1999 has been confirmed. Both had then travelled to Saudi Arabia or the Gulf, and probably to Afghanistan, towards the end of the year and, when the CIA picked them up, appeared to be heading back to the USA. The pair was watched by Malaysian intelligence when they met several senior local militants, including Hambali, at a flat in Kuala Lumpur in early January 2000. Also attending the meeting was Tawfiq bin Atash, a veteran militant with close links to bin Laden who was to be involved in the bombing of the *USS Cole* nearly ten months later. Both al-Midhar and al-Hazmi re-entered the USA on 15 January and based themselves in San Diego where they set about trying to learn to fly.

The third group of men among the hijackers was the Muscle; they arrived in America, in ones and twos, between 23 April and 29 June 2001.[25] They were young (the exact ages of many of them are still to be determined), almost all were Saudi Arabian and not one had any previous record of involvement with terrorism. Most of them came from the south-western Saudi provinces of Asir and al-Baha. Asir has always been apart from the rest of the kingdom. Its high, rainy coastal mountains are very different from the parched desert of the interior. Despite the burgeoning local tourist industry, Asir is backward economically. It was the last province to come under the rule of the Saud kings in Riyadh and, without oil itself, has been denied many of the financial benefits of other areas. Many of its inhabitants have turned to the government for jobs, seeking employment in the military and security services where they hold lower and middle-ranking jobs.[26] Resentment at the monopolisation of power and wealth by the dominant Saudi tribes in the richer provinces has led to a strong local tradition of political opposition. Many of the tribes of Asir are more closely related to those of the Yemen than those of the Saudi Arabian ruling classes and this exacerbates their marginal status within the kingdom. Asir is also a province of profound religious conservatism. Safar bin Abd al-Rahman al-Hawali, the leading dissident cleric whose mix of political and religious criticism was an influence on bin Laden in the early 1990s, was born in al-Baha. Asir was known as one of the main recruiting grounds during the war against the Soviets in Afghanistan and received many of the returning veterans.[27]

And most of the Muscle, though educated and from relatively prosperous backgrounds, appear to have been socially marginalised in some way beyond their more general marginality within Saudi Arabia as Asiri. Two, Wail, 25, and Waleed al-Shehri, 21, came from the Asir town of Khamis Mushayt, where their father was a wealthy car dealer. He lost contact with his sons after they had gone to the holy city of Medina to seek help for the elder's chronic depression.[28] The treatment was to be 'some verses from the Qur'an' read by 'their sheikh'. The two young men rang home only once and were vague about when they would return.

According to several accounts, they had already told friends they hoped to travel to Chechnya.[29] From Medina, the brothers appear to have travelled to Afghanistan and appear to have followed the standard path, spending time at Khaldan camp and then at al-Farooq.[30] Also at al-Farooq was Abdulaziz al-Omari. Al-Omari came from al-Makwah, a town just north of Asir and had studied at Mohammed ibn Saud University in Buraydah, known locally for its radical dissident preachers, notably the charismatic and prolific Salman al-Auda. Buraydah is deeply conservative and one of the poorest areas of Saudi Arabia. Mamoun Fandy calls it 'fertile ground for the elaboration of a discourse of resistance coloured in religion'.[31] Al-Omari was the student of one such radical young alim, Suleiman al-Alwan, and is believed to have acted as imam at the al-Farooq camp.[32] There were several other students among the Muscle. Majed Moqed, the son of a tribal headman near Medina who died on flight AA77, had attended Mohammed ibn Saud University in Buraydah too. Ahmed al-Nami, who died on UA93, had been to King Khalid Islamic law school in Abha, the provincial capital of Asir.[33]

Three other youths from al-Shehri's hometown, Khamis Mushayt, died on the planes. Two, Ahmed and Hamza al-Ghamdi, were brothers. They had left home in 1999 or 2000 and had told their parents and friends they were going to Chechnya.[34] Both were said to be religiously observant.

The exact details of how the Saudi volunteers were inducted into the September 11th plot is unclear. It seems that during 2000 a dozen or so volunteers were picked out from the thousands of recruits in the training camps in Afghanistan at the time by senior figures from within the 'al-Qaeda hardcore'. Al-Farooq, the camp where the most motivated and capable of the volunteers were sent, would have been an obvious place to look. Saudi citizens were useful because they would be able to exploit the good relations of the kingdom with the USA to easily obtain visas. One obvious place to find Saudis were the guesthouses run specifically for them in Kandahar. There is certainly evidence that, once selected, the recruits for the hijacking were moved to the city and given special training there. One, Ahmed al-Haznawi, the son of a cleric in a mosque in al-Baha, recorded a 'martyrdom video' in March 2001. 'It is time to kill the Americans on their own ground,' al-Haznawi, wearing combat dress and a black and white headdress, said in the film.

The decision to attack the USA on its home territory (the diplomatic niceties of the sovereignty of individual embassies notwithstanding) rather than abroad appears to have been taken between the end of 1998 (when Abu Doha applied for assistance for Ahmed Ressam) and late

1999 at a series of meetings in Khost, Kandahar, Jalalabad or possibly Kabul. We cannot say with any great certainly who attended these meetings but it appears they included bin Laden himself, al-Zawahiri, Mohammed Atef, Abu Zubaydah, Saif al-Adel and Khalid Shaikh Mohammed, i.e. the key members of the small band constituting the 'al-Qaeda hardcore' in Afghanistan at the time.

So far, few details have emerged of the exact planning that went into the September 11th operation. In a discussion with a Saudi cleric recorded in Afghanistan some time after September 11th and released by the American government in early December 2001, bin Laden made clear that he was unaware of the operational details of the plan, though he had knowledge of its broad objectives. He had, he said, used his civil engineering experience to calculate the damage the planes would do when they struck the towers. This is corroborated by the statements made by Ramzi bin al-Shibh, one of the Hamburg cell, when interviewed by an al-Jazeera journalist while in hiding in Karachi in the late summer of 2002.[35]

Al-Shibh was interviewed with Khalid Shaikh Mohammed. After the fire that had exposed Ramzi Yousef and the Bojinka plot, Shaikh had made his way, possibly via the Su-Casa guesthouse, from the Philippines to Doha, Qatar, where he had powerful friends in the government. He was a guest of the Qatari minister for religious affairs and spent 1995–6 raising funds among wealthy and devout businessmen in the Gulf. He lived openly and travelled widely. American investigators have tracked his movements through Italy, Egypt, Singapore, Jordan, Thailand and the Philippines.[36] When the FBI tried to arrest him in Qatar in 1996, he was tipped off and fled to Afghanistan, about the only place where he knew he would be safe. As noted before, Khalid Shaikh Mohammed is typical of many of the senior activists who emerged after the war against the Soviets. Using his own connections and backers, he tried to build up his own independent operations, only joining forces with bin Laden at a relatively late stage. It is likely that, having collectively taken the broad strategy decision to strike the mainland in late 1999, bin Laden and al-Zawahiri then left lieutenants such as Shaikh or Mohammed Atef to sort out the details, picking and choosing from the plans that were being put to them by volunteers, suggesting others of their own. In his interview with al-Jazeera, Shaikh claimed the idea for an attack using planes as bombs was his own. This is certainly possible given his previous involvement in Ramzi Yousef's operations in the Philippines, but does not make it any less likely that the Hamburg cell had also evolved a similar plan simultaneously and independently.

One possible scenario, which marries the various conflicting interpretations of the evidence, is that the Hamburg cell, having formulated its idea, approached the al-Qaeda hardcore with it at a particularly auspicious time. In late 1999, following the strategy meeting, the group's senior military planners were trying to sort out the details of a series of attacks on America. Their ideas had so far centred on al-Hazmi and al-Midhar, who may have originally been sent to America to play some kind of role in the Millennium plot, and the arrival of the Hamburg cell members with their own ideas to use planes to attack American was fortuitous for them. Al-Qaeda in Afghanistan had access to cash, expertise, training facilities and leadership capabilities that were beyond Atta and his band. But, Khalid Shaikh Mohammed told al-Jazeera, though al-Qaeda 'had scores of volunteers... [their] problem at the time was to select suitable people who were familiar with the West'.[37] With Atta and his friends as a nucleus, the plot was expanded. Al-Hazmi and al-Midhar were linked into the new plan but kept apart for clear security reasons. The various teams would only come together at a very late stage.

Bin Laden and his close associates may have been short of 'suitable volunteers' but they were not short of funds. Since September 11th, investigators have worked hard to uncover the networks that funded terrorist operations across the world. The picture that emerges is of a vast and complex global network of charities, government aid organisations, private businesses, banks and accounts that are used to raise, hold and transfer cash to fund terrorism. The cash itself comes from a variety of sources. Some is diverted, often with the cognisance and approval of the donors, from collections from congregations in mosques or elsewhere. Giving *zakat* is one of the fundamentals of Islam and very substantial sums are raised in this way. Other funds come in private donations from wealthy individuals: Gulf merchants, Qatari, Emirati or Saudi princes and other sympathisers from all over the world. Once again, sometimes these funds are used for legitimate relief and social work, sometimes for da'wa or proselytisation, sometimes they are diverted to buy equipment or facilitate the travel of mujahideen to Kashmir, Chechnya, Bosnia or elsewhere and occasionally they are drawn on, by those with the connections and the credibility, for terrorist actions. Single organisations, such as the Saudi International Islamic Relief Organisation, can fulfil all these roles at once.[38]

The amount of money in the system at any one time, and thus potentially available to fund terrorist operations, is huge. As ever, bin Laden appears as one element among many. Enaam Arnaout, a Syrian currently living in America, is alleged to be one of the key figures in the global network of financing terror though he denies all the charges against him. According to the US government indictment, while working with bin Laden and Azzam in the MAK in Pakistan in the mid 1980s, Arnaout, though serving as a 'director of communications' at bin Laden's 'lion's den' training camp, was closest to Hekmatyar's Hizb-e-Islami, for whom he bought weapons and other materiel. Much of the money for the purchases was channelled through a charity called the Benevolence International Foundation (BIF), of which Arnaout was executive director. During the early and mid 1990s,the indictment alleges, Arnaout provided a satellite telephone and organised and funded special training for mujahideen from Hekmatyar's faction in 1991–2 at a camp near Khost. He also produced fundraising and recruitment videos for the Islamic militants in Bosnia, procured money and equipment for Chechen guerrillas and facilitated the movement of senior militant figures, including men close to bin Laden, around Europe and the Middle East. A 'list of [BIF's] wealthy sponsors from Saudi Arabia' found in Bosnia 'include[d] references to… bin Laden' among several others. The sort of sums the BIF was dealing in was revealed by a bank transfer between an account in Switzerland and one in the USA, wired sometime between June 2000 and September 2001, for $1,414,406.[39] Hundreds of such transactions occur everyday and give a useful indication of how much cash there is available. Even if bin Laden had ever received substantial funds from his inheritance they would be dwarfed by the sort of money habitually disbursed by even medium-sized Saudi charities.

The September 11th attacks cost around $500,000. This may have been drawn from funds already hidden in accounts held within the Islamic banking system by associates of bin Laden or may have been raised specifically from one or several individual donors. The money was sent to the hijackers by individuals in Dubai.[40] Al-Shehhi, al-Hazmi and al-Midhar were all sent money through the city. In July 2000, shortly after arriving in America, al-Shehhi opened a joint checking account with Atta at SunTrust bank in Florida which, over the next three months, received four money transfers totalling $109,500, considered the 'primary funding' for the September 11th operation by the FBI. The transfers were again sent from Dubai. Many of the Muscle appear to have been given cash funds, converted into travellers cheques, when they transited Dubai on their way from Saudi Arabia to America. Others simply used foreign checking accounts or credit cards at Saudi Arabian or Emirati banks. Much of the money went through Faiz Ahmed, an Emirati who was the only non-Saudi member of the Muscle. The September 11th group does not appear to have used *hawala*, the traditional, untraceable, trust-based banking system.

At the risk of increasing the *dramatis personae* in this chapter beyond manageable limits, three other individuals must swiftly be mentioned when examining the evolution and execution of the September 11th plot. They are Zacarias Moussaoui, the Frenchman recruited by bin al-Shibh to be a pilot for one hijacked jet when it became apparent that al-Shibh himself was not going to get a visa to travel to the USA; Mohammed Hayder al-Zammar, a middle-aged and bombastic Syrian-born Islamic activist and veteran of the war in Afghanistan who appears to have been influential in radicalising Atta and his young friends in Hamburg; and Abu Qatada, the London-based ideologue, whose work, along with that of Abdallah Azzam was favoured by the Hamburg cell.

Moussaoui, who, were it not for the appalling nature of his ambitions, would be very difficult to take seriously, was arrested after behaving suspiciously at a flight simulator in Minnesota in August 2001. He had failed to learn the requisite skills at his first flight school, where he had registered as Zuleiman Tango Tango, and tried elsewhere. Senior al-Qaeda figures, such as Khalid Shaikh Mohammed, who is thought to have met Moussaoui in Afghanistan, were concerned by the Frenchman's poor tradecraft and eccentricities and were apparently unsurprised when he was arrested.[41] The trip in 2000 was Moussaoui's second trip to Afghanistan. In early 1998, he had made his way independently to Khaldan camp.[42] Moussaoui, who was born in Narbonne in southern France, appears to have been inducted into radical Islam when he came into contact with Qutada and his circle after moving to London in the early 1990s.[43] Though of Moroccan descent, Moussaoui thus became involved in the work of Algerian GIA and GSPC supporters in the UK.

By going through an established group with a local and tradional with a local and international agenda, Moussaoui was following a more traditional route to the al-Qaeda hardcore than the members of the Hamburg cell. The latter were not in any way affiliated to extant military organisations. Al-Zammar may have played the familiar 'older man' role (as Abderraouf Hannachi had for Ressam, Abu Hosha had for Hijazi, Abu Qutada had for Beghal and Beghal himself had for others), but the members of the Hamburg cell were never inducted into the Algerian, Egyptian, or indeed any other local struggle. Instead they went straight to the al-Qaeda hardcore. From the outset, their targets were America and other representatives of global kufr, rather than the regimes in their own country. Though Atta loathed Mubarak's government in Egypt, there is little evidence that the others in the Hamburg cell harboured any great ill will towards the political leaders of their own respective homelands. Their hatred was primarily directed at the West. This mirrors bin Laden's own ideological and strategic shift and is a radical and important shift with profound implications for the future face of modern Islamic militancy.

By the late summer of 2001 the final arrangements for the September 11th attacks were being made. Al-Hamzi and al-Midhar had proved incapable of piloting a hijacked jet so a replacement pilot was found for the San Diego-based cell. This was Hani Hanjour, a rich and weak-willed Saudi who had drifted around the USA and Saudi Arabia for a decade, dreaming of being an airline pilot. Moussaoui, arrested in August, was not replaced, if indeed he was ever going to fly. Atta had spent the previous year travelling around Europe and the USA, managing the operation and coordinating with al-Shibh and others. There is no evidence to suggest that there was another 'in-country' commander, superior to Atta, in the USA. In the last weeks of August, Atta organised the concentration of the teams nearer their targets and conducted last-minute surveillance and research. Towards the end of August 2001, the 19 men began moving into a series of motels, hotels and apartments along the length of the American east coast.

At 3am on 29 August, Atta called al-Shibh in the Marienstrasse flat in Harburg to tell him which date had been selected for the attack.[44] Over the next few days, around 20 men connected with the hijackers left Hamburg. Several of them remain unidentified. Bahaji flew to Islamabad.[45] Al-Shibh cleared the flat and left too. On 6 September in Afghanistan, bin Laden received notice that the plan was going ahead.[46] On the evening of 10 September, all the hijackers were in position. Each group had a copy of a letter, probably dictated to Abulaziz al-Omari by Atta. 'When you board the plane,' the letter said, 'remember that this is a battle in the sake of God, which is worth the whole world and all that is in it.' The hijackers were reminded that, as martyrs, they would be rewarded with paradise: 'And when zero-hour comes, open your chest and welcome death in the cause of God… And let your last words be "There is no God but God and Mohammed is his messenger".'[47]

CHAPTER SIXTEEN

THE WAR ON TERROR

On the horizon, the hills were sharp against a pale stormy sky. Beneath them was a huge gravel plain that was blank and grey and featureless but for the odd village of low, flat-roofed houses and an occasional stand of slender ash trees with very yellow leaves. In the middle of the plain were Major Garry Green of 45 Royal Marine Commando, two enormous rubber bladders full of aviation fuel, several score British soldiers, five eager if slightly bewildered Afghan coalition fighters, a bearded American special forces man, four huge piles of very large camouflaged boxes and a small pack of journalists.

It was April 2002 and the 'War on Terror' was in full swing. With a dozen other reporters, I had flown out of Bagram, the main airbase 30 miles north of Kabul, in a British Royal Air Force Chinook. We had swept low over the Shomali plains, skirted the capital's western suburbs and then dropped through the hills that circle the city and out into Logar province. The Ministry of Defence had refused to tell us where the British component of 'Operation Mountain Lion', the US-led coalition's campaign to clear Afghanistan of 'AQT' (al-Qaeda and Taliban), had been deployed but, as the Chinooks circled above the landing zone, it was easy to work out where we were.

On the southern horizon, beyond the town of Gardez, were the Shah-e-Kot mountains where the Americans had clashed with 'AQT' two months previously in the only set-piece engagement since Tora Bora. The US-led forces had found the resistance from a few hundred former Taliban and foreign fighters unexpectedly stiff and had suffered relatively heavy casualties. It was in the aftermath of that confrontation that fresh British combat forces had been deployed. On the eastern horizon, I could see the hills I had driven through on my way to Khost six months before.

The British troops had set up a forward base to allow helicopters to refuel close to the combat zone and to provide a staging post for troops on their way to the fighting. There was, Major Green told us, a significant risk of a mortar or rocket attack. But it was nothing like the fighting in the autumn or indeed any other conflict that I have ever covered. There was no 'crack-thump' of artillery, no rattling small-arms fire, no smoke, no flames and no streams of scared refugees. We watched the distant hills. Even through binoculars they revealed no more than fissured gulleys, scrubby forest and interminable scree slopes.

A Royal Marines mortar and heavy machine-gun troop was sitting on the ground waiting for their transport. Their rucksacks were vast, swollen with ammunition, rations and huge metal bits of weapon. They weighed, the men proudly said, as much as 140lbs. Their desert battle fatigues had been softened by dust and sweat and hung heavily from their bodies. The men smoked and watched the hills and spoke in quiet voices.

More helicopters rotored in and out. The soldiers guarding the base scanned the middle distance through their gun sights. The brand new, heavily armed desert jeeps were lined up beside the camouflage nets. There were dark rain clouds in the south and shafts of light flickered through them and played over the plain.

For several weeks, the Royal Marines scoured sections of Afghan hillside, finding very little except old arms caches and truculent shepherds. Elsewhere in the country, thousands of American troops were engaged on similar missions, dubbed 'clean and sweep' to avoid the Vietnam-era connotations of 'search and destroy'. I spent several weeks at Bagram as a guest of the 10th Mountain Division and every evening I went for a run. I would jog out of the journalists' tent in the 101st Airborne's encampment, past the Spanish medical teams, past the Royal Marines and their six 105mm guns, and out onto the old Soviet-built airstrip where long lines of helicopters, Apaches, Blackhawks, Chinooks, and A10 Tankbuster jets gleamed in the low evening light. During the night, we slept fitfully, woken by the aircraft ferrying special forces troops out into the hills.

Allied troops had moved into Bagram within days of the fall of Kabul. During the spring of 2002, as the structures of the camp gradually grew more permanent, the aims of the military operations subtly changed too. At Tora Bora the objectives had been explicit: find, capture or kill bin Laden and as many of his men and his Taliban allies as possible. By May, American and British military planners were talking about 'denying' territory to the militants instead. Their job, they said, was to keep Afghanistan 'al-Qaeda-free'. It was a tacit admission that most of the people they had wanted to catch had escaped. It was clear that hunting them was a job for which the hardware that had been assembled at Bagram was particularly ill suited.

The failure of the Marines to get a single confirmed 'kill' was understandable. The task they had been expected to complete was unrealistic. The professionalism of the soldiers themselves and the achievements of the competent, popular and successful United Nations peacekeeping mission in Kabul were forgotten. This was a pity because the war, though it tragically cost the lives of many civilians in Afghanistan, gave the country its best opportunity for several decades to build a peaceful and secure future.[1] The foreign militants who were causing so much trouble and were so loathed by most Afghans were expelled, the Taliban, whose increasing radicalism outweighed the enhanced security they brought, were removed from power and the interference of regional powers, notably Pakistan, Iran and Saudi Arabia, in the country's internal politics was, and at the time of writing still is, largely curtailed. Millions of refugees, exiled from their homes for up to 25 years, are returning. In the autumn of 2001, I had been deeply concerned about the prospect of a ground war in Afghanistan. When, a year to the day after the start of the hostilities, I visited a girls' school in Jalalabad and saw hundreds of neatly uniformed pupils being taught under the trees in the playground because the classrooms were all full, I knew I had been wrong.

It is, of course, early days yet. The amount of money contributed by Western powers, given the sums spent on fighting in the country in the last 20 years, has been miserly. The shortsighted abandonment of Afghanistan at the end of the 1980s risks being repeated. Many Afghans are becoming angry at the slow pace of change and this growing resentment has been exacerbated both by the strong sense that the government is a puppet of Washington and by insensitive behaviour by American troops. Though Kabul has been transformed as a city, huge swathes of countryside are still acutely deprived. People are still dying of hunger-related diseases and exposure in the provinces. There is, and will be for some time, a significant risk that extremists will garner sufficient support to become a serious threat. Certainly the number of attacks on international bases is rising. It is now impossible to drive alone through much of the country, as I did without a second thought when the Taliban were in power. Life in the poorest state in Asia is still hard and dangerous.

But, as one Western diplomat wryly told me in Kabul in the summer of 2002, 'Afghanistan is not Sweden'. Indeed, in many ways an old pattern has reasserted itself in the country. There is a Durrani Pashtun head of state in Kabul, whose power depends on patronage and works funded by foreign powers; strong particularist powers in the provinces have an uneasy relationship, rooted in mutual benefit and mutual competition, with the metropolis; there is a wide gulf between the cities, especially Kabul, and the countryside; a strong degree of ethnic tension continues, and there is continuing bloodletting as rival warlords jockey for position. None of these things is new in Afghanistan. Many have been exacerbated by decades of war. However, the simple fact remains that Afghanistan's 25 million people have a better chance of a better future than they have had for a long time.

But what about the rest of the 'War on Terror'? How has 'al-Qaeda', however defined, fared in the aftermath of the war in Afghanistan? And how will it fare in the aftermath of the conflict in Iraq and future wars?

President George Bush is reported to keep a list of around two dozen senior 'al-Qaeda figures' in his desk in the Oval office. These are the hardest of the 'al-Qaeda hardcore'. He crosses them off the list as they are killed or captured. One of the first names to be struck through was that of Mohammed Atef, bin Laden's veteran military commander, who was killed by a missile strike on the outskirts of Kabul in November 2001. Anas al-Liby, another senior figure linked to the 1998 embassy bombings and other attacks, was almost certainly killed on the Shomali plains around the same time. Other less well known, more junior figures are now dead too. In September 2001, Algerian security forces had killed Emad Abdelwahid Ahmed Alwan, bin Laden's emissary to north Africa. Two months later, Qaed Salim Sinan al-Harethi, a Yemeni linked to the strike on the *USS Cole*, was obliterated by a Hellfire missile fired from a pilotless drone over the Yemen in November 2002. Many senior men have been captured. In March 2002, Abu Zubaydah was seized in a safe house in the eastern Pakistani city of Faisalabad. In September 2002, Ramzi bin al-Shibh, his location possibly betrayed by his boastful interview with al-Jazeera, was captured after a gun battle in Karachi. Khalid Shaikh Mohammed is now believed to be in custody too. More junior cadres who were wanted for their involvement in a whole series of different plots have been picked up. They range from Mohammed Khalim bin Jaffar, the man whose video of US targets in Singapore was found in the ruins of Atef's home in Kabul, to Abd al-Rahim al-Nashiri, identified as al-Qaeda's chief in the Gulf.

There has also been the physical damage to the group. The system of camps in Afghanistan, built up over nearly two decades, has been entirely lost to the Islamic radical movement. So has much hardware and research. A secure base from which to plan and organise was destroyed. There is nowhere else that is in anyway comparable to Taliban-run Afghanistan and nor is there likely to be in the coming decades. This has left the 'al-Qaeda hardcore' with few places to hide. Those senior activists still at liberty have to work with constant fear of arrest or surveillance. Coordination and planning are vastly more difficult. Few states will risk sheltering them. Only a small number of lawless zones – in parts of Africa, Bangladesh, the Indonesian archipelago, along the Afghan-Pakistan border, Chechnya and amid the high mountains of central Asia – remain as possible refuges. The missile strike that killed al-Harethi was an indication of what the future holds for the remaining members of the 'al-Qaeda hardcore'.

In short, the operations of late 2001 put an end to the concentration of Islamic militant leadership, volunteers and infrastructure in Afghanistan that had come about in the late 1990s. It was shown to have been merely a transient phase in the history of Islamic militancy, comparable, to an extent, to the concentration of radical activists in Pakistan between 1988 and 1992. By the beginning of 2002, the physical assets were destroyed, the personnel scattered.

Like particles after the Big Bang, still travelling long after the explosion, or an engine running down slowly after power has been cut off, the pattern of militancy and the style of terrorist attacks established during the late 1990s continued unchanged for some time. In late November 2001, while at Tora Bora, bin Laden told his associates to disperse. Money was given to anyone with a viable plan to launch attacks on Western interests. It took a few months for the results of this decision to become apparent but, in May 2002, three Saudis who had been planning to pilot small powerboats loaded with explosives into British and American warships as they passed through the Straits of Gibraltar were arrested in Morocco. They were led by Zuhair Hilal Mohammed al-Tubaiti, the man who had been told to go and do some homework when he had asked bin Laden's aides for a 'martyrdom operation' a year previously. As the American jets had roared over Tora Bora he had been given $5,000 by Ahmed al-Moula al-Billal, the bin Laden lieutenant who had previously brushed him off, and told to get on with whatever attack he could manage. Al-Tubaiti had escaped Afghanistan into Iran in December 2001. He then flew to Morocco, arriving on 13 January on a flight from Tehran via Rome. In Morocco, he recruited several accomplices. Along with the attack on British and American warships in the Straits of Gibraltar, al-Tubaiti planned to blow up a café and attack public buses. He was arrested by Rabat's intelligence service before he could implement any of his schemes.[2]

A month before al-Tubaiti's arrest, a huge truck-bomb exploded outside a 2,000-year-old synagogue in Djerba, Tunisia. This attack too had originated in Afghanistan during the last days of the fighting of autumn 2001. Twenty-one people, mainly tourists, were killed. The bomber was a 24-year-old drifter and former smuggler called Nizar Nouar, who came from a local lower middle-class Tunisian family. He had no radical history but had spent time in Montreal, Canada, where he may have become involved in Algerian radical groups. He also had radical Muslim friends in Germany. His family believe he had spent 2000 and 2001 in Afghanistan. As the Taliban collapsed, Nouar, like al-Tubaiti, appears to have been given a sum of money and sent off to set in train terrorist operations. Investigators quickly established that he had called a number linked to Khalid Shaikh Mohammed a few hours before he died.[3] Shaikh appears to have used his contacts among European militants, largely connected to Egyptian and Algerian groups, to source the material needed for the attack. In May, Ahmed al-Moula al-Bilal surfaced on the Pakistan-Afghanistan border to give an interview to an Arabic newspaper in which he claimed the attack in the name of 'al-Qaeda', one of the few examples of the group publicly using the name to describe themselves.[4]

The involvement of Khalid Shaikh Mohammed was interesting. The veteran activist had operated for a long time without a solid base before moving to Afghanistan in 1996 and, in the aftermath of the war there, was reverting to what he had always done best, drawing together the different elements necessary to create an attack. In the summer of 2001, he gave his extraordinary interview, with Ramzi bin al-Shibh, in Karachi. Bin al-Shibh was arrested eight weeks afterwards; Shaikh stayed ahead of his pursuers for another eight months. Osama bin Laden and Ayman al-Zawahiri are still free.

Beyond the 'al-Qaeda hardcore' was the 'network of networks'. How have they fared? The vast majority of those foreigners in Afghanistan, as we saw in preceding chapters, were not connected to al-Qaeda at all but were involved with the Harkat-ul-Mujahideen, the Islamic Movement of Uzbekistan, the Taliban themselves or other groups. As had happened between 1989 and 1992, the dispersal of those militants who had been in Afghanistan, above and beyond those with bin Laden or close to him, caused significant radicalisation wherever they ended up. HUM cadres in Kashmir and elsewhere in Pakistan sparked a new wave of sectarian killing and activity in Kashmir. The Arabs who made their way to Chechnya galvanised groups there. In Algeria, a new influx of Yemenis and other foreigners was held responsible for the ambush of a military convoy in November 2002, in which more than 40 soldiers died. It was the most effective single strike by militants there for years.

The case of one militant who had fled Afghanistan was highlighted in February 2003 when US Secretary of State Colin Powell set out the American case for attacking Iraq before the United Nations. Abu Musab al-Zarqawi, a Jordanian militant who had been running his own small group in Afghanistan since the mid-1980s, was forced to leave the country in March 2002. Al-Zarqawi had operated independently of bin Laden, running his own training camp near Herat. It was a small operation and al-Zarqawi was not considered a significant player in Afghanistan at the time. It is likely he had some contact with bin Laden but never took the bayat and never made any formal alliance with the Saudi or his close associates. He was just one of the thousands of activists committed to jihad living and working in Afghanistan during the 1990s. Wounded in the fighting at Shah-e-Kot, he fled first to Iran, which expelled him into northern Iraq. From there, according to the Americans, he sought medical treatment in Baghdad where he remained. Powell called al-Zarqawi a 'bin Laden associate', revealing either a wilful misconception of the sheer variety of activists and radical groups that were based in Afghanistan in the late 1990s or genuine ignorance about the real nature of modern Islamic militancy and, by extension, that of 'al-Qaeda'.[5]

Bin Laden has attempted to keep abreast of the shifts caused by this new diaspora of Arab Afghans among the modern Islamic militant movement by sending emissaries to try to build his influence among the newly emergent groups and with new leaders. But he has not been very successful. The sense among activists now is that, though his iconic value remains, bin Laden's time as an effective player in radical activism has passed. The GSPC has rejected his advances. They are not the only group to do so.

Following September 11th, security forces around the world made huge efforts to break groups in their respective countries. They scored many notable successes. Ibn Khattab, the famous Saudi-Jordanian leader, was killed in Chechnya. In Egypt, any militancy that might have survived the crackdowns of the mid and late 1990s was crushed. In Pakistan, a confused situation prevailed as the military government tried to reverse, at least in part, the policy of nearly 20 years and rein in, if not entirely eradicate, the terrorists and militants that had been acting as Islamabad's proxies for so long. In the Philippines, the Abu Sayyaf group suffered under American-aided military offensives. All across Europe, the police, bolstered by new legislation, rounded up activists. In Britain, Abu Qutada was arrested and imprisoned along with scores of others militants. Finsbury Park Mosque was raided in January 2003. One result of the crackdowns, accelerating a process that has been going on for years, is the shift of jihadi activity to less well-policed, more peripheral regions where the material, space and targets the militants seek are all available.

But the temptation to see these groups, 'the network of networks', as 'bin Laden-linked' or part of al-Qaeda must be resisted. 'Al-Qaeda', or even bin Laden, may perform a specific function for many of them at specific times but Algerian, Chechen and Indonesian groups are rooted in specific local contingencies and causes. Islamic militancy is a broad-based, multivalent, diverse movement. It goes far beyond the deeds or words of one man or one small organisation.

In the aftermath of September 11th, the Bush administration was swift to move against those they felt were sponsoring or financially facilitating terrorism. The Americans publicly identified 300 individuals and entities and within months $112m had been frozen in accounts all over the world. Yet over the following year only another $10m was seized. In September 2002, the United Nations committee monitoring 'al-Qaeda' announced that the group's financial backers in North Africa, the Middle East and Asia were still managing at least $30 million in investments, with some estimates going as high as $300 million.[6] The committee noted that private donations to the group were continuing 'largely unabated'.[7] The FBI designated nine men as key terrorist financiers: seven Saudis, a Pakistani and an Egyptian.[8] But to pick out individuals is ludicrous. The basis for the funding of modern Islamic terrorism, whether committed by individuals linked to bin Laden or any other group or acting on their own, is the sympathy felt for the cause among millions of Muslims worldwide. Stopping the activities of seven men will do nothing to stop the problem. The FBI and US Treasury estimate that as much as $100 million has flowed from private sources within Saudi Arabia alone to 'terrorist groups 'in recent years, let alone from other Gulf countries. Huge sums flow from devout, and not-so-devout, Muslims into Islamic charities from all over the world. Much of this money is spent on spreading hardline Wahhabi-style Islam, some is spent on relief for needy Muslims, some is diverted to fund terrorism.[9] Since September 11th, donations to radical movements, all over the Islamic world, have substantially increased.

On 12 October 2002, three bombs exploded in Bali killing more than 180 people. The most devastating destroyed a nightclub full of Western holidaymakers. The details of the plot are still being uncovered but it appears that a group of around a dozen local Indonesian Islamic activists, many related to each other, were behind the attack. According to the Indonesian intelligence service, they were directed by Hambali, the veteran militant with links to the 'al-Qaeda hardcore'. But according to the Indonesian police, and most other analysts, the Bali group was a radical splinter-group within the nebulous Southeast Asian network known as Jemaa Islamiyya and was largely 'home-grown'. The group, composed largely of young men who had no previous involvement in terrorism, were not 'recruited' but came together of their own accord. They decided to go ahead with a campaign of violence directed at local Western targets in late September 2002, despite the opposition of more moderate senior figures within Jemaa Islamiyya. The more junior members of the group appear to have been recruited only weeks before the attack itself. Local police are adamant that no link with 'al-Qaeda' has been proven. There certainly appears to have been no 'al-Qaeda' master-bomber, no coordination by any close associate of bin Laden and no recruitment. The plan appears to have been the bombers' own.[10]

This makes Bali significant. If recent Islamic terrorist attacks can be located on a scale with those entirely organised and executed by relatively senior al-Qaeda cadres at one end and those conducted with no input from anyone from the 'al-Qaeda hardcore' at the other, most of the attacks during 2002, including the attempt in Morocco, the attack on the synagogue in Tunisia and, possibly, the car-bombing of Israeli tourists at a hotel in Mombassa in November, would be clustered in its middle. Like the majority of attacks since the mid-1990s, they involve 'al-Qaeda' but only in terms of providing the practical support necessary for self-motivating groups or individuals to fulfil their terrorist ambitions. Bali, a major attack involving sophisticated techniques and motivated by a profound hatred of anything that represented the West and kufr, was an attack *in the style of al-Qaeda*, but apparently not involving the group itself and would thus be placed further down the scale. As there was no one, in Afghanistan or elsewhere, to go to for training and support, the Bali bombers did it on their own.[11]

Along with the bigger attacks, there has been a steady background hum of violence directed at Western targets. If these too are placed on our scale, a clear pattern begins to emerge. Very few of these strikes involve the 'al-Qaeda hardcore' in any meaningful way. Indeed, as 2002 turned to 2003, the involvement of bin Laden and his associates seems to drop away entirely. The markers on our scale all begin to shift to one end.

In May 2001 in Karachi, a bomb on a bus placed by a group related to Harkat-ul-Mujahideen, the Pakistani group, killed 11 French submarine engineers.[12] It was only one of a series of attacks in Pakistan. The most serious included an attempt to blow up a US consulate and an attack on a school. Both involved groups of local militants. There have been bombings in the Philippines; two local men shot and killed a US Marine at a training facility in Kuwait; and an explosives-laden boat rammed a French oil tanker off the Yemen. The latter is the only attack that can be linked to 'al-Qaeda', though no proof has yet emerged of a connection. In Jordan, an American embassy worker was shot dead. The attack was blamed on Abu Musab al-Zarqawi, someone whose links with 'al-Qaeda' are tenuous at best. Ten men arrested in Jordan in March 2002 for conspiring to carry out terror attacks against US and Israeli targets had, security officials stressed, 'no links to al-Qaeda'.[13] In Afghanistan, rockets are being fired at American troops on an almost daily basis, but by local Afghan militants, or local Afghans paid by militants, who have nothing to do with bin Laden. In Yemen in December 2002, three American missionary doctors were shot and killed by someone who admired bin Laden but was not in contact with any al-Qaeda operatives.[14]

These attacks, following the destruction in Afghanistan of the autumn of 2001, were met with a degree of surprise. Headlines announced 'the return of al-Qaeda'. If the threat from modern Islamic terrorism is conceived of as a single organisation led by an identifiable commander, then this apparent astonishment is comprehensible. If the 'al-Qaeda hardcore' is recognised for what it is, one element of the many that comprise contemporary Islamic militancy, then it is not. For these low-level 'freelance' attacks, complemented by occasional larger attacks by independent groups such as the one that formed so swiftly in Bali, are the future of modern Islamic terrorism. They are the future of the 'war on terror' too.

At first glance, bin Laden's position looks weak. Though his exact location is unknown, he is likely to be hiding among the Pashtun tribes along the mountainous Afghan-Pakistani frontier south of Khost and north of the Pakistani city of Quetta. He was last seen in Jalalabad on 14 November 2001, a day or so before the Taliban evacuated the city. A month later, his voice was heard on a radio during the fighting at Tora Bora, though this may have been a decoy. There are several unconfirmed reports that he and al-Zawahiri were near Khost and Gardez in the spring of 2002. Since then, his appearances have been limited to increasingly infrequent taped statements.

But from bin Laden's point of view, the war is going very well. On 27 December, even as everything he had built over the preceding five and a half years appeared to be collapsing around him, bin Laden issued a confident call to arms. 'Regardless if Osama is killed or survives,' he said, 'The awakening has started, praise be to God.'[15]

Bin Laden has always aimed to radicalise and mobilise those Muslims who have shunned his summons to action. This has been the critical problem for radical Islamic activists for three decades. Bin Laden's sponsorship of terrorist attacks has always been a means to an end. The destruction of life and property was only a useful bonus. The main consideration has always been proving that there is a cosmic battle between good and evil underway and that Islam, and thus all that is seen as good and righteous and just, is in desperate peril. Once the umma are convinced of this, bin Laden thinks, the world's Muslims will rise up, return to the true path and, having thus earned the blessing of God, cast off the shackles that have been laid upon them by what he sees as centuries of 'humiliation and contempt'. According to bin Laden, their struggle, which will be a violent one, will be rewarded with victory.

If bin Laden's aim is to radicalise and mobilise, then one would surmise that the aim of those running the war on terror would be to counter those efforts. A swift survey of popular newspapers in the Islamic world (and beyond) or of Friday sermons in the Middle East's mosques or a few hours spent in a bazaar or a *shouk* or a coffee shop or kebab restaurant in Damascus, Kabul, Karachi, Cairo, Casablanca or indeed in London or New York shows clearly whose efforts are meeting with greater success. Bin Laden is winning.

The world is a far more radicalised place now than it was prior to September 11th. Helped by a powerful surge of anti-Americanism, by Washington's incredible failure to stem the haemorrhaging of support and sympathy prompted by the attacks of 2001 and by modern communications, the language of bin Laden and his concept of the cosmic struggle has now spread among tens of millions of people, particularly the young and angry, around the world. It informs their views and, increasingly, their actions. In Indonesia in November 2002, days after the Bali bombing, I saw young Islamic activists wearing bin Laden T-shirts. There were pro-Palestinian slogans on many walls in Jakarta. Hundreds of thousands of young men log onto to jihadi websites across the world each day. Once the anger and resentment of young men and women throughout the Islamic world was voiced in the language of relatively moderate political Islamists. Now the slogans are those of bin Laden, al-Zawahiri, Abu Qatada, Sheikh Abdel Omar Rahman and the other public ideologues of the most radical extreme of modern militancy. The brand of activism, articulated in Islamic terms and justified by reference to the Islamic tradition personified by bin Laden, is fast becoming a global discourse of dissent.

This has two consequences. The first is an ideological convergence among extant groups, among the 'network of networks'. This can be detected everywhere. Organisations (and individuals) with no previous interest in 'global jihad' now have vastly broadened perspectives. Where once groups focused on local concerns, now they look on all that is kufr as their target. Algerian activists arrested in France in late 2002 were planning to attack the Russian embassy in Paris in revenge for atrocities committed by Moscow's troops in Chechnya. In Pakistan, Abu Zubaydah was captured at a safe house belonging to the Sipa-e-Sahaba Pakistan (SSP), a group previously interested only in a local sectarian agenda. The backgrounds and demands of the men who kidnapped *Wall Street Journal* reporter Daniel Pearl in January 2002 are further evidence of the convergence of local groups. The kidnappers were led by Omar Saeed Sheikh, the British-born Pakistani whose release had been forced by the HUM hijackers of the Indian plane two years previously. It is thought that Pearl was actually killed by a Yemeni who had been fighting in Afghanistan. Other conspirators included members of at least three different Pakistani groups, none of which had ever shown much previous interest in international jihad. Palestinian groups are completing their journey from secular leftist thought to jihadi Salafism. Their struggle, in a way that has never previously been the case, is being seen, along with Kashmir, Chechnya and even Iraq, as part of one titanic battle. Overcoming the fitna, or the factionalism and parochialism, of militant groups, was one of the main reasons bin Laden set up 'al-Qaeda'. He is finally achieving that aim.

The second result of the new radicalisation is that a whole new cadre of terrorists is being created. The third definition of 'al-Qaeda' outlined in my introduction was the ideology and the idea of modern radical Islamic militancy, the resonance of the ideas of bin Laden, al-Zawahiri and their lieutenants among the broader movement of Islamic activism. It was 'al-Qaeda-ism'. Though the hardcore is scattered, and the network of networks suffering under the pressure exerted by local security services, the craving for jihad that sent tens of thousands of young men to seek training and jihad in Afghanistan is flourishing. In the post-September 11th environment, the message of bin Laden makes sense for millions.

It is from these millions that the new wave of terrorists will come. They will be 'freelance' operators who have no obvious connection to any existing group. They will have no previous involvement in terrorism. They may not have access to sophisticated explosives, automatic weapons or rockets, but once they have accepted bin Laden's worldview they will be committed to finding the resources necessary to launch their own violent jihad, whether their weapons be castor beans cooked up to form a basic poison in a flat in north London, a kitchen knife plunged into the chest of a policeman in Manchester or an aircraft full of fuel and passengers. For these men, as for Mohammed Atta, jihad is a profoundly felt religious duty. It brings them something that nothing else can. They will not be diverted from it by a few extra bollards outside an embassy or by the destruction of a training camp in a far-off country.

CONCLUSION

I met Didar in northern Iraq in August 2002. I was investigating the Ansar ul Islam group post-September 11th. In the aftermath of the war in Afghanistan, scores of Arabs fighters who had been with the Taliban, bin Laden and others made their way to the scrubby hills above Halabja and catalysed renewed violence.

Didar was born, he said, in 1985 in the sprawling city of Arbil, the capital of the *de facto* mini-state of Iraqi Kurdistan, where the Kurdish Democratic Party (the KDP), who run the western half of the enclave, have their headquarters. It is a big, busy place and, in August at least, is extremely hot. The KDP's rivals, the Patriotic Union of Kurdistan (PUK) are based in the smaller, quieter eastern city of Sulaimaniya, which was where I was talking to Didar.

Didar had five brothers and three sisters. His father, once a shopkeeper, was unemployed but, as two of his sons were (illegally) in Britain and sent back money on a regular basis, the family had a good standard of living. They lived in their own house and owned a car. All the children went to school and Didar, the sixth child, studied until he was 14. His favourite subject was Arabic. He also did Geography, History and Science but didn't like them.

Didar's upbringing was not particularly religious, he said. Like most Kurds he went to the mosque to pray several times a week and kept the fast at Ramadan but little else. Nor had he been involved in politics though, he said, he felt strongly that things were not right with the world from his early teens. His education, he said, was unlikely to get him a decent job. He played football a lot but had few male friends and no girlfriends. When he left school in 1999, without employment, he 'didn't have much to do so started going to the mosque a lot'. Soon he was spending every evening there and was invited to join a Qur'anic study group. He enjoyed the meetings and liked being with his new friends. Didar's teacher at the mosque, a man about twice his age, gave him books and pamphlets to read. Some were Wahhabi tracts published with subsidies from the Saudi Arabian government. Others were reprints of Abdallah Azzam's works. His teacher explained Azzam's doctrine that jihad was the duty of every Muslim man and told him that men like Osama bin Laden were true Muslims whose examples should be followed. He introduced Didar to other young men with similar ideas. Didar felt welcome and was happy with his new group of friends. He told me:

> We felt we could change things. We could make everything come right in our homeland. What Osama and my teacher said was true. If everybody did what it said in the Qur'an then everything would be ok. It was only the atheists in government who were stopping that and their supporters among the Jews and the Crusaders. We had to fight them all.

One of his new associates, Hisham, became a good friend. Soon they were talking about the new party they would form that they hoped would be part of al-Qaeda. 'We would be warriors and strong and everyone would be proud of us,' Didar said.

In November of 2001, Didar was told by his teacher that a group called Ansar ul Islam had announced a jihad in Kurdistan. He had not heard of the organisation before. 'I was very excited. I wanted to be a part of it very much,' Didar said. The two men took a bus across the mountains to Sulaimaniya and then another bus out towards Halabja. As they neared the city they got off and picked up a taxi up to the headquarters of the group.

Ansar ul Islam's base was surrounded on three sides by the PUK's peshmerga. On the fourth side was the Iranian border. Around 40 Arabs had recently arrived. There were around 500 Kurds.

The first man Didar met was Abu Abdullah Rahman al-Shami, the Kurd who had spent most of the 1990s in Afghanistan before returning to Kurdistan a few months previously as an emissary of bin Laden. Ali Wali, another Kurd who had spent time in the Afghan camps, was running the training of new recruits, and for the next three months Didar was instructed in basic infantry tactics, explosives, urban warfare and assassinations. The training followed the syllabus that had been taught to the group's representatives who had made it to Afghanistan in the previous year. On the wall of one of their dormitories, Didar said, was a rough mural of bin Laden standing above a burning World Trade Center with a Kalashnikov in his hand.

Every morning the recruits would rise for morning prayers and then run until the sun came over the horizon. They spent the rest of the day training, in lectures or reading the Qur'an. The idea of *ishtishad,* or 'martyrdom operations' was first raised by the Arab instructors but it was Didar's friend, Hisham, the 22-year-old he had met in the mosque at Arbil, who starting talking about suicide seriously.

> Hisham said we should do it together. He quoted all the verses of the Qur'an and repeated the prophet's teaching on ishtishad and every day we talked about it. Especially after two of our group were martyred when they attacked the [PUK forces] in Halabja. I decided that I wanted to do this too. I knew that PUK people were kufr and our duty was to fight against the kufr to free the umma. I told Abu Abdullah, that I was ready and then during the night they called me on the radio and asked me to come to them. I drove to Biyara, the village where they were, and they showed me the jacket and showed me how it worked. Then we had lunch.

Didar was talking to me in the office of the PUK security chief. The chief went to a cupboard and pulled out the jacket that had been taken off Didar when he had been arrested. It had two slabs of TNT over the chest and in the small of the back and was made of blue nylon. A belt contained more explosives. There were two metal switches, one for the jacket and one for the belt. I sat and clicked them back and forth, listening to the metallic tick, as Didar continued.

> 'After seeing the jacket I went back to our base.'
>
> 'What date was it?'
>
> 'It was the 12th of June,' he said. 'Because it was during the World Cup.'
>
> 'You were watching the World Cup?'
>
> 'There were no televisions because they were *haram* [forbidden]. But I was following it in the newspapers.'
>
> 'What was your favourite team?'
>
> 'England. Michael Owen and I like David Beckham and David Seaman.'

'England is your favourite team and you are about to blow yourself up in the jihad against kufr?'

✓ 'Politics is one thing. Football is something else.'

After lunch with Abu Abdullah, Didar was driven to a house on the outskirts of Halabja. He was told that when he heard shooting the next morning he was to make his way to the local PUK office and blow himself up. He had dinner at the house of a sympathiser. Then they watched a Jackie Chan film on DVD.

'I didn't dream. I slept fine. I knew I was going to paradise so I was very calm.'

'Didn't you think about your mother?'

'Just about paradise.'

'Did you have an alarm clock?'

'I woke up at 3am and put the jacket on with the help of the owner of the house. But there was no shooting so I thought the plan had gone wrong so I took it off again and went back to Biyara. I was sad that I was not able to die. I went to Abu Bakr al-Tauhidi and spent three days with him. He spoke to me about ishtishad and faith and jihad and my duty. On the third day after morning prayer I went in a car to Said Sadiq again and went to the same house and I slept until lunchtime and then prayed and ate and then waited until *Ushr* prayers and then put on my jacket and went with my host to the bus stop. It was just after five pm I think but I had no watch. I was calm and not at all nervous. I was thinking about paradise. He paid one dinar to the driver and I got on the bus that went through the bazaar and I got down just before the PUK office and walked up to it with the switch in my pocket and my hand on it. I walked up to the peshmerga at the door and gave him the name of a man who I thought would be inside and said I had come to see him and he said what is that underneath your shirt and he spoke with the accent of my home town and I said nothing and he asked again and I said "It's TNT", and then they arrested me.

Analysis of the backgrounds of the thousands of individuals of whom the modern Islamic militant movement is composed is a fraught business. It is very difficult to impose some kind of analytic order on the huge variety of different people involved with their diverse motives, backgrounds, experience and culture. However, two broad groups can be distinguished among modern militants.

The first can be termed intellectual activists. These are men who can justify their attraction to radical Islam in relatively sophisticated terms. They share many common elements, particularly regarding their backgrounds, with more moderate political Islamists. This group would include Gulbuddin Hekmatyar, Dr Ayman al-Zawahiri, bin Laden himself, Khalid Shaikh Mohammed, Omar Saeed Sheikh, Abu Doha, Abu Qutada, arguably Mohammed Atta and many others. These people are drawn from the same social groups who were involved in the earliest Islamist movements of the colonial period. They dominated Islamic militant leadership cadres in the 1970s and 1980s, as well as filling the ranks of more moderate organisations. They also share many common elements with radical political activists on both the left and the right. In fact, they do not just fit a particular model of Islamic activist over recent decades, they fit a model of revolutionary cadres over several centuries. There is no space here to look at the similarities in background between Egyptian Islamists in the 1970s, Russian anarchists, Bolshevik or French revolutionaries but it is striking how often it is elements from the newly educated lower middle classes who are so often at the forefront of calling for change, even if change is justified by retrospective appeal to a nostalgically imagined 'just' golden age.

These are men who are articulate, intelligent and relatively worldly. They have aspirations and experience profound resentments when those aspirations are frustrated. When their expectations cannot be met, they perceive it as an injustice. If there are no effective ways to resolve the problem within the bounds of state-sanctioned political or social activism then alternatives are sought. Radical Islamic militancy is one.

The concept of injustice is key. It is not absolute deprivation that causes resentment but, as many scholars have noted, deprivation following a period of aspiration-raising relative prosperity. In very general terms, and over the long term, the history of the Middle East and the Islamic world can be read in these terms. A lengthy period of international political and cultural dominance has left a legacy of expectation that is very much at odds with the region's current subordinate status. The recent economic success of East Asia, for example, is felt as *wrong*. It is not fair, right or just. It is humiliating.

This model of expectation, disappointment and perceived injustice works over a shorter time span too. The expectations of the populations of many Middle Eastern countries were raised hugely as the Western imperialist system fell apart and the old regimes that had governed so incompetently and repressively were overthrown. However, expectations of democracy and prosperity were swiftly disappointed. The number of militants whose fathers were involved in anti-colonial struggles is significant. So too is the number whose families unexpectedly suffered under the post-colonial regimes. Their sense of injustice is profound.

In the short term, aspirations have been raised hugely both by the extension of education to so many and by the exposure of virtually everyone in the Islamic world to images of the West, with its apparent democracy, sexual opportunity, freedom of opportunity and wealth. Again the model of expectation, disappointment and perceived injustice fits the experience of millions of graduates, provincial immigrants to cities, doctors who drive cabs, ambitious civil engineers who teach basic arithmetic. It matches the experience of the 17-year-old Pakistani lower middle-class youth torn between the mullah and MTV. If he accepts his desire to be part of the Westernised world he will have to address the fact that he is unlikely ever to enjoy anything more than an ersatz, inferior version of the 'Western' life enjoyed by his equivalent in London or Los Angeles. His clothes will never be as up to date, his skin will never be the right colour, his chances of pre-marital sex will always be infinitesimally lower. An alternative course is to reject the West and all it stands for in favour of the affirming, empowering certainties of radical Islam.

The second group of activists emerged at the end of the 1980s and became increasingly dominant though the 1990s. They are less educated, more violent and follow a more debased, popularised form of Islam. They are more unthinkingly radical, bigoted and fanatical. Instead of being drawn from frustrated, aspirant groups within society they are more often drawn from its margins, from those who have few expectations to be disappointed. This was very clear in Algeria in the mid-1990s, where the most violent groups among the GIA drew the mass of their recruits from the poorest and most brutalised elements in society; in Pakistan where, in the same period, the various political Islamist groups found themselves forced to cede ground to the Deobandi medressa boys; and in Kashmir where the teachers and doctors who formed the leadership cadres of Hizb-ul-Mujahideen have now been forced aside by the semi-educated militants of the new Jihadi groups. The same is true in Egypt, Morocco, Tunisia, Jordan, Saudi Arabia and in Southeast Asia.

The shift can also be seen in the West. At the beginning of the 1990s, most of the Islamic activists living in London, or 'Londonistan' as it was called by critics of the British government's liberal asylum policy, were highly politicised, educated and relatively moderate. By the end of the decade, militants in the West included far more men like Richard Reid, a British petty criminal who tried to blow himself up on a transatlantic jet in December 2001, or Nizar Trabelsi, a former drug addict and refugee. These were poor, unemployed, angry people. The number of former convicts or asylum seekers, both marginalised from mainstream society, among recently recruited Islamic militants is striking. Significantly, British security officers charged with countering Islamic terror in the UK have made the monitoring of mosques frequented by young Afro-Caribbean first or second-generation immigrants a priority.[1]

These two groups are not rigidly defined and individual activists can show elements of both or neither. Men like bin Laden, al-Zawahiri and Abu Qutada have managed, despite their own backgrounds, to assume leadership of large numbers of men drawn from the most violent militant elements. But, despite the flaws inherent in any broad-brushed approach, this analysis may help us understand why terrorists act as they do.

Modern Islamic terrorists are made, not born. There are various stages in that process of creation. The route to terrorism starts with a feeling that something is wrong that needs to be set right. This can be a real problem or merely a perceived injustice (or indeed both). The second stage is the feeling that the problem, whether cosmic or purely personal, cannot be solved without recourse to a mode of action or activism beyond those provided for by a given society's political or legal framework. The third stage changes the individual from being an activist, even a militant, into a terrorist. It involves the acceptance of an ideology or the development of a worldview that allows the powerful social barriers that stop most people from committing acts of violence to be overcome. If recruits are to be diverted from terrorism it is this process that we need to counter.

The root causes of modern Islamic militancy are the myriad grievances that lead to the first step on the road to terrorism being taken. Social and economic problems are critical. Such problems are growing more, not less, widespread and profound throughout the Islamic world. The economies of states from Morocco to Indonesia are in an appalling state. Population growth continues unabated. Unemployment, particularly among critical groups such as graduates, is still rising fast. Housing is crowded and sanitation basic in many cities. The gulf between the rich and the poor is increasing.

But these problems alone do not cause terrorism. If individuals have faith in a political system, a belief that they can change their lives through activism that is sanctioned by the state or understand and accept the reasons for their hardships, they are unlikely to turn to militancy. But there is little reason to be optimistic about the possible development of alternatives that might divert the angry and resentful from radical Islam in the near future. Only in a few small Gulf states has there been any genuine move towards reform in recent years. One of the reasons for the evolution of a more radical, debased and violent form of protest is the tendency of governments in the Middle East to crush moderate movements. Because they are scared of radical Islam taking power, the regimes block democratic reform. Because there is no reform, radical Islam grows in support. As national Islamic movements, moderate or violent, are crushed or fail, anger is channelled into the symbolic realm and into the international, cosmic, apocalyptic language of bin Laden and his associates.

This is the biggest threat of all. This is the crucial third stage that turns an angry and frustrated young man into a terrorist. This is the moment when an individual begins to conceive of doing something more than shouting slogans or waving banners. And it is here that the newly dominant, globalised 'al-Qaeda', as a universally transportable, universally applicable ideology and worldview, is so important. To overcome the behavioural norms that restrain most balanced citizens in any society from acts of appalling brutality, particularly against those usually considered civilians, a powerful legitimising discourse is needed. The ideologues of modern 'Jihadi Salafi' Islamic radicalism with their vision of a cosmic struggle between good and evil, belief and unbelief, the true faith and its opponents provide one.

The situation is far worse than when bin Laden began to come to prominence. The legitimising discourse, the critical element that converts an angry young man into a human bomb, is now everywhere. You will hear it in a mosque, on the internet, from friends, in a newspaper. You do not have to travel to Afghanistan to complete the radicalising process; you can do it in your front room, in an Islamic centre, in a park. For an increasing number of people, the 'Jihadi Salafist 'al-Qaeda-ist' worldview explains everything. It makes sense. There is a battle going on between good and evil, between right and wrong, between justice and injustice. We are all soldiers on the frontline. There are no civilians. This is their worldview.

The camps in Afghanistan may be gone but the reasons the volunteers travelled there persist. Do we honestly think that, because Afghanistan is no longer a viable destination, they will not seek other places or other ways to learn the skills necessary to fight their own personal jihad? Insurgencies and terrorism in Chechnya, Uzbekistan, Tajikistan, Kashmir, Algeria, Egypt, Jordan, Indonesia, Malaysia, the Philippines and elsewhere continue. Everywhere there is fertile ground for fanatics to find material support and willing helpers.

Our societies are open societies. Armouring ourselves may seem useful in the short term, comforting in the mid-term, but is, in the long term, impossible. We need to think again about our approach. We need to counter the twisted vision of the world that is becoming so prevalent. Every time force is used it reinforces that vision by providing more evidence of a 'clash of civilisations' and a 'cosmic struggle.' Every use of force is another small victory for bin Laden.

Of course the 'war on terror' should have a military component. It is easy to underestimate the sheer efficacy of military power in achieving specific immediate goals. Hardened militants cannot be rehabilitated and need to be made to cease their activities, through legal processes or otherwise. But if we are to win the battle against terrorism our strategies must be made broader and more sophisticated. Military power must be only one tool among many, and a tool that is only rarely, and reluctantly, used. Currently, military power is the default, the weapon of choice. In fact, the greatest weapon available in the war on terrorism is the courage, decency, humour and integrity of the vast proportion of the world's Muslims. It is this that is restricting the spread of 'al-Qaeda' and its warped worldview, not the activities of counter-terrorist experts. Without it we are lost. There is indeed a battle between the West and men like bin Laden. But it is not a battle for global supremacy. It is a battle for hearts and minds. And it is a battle we, and our allies in the Muslim world, are losing.

I have tried to explain the nature of modern Islamic terrorism and examine some of its root causes. All are the results of historical processes, none is inevitable and all can be acted on by well-judged, properly executed policies. The causes of terrorism must be addressed, a careful analysis of the phenomenon that comprises the threat against us must be undertaken, moderate Muslim leaders must be engaged, the spread of hardline strands of Islam rolled back, and an enormous effort to counter the growing sympathy for the 'al-Qaeda' worldview must be made. All this will follow a single, substantial paradigmatic shift in the way the threat facing us all is currently understood and addressed. This is not about one man or one organisation.

All terrorist violence, 'Islamic' or otherwise, is unjustifiable, unforgivable, cowardly and contemptible. But just because we condemn does not mean we should not strive to comprehend. We need to keep asking why.

NOTES

Introduction: The Shadow of Terror

1. Interviews with Saudi intelligence officers, Peshawar, October 2001; with senior former Taliban, Peshawar, June 2002.
2. Interviews with eyewitnesses in Jalalabad, November 2001; with Mullah Jan Mohammed, Maulvi Abdul Qabir's private secretary, Peshawar, June 2002.

Chapter One: What Is al-Qaeda?

1. The French scholar Oliver Roy points out that the fundamental unit of the Afghanistan resistance movement was, in varying local dialects, the *komite, qarargah* ('the base' in Panjshiri), the *markaz* (an Arabic-derived word meaning 'the centre' among the Pashtun), etc. Roy, *Islam and Resistance in Afghanistan*, p.160. In 2002, Arabic-language newspapers referred to the base at Bagram where the British and American soldiers hunting bin Laden and the Taliban were based as 'al-Qaeda Bagram'.
2. Quoted in Gunaratna, *Inside Al-Qaeda*, p.3.
3. Others, primarily Saudi Arabian intelligence sources, say that the root of the 'al-Qaeda' name can be traced back to 1988 when, a year before leaving Afghanistan, bin Laden set up a database to record the identities and the movements of the volunteers coming through the guesthouses in Peshawar. They say his primary motivation was to be able to answer the queries of families whose relatives had gone missing. In Arabic such a database could be called 'al-Qaeda', using 'base' as in the English word 'database'. Interview with Saudi intelligence source in Pakistan, September 2001.
4. *The Encyclopedia of Jihad*, vol. I, author collection. The dedication reads: 'To our much loved brother Abu Abdullah Osama bin Laden who shared in the jihad of Sheikh Abdallah Azzam and in the creation of

the Office of Services. Who has committed himself every day to jihad. I pray to God to give him still more will and courage to serve Islam, Muslims, jihad and the mujahideen.'

5. Gunaratna, *Inside Al-Qaeda*, p.36.
6. Reeve, *The New Jackals*, p.48; Gunaratna, *Inside Al-Qaeda*, p.36.
7. Benjamin and Simon, *The Age of Sacred Terror*.
8. US Department of State, Office of the Coordinator for Counterterrorism, *Patterns of Global Terrorism 1995*, April 1996.
9. CIA memo, 'Usama bin Laden: Islamic extremist financier', released after 1998 bombings of east African embassies, p.1, author collection.
10. US Department of State, *Patterns of Global Terrorism 1997*, 1998.
11. Address by President Clinton on military actions against terrorist sites in Afghanistan and Sudan, 20 August 1998, author collection.
12. USA vs Usama bin Laden, New York Southern District Court, transcript day 19; direct examination of Agent Perkins, 19 March 2001.
13. Interview, Sulaimaniya, Iraq, August 2002.
14. Interview with Algerian security officials, London, October 2002.
15. Interview with former AIS activists, Algiers, August 2001.
16. US State Department, *Patterns of Global Terrorism 1997*.
17. *Herald*, Karachi, May 2002.
18. Michael Smith, 'Bin Laden hunted by SAS in Kashmir', *Daily Telegraph*, 23 February 2002.
19. In 1998, I was the victim of a classic intelligence operation when I was fed, and published, false information about bin Laden and the heroin trade.
20. Jason Burke, 'Diary', *London Review of Books*, 19 September 2002.
21. Dickinson, *Behind the Mask of the Terrorist*.
22. Hala Jaber, 'Ryanair gunman: I was not going to crash plane', *Sunday Times*, 13 October 2002.
23. On one occasion, he spent several hours briefing an Arab journalist in secret 'off the record' in Kabul. Nothing was to be printed, he told the frustrated correspondent, because he did not want to get in trouble. Interview with Arab journalist based in Islamabad, June 2002.
24. US State Department, *Patterns of Global Terrorism 1995*.

Chapter Two: September 11th, Terror and Islam

1. Letter published around September 2002, author collection. There is some doubt over whether the letter is actually the work of bin Laden himself. There are several Qur'anic references in it that are erroneous, mistakes bin Laden would be unlikely to make. However, even the fact that sympathisers or associates might be concerned by global warming is significant.

2. Excerpts from *Knights Under the Banner of the Prophet* were translated and published by *al-Sharq al-Awsat*, the Arabic-language newspaper, 20 December 2001. The author obtained a copy in Peshawar in June 2002, believed to have been published in early 2002.
3. Fandy, *The Politics of Dissent*, p.191.
4. Ferguson, 'Clashing Civilizations', in Strobe Talbott and Nayan Chanda (eds), *The Age of Terror*, p.120.
5. Juergensmeyer, *Terror in the Mind of God*, p.147.
6. Ibid. p.155.
7. Roy, *The Failure of Political Islam*, p.13.
8. Akbar, *Islam Today*, p.45.
9. Gibreel, 'The Ulema: Middle Eastern Power Brokers', *Middle East Quarterly*, Fall 2001, vol. VIII, no. 4.
10. Ruthven, *Islam in the World*, p.280
11. Sura 3:193 (excerpt): 'Lord, forgive us our sins and remove from us our evil deeds and make us die with the righteous… Those that fled their homes or were expelled from them, and those that suffered persecution for My sake and fought and were flain: I shall forgive them their sins and admit them to gardens watered by running streams, as a recompense from God; God dispenses the richest recompense' (Dawood translation).
12. It was in fact 220 miles from Mecca to Medina.
13. 'The last will of Abdallah Yusuf Azzam', Khorasan publications, date unknown, author collection.
14. 'The real meaning of Jihad', e-mail circular, November 2002. Author collection.
15. Esposito, *Unholy War*, p.64.
16. Qutb, *Milestones*.
17. Ibid. pp.46, 48.
18. Ibid. p.49.
19. Ibid. p.131.
20. Global Islamic Media, January 2002: http://groups.yahoo.com/group/abubanan.
21. Roy, *The Failure of Political Islam*, p.156.
22. The others are prayer, fasting, the donation of a certain amount of money each year to charity and the pilgrimage to Mecca, known as *haj*. Many of the more militant thinkers have said that jihad is the 'sixth pillar'.
23. Translation of letter left by the hijackers, *Los Angeles Times*, accessed www.ict.org.il/documentes/documentdet.cfm?docid=57.
24. http://www.waaqiah.com/zawahariinterview.htm.
25. Transcript of al-Jazeera documentary aired 10 June 1999, featuring interview recorded earlier that year in Afghanistan.
26. Al-Zawahiri, *Knights Under the Banner of the Prophet*.

27. Kepel, *Jihad*, p.282.
28. Quoted in Ruthven, *Fury*, p.204.
29. 'Bin Laden's warning': full text, BBC online, 7 October 2001.
30. Baudrillard, *The Spirit of Terrorism*, p.10.
31. Bernard Lewis, 'The revolt of Islam', *New Yorker*, 19 November 2001.

Chapter Three: Radicals

1. Though the idea of Mohammed bin Awad bin Laden working with his hands to build up enough capital for his first venture is often repeated, Osama himself hints that he was considerably better off and started contracting immediately in his interview with al-Jazeera correspondent Jamal Isma'il, aired June 1999.
2. Hiro, *War Without End*, p.121.
3. Al-Rasheed, *A History of Saudi Arabia*, p.10.
4. Cooley, *Unholy Wars*, p.117.
5. Interview with bin Laden family member, London, July 2001. Phone interview with Saudi business associate in Riyadh, February 2002.
6. Interview with bin Laden family member, London, July 2001.
7. Mary Anne Weaver, 'The real bin Laden', *New Yorker*, 24 January 2001.
8. Interview with bin Laden family member, London, September 2002; Jane Mayer, 'The house of bin Laden', *New Yorker*, 12 November 2001.
9. Bin Laden gave this date to Jamal Isma'il of al-Jazeera in an interview aired 10 June 1999.
10. www.pbs.org. The document appears to have come from Saudi or Kuwaiti intelligence sources.
11. Sam Lister, 'Bin Laden was the perfect pupil, says his old teacher', *The Times*, 22 September 2001.
12. Interview with friend of bin Laden family, London, June 2001. Ghazi al-Gosaibi, the former Saudi Ambassador to London, has estimated bin Laden's fortune at not more than $30m. Jason Burke, 'Fight to the Death', *The Observer*, 27 October 2001.
13. Fandy, *Saudi Arabia and the Politics of Dissent*, p.27.
14. Interview with bin Laden family member, September 2002.
15. Interview with former bin Laden family retainer. See also Burke, 'Fight to the Death', *The Observer*, 27 October 2001.
16. Interviews with friends of bin Laden family, London, 2001, 2002. Pictures apparently showing bin Laden on holiday in Sweden or Britain are unreliable. He may have spent short periods on holiday in Europe but this is unlikely.
17. Bin Laden interview with al-Jazeera, broadcast 10 June 1999.
18. Kepel, *Jihad*, p.314.
19. The opening verse of the Qur'an, the *fatahah*: 'Guide us in the straight

path, the path of those whom Thou has blessed, not of those against whom Thou art wrathful, nor of those who are astray.' Also, verse 6 (cattle):153, 'This is My path, straight so do you follow it and follow not lest they separate you from this path'.

20. Ruthven, *A Fury For God*, p.73.
21. Quoted in Esposito, *Unholy War*, p.52.
22. Biographical details from the Jamaat Islami website, http://www.jamaat.org/overview/founder.html. Such denial of the ulema's monopoly on religious authority has been a hallmark of both Muslim revivalist movements and modern political Islamism. It is also worth remembering what a feature such anticlericalism has been in Christian religious revivalist movements, particularly those of sixteenth and seventeenth-century Europe. Martin Luther's 'justification by faith alone' (i.e. without the intercession of the clergy) is only the most obvious example of many.
23. The division is rooted in pure practicalities. In the absence of a true Islamic society run by truly virtuous men, the best the umma could hope for was to be ruled in accordance with the Shariat. It was in fact better to suffer a bad ruler than to risk *fitna*, or division, and disorder by opposing him. The key concept here is zulm, or tyranny. It is not when a leader rules unrepresentatively or undemocratically that he should be opposed but when he rules unjustly.
24. Ruthven, *A Fury for God*, p.68–69.
25. Kepel, *Jihad*, p.34.
26. Ruthven, *A Fury for God*, p.95.
27. Ibid. pp.76–8.
28. Esposito, *Unholy War*, p.57.
29. Qutb, *Milestones*, p.119.
30. Ibid. p.5.
31. Ibid. p.6.
32. Ibid. p.13.
33. Ibid. p.8.
34. Ibid. pp.8–9.
35. Ibid. pp.21–22, 25.
36. Ibid. p.25.
37. Ibid. p.9.
38. Ibid. p.16.
39. Ibid. p.7.
40. When the Prophet Mohammed accepted the leadership of the people of Medina, the power of several tribal leaders was reduced. They outwardly accepted Islam to preserve their status but inwardly detested Mohammed and his message. They eventually abandoned Mohammed

on the battlefield when he was already heavily outnumbered. They are the hypocrites or *munafiqun*.

41. Interview with bin Laden family member, London, July 2002.

Chapter Four: Mujahideen

1. Cooley, *Unholy Wars*, p.43.
2. Interview with *al-Quds al-Arabi*, 1993.
3. Interviews with senior Islamic leaders in Peshawar, June 2002.
4. Interviews with former associates of bin Laden, mujahideen, neighbours, Peshawar, 1998–2001.
5. Interview with Ahmed Zaidan, editor of *al-Jihad* from 1986, Islamabad; also Zaidan, *The Afghan Arabs*, pp.36–50.
6. Weaver, 'The real bin Laden'.
7. Interview with former Algerian fighter, Algiers, August 2001.
8. Multiple interviews with former fighters, Peshawar, 1998; Jordan, 2001; Mullah Majjed Ismael, Sulaimaniya, Iraq, August 2002.
9. Interview with former mujahideen commander, Peshawar, 1998.
10. Multiple interviews with former associates, mujahideen, neighbours, Peshawar, 1998–2001.
11. Interviews with former associates, Peshawar, 2001, 2002.
12. Interview with Hameed Gul, director general of ISI, 1987–89, Rawalpindi, May 2002. Saudi airlines offered a 75 per cent discount on (one-way) flights to Pakistan for aspirant Arab mujahideen, and though the bulk of non-US funds went to the Afghan fighting groups or was disbursed for proselytisation and relief work, some did fund the Arab volunteers; interview with former mujahideen, Peshawar, November 2001.
13. Interesting discussions of international reactions to the Iranian Revolution can be found in Martin, *Creating an Islamic State*, Chapter IX, pp.188–96; and Esposito (ed.), *The Iranian Revolution*.
14. Rubin, *The Political Fragmentation of Afghanistan*, pp.180–1.
15. Multiple interviews with former mujahideen commanders, Afghan journalists who covered the war, Peshawar, 1998–2002.
16. Milton Bearden, 'Afghanistan, Graveyard of Empires', *Foreign Affairs*, November/December 2001.
17. Interview with Algerian mujahideen, Algiers, August 2001.
18. Interview with Mohammed Din Mohammed, former Hizb-e-Islami (Khalis) deputy leader, Peshawar, October 2001.
19. Michael Barry, *Le Royaume d'Insolence*, quoted in Rubin, *The Political Fragmentation of Afghanistan*, p.38.
20. Dupree, *Afghanistan*, p.104.
21. In much of southwest Asia, as in the rest of the Islamic world, leaders within the mystic Sufi branch of Islam, possibly named after the woollen

cloak worn by some of its earliest practitioners, are venerated as a source of blessing and holiness. Salafi and Wahhabis see this as *shirk* or polytheism and an appalling deviation from the true path.

22. Marsden, *Taliban*, p.32 and interview with the author, July 2002. Multiple interviews with Afghan mujahideen, politicians including Mohammed Nabi Mohammedi (August 1998), Afghanistan and Pakistan, 1998–2002.
23. Rashid, *Taliban*, p.13.
24. Magnus and Naby, *Mullah, Marx and Mujahed*, p.215.
25. Rubin, *The Political Fragmentation of Afghanistan*, p.71.
26. Ibid. p.70.
27. Ibid. p.76.
28. Roy, *The Failure of Political Islam*, pp.110, 118.
29. Rubin, *The Political Fragmentation of Afghanistan*, p.93.
30. Interview with senior aide of Qazi Hussein Ahmed, Islamabad, May 2002; profile of Qazi Hussein Ahmed, Jamaat Islami website.
31. Rubin, *The Political Fragmentation of Afghanistan*, pp.84, 101.
32. Multiple interviews with former Sayyaf associates, former Hizb-e-Islami activists, former mujahideen, Peshawar, Kabul, 1999–2002.
33. Rashid, *Taliban*, pp.18–19.
34. An interesting feature of the refugees' flight from Afghanistan was how it was legitimised by a reference to the example of the Prophet's hijra.
35. Statistic provided by UNHCR to author, July 2002.
36. Haqqani eventually married an Emirati princess.
37. Rubin, *The Political Fragmentation of Afghanistan*, p.221.
38. Interviews with Haji Zargoon, Jalalabad, November 2001; Said Pahlwan, Peshawar, October 2001.
39. Lamb, *Waiting for Allah*, p.220.

Chapter Five: Heroes

1. Al-Zawahiri's own book, *Knights Under the Banner of Islam*, described his arrival in Pakistan with two other Egyptian doctors. See also: Lawrence Wright, 'The Man Behind bin Laden', *New Yorker*, 16 September 2002; interview with Mahfouz Azzam, al-Zawahiri's great uncle and lawyer, *The Guardian*, 11 September 2002.
2. Multiple interviews with former mujahideen, political activists and retired Pakistani army officers and bureaucrats in Peshawar, Islamabad and Lahore, 1998–2001; Ruthven, *A Fury for God*, pp.202–11; Kepel, *Jihad*, pp.144–-5.
3. Abdallah Azzam, 'Last Will', Khorasan Publications, publication date unknown, author collection.
4. Quoted in Esposito, *Unholy War*, p.7.

5. Information from www.Azam.com, accessed September 2002.
6. Interview with former Maktab al-Khidamat employee, Peshawar, October 2002.
7. Many Kurds, who had been forced to flee Iraq by Saddam Hussein during the early and mid-1980s, when they were perceived by Baghdad as a potential fifth column aiding Tehran, were recruited by Saudi dissidents, including the followers of Juhaiman and the rebels who seized Mecca, who had set up secret *medressas* and were teaching Wahhabism in the refugee camps in Iran; author interview with Mullah Majjed Ishmail Mohammed (who spent 1988 to 1994 in Pakistan), Sulaimaniya, Iraq, August 2002.
8. Roy, *The Failure of Political Islam*, p.66. According to Milton Bearden, the CIA station chief at the time, 'there were genuine volunteers on missions of humanitarian value, there were adventure seekers looking for paths to glory, and there were psychopaths'. Milton Bearden, 'Afghanistan, Graveyard of Empires', *Foreign Affairs*, November/December 2001. It is interesting to note how the Afghan jihad had replaced Palestine as the cause that was most attractive to young Muslims. The shift in focus was ideological (from the Left to Islam) as well as geographical. Given historic Soviet backing for the Palestinian cause supporting both was clearly difficult.
9. Interviews with mujahideen, former Hizb-e-Islami activists, Peshawar, 1998, 2001, 2002.
10. Mary Ann Weaver, 'Blowback', *Atlantic Monthly*, May 1996.
11. Interview with former mujahideen and activist, Peshawar, October 1998.
12. James Bruce, 'Arab veterans of the Afghan war', *Jane's Intelligence Review*, April 1995.
13. Wright, 'The Man Behind bin Laden'.
14. Lester W Grau and Ali Ahmad Jalali, Foreign Military Studies Office, *Journal of Slavic Military Studies*, vol. 14, September 2001, Number 3; sketch maps of the base can be found at http://call.army.mil/fmso/FMSOPUBS/ISSUES/zhawar/zhawar.htm.
15. Mohammed Yousaf and Mark Adkin, *The Bear Trap*, p.166; Grau and Jalali; author interviews with visitors to Zhawar Khili in the late 1980s and subsequently.
16. Some activists say that it was Maktab al-Khidamat itself that funded Khaldan.
17. CNN interview, 1997.
18. Jamaal Isma'il, an al-Jazeera correspondent who was associated with the Arabs during the Afghan war, said it was late 1986 or 1987 in a documentary broadcast in 1999. However, Afghan former mujahideen and activists have told the author it was later. Several have also denied

that it was a bin Laden camp at all. Instead, they say, it was run by various Arab groups under the auspices of Hekmatyar and Sayyaf.

19. Interview with former Sayyaf fighter, June 2001.
20. Interview with former mujahideen commander, Peshawar, 2001.
21. Jalaluddin Haqqani, for example, often disappeared to the Gulf for protracted fund-raising trips, either to Saudi Arabia or to Kuwait to see his in-laws.
22. Yousaf and Adkin, *The Bear Trap*, p.166.
23. Multiple interviews, Peshawar, September to November 2001.
24. Multiple interviews, Peshawar, September to November 2001.
25. Multiple interviews with former mujahideen, 1998–2001.
26. Al-Zawahiri, *Knights Under the Banner of Islam*; bin Laden interview with al-Jazeera broadcast 10 June 1999.
27. Interview with bin Laden associate, interview with Mohammed Said Pahlwan, Peshawar, October 2002.
28. Multiple interviews in Pakistan, Afghanistan, Algiers, 1998–2002.
29. Yousaf and Adkin, *The Bear Trap*, pp.8–9.
30. Interviews with Qazi Amin Wiqad, Hekmatyar's asst, Hizb, Peshawar, September 2001; Mohammed Din Mohammed, October 2002.
31. Mohammed Din Mohammed, Peshawar, October 2002.
32. Interview with former fighter, former Hizb-e-Islami activist, Peshawar, October 2001.
33. Interview with former bin Laden associate, Sayyaf commander, Peshawar, October 2001.
34. Multiple interviews with Afghan mujahideen, Pakistani ISI officers, former 'Arab Afghan' fighters, Afghanistan, Pakistan, Algeria, London, 1998–2002.
35. Roy, *The Failure of Political Islam*, p.74.
36. Kepel, *Jihad*, p.9; Ruthven, *Islam in the World*, p.442.
37. Jamal Ahmed al-Fadl, called as prosecution witness, USA vs Usama bin Laden, New York Souther District Court, transcript days 2 and 3.
38. Multiple interviews with senior Sayyaf and Hizb-e-Islami commanders, Peshawar, December 1999, September–November 2001, July and October 2002.
39. Oath-taking, or 'making bayat', was a common practice among groups in the jihad.

Chapter Six: Militants

1. Sara Dixon, 'From life-saver to life-taker', *Redbridge Guardian*, 19 July 2002.
2. Nick Fielding, 'The British Jackal', *Sunday Times*, 21 April 2002; interviews with Aitchison old boys in Lahore, June 2002.

3. Fielding, 'The British Jackal'; interviews with HUM activists, Lahore, 1998.
4. Between 1955 and 1970 population growth across the Muslim world approached 50 per cent. Pakistan was no exception. Kepel, *Jihad*, p.66.
5. Cooley, *Unholy Wars*, p.49.
6. Barbara Metcalf, *Traditionalist Islamic Activism: Deoband, Tablighis and Talibs* (Social Science Research Council, New York).
7. Rashid, *Taliban*, p.88.
8. Ibid. p.89.
9. Owen Bennett Jones, *Pakistan*, p.32; multiple interviews with senior Deobandi ulema, Kohat, Akora Khattak, Peshawar, Lahore, 1998–2000.
10. Tariq Rahman, 'Language, Religion and Identity in Pakistan: Language-Teaching in Pakistan', *Medressas: Ethnic Studies Report*, vol. XVI, no. 2, July 1998.
11. Multiple interviews with former army officers who witnessed such training, senior SSP cadres, Islamabad, Kohat, Peshawar, Lahore, 1998–2002; Azmat Abbas, 'Tentacles of Hatred', *Herald*, September 2001; interviews with former Harkat-ul-Mujahideen officials, Lahore, Islamabad, 1998–2000.
12. In October 2001, a diary allegedly written by Sheikh surfaced amid court documents relating to his arrest for kidnapping Westerners in New Delhi. The 35-page diary, which Sheikh had apparently written in jail after his conviction, details his training and subsequent activities. The diary is almost certainly a forgery by the Indian intelligence services. It was 'discovered' and swiftly released to the Indian newspapers at a time when New Delhi were extremely nervous about the sudden popularity of Pakistan in the aftermath of Islamabad's decision to back the 'War on Terror'. It seems unlikely that Sheikh would write such a comprehensive confession of his own operations, particularly as he had not actually been convicted of any offence by the Indians at the time the diary was meant to have been written. The diary states that, before being dispatched to New Delhi in 1994, Sheikh was told of the capture of British hostages in Kashmir, an event that actually took place a year later. The 'diary' appears to be based on Sheikh's own interrogation and the interrogations of other captured militants during this period. Apparently correct in many details, it is nonetheless a forgery, albeit a useful one.
13. Multiple interviews with Harkat cadres, Lahore, Rawalpindi, Islamabad, Muzaffarabad, 1998–2001.
14. Notebooks found by author at Darunta, Farm Hadda, Khost, November 2001; multiple interviews with former mujahideen, Pakistan, Afghanistan, Algeria, 1998–2002.
15. Multiple interviews with Harkat cadres, Lahore, Rawalpindi,

Islamabad, Muzaffarabad, Skardu, 1998–2001.

16. USA vs Usama bin Laden, New York Southern District Court, direct examination of Agent Perkins, 19 March 2001.
17. Amanullah Khan, the then leader of the JKLF has confirmed these details to both Alexander Evans and Owen Bennett Jones; author interviews with both. The fact that senior JKLF leadership cadres were living in the UK is worth noting. The British tradition of welcoming dissidents of all types occasionally (critics would say often) shades into providing a haven for known terrorists. Such havens are essential to any radical group.
18. Eyewitness accounts from former mujahideen, author interviews, Rawalpindi, Peshawar, June 2002.
19. In 1992, Pakistan was put on the US State Department 'watch list' of countries sponsoring terrorism when the ISI obstructed plans to buy back the unused Stinger missiles from commanders loyal to Hekmatyar. Following the removal of ISI officers named by the US, Pakistan was removed from the list in July 1993.
20. Alexander Evans, 'Talibanising Kashmir?', *World Today*, December 2001.
21. Alexander Evans, *Monterey Institute Project*, draft chapter kindly made available to the author; interview with General Mirza Aslam Beg, Islamabad, July 2002.
22. Trevor Matthews, 'Daniel Pearl's kidnapper nearly got me too', *The Guardian*, 13 February 2002.

Chapter Seven: Terror

1. Statements to 1998 Congressional Hearings on Intelligence and Security, Senate Judiciary Committee, 24 February 1998.
2. Interviews with journalists and mujahideen eyewitnesses, Haji Zahir Qadir, Peshawar and Jalalabad, 2001–2, London, 2003. L'Hossaine Khertchou, the Moroccan-born former chef who was a government witness in the trials for the 1998 bombings fought Dr Najibullah's Communists. Many of his fellow fighters belonged to the extremist groups associated with the extreme strand of contemporary Islamic militancy dubbed 'Takfiri wal Hijra' (Excommunication and Exile) by investigators in Egypt. A group of Takfiris were later to contest bin Laden's claim to pre-eminence among Islamic militants in Afghanistan on the basis that he was too moderate.
3. Interview with former employee, Peshawar, October 2002.
4. CIA memo, compiled 1996, released 1998, author collection; interview with former MAK official, Jalalabad, September 2002; Embassy trial testimony of L'Hossaine Khertchou, 21 February 2001.
5. Embassy trial testimony of L'Hossaine Khertchou, 21 February 2001;

details from Ali Mohammed plea agreement and transcript of appearance by Ali Mohammed before Judge Sand on 20 October 2000, Southern District Court, New York; see also Chapter Ten, note 13.

6. Multiple interviews with former mujahideen, Hizb-e-Islami and Sayyaf activists, Pakistan and Afghanistan, 1998–2002; embassy trial testimony of L'Hossaine Khertchou, 21 February 2001.
7. Interviews with former mujahideen commanders from both Hizb-e-Islami factions and Sayyaf's group, Jalalabad, September 2002, Peshawar, June and September 2002.
8. Testimony of FBI Agent John Anticev, US Embassy trial, New York, 22 February 2001.
9. Interview with Rahamullah Bariali, Abdul Haq's brother, Jalalabad, October 2002. Abdul Haq wrote in 1991.
10. 'Osama bin Laden: Islamic Extremist Financier', CIA memo, *ca.*1996, p.2.
11. Reeve, *The New Jackals*, pp.112–3.
12. Ibid. pp.118–120, 135; Ian Katz, 'Bomb mastermind studied in Britain', *The Guardian*, 11 February 1995.
13. Multiple interviews with former students at the university, Peshawar, September 2002, London, 2002, 2003.
14. Jamal al-Fadl has claimed that he saw Ramzi in 'Sadda' camp, also run by Sayyaf. USA vs Usama bin Laden, trial transcript day 7, cross-examination of Jamal al-Fadl, 20 February 2001. Al-Fadl has told contradictory stories about seeing Ramzi. Interview with Libyan activist, London, February 2003.
15. Interviews with former mujahideen, Peshawar, June 2002; Insight, 'God's Warrior', *Sunday Times*, 13 February 2002.
16. Government statement during Appeal of USA vs Mohammed Salameh and others, US 2nd Circuit Court of Appeals, 18 and 19 December 1997.
17. Statements to US Congressional Hearings on Intelligence and Security, 24 February 1998.
18. Reeve, *The New Jackals*, pp.48–49.
19. Ibid. pp.52–53.
20. Khalid Ahmed, 'Fundamental Flaws', in Ali et al, *On the Abyss: Pakistan After the Coup*, p.94; Bennett Jones, *Pakistan*, p.22.
21. Amir Mir, 'Faith that kills', *Newsline*, October 1998; 'The Jihad within', *Newsline*, May 2002.
22. Reeve, *The New Jackals*, pp.64–5.
23. Ibid. pp.77–105; Doug Struck, Howard Schneider, Karl Vick and Peter Baker, 'Borderless network of Terror', *Washington Post*, 23 September 2001.
24. Bin Laden interview with CNN, 1997.

25. Judith Miller, 'Bin Laden relative linked to 1993 Trade Center bombers, affidavit says', *New York Times*, 2 May 2002.
26. Mark Huband, 'Bankrolling bin Laden', *Financial Times*, 28 November 2001.
27. Jane Mayer, 'The House of bin Laden', *New Yorker*, 12 November 2001. Mayer was told by a senior Saudi diplomat that 'a brother in law... in Saudi Arabia [is] not even considered part of the family'.
28. The FBI (www.fbi.gov/mostwanted/) give both dates.
29. Terry McDermott, Josh Meyer and Patrick J McDonnell, 'The plot and designs of al-Qaeda's engineer', *Los Angeles Times*, 22 December 2002.
30. Interview with Benazir Bhutto, Naudero, Pakistan, April 1999.
31. Reeve, *The New Jackals*, p.49.
32. Terry McDermott, Josh Meyer and Patrick J McDonnell, 'The plot and designs of al-Qaeda's engineer', *Los Angeles Times*, 22 December 2002.
33. Terry McDermott, 'How terrorists hatched a simple plan to use planes as bombs', *Los Angeles Times*, 1 September 2002.
34. Christopher John Farley, 'The man who wasn't there', *Time*, 20 February 1995; Reeve, *The New Jackals*, p.106.
35. James Bruce, 'Arab veterans of the Afghan war', *Janes*, April 1995; testimony of FBI Agent Anticev, US Embassy trial, New York, 22 February 2001.
36. Rahimullah Yusufzai, *News*, 8 December 1995.

Chapter Eight: Seekers

1. Interview with Mullah Mohammed Hassan Akhund, governor of Kandahar, Kandahar, August 1998; multiple interviews with Taliban diplomats in Islamabad and Peshawar, 1998–2000; multiple interviews with Taliban ministers in Kabul, August 1998, September 1998, December 1999. Significantly even enemies of the Taliban support this explanation. Mohammed Din Mohammed, the Hizb-e-Islami deputy leader who was ousted by the Taliban from Jalalabad, told me in Peshawar in October 2001: 'An anarchy emerged and people came together. Not just Pashtuns. I saw hundreds of Badakshis even going to the Taliban in hope they would solve their problems. As fighting prolonged and the Taliban could not defeat the northern alliance so people who joined them for peace were disappointed so they left. The Taliban's popularity was because of fighting between Rabbani and Hekmatyar and other commanders who committed robbery.'
2. Anthony Davies, in William Maley (ed.), *Fundamentalism Reborn?*; Peter Marsden, private communication to the author.
3. Kepel, *Jihad*; Ruthven, *Islam in the World*; Roy, *The Failure of Political Islam*.
4. Olivier Roy, in Maley, *Fundamentalism Reborn?*, p.20.

5. One result of the destruction of centuries-old irrigation systems was the shift from fruit and arable production to opium, a crop that needs a sixth of the water that wheat requires.
6. Rashid, *Taliban*, p.41.
7. Interviews with senior Taliban officials and ulema who were at this meeting, Peshawar, Jalalabad and Kandahar, 1998–9. The Taliban were not entirely an innovation. Units composed of talibs, as students at Afghanistan and Pakistan's network of medressas, had always existed. During the war against the Soviets they had fought, usually under the command of alim. They had maintained a discrete identity during operations and had showed a willingness to die not usually shared by other mujahideen.
8. Rubin, *The Political Fragmentation of Afghanistan*, p.39; Roy, *Islam and Resistance in Afghanistan*, p.35.
9. It is wrong to overemphasise the detail here. Mullah Omar and many of his early comrades were from the Hotaki tribes and thus Ghilzai.
10. Rashid, *Taliban*, p.29.
11. The two best-known medressas were the Haqqania medressa at Akora Khattak and the Jamiat ul Uloom i Islamiya Binoria in Karachi. The former, which, by the mid-1990s, had accomodation for 2,000 students and facilities for 3,000, provided dozens of senior Taliban leaders who often returned to attend *dastarbandi*, turban-tying or graduation ceremonies. The Binoria school had room for 8,000 students. Though Mullah Omar never studied there as often reported, many other Taliban did. Smaller medressas were established by men like Javed Ibrahim Parachar, a tribal leader and Islamic judge in the frontier town of Kohat. He started the 1980s with one medressa teaching 100 pupils. By the middle of the next decade he was running four with a total of more than 1,000 pupils. Parachar is a Pakistani, but also a Pashtun and a Deobandi, and it was these ties that proved crucial in the early days of the Taliban. In late 1994, after being approached by senior Deobandi clerics, Parachar started sending his students across the border to fight for the new group. Hundreds of other clerics did the same. Author interview with Javed Parachar, Kohat, June 2002. Interview with Sami-ul Haq, leader of Haqqania medressa, September 1998; interview with senior teaching staff at Binoria medressa, Islamabad, June 2002.
12. Interviews with UNDCP officials, Islamabad, 1999.
13. Maley, *The Afghanistan Wars*, pp.235–6.
14. Interviews with senior British officials, Islamabad, 1998, UNDCP officials, Islamabad, 1999.
15. Interviews with UNDCP officials, Islamabad, 1999.
16. Interview with Iranian drug smuggler, Sulaimaniya, Iraq, August 2002,

with UNDCP officials and British customs and excise officials, Islamabad, September 1999; Burke, 'The desert village that feeds UK heroin habit', *The Observer*, 12 December 1999.

17. Interviews with Western diplomats, London, September 2002. Mohammed Ilyas Khan, 'The ISI-Taliban Nexus', *Herald*, November 2001.
18. It was Fazl-ur Rehman, the leader of the Deobandi political party in Pakistan, who arranged for a series of Arab princes to go bustard hunting with the Taliban in the desert around Kandahar in the spring of 1994. Rashid, in Maley, *Fundamentalism Reborn?*, p.76.
19. Interview with British diplomat, London, September 2002.
20. Interview with Jaffar, Intercontinental employee since 1969, August 1998.
21. Multiple interviews with taliban. Two that were particularly useful were with Maulvi Mahmud Waziri Abdurrahman, Minister for Internal Affairs, and Ahmad Hotaqi, the Taliban's Deputy Information Minister, Kabul, August 1998.
22. Maley, *The Afghanistan Wars*, p.10.
23. Esposito, *Unholy War*, p.131; Martin, *Creating an Islamic State*, p.156.
24. A similar distortion took place during the early days of the Iranian Revolution. Few reporters were prepared, or able, to travel into the rural areas and thus relied over-heavily on middle-class elite sources for information. This is described in Martin, *Creating an Islamic State*, p.177.
25. Esposito, *Unholy War*, p.131.
26. Kepel, *Jihad*, pp.170, 117.
27. The seclusion of women after puberty in Afghanistan has resulted, particularly in the Pashtun areas, in a rich tradition of male homosexuality celebrated in poems such as the famous, and oft-quoted couplet: 'I saw a boy across a river with a bottom like a peach, but alas I could not swim.' There are even crude Afghan jokes about 'the crows flying over Kandahar with one wing behind their backs'. Purdah was, of course, reinforced in the chaotic and threat-filled world of the refugee camps.
28. Roy, *The Failure of Political Islam*, p.58.
29. Nancy Hatch Dupree, in Maley, *Fundamentalism Reborn?*, p.163.
30. I recommend Latifa, *My Forbidden Face* for an excellent insight into the attitudes and experiences of middle-class, educated, politically conscious Kabuli women in the early days of the Taliban's rule in the city. There are, for obvious reasons, no similar accounts written by rural Pashtun peasant women in Oruzgan province.

Chapter Nine: Home

1. Interview with Mohammed Din Mohammed, who was present at the meeting. Peshawar, October 2002. There is some debate over whether bin Laden was received by Crown Prince Sultan or Prince Turki al-

Faisal. Mohammed Din Mohammed and the majority of sources consulted insist it was the former.

2. Al-Jazeera television, 10 July 2002, interview with Sheikh al-Awaji; Bergen, *Holy War, Inc.*, p.85.
3. Interviews with senior Hizb and Sayyaf commanders, Peshawar, October 2001.
4. Al-Rasheed, *A History of Saudi Arabia*, p.168.
5. Schneider, 'Saudi Missteps Helped Bin Laden Gain Power', *Washington Post*, 15 October 2001.
6. Interview with Peter Arnett, CNN, March 1997.
7. Fandy, *Saudi Arabia and the Politics of Dissent*, p.183.
8. Ibid. p.180.
9. Ibid. p.183.
10. Jacquard, *Les Archives Secrètes d'al-Qaida*, p.346.
11. Brian Whitaker, 'Violence dominates lawless province', *The Guardian*, 19 December 2001.
12. Bergen, *Holy War, Inc.*, pp.185, 188–9; Jamal Kashoggi, 'How we hit the Americans in Aden', *al-Hayat*, 21 February 1994.
13. Shelagh Weir, 'A Clash of Fundamentalisms: Wahhabism in Yemen', *Middle East Research and Information Project*, July–September 1997.
14. Brian Whitaker kindly made several chapters of his forthcoming book on the Yemen available to me.
15. Bergen, *Holy War, Inc.*, p.188.
16. Ibid. p.86.
17. Bin Laden told al-Jazeera this in 1999.
18. Documentary on bin Laden, broadcast, June 1999, on al-Jazeera; London *al-Quds al-Arabi*, 24 November 2001.

Chapter Ten: Flight

1. Interview with Libyan Islamic activist who was in Khartoum between 1992 and 1995, London, February 2003. His eyewitness account of bin Laden's house is confirmed in Corbin, *The Base*, p.35. Corbin's book is not annotated, so I have only used material that appears to have been collected firsthand by the writer or that is identifiably from another work. London *al-Quds al-Arabi* interview with Mahjub al-Aradi, bin Laden's gardener in Sudan, published 24 November 2001, was also helpful. Charles Sennott of the *Boston Globe* visited the house while bin Laden was there and confirmed the details to the author.
2. Interview with Libyan Islamic activist, London, February 2003.
3. Al-Fadl testimony, New York, February 2001.
4. Kepel, *Jihad*, p.177.
5. Ruthven, *Islam in the World*, p.321.

6. Kepel, *Jihad*, pp.178–9; Huband, *Warriors of the Prophet*, pp.150–3.
7. *Al-Quds al-Arabi*, 24 November 2001.
8. Bin Laden gave his first interview to a Western journalist, Robert Fisk of the *Independent*, while building the 'challenge highway' in 1993. London *al-Quds al-Arabi*, 24 November 2001.
9. Al-Fadl testimony, USA vs Usama bin Laden, 5 February 2001.
10. Al-Ridi testimony, USA vs Usama bin Laden, 7 February 2001.
11. Al-Fadl testimony.
12. Also in the Sudan at the time was Carlos the Jackal. He was handed over to the French in 1994.
13. Ali Mohammed was born in Egypt in 1952, served 13 years in the Egyptian army, rising to the rank of major and obtaining a degree in psychology. He was discharged in 1984, moved to the USA, married an American and enlisted in the American army. By 1988, despite having used his leave to travel to Afghanistan to fight, he was teaching seminars on Islam at the Fort Bragg special forces school. He left the army in 1989 and gave courses in basic military tactics to Islamic radicals in New York. In 1991 and 1992, he returned to Afghanistan to train militants there. Ali Mohammed is an extraordinary figure whose complex career (he was finally arrested in September 1998 in America) shows the difficulty of trying to pigeonhole terrorists as members of one or other organisation. He seems to have worked for, or with, anyone with the requisite facilities or cash. Details from Ali Mohammed plea agreement and transcript of appearance by Ali Mohammed before Judge Sand, Southern District Court, New York, on 20 October 2000.
14. Al-Fadl testimony; Cooley, *Unholy Wars*, p.122.
15. Testimony of FBI Agent Anticev, Embassy Bombings trial, New York, 22 February 2001.
16. Testimony of L'Hossaine Kertchou, USA vs Usama bin Laden, 26 February 2001.
17. CNN interview, transcript available on CNN website.
18. Scott Peterson of the *Christian Science Monitor*, private communication to the author, August 2002.
19. Transcript of day 36, US Embassy trials, New York, 30 April 2001.
20. Weaver, 'The Real bin Laden', *New Yorker*, 24 January 2000.
21. Scott Peterson, private communication with the author; Mark Huband, *Warriors of the Prophet*, p.41.
22. Bergen, *Holy War, Inc.*, p.89.
23. Al-Fadl testimony.
24. Wright, 'The Man Behind bin Laden'.
25. Cooley, *Unholy Wars*, pp.32, 43; Hiro, *War Without End*, p.69.
26. Ibid. p.75.

27. 'Da'wa' means making bad Muslims better Muslims as well as converting those from other faiths.
28. Hiro, *War Without End*, p.91.
29. Al-Fadl testimony.
30. Al-Fadl testimony.
31. The man in charge of the assassination attempt was Mustafa Hamza, an al-Gamaa al-Islamiyya senior operative who, though he was not a member of 'al-Qaeda', was working in one of bin Laden's businesses in Khartoum.
32. Fandy, *Saudi Arabia and the Politics of Dissent*, pp.1–3; Hiro, *War Without End*, p.173; Reuters, 25 October 1996.
33. Indictment, United States District Court of Virginia, USA vs Ahmed al-Mughassil et al, June 2001.
34. CNN interview, 1997.
35. Interview with Libyan activist in the Sudan at the time, London, February 2003.
36. Hiro, *War Without End*, p.174; Barton Gellman, 'Sudan's Offer to Arrest Militant Fell Through After Saudis Said No', *Washington Post*, 3 October 2001.
37. Benjamin and Simon, *The Age of Sacred Terror*, p.246.

Chapter Eleven: Struggle

1. Testimony of Agent Stephen Gaudin, USA vs Usama bin Laden, transcript day 14, 7 March 2001.
2. Interviews with close associates of Mujahed and Saznoor, Peshawar, October 2001; interviews with Mohammed Said Pahlwan, former Sayyaf commander, Peshawar, November 2001.
3. Interview with Mohammed Said Pahlwan, Haji Din Mohammed, Peshawar, November 2001; neighbours of Bagh Zahera in Jalalabad, October 2002.
4. CNN interview, 1997.
5. Reuel Marc Gerecht, 'The Gospel according to Osama bin Laden', *Atlantic Monthly*, January 2002.
6. A full translation of Abdul Bari Atwans' interview with bin Laden, first published in December 1996, appeared in *The Guardian*, 21 November 2001.
7. Rahimullah Yusufzai, 'Exporting Jehad', *Newsline*, September 1998; interviews with former Hizb-e-Islami activists, Peshawar, June 2001.
8. Behroz Khan, 'Afghanistan's nation of Islam', *Newsline*, September 1998; interview with Behroz Khan, September 2001; interviews with police chief and other officials in Khost, November 2001.
9. At least that is what people in Khost told me.

10. Qutb developed this with his radical 'Takfiri' doctrine. Combining Qutb with the practical experience of insurrection and resistance gained in their own country and in Afghanistan, the al-Gamaa al-Islamiyya in Egypt in the late 1980s and early 1990s made securing control of areas of territory a key part of their insurrectional strategy. Such captured or 'liberated' zones could be Islamicised.
11. Testimony of Agent Gaudin.
12. Letter in author collection.
13. Various letters; letter dated 24 April 1998, all author collection.
14. Letter in author collection.
15. Testimony of Agent Gaudin, USA vs Usama bin Laden, New York, 2001.
16. Letter obtained in Peshawar, September 1998, author collection.
17. Communiqué, 21 May 1998, author collection.
18. Benjamin Orbach, 'Usama bin Ladin and al-Qaida: origins and doctrines', *Middle East Review of International Affairs*, vol. 5, no. 4, December 2001.
19. Rahimullah Yusufzai, 'Myth and man', *Newsline*, September 1998.
20. John Miller interview, May 1998, ABCnews.go.com/sections/world/DailyNews/miller_binladen_980609.html.
21. Interview with Alex Yearsley of *Global Witness*, London, June 2002.
22. David Pallister, 'Fax to newspaper warned of threat to Great Satan', *The Guardian*, 12 August 1998.
23. Testimony of Agent Gaudin, USA vs Usama bin Laden, New York, 2001.

Chapter Twelve: Global Jihad

1. 'Bin Laden getting support', *Associated Press*, 29 October 1999.
2. In his book, *Knights Under the Banner of the Prophet*, al-Zawahiri explains: 'The problem of finding a secure base for jihad activity in Egypt used to occupy me a lot, in view of the pursuits to which we were subjected by the security forces and because of Egypt's flat terrain which made government control easy, for the River Nile runs in its narrow valley between two deserts that have no vegetation or water. Such a terrain made guerrilla warfare in Egypt impossible and, as a result, forced the inhabitants of this valley to submit to the central government and be exploited as workers and compelled them to be recruited in its army.'
3. Alan Cullison and Andrew Higgins, 'Computer in Kabul Holds Chilling Memos', *Wall Street Journal*, 31 December 2001.
4. Multiple interviews with senior Taliban officials, Kabul, Kandahar, Herat and Jalalabad, 1998–9.
5. Interview with senior Taliban official present at meeting, Peshawar, October 2001.
6. Interview with former Taliban official, Peshawar, October 2002.

7. Quoted in Roy, *The Failure of Political Islam*, p.208.
8. Ibid. p.36.
9. Abu Qutada fatwa, author collection, obtained in Peshawar, September 2001.
10. Lecture by Dr Xavier Raufer, Research Director, Institute of Criminology, University of Paris, 21 November 2002, RUSI, London.
11. Bergen, *Holy War, Inc.*, p.209.
12. Cullison and Higgins, 'Computer in Kabul Holds Chilling Memos'.
13. Cullison and Higgins, 'A Once-Stormy Terror Alliance Was Solidified by Cruise Missiles', *Wall Street Journal*, 2 August 2002.
14. Interview with Saudi intelligence officer, Peshawar, August 1998.
15. Multiple interviews with senior Taliban and Pakistani officials, Islamabad, Peshawar and Kabul, 1999–2000, 2001.
16. *Nida ul Momineen*, October 1998, author collection.
17. Bergen, *Holy War, Inc.*, p.179.
18. Burke, 'Revealed: Secret hideout of world's most feared terrorist', *The Observer*, 4 July 1999.
19. Amir Mir, 'Faith that Kills', *Newsline*, October 1998; interview with Pakistani government minister, Lahore, Islamabad, December 1998; multiple interviews with senior police officers, Lahore, February 1999.
20. Azmat Abbas, 'Tentacles of Hatred', *Herald*, September 2001.
21. Ismail Khan, 'Taliban close down three camps', *News*, 19 June 2000.
22. Ansar Abassi, 'Taliban close down training camp', *Dawn*, 6 September 2000.
23. Statement at press conference at Holiday Inn, Islamabad, 22 August 1998.
24. Behroz Khan, 'Remains of the day', *Newsline*, September 1998; interview with Bakht Zamin, HUM commander, Mansehra, Pakistan, October 1998.
25. A useful commentary is by Brigadier (retd) Shaukat Kadir, 'An analysis of the Kargil Conflict', *RUSI Journal*, April 2002, who spoke to the author in June 2002.
26. The best analysis of Central Asian Islamic militancy can be found in Rashid, *Jihad: The Rise of Militant Islam in Central Asia*.
27. Multiple interviews with Taliban ministers, officials, Jalalabad, Kabul, Kandahar, Herat, 1998–2000.
28. Benjamin and Simon, *The Age of Sacred Terror*, pp.272–3.
29. Multiple interviews with Taliban officials and opium farmers in Afghanistan, Western diplomats, UNDCP and British Customs and Excise officials in Islamabad, autumn 1999.
30. Interview with senior United Nations education specialist, Jalalabad, October 2002; Burke, *India Today*, November 1999.
31. Interview with Amir ul Momineen by Nazir Leghari and Mufti Jamil Khan, published in *Taliban, an exemplary rule of an exemplary state*, by the

Ahle Sunnat Wal Jama'at. The exact date of the interview and publication are unclear from the document, in the author's collection, but from the text can be inferred to have taken place sometime in early 1996.

32. *Islamic Emirate Magazine*, first issue, July 2000, p.14.
33. *Newsline*, January 1999.
34. *Islamic Emirate Magazine*, p.3.
35. Tim Judah, 'The Taliban Papers', *Survival*, vol. 44, no. 1, Spring 2002.
36. Timothy Roche, Brian Bennett, Anne Berryman, Hilary Hylton, Siobhan Morrissey and Amany Radwan, 'The Making of John Walker Lindh', *Time*, 29 September 2002.
37. Ibid.
38. John Walker Lindh indictment, 5 February 2002, in the United States District Court for the Eastern District of Virginia, USA vs John Philip Walker Lindh.
39. Ibid.
40. Interview with senior Taliban foreign ministry official, Peshawar, September 2001.
41. Janine di Giovanni, 'Radicals abroad urged destruction of Bamiyan Buddhas', *The Times*, 24 November 2001; Fatwa of Sheikh Ali Bin Khodeir al-Khodeir, dated February 2001, reproduced in Jacquard, *Les Archives Secrètes d'al-Qaida*, p.312.
42. Tim Judah, 'The Taliban Papers', *Survival*, vol. 44, no. 1, Spring 2002, pp.68–80.
43. Interviews with arms dealers, Peshawar, September 2001; see Burke, in 'War on Terrorism: Special Edition – The Afghan Connection', *The Observer*, 23 September 2001.
44. Cullison and Higgins, 'Computer in Kabul Holds Chilling Memos'.
45. Anderson, *The Lion's Grave*, p.187; 'Massoud conscious, stable after attack', *Associated Press*, 10 September 2001. I spent time with Massoud in the summer of 1999 in the Panjshir and found him to be one of the most charismatic people I had ever met. I was genuinely saddened by his death.

Chapter Thirteen: The Millennium Plot

1. Complaint filed against Ahmed Ressam in US District Court in Seattle, CASE NO. 99-547M. Application for arrest warrant of Samir Ait Mohammed, by Adam S Cohen, FBI, 26.10.2001, Southern District, New York.
2. Judith Miller, 'Holy Warriors: Dissecting a terror plot from Boston to Amman', *New York Times*, 15 January 2001.
3. Hal Bernton, Mike Carter, David Heath and James Neff, 'The Terrorist Within', *Seattle Times*, 23 June–7 July 2002.

4. General Paul Aussaresses, *Service Speciaux*, Perrin, Paris, 2001.
5. Scott Johnson, 'Tale of the Wayward Son', *Newsweek*, 8 May 2000.
6. Bernton, Carter, Heath and Neff, 'The Terrorist Within'; Scott Johnson, 'Tale of the Wayward Son'.
7. Kepel, *Jihad*, p.160.
8. Cooley, *Unholy Wars*, pp.197–8.
9. Kepel, *Jihad*, p.161.
10. Testimony of Ahmed Ressam, USA vs Mokhtar Houari, 3 July 2001.
11. Roy, *The Failure of Political Islam*, p.24.
12. Omar Belhouchet, editor of *El Watan*, quoted in Bernton, Carter, Heath and Neff, 'The Terrorist Within'.
13. Interview with Algerian former mujahideen, Algiers, August 2001.
14. Interview with senior security official, Algiers, August 2001.
15. Bernton, Carter, Heath and Neff, 'The Terrorist Within'.
16. Testimony of Ahmed Ressam, USA vs Mokhtar Houari, 3 July 2001.
17. Website at www.assuna-annabawiyah.org.
18. Multiple interviews with former AIS fighters in Algiers, August 2001.
19. Al-Fadl testimony, USA vs Usama bin Laden, 2001, transcript day two.
20. Conversations with activists conducted by senior Arab journalist and relayed to the author, October 2002.
21. Interview with senior member of Libyan Fighting Group, London, February 2003. The activist also related how ibn Khattab, the Chechnyan commander, attempted to make contact with the GIA. They told him they would be pleased to see him – if he signed up as a foot soldier.
22. GIA videos circulated 1994–5, author collection. See also Jason Burke, David Leppard and Tim Kelsey, 'Islamic terror videos sold in Britain', *Sunday Times*: 'Insight', 29 December 1996.
23. Testimony of Judge Jean-Louis Brugiere, trial of Ahmed Ressam, Los Angeles, 2 April 2001.
24. Bruce Crumley, 'Fighting terror: Lessons from France', *Time*, 24 September 2001; Patricia Tourancheau, 'A Paris, faux papiers au cœur d'un réseau islamiste', *Liberation*, 28 September 2001.
25. 'Bin Laden linked to Paris plot', CNN, 3 October 2001.
26. Testimony of Ahmed Ressam, USA vs Mokhtar Houari, 3 July 2001.
27. USA vs Abu Doha sealed complaint, US Southern District Court, New York, 2 July 2001; testimony of Ahmed Ressam, USA vs Mokhtar Houari, 5 July 2001.
28. I am grateful to Ben Brown for showing me the notebook in Jalalabad, November 2001.
29. Testimony of Ahmed Ressam, USA vs Mokhtar Houari, 5 July 2001; Judith Miller, 'Holy Warriors: Killing for the Glory of God, in a Land Far From Home', *New York Times*, 16 January 2001.

30. 'Terror suspect: an interview with Osama bin Laden', ABC news, transcript at www.abcnews.go.com.
31. USA vs Abu Doha, indictment, sealed complaint, US Southern District Court, New York, 2 July 2001.
32. Testimony of Ahmed Ressam, USA vs Mokhtar Houari, 5 July 2001. Further funds were allegedly provided by Abu Qutada, the cleric in London. See Burke, Amman and Bright, 'Cleric hits back over bomb plot claims', *The Observer*, 19 December 1999.
33. Judith Miller, 'Holy Warriors: Dissecting a terror plot from Boston to Amman', *New York Times*, 15 January 2001.
34. First supplemental affidavit, Frederick W Humphries II, special agent FBI, 8 August 2001, Seattle, Washington, author collection.
35. Testimony of Judge Jean-Louis Brugiere, trial of Ahmed Ressam, Los Angeles, 2 April 2001.
36. USA vs Abu Doha sealed complaint, US Southern District Court, New York, 2 July 2001.
37. Judith Miller, 'Holy Warriors: Dissecting a terror plot from Boston to Amman'; 'Death Sentence for Jordan Terror Suspect', BBC News, 11 February 2002.
38. Ambassador Michael Sheehan, Coordinator for Counterterrorism, Office of the Coordinator for Counter-terrorism, Testimony Before the House International Relations Committee, Washington, DC, 12 July 2000.

Chapter Fourteen: The Holy War Foundation

1. Jason Burke, 'Bin Laden and son: The grooming of a dynasty', *The Observer*, 23 September 2001; interview with Ahmed Zaidan, al-Jazeera journalist present at wedding, Islamabad, June 2002. Bin Laden's mother and two brothers flew into Kandahar from Saudi Arabia for the occasion.
2. US State Department, *Patterns of Global Terrorism: 1999 Middle East Overview*, April 2000.
3. Brian Whitaker, 'Al-Qaida link to tourists' kidnap', *The Guardian*, 13 October 2001; Brian Whitaker, 'War in Afghanistan: Violence dominates lawless province', *The Guardian*, 19 December 2001; Bergen, *Holy War Inc.*, p.201.
4. 'US finds link between bin Laden and Cole bombing', CNN, 8 December 2001.
5. Bergen, *Holy War Inc.*, p.208.
6. Mark Hosenball and Daniel Klaidman, *Newsweek*, 25 February 2002.
7. John Miller, 'Yemen Probe Uncovers Bin Laden Links and Missteps by Cole Bombers', ABC News, 8 December 2001.

8. Brian Whitaker, 'Yemen bombers hit UK embassy', *The Guardian*, 14 October 2000.
9. 'Bin Laden watches over Yemen flock', *Intelligence newsletter* (online), no. 366, 23 September 1999.
10. Bergen, *Holy War Inc.*, p.197.
11. Saudi Arabian security sources in Islamabad; author telephone interviews, January 2001.
12. Cullison and Higgins, 'Computer in Kabul Holds Chilling Memos'.
13. Jason Burke, 'Algeria tries to forget its dark, tortured past', *The Observer*, 12 August 2001.
14. Florence Beaugé, 'En Algérie, les islamistes armés se sont restructurés en trois formations', *Le Monde*, 30 October 2002.
15. Interview with Algerian security source, London, 2002.
16. 'Saudi terrorist mastermind behind Algerian group', AFP, 15 February 1999.
17. Interviews with senior Algerian security officers, London and Algiers, 2001.
18. 'Ben Laden au secours de Hattab', *Le Matin*, 26 November 2002; El Watan, 'Un dirigeant d'al-Qaïda tombe en Algérie', *Mounir B*, 26 November 2002; interviews with *al-Hayat* journalists, London, August 2002; interviews with Algerian security officers, Algiers, August 2001; Jason Burke, Ed Vulliamy, James Astill and Nick Pelham, 'Terror that haunts Africa', *The Observer*, 30 November 2002.
19. Jonathan Schanzer, 'ALGERIA'S GSPC AND AMERICA'S "WAR ON TERROR"', *Washington Institute, POLICYWATCH*, Number 666, 2 October 2002.
20. Indictment of Marouf, Essid Sami et al, case number 13016/99, Public Prosecutor's Office, Milan, author collection; Frances Kennedy, 'Two men suspected of recruiting Islamic militants are arrested in Milan', *Independent*, 30 November 2001.
21. Bruce Hoffman, Rand Corporation, testimony to House and Senate Select Committee on Intelligence, 8 October 2002, p.15.
22. Paul Harris, Burhan Wazir and Kate Connolly, 'British Plotter planned al-Qaeda bomb massacre', *The Observer*, 21 April 2002.
23. Patricia Tourancheau, 'Une filière tombe en France, Sa cible probable: l'ambassade des Etats-Unis', *Liberation*, 26 September 2001; Marie-France Etchegoin, 'Düsseldorf, Londres, Kaboul, l'itinéraire d'une conversion à la guerre sainte', *Le Monde*, 19 October 2001; 'Qui est Djamel Beghal?' *Nouvel Observateur*, no. 1928, 18 October 2001; interrogation report of Djamal Beghal, M. Jean-Louis Brugiere, premier vice-president charge de l'instruction au tribunal de grande instance de Paris, September 2001, author collection.

24. Interrogation report of Djamal Beghal, author collection.
25. Ibid.
26. Interviews with British and French intelligence officers, London and (by phone) Paris, October 2002.
27. Hiro, *Dictionary of the Middle East*, pp.135–6; interviews in Sulaimaniya, Iraq, August 2002; interviews with PUK officials in London, December 2002.
28. Krekar was born in 1956 in an outlying district of Sulaimaniya. In 1978 he went to university in Arbil and went on to take a masters in Modern Science in Pakistan. Assad Mohammed Ameen Herki, who is also known as Mullah Aso and is a science graduate from Mosul University, was born around 1957, went in 1988, as did Satbun Mahmud Abdul Latif al-Aiai, aka Abu Wa'el, an Arab law graduate from Ramadi, 100 miles west of Baghdad. Profiles compiled from interviews with Islamist prisoners and intelligence documents in Sulaimaniya, August 2002.
29. Interview with senior PUK intelligence officer, Sulaimaniya, August 2002.
30. Interview with former student at Arbil University, Chamchamal, August 2002.
31. Interview with Fawzi Hariri, senior KDP official, Salahaddin, August 2002.
32. Interview with senior PUK official, Sulaimaniya, August 2002.
33. Interview with Mullah Majjed Ismail Mohammed, Sulaimaniya, Iraq, August 2002.
34. Interview with PUK intelligence official and Islamist prisoners, Sulaimaniya, August 2002.
35. The IMK already had a strong presence in city, partly because of Mullah Uthman Ali Aziz and his family's roots nearby, but largely because of the strong Iranian religious influence on the area. Ali Aziz also wanted an enclave close to the Iranian border so he and his allies within the IMK would have an escape route should the PUK and the KDP decide to renew its military attack on the movement. Halabja was thus perfect. The PUK, embroiled in a vicious and bloody armed struggle with the KDP, was in no position to resist the Iranian and IMK demands.
36. Interviews with senior KDP and PUK officials in Sulaimaniya, Dohuk, Salahaddin, August 2002; Hiro, *Dictionary of the Middle East*, pp.135–6.
37. Author collection.
38. Multiple interviews with Ansar ul Islam militants, IMK activists, PUK security officials, Sulaimaniya, August 2002.
39. Multiple interviews with Ansar ul Islam militants, PUK security officials, Sulaimaniya, August 2002.
40. Multiple interviews with Ansar ul Islam militants, PUK security officials, Sulaimaniya, August 2002.

41. According to some, al-Shami brought a substantial amount of money with him. I was, however, unable to confirm this.
42. Rohan Gunaratna, 'The Singapore Connection', *Jane's Intelligence Review*, March 2002, pp.8–11.
43. Interview with senior officer Banden Intelligens Nasional, Jakarta, October 2002; Raymond Bonner, 'Indonesian Cleric Is Suspected of Being a Terrorist Leader', *New York Times*, 3 February 2002.
44. Terry McDermott, 'How terrorists hatched a simple plot to use planes as bombs', *Los Angeles Times*, 1 September 2002.
45. Rajiv Chandrasekaran, 'Clerics Groomed Students for Terrorism', *Washington Post*, 7 February 2002.
46. Daniel Klaidman and Melinda Liu, 'A good place to lie low', *Newsweek*, 4 February 2002.
47. Romesh Ratnesar, 'Confessions Of An Al-Qaeda Terrorist', *Time*, 15 September 2002.
48. Interview with senior officer Baden Intelligens Nasional, Jakarta, October 2002; Derwin Pereira, 'Jakarta team in Pakistan to track Hambali', *Straits Times*, 22 March 2002.
49. I am indebted to *The Guardian*'s Southeast Asia correspondent John Aglionby for much of this analysis. Also Seth Mydans, 'Islam Grows Rigid', *New York Times*, 29 December 2001; Government of Australia, *Current Issues Brief* 6, 2001–2; Indonesia and Transnational Terrorism, Chris Wilson, Foreign Affairs, Defence and Trade Group, Australian Parliament; RC Paddock, 'Indonesian Extremist Backs Terror Southeast Asia', *Los Angeles Times*, 23 September 2001.
50. Moroccan ministry of justice, interrogation report of al-Tubaiti, Casablanca, 19 June 2001, author collection.

Chapter Fifteen: September 11th

1. Statement of FBI Director Robert S Mueller III, the Senate Select Committee on Intelligence website, 26 September 2002, http://intelligence.senate.gov/0209hrg/020926/witness.htm.
2. The exact number of dead is still uncertain. Early estimates have been consistently revised downwards as missing people have been identified. The final total is likely to be 3,000 or just under, of whom around 2,700 died in the World Trade Center itself.
3. 'Many Say US planned for terror but failed to take action', *New York Times*, 30 December 2001; Michael Elliott, 'Could 9/11 have been prevented?', *Time*, 4 August 2002; CIA Director George J Tenet, testimony before Senate Select Committee on Intelligence, CIA website, 18 June 2002.
4. Joint Inquiry Staff Statement, part 1, Eleanor Hill, Director, Senate Select

Committee on Intelligence, 18 September 2002.

5. Reproduced in Jacquard, *Les Archives Secrètes d'al-Qaida*, p.322.
6. Carlyle Murphy and David B Ottaway, 'Some light shed on Saudi suspects', *Washington Post*, 25 September 2001.
7. Corbin, *The Base*, p.114.
8. Terry McDermott, 'A Perfect Soldier', *Los Angeles Times*, 27 January 2002.
9. Ibid.
10. Insight, 'The road to ground zero', part 1, *Sunday Times*, 6 January 2002.
11. Australian Broadcasting Corporation, *Four Corners*, interview with Volker Hauth, Hamburg, 18 October 2001, broadcast 12 November 2001.
12. Christopher Walker, 'Egypt cracks down on non-violent Muslim brothers', *The Times*, 27 July 1995; Kepel, *Jihad*, p.277.
13. Australian Broadcasting Corporation, *Four Corners*, interview with Ralph Bodenstein, Beirut, Monday 15 October 2001; interview with Volker Hauth, Hamburg, 18 October 2001, broadcast 12 November 2001.
14. Atta's will, 4 October 2001, translated by ABC News, http://abcnews.go.com/sections/us/DailyNews/WTC_atta_will.html.
15. Insight, 'God's Warrior', part 1, *Sunday Times*, 13 January 2002; Corbin, *The Base*, p.133
16. Kay Nehm, German Chief Prosecutor, press conference, Berlin, 29 August 2002.
17. CIA Director George J Tenet testimony before Senate Select Committee on Intelligence, CIA website, 18 June 2002.
18. Kay Nehm, German Chief Prosecutor, press conference, 29 August 2002.
19. Doug Frantz and Desmond Butler, 'Germans lay out early qaeda ties to 9/11 hijackers', *New York Times*, 24 August 2002.
20. Nehm, press conference.
21. Yosri Fouda, 'The Masterminds', *Sunday Times*, 8 September 2002.
22. CIA Director George J Tenet testimony before Senate Select Committee on Intelligence, CIA website, 18 June 2002.
23. Michael Isikoff and Daniel Klaidman, 'The hijackers we let escape', *Newsweek*, 5 June 2002.
24. Fouda, 'The Masterminds'.
25. FBI Director Robert S Mueller III, Senate Select Committee on Intelligence website, 26 September 2002.
26. Murphy and Ottaway, 'Some light shed on Saudi suspects'.
27. Fandy, *The Politics of Dissent*, p.62.
28. Molouk Y Ba-Isa and Saud al-Towaim, 'Another hijacker turns up in Tunis', *Arab Times*, 1 October 2001.
29. Interviews by al-Watan, published in Murphy and Ottaway, 'Some light shed on Saudi suspects'; Insight, 'The highway of death', *Sunday Times*, 27 January 2002.

30. Interview with Saudi intelligence source, Peshawar, September 2001.
31. Fandy, *The Politics of Dissent*, p.91.
32. Insight, 'The highway of death'.
33. Corbin, *The Base*, p.210.
34. Molouk Y Ba-Isa and Saud al-Towaim, 'Another hijacker turns up in Tunis'.
35. Fouda, 'The Masterminds'.
36. Terry McDermott, Josh Meyer and Patrick J McDonnell, 'The plot and designs of al-Qaeda's engineer', *Los Angeles Times*, 22 December 2002; Terry McDermott, 'The Plot', *Los Angeles Times*, 1 September 2002.
37. Fouda, 'The Masterminds'.
38. The Somali and Bosnian offices of the IIRO were shut down after it became clear they were acting as support offices for terrorist cells linked to bin Laden. Other charities came under scrutiny in the years before September 11th. One, called Mercy International and funded by 'Saudi merchants' according to witness testimony from the trial of the 1998 Embassy bombers, was a key conduit for funds for the attacks in Dar-es-Salaam and Nairobi. Claim, decedent john doe vs al-Baraka Investment and Development Corporation et al, in the US District Court of Colombia, civil action, third amended complaint, 2002.
39. USA vs Enaam Arnaout, US District Court, Northern District of Illinois, no. 02 CR 892, April 2002. Arnaout was indicted on 30 April 2002 on perjury charges.
40. Statement of Matthew A Levitt to International Trade and Finance Subcommittee, US Senate Committee on Banking, Housing and Urban Affairs, 1 August 2002; statement of FBI Director Robert S Mueller III, Senate Select Committee on Intelligence website, 26 September 2002.
41. Susan Schmidt, 'Moussaoui Linked to Plot', *Washington Post*, 20 November 2001.
42. Indictment, USA vs Zacarias Moussaoui, US District Court for the Eastern District of Virginia, December 2001.
43. Antony Barnett, 'Bin Laden man's mother blames British extremists', *The Observer*, 28 July 2002.
44. Fouda, 'The Masterminds'.
45. Bahaji's disembarkation card at Islamabad is reproduced in Jacquard, *Les Archives Secrètes d'al-Qaida*, p.345.
46. Transcript of video of meeting with Saudi cleric, date and location unidentified. The cleric has been identified as a veteran of the war in Afghanistan, Bosnia and Chechnya, from Asir, called Khaled al-Harbi.
47. Archives at www.ict.org.il/documents/ originally translated by the *Los Angeles Times*.

Chapter Sixteen: The War on Terror

1. Though few estimate more than 800 civilians were killed by the air-strikes themselves, the war caused the death of many tens of thousands more through hunger, disease and exposure.
2. Moroccan Ministry of Justice Press Release on the International Terrorism Case, Casablanca, 19 June 2002.
3. Doug Frantz and Desmond Butler, 'Germans lay out early qaeda ties to 9/11 hijackers', *New York Times*, 24 August 2002.
4. 'One year on: the hunt for al-Qaida', *The Guardian*, 4 September 2002; BBC online, 'Al-Qaeda "responsible" for Tunisia blast', 18 May, 2002.
5. Colin Powell's speech, 5 February 2003, was broadcast live around the world and excerpted in most major English-language newspapers the following day; interviews with Afghan and Libyan former activists, London and, by telephone, Pakistan, February 2003.
6. Reuters, 'Al-Qaeda Has Access to Millions, UN Says', 29 August 2002.
7. Colum Lynch, 'Al Qaeda Is Reviving, U.N. Report Says', *Washington Post*, 18 December 2002.
8. Douglas Farah, 'Saudis Face U.S. Demand On Terrorism', *Washington Post*, 26 November 2002.
9. Matthew Levitt, 'Saudi financial counter-terrorism measures, smokescreen or substance?', *Washington Institute, Policywatch*, no. 687, 10 December 2002.
10. Rory Callinan, 'Lessons of terror at school in the jungle', *Courier Mail*, 13 December 2002; International Crisis Group, 'How the Jemaa Islamiyya terrorist network operates', 11 December 2002; Simon Elegant, 'Unmasking Terror', *Time Asia*, 18 November 2002; 'The family behind the bombings', *Time Asia*, 25 November 2002; telephone interview with Indonesian intelligence and police officials, January 2002.
11. The Kenya attack involved a suicide car bomb detonated outside a tourist hotel in Mombassa patronised almost exclusively by Israelis. Most of the 13 killed were local Kenyan workers. Simultaneously two surface-to-air missiles were fired at a charter passenger jet full of Israeli tourists taking off from Mombassa airport. So far, few details of the plot have emerged and so it is difficult to gauge who was behind it. Bin Laden has been criticised for not acting against Israeli targets and for ignoring the Palestinian conflict, and the attack may have been orchestrated by the remaining elements of the 'al-Qaeda hardcore' with the aim of appropriating the Palestinian struggle for the mainstream of Sunni jihadi Salafi militancy. Alternatively, the attack may have been the work of a local group who, independent of any outside elements, chose what they saw to be a suitable target, according to the agenda

that bin Laden and others have set, and were able to source the necessary material themselves. At the time of writing, it is simply impossible to say.

12. Reuters, 'Pakistan holds militant for killing of 11 French', 28 December 2002.
13. Jamal Halaby, 'Military court opens trial of 10 suspected terrorists', *Associated Press*, 11 September 2002.
14. Reuters, 'Three Americans shot dead at hospital in Yemen', 30 December 2002.
15. Osama bin Laden, videoed speech broadcast by al-Jazeera, 27 December 2001.

Conclusion

1. Interview with senior Scotland Yard policeman, London, November 2002.

SELECT BIBLIOGRAPHY

Aburish, Said, *The Rise, Corruption and Coming Fall of the House of Saud* (Bloomsbury, 1995)

———, *Saddam Hussein: The Politics of Revenge* (Bloomsbury, 2000)

Akbar, Ahmed, *Jinnah, Pakistan and Islamic Identity: The Search for Saladin* (Routledge, 1997)

———, *Islam Today: A Short Introduction to the Muslim World* (I.B.Tauris, 1999)

Akbar, MJ, *The Shade of Swords* (Routledge, 2002)

Akhund, Iqbal, *Trial and Error: The Advent and Eclipse of Benazir Bhutto* (Oxford University Press Pakistan, 2000)

Alexander, Yonah and Michael S Swetnam, *Usama bin Laden's al-Qaida: Profile of a Terrorist Network* (Transnational Publishers Inc., 2001)

Ali, Tariq et al, *On the Abyss: Pakistan After the Coup* (HarperCollins India, 2001)

Anderson, John Lee, *The Lion's Grave* (Atlantic Books, 2002)

Arberry, Arthur (trans.), *The Quran*, (Oxford University Press, 1964; first publ. Allen & Unwin, 1955)

Armstrong, Karen, *Islam: A Short History* (Phoenix, 2000)

———, *Holy War: The Crusades and Their Impact on Today's World* (Anchor Books, 2001)

de Aussaresses, Paul, *Service Speciaux* (Rocher, 2001)

al-Banna, Hassan , *Letter to a Muslim Student* (The Islamic Foundation, 1995)

Barthorp, Michael, *Afghan Wars* (Cassell and Co., 1982)

Baudrillard Jean, *The Spirit of Terrorism* (Verso, 2002)

Benjamin, Daniel and Stephen Simon, *The Age of Sacred Terror* (Random House, 2002)

Bennett Jones, Owen, *Pakistan* (Yale University Press, 2002)

Bergen, Peter, *Holy War, Inc.: Inside the Secret World of Osama bin Laden* (Wiedenfeld & Nicholson, 2001)

Bhutto, Benazir, *Daughter of the East* (Mandarin, 1988)

Bloom, Jonathan and Sheila Blair, *Islam: A Thousand Years of Faith and Power* (Yale University Press, 2002)

Bocharov, Gennady, *Russian Roulette* (Hamish Hamilton, 1990)

Bodansky, Yossef, *Bin Laden: The Man Who Declared War on America* (Forum, 1999)

Borovik, Artyom, *The Hidden War* (Atlantic Monthly Press, 1990)

Bowden, Mark, *Black Hawk Down* (Penguin, 1999)

Cloughley, Brian, *A History of the Pakistan Army: Wars and Insurrections* (Oxford University Press Pakistan, 2000)

Cooley, John, *Unholy Wars: Afghanistan, America and International Terrorism* (Pluto Press, 1999)

Corbin, Jane, *The Base* (Simon & Schuster, 2002)

Cordovez, Diego and Selig S Harrison, *Out of Afghanistan: The Inside Story of the Soviet Withdrawal* (Oxford University Press, 1995)

Dickinson, Adam, *Behind the Mask of the Terrorist* (Mainstream Publishing, 2001)

Duncan, Emma, *Breaking the Curfew: A Political Journey Through Pakistan* (Arrow, 1989)

Dupree, Louis, *Afghanistan* (Oxford University Press Pakistan, 1998)

Durrani, Tehmina, *My Feudal Lord* (Corgi, 1994)

Edwards, David, *Heroes of the Age: Moral Fault Lines on the Afghan Frontier* (University of California Press, 1996)

Esposito, John L, *The Islamic Threat* (Oxford University Press, 1992)

———, *Unholy War: Terror in the Name of Islam* (Oxford University Press, 2002)

———, (ed.), *The Iranian Revolution: Its Global Impact* (University Press of Florida, 1990)

Ewans, Martin, *Afghanistan* (Vanguard Books, 2001)

Fandy, Mamoun, *Saudi Arabia and the Politics of Dissent* (Palgrave, 1999)

Fox, Robin Lane, *Alexander the Great* (Penguin, 1973)

French, Patrick, *Liberty or Death: India's Journey to Independence and Division* (HarperCollins, 1997)

Griffin, Michael, *Reaping the Whirlwind* (Pluto Press, 2001)

Guillaume, Alfred, *Islam* (Penguin, 1954)

Gunaratna, Rohan, *Inside al-Qaeda* (Hurst, 2002)

Halliday, Fred, *Islam and the Myth of Confrontation* (I.B.Tauris, 1995)

———, *Two Hours That Shook the World* (Saqi Books, 2002)

Hiro, Dilip, *Islamic Fundamentalism* (Paladin, 1988)

———, *Dictionary of the Middle East* (Macmillan, 1996)

———, *War Without End* (Routledge, 2002)

Hoffman, Bruce, *Inside Terrorism* (Victor Gollancz, 1998)

Hoge Jr., James F and Gideon Rose (eds), *How Did This Happen? Terrorism and the New War* (PublicAffairs Ltd, 2001)

Hopkirk, Peter, *The Great Game* (Oxford University Press, 2001)

Horne, Alistair, *A Savage War of Peace: Algeria 1954–1962* (Macmillan, 1977)

Huband, Mark, *Warriors of the Prophet* (Westview Press, 1998)

Huntington, Samuel P, *The Clash of Civilizations and the Remaking of World Order* (Free Press, 2002)

Jacquard, Roland, *Les Archives Secretes d'al-Qaida* (Jean Picollec, 2002)

James, Lawrence, *Raj: The Making and Unmaking of British India* (Little, Brown, 1997)

Jenkins, Brian, *Countering al-Qaeda: An Appreciation of the Situation and Suggestions for Strategy* (Rand Corporation, 2002)

Juergensmeyer, Mark (ed.), *Violence and the Sacred in the Modern World* (Frank Cass, 1992)

______, *Terror in the Mind of God* (University of California Press, 2000)

Kepel, Giles, *The Prophet and Pharaoh: Muslim Extremism in Egypt* (Saqi Books, 1985)

______, *Jihad: The Trail of Political Islam* (I.B.Tauris, 2002)

Khan, Roedad, *Pakistan: A Dream Gone Sour* (Oxford University Press Pakistan, 1998)

Lamb, Christina, *Waiting for Allah* (Penguin, 1992)

Laquer, Walter, *Terrorism* (Little, Brown, 1977)

Latifa, *My Forbidden Face* (Virago, 2002)

Levi, Peter, *The Light Garden of the Angel King* (Collins, 1972)

Lewis, Bernard, *The Middle East* (Phoenix Press, 2001)

______, *The Arabs in History* (Oxford Paperbacks, 2002)

______, *What Went Wrong? The Clash Between Islam and Modernity in the Middle East* (Phoenix Press, 2002)

Maalouf, Amin, *The Crusades Through Arab Eyes* (Knopf Publishing Group, 1985)

Magnus, Ralph H and Eden Naby, *Mullah, Marx and Mujahed* (HarperCollins India, 1998)

Maley, William, *The Afghanistan Wars* (Palgrave Macmillan, 2002)

______, (ed.), *Fundamentalism Reborn? Afghanistan and the Taliban* (Vanguard, 1998)

Marsden, Peter, *Taliban* (Zed Books, 1998)

Martin, Vanessa, *Creating an Islamic State* (I.B.Tauris, 2000)

Metcalf, Barbara, *Islamic Revival in British India: Deoband, 1860–1900* (Princeton University Press, 1982)

Oliveti, Vincenzo, *Terror's Source* (Amadeus Books, 2002)

Qutb, Syed, *Milestones* (American Trust Publications, 1990)

Randal, Jonathan C, *Kurdistan: After Such Knowledge What Forgiveness* (Bloomsbury, 1998)

al-Rasheed, Madawi, *A History of Saudi Arabia* (Cambridge, 2002)

Rashid, Ahmed, *The Resurgence of Central Asia: Islam or Nationalism?* (Zed Books, 1994)

______, *Taliban* (I.B.Tauris, 2001)

______, *Jihad: The Rise of Militant Islam in Central Asia* (Yale, 2002)

Reeve, Simon, *The New Jackals* (Andre Deutsch, 1999)

Rehman, Shahid ur, *Who Owns Pakistan?* (Mr Books, 1998)

Richards, DS, *The Savage Frontier* (Macmillan, 1990)

Rodinson, Maxime, *Mohammed* (I.B.Tauris, 2002)

Roy, Olivier, *The Failure of Political Islam* (I.B.Tauris, 1994)
______, *Afghanistan: From Holy War to Civil War* (Princeton, 1995)
______, *Islam and Resistance in Afghanistan* (Cambridge, 1990)
Rubin, Barnett, *The Political Fragmentation of Afghanistan* (Yale, 2002)
Ruthven, Malise, *Islam in the Modern World* (Penguin, 1984)
______, *A Fury for God* (Granta, 2002)
Saad-Ghorayeb, *Hizbullah* (Pluto Press, 2002)
Said, Edward, *Covering Islam: How the Media and Experts Determine How We See the Rest of the World* (Vintage, 1997)
Schofield, Victoria, *Every Rock, Every Hill* (Century, 1987)
______, *Kashmir in the Crossfire* (I.B.Tauris, 1996)
______, *Kashmir in Conflict: India, Pakistan and the Unending War* (I.B.Tauris, 2002)
Spear, Percival, *A History of India* (Penguin, 1990)
Stern, Jessica, *The Ultimate Terrorists* (Harvard, 2000)
Talbott, Strobe and Nayan Chanda, *The Age of Terror* (Perseus Press, 2002)
Thakur, Sankarshan et al, *Guns and Yellow Roses: Essays on the Kargil War* (HarperCollins India, 1999)
Tibi, Bassam, *The Challenge of Fundamentalism* (University of California Press, 1997)
Turkaaya, Ataov, *Kashmir and Neighbours* (Ashgate, 2001)
Urban, Mark, *War in Afghanistan* (Palgrave Macmillan, 1987)
Whitlock, Monica, *Beyond the Oxus: The Central Asians* (John Murray, 2002)
Wolpert, Stanley, *Zulfi Bhutto of Pakistan: His Life and Times* (Oxford University Press, 1993)
______, *Jinnah of Pakistan* (Oxford University Press, 1993)
Woodward, Bob, *Bush at War: Inside the Bush White House* (Simon and Schuster, 2002)
Yermakov, Oleg, *Afghan Tales: Stories From Russia's Vietnam* (W. Morrow & Co., 1993)
Yousaf, Mohammed and Mark Adkin, *The Bear Trap: Afghanistan's Untold Story* (Pen & Sword Books/Leo Cooper, 1992)
Zaidan, Ahmed Muaffaq, *The Afghan Arabs: Media at Jihad* (PFI Islamabad, 1999)
Zaman, Mohammed Qasim, *The Ulema in Contemporary Islam: Custodians of Change* (Princeton University Press, 2002)
al-Zawahiri, Ayman, *Knights Under the Banner of the Prophet* (trans. & publ. by *al-Sharq al-Aswat*, the Arabic-language newspaper, 2001)
Ziring, Lawrence, *Pakistan in the Twentieth Century: A Political History* (Oxford University Press Pakistan, 1998)

INDEX